VIOLENCE AND DIPLOMACY IN LEBANON

The Troubled Years, 1982–1988

Elie A. Salem

I.B. Tauris Publishers
LONDON · NEW YORK

Published in 1995 by
I.B.Tauris & Co Ltd
45 Bloomsbury Square
London WC1A 2HY

In the United States of America
and Canada distributed by
St Martin's Press
175 Fifth Avenue
New York NY 10010

A full CIP record for this book is available from the
British Library

Library of Congress catalog card number 94–60697
A full CIP record for this book is available from the
Library of Congress

ISBN 1–85043–835–8

Set in Monotype Sabon by Ewan Smith
Printed and bound in Great Britain by
WBC Ltd, Bridgend, Mid Glamorgan

Contents

Preface

In these memoirs I record the main political and diplomatic events in Lebanon between 1982 and 1988.

The 1980s were the troubled years for Lebanon. The Israeli army had occupied the capital, Beirut, and deployed beyond it in the towns and villages to its north and north-east. The militias of the conflicting parties pretty much controlled their respective domains. The Syrian army, PLO units and Hizballah forces were also deployed in most of the areas not under direct Israeli military occupation.

The Cold War was at its height, and the USA and USSR were fiercely competing for influence and land in the Middle East. To Ronald Reagan, the Soviet Union was then the 'evil empire', while to Moscow the United States was the imperialist country bent on world domination. Israel and Syria, Lebanon's two powerful neighbours, were pitted against each other in alliances with the USA and USSR respectively.

It was our policy in the 1980s to disentangle Lebanon from the heated regional and international vortex into which it had fallen. As the state was weak and the army and internal security forces relatively ineffective in the presence of massive foreign forces in our country, we had to rely largely on diplomacy to free our territory, to regain state authority and to start the process of reconstruction.

While these memoirs describe the unfolding of events, they also reflect my feelings, my hopes and frustrations as a Lebanese citizen trying to find a way out of the labyrinth.

I wish to express my indebtedness to and admiration for my wife, Phyllis Sell Salem, who, although American by birth, chose Lebanon as her home, stayed by my side 'under fire' throughout the war, and never once wavered in her love for and loyalty to Lebanon. My children, Elise, Nina, Adib and Paul, also gave me solace and support and an added reason to persist in the job in spite of the seemingly endless obstacles in the way.

I must also express my gratitude to my assistant, Ms Itamar Diab, who shared in virtually all the meetings and discussions I held as foreign minister (1982–84) and as adviser to the president on foreign affairs (1984–88), and kept such an extensive record as to make the writing of this account relatively easy.

Special thanks are also due to Dr Nadim Shahadeh of the Centre for Lebanese Studies at Oxford, and to Ms Anna Enayat of I.B.Tauris, for their encouragement and support.

As memoirs are truly the responsibility of their authors, I alone assume responsibility for all flaws, omissions and errors that are bound to permeate as complex and kaleidoscopic a subject as Lebanon in the turbulent 1980s.

Elie A. Salem
Ba'bda, 2 August 1994

Introduction

On 7 June 1982, as I took refuge alone in a supposedly safe corner in my faculty home on the campus of the American University of Beirut, a shell fired from an Israeli ship a few kilometres offshore hit our living room. The impact left a gaping hole in the wall and sent debris flying throughout the house. Thrown on the floor by the explosion, dazed and half-unconscious, I struggled to regain my senses and crawl to the university observatory close by. I finally made it there in a curious mood of fear and courage, concern and carelessness. In moments of great danger a certain inexplicable destiny seems to direct one's thoughts and actions.

This episode happened in the wake of the Israeli invasion of Lebanon. I mention it not for its uniqueness, but rather for its averageness. It was the kind of event that became almost routine in the life of the Lebanese people during their long and devastating war. Violence, terror and death became part of our daily existence.

I lived the Lebanese war and experienced its turbulent course. I observed it closely, between 1982 and 1988, and recorded its events and the feelings these events engendered. Lebanon's war, like all wars, raises the universal questions of order and anarchy, man and the state, peace and war, and love and hate.

Ours was a war of killings, kidnappings, dislocations of population, destruction of property, the denigration of national symbols, and the dangerous mixing of religion and politics. It was a conflict sustained by the collapse of the state and by the unleashing of passion – the deep, wild, irrational force that the Greeks called *thumos*.

Almost every Lebanese has experienced anarchy, witnessed violence, and stared death in the face. Two youths fight; one draws a gun and shoots the other, who falls dead at his father's feet. The father cries, buries his son, and goes on. It does not enter his mind to call the police. What police? What investigation? What state? An official performs his duty

1

according to his conscience. He is asked to bend his conscience. He refuses. Next day he is found dead in the boot of his car. The family buries him. Everyone knows that in times of anarchy there is no accountability. The state is dead and everything is allowed.

In this Lebanon was not unique. Thomas Hobbes wrote *Leviathan* in the seventeenth century as a commentary on the English civil war, arguing that only a strong state administering the law could prevent society from falling back into an anarchy which made life 'nasty, brutish and short'. The great Arab historian Ibn Khaldun, who pre-dated Hobbes by two hundred years, said that government must inspire awe, or *haibah*. It is this awe which leads to compliance and civility among civilians. No *haibah* meant no order, no law, and no civility.

In Lebanon, it was the opponents of the state who commanded awe. They created a persistent tension which transformed people. Planning came to a halt. Since death might come at any moment, people lived well, even beyond their means. In the Middle Ages, we are told, a rumour about the imminent arrival of Christ led people to spend lavishly, for time would end soon. The wildest parties in Beirut were held under intense shelling. People tended to socialize more, drink more, and work together more in small groups. Friendship replaced statehood: no individual was better than the other. Little things acquired great importance, often at the expense of more important issues.

It is not my intent to write an account of the Lebanese crisis. Instead, I hope to write an account from my perspective as Lebanese foreign minister, and then adviser on foreign affairs to the president of the republic, Amin Jumayyil. I write as a witness to the fate of a small country that has fallen victim to both internal and regional contradictions; as a witness to a liberal democratic system struggling against the gravitational pull of a region in conflict, and, perhaps, as a witness to the neglect that befalls the weak in the world of the strong.

Perhaps it is only fitting to begin my account with Bashir Jumayyil, my first curious encounter with the politicians and militias of the war. Wars produce and consume their own heroes. A young man joins the ranks, sees opportunities, takes risks, and rises to the top always encountering and surmounting dangers that might put an end to his ambitions, and to his life. The greater the danger surmounted, the greater the heroic role. Of Pierre Jumayyil's two sons, the younger Bashir was destined to play this role.

In his schooldays Bashir was a short, squat, unassuming young man with an average academic record and passionate partisan political views. He grew up fast during the Lebanese war, distinguished himself as a fighter, and soon matured beyond his years. He was in every way a product of the war. His mentors were the philosopher Dr Charles Malik, the historian Fuad Iphrem Bustani, his father Sheikh Pierre Jumayyil, and former President Kamil Sham'un. These were the patron saints of the Christian community during the war, and Bashir was their disciple.

Charles Malik, though a Greek Orthodox by birth, was a proponent of Catholic thought and an admirer of St Thomas Aquinas. He provided the Christians with the philosophic grounds for their struggle, which he expounded effectively. He was charismatic, eloquent, doctrinaire, and utterly uncompromising. He drank long and deep from the Western fountains of learning at Harvard, and appropriated Christian thought in a manner that left little room for Arabism and Islam.

Fuad Iphrem Bustani provided Bashir with historical depth by connecting modern Lebanon, through measured stages, with the Phoenician city-states of antiquity. He set Lebanon apart from the Arab states and the Arab legacy, which corresponded with the ideological needs of the Maronite minority.

Pierre Jumayyil was the mystical politician who had succeeded, through his Kata'ib party, in rallying Lebanon's Maronites around a movement which worked for a free and independent Lebanon presumably under Maronite tutelage. To him and to his two sons, Amin and Bashir, Lebanon was something to be revered; it was an icon, an object of love which required neither explanation nor rationalization. Kamil Sham'un was the consummate politician. The former president of Lebanon was the irrepressible pragmatist and architect of alliances; a strategist on whom the burden of political direction of the Christian community fell.

Bashir took elements from each of them, and moved beyond. Though his manner was informal and charming, his method was cool and calculated. His love of power and his pursuit of it were phenomenal. He was impatient with his father's old-fashioned way of doing things and with his older, more intellectual brother, Amin. He wanted to take by force what his brother had by tradition: the right to preside over his father's Kata'ib party and its militia. Once that was secured, he could hope to become the leader of the Christian community and, ultimately, capture the presidency of the republic and reconstitute Lebanon according to his own vision. This was a mixture of idealism and pragmatism, which changed and grew in the light of his experience. He wanted a strong presidency, a strong army under his command, and a radically reformed bureaucracy. In time Bashir took control of the Kata'ib militia, broadened it to include other smaller Christian militias, and recast it under the name of the Lebanese Forces (LF). He did not hide his contacts with the Israelis. Israel hoped to use him as a means to fight the PLO, while by 1982 Bashir was hoping to use Israel to become Lebanon's president.

I learned of his intentions under somewhat inauspicious circumstances.

Bashir had been planning his presidency for some time and his men were working towards that objective in Lebanon, Europe and the United States. The American Enterprise Institute, a conservative Washington think-tank, had invited me to give a talk on Lebanon in the spring of 1982. When Bashir heard about this, he was furious: Washington was his terrain, and no one could venture there without liaising with him and espousing his particular line.

Before my departure, he sent me a strong message to this effect. No person living in Lebanon during the war would ignore a message from a militia leader. I recalled meeting Bashir at a dinner at Charles Malik's residence early in the war, and I remembered him as quiet, intense, and a bit shy. He struck me as someone biding his time. What impressed me most about the evening, however, was that Malik, who was known for having a rather large ego, talked of the boyish, untested Bashir as the leader and saviour of the Christian community.

Malik and I were distant relations from Bterram in North Lebanon. Although he had great influence on me intellectually, politically we differed greatly. We agreed on the fundamentals of Lebanon and of the Christian presence in the Middle East, but we were often far apart on details and method. Malik tended to extol the Graeco-Roman-Christian tradition, and to play down the role of the Arabs and Islam in the continuum of civilization. His ideological and political benchmarks were America and the Church, whether Roman Catholic or Greek Orthodox. I came from a different background. In college I had studied Islam and written extensively about it. I admired the Arab cultural tradition, which spanned some seven centuries and which attained the highest level of universality in most fields of learning. While fiercely committed to Lebanon's independence, sovereignty, and liberal democratic order, I never doubted that Lebanon was an Arab country and an heir to a great Arab tradition, as it was to the Graeco-Roman-Christian tradition.

At any rate, after hearing of Bashir's reaction to my forthcoming Washington trip, I confided in a colleague of mine from the American University of Beirut who was a close friend of Bashir's. He suggested a private lunch at his house to settle the matter. On the appointed day I arrived on time, and Bashir, as befitted his leadership status, arrived a bit late. When he arrived, he shook my hand strongly, a clear indication of his power, and said: 'Let's get down to business. You are going to Washington; this capital is important to me. I am running for president.' I asked whether he was intending to run now, or in six years' time. 'It's now or never', he answered.

This came as a surprise to me. Here was a young and partisan militia-man, feared in the Muslim half of Lebanon, and at best a possible regional leader, and yet he seriously believed he could be elected to the presidency. There was no hint of doubt in his voice. His determination was complete. He continued, resenting my naïve interruption: 'The American Enterprise Institute is an important forum for me. Your speech must correspond to my views fully or you will not go.'

As Bashir lectured, my mind wandered. I had been a professor for many years; this young man could be my student; he was harassing me on politics, a subject not unfamiliar to me. He was demanding that I conform to his ideas, but I felt that his ideas were still unformed, his knowledge incomplete, and his experience limited. I interrupted Bashir and said, half in earnest, half in jest, that I was 20 years his senior; as a professor, my job was to reflect rationally on the issues he was raising. I had read his party's statements on Lebanon, and while I agreed with some, I disagreed with others. My commitment to Lebanon was absolute. In the event of a conflict of views, I expected that (and here I allowed the jest to widen) Bashir would conform with me rather than the other way around.

Bashir rose from his chair and embraced me, saying that I was right. Somehow, after this, we became friends. The more we met and talked the more incongruous the friendship seemed and the more imperative it became, for him as well as for me. For the first time I found myself sucked into the violent vortex of Lebanese politics. It is one thing to observe the political scene and write about it and another to participate in it. The politics I knew were the politics of a university which, though non-violent, were often no less intricate than the politics of Lebanon.

I took great risks in crossing from West Beirut, where I lived, to East Beirut, where Bashir lived. I flattered myself in thinking that it was up to someone like me to try to persuade Bashir to see Lebanon from a wider perspective. For virtually a decade this young man had heard only one voice and one version of Lebanon; this was good enough for a militia leader, but not for someone who aspired to the presidency.

Bashir already had in place a team of dedicated young men and women working for his presidency. They were intelligent and fervently loyal to their leader. Bashir was presented as a hero, saviour, reformer and liberator. His hopeful speeches, assailing all those who endangered Lebanon, were listened to by both Christians and Muslims. He became the central figure of Lebanese politics. He openly said what others would not dare whisper, and acted in defiance of accepted norms. He seemed honest, naïve and tragic. Since Lebanon's war was bigger than Lebanon itself, Bashir's readiness to take on the challenge and to liberate Lebanon's 10,453 square kilometres, a slogan which he created, was met with admiration, tempered by scepticism. He could run all he wanted, most said, but he could not be elected.

My friendship with Bashir rested on shaky ground. We disagreed on Israel, Syria, the United States, and on internal political reforms; in fact we disagreed on almost everything. Yet there were two things about him that I liked: one was his uncompromising attitude towards corruption in government; the second was his style. In Lebanon, corruption was often the norm in government rather than the exception. It was an accepted fact that many politicians used their positions to make money, and with money they strengthened their position. Bashir's style was one I somewhat ambivalently admired. I liked his passion, his faith, his ability to express himself in simple colloquial words. I liked his informality, his Lebanese *hamshariyyah* or nonchalance, his seriousness of purpose, and his desire to cut to the substance of a matter with minimum attention to form. Bashir would start with an extremist position, one intended to shock, and then would end up with a rational conclusion. He spoke as much with his eyes, hands and fists as with his tongue. He was always in a hurry, as if he knew that time was limited. Yet there was also a hard coolness to his style. He did not hesitate to push his enemies and competitors out of the way. He tolerated no opposition and no competition.

Bashir's relations with Israel derived from the fear within the Christian community that the PLO, allied with the predominantly Muslim National Movement, would destroy Lebanon, and with it the freedoms enjoyed by its Christian communities. Israel thus became an instrument for Bashir, first to defeat the Palestinians and their allies, and then to help him become president. His pursuit of power was such that none of the methods used to achieve it was questionable. His person would always purge the impurities of his method.

As regards the United States, I believe Bashir overestimated Washington's power and determination in Lebanon. Somehow this young Francophile had fallen in love with the USA, and love is often blind. He was willing to go far with the United States. If the Soviets were in Syria, he argued, the Americans should be in Lebanon. I thought this was a dangerous proposition. Lebanon was not Syria. Our heterogeneous society necessitated a more cautious policy, and demanded disengagement from superpower rivalries, rather than deeper engagement.

On 23 August 1982, Bashir was elected president. By persuasion he ensured that the necessary parliamentary quorum of 62 deputies would exist to permit elections. Fifty-seven deputies voted for Bashir, while five others cast blank ballots. His partisans celebrated as if a new day of hope and destiny had dawned. His enemies, and they were many, were thunderstruck. Israel was delighted. Bashir had promised Israel the moon, and now he had to deliver. The Israelis were to soon to learn, however, that this upstart had tricked them. Prime Minister Menachem Begin and

Defence Minister Ariel Sharon bitterly realized that Bashir would not sign a peace treaty with them as they had hoped. Instead, Bashir began to cultivate relations with his traditional Muslim rivals, and soon he began winning support in West Beirut. Perhaps he was dissimulating at a time when he was anxious to broaden and consolidate his power base. His pragmatism was boundless.

The foreign media swarmed around him, curious about his meteoric rise, and anxious to know where he stood on the complex issues of his tortured land. He agreed to give a pre-recorded private interview to one of the leading American TV stations and asked me to be present. He told me he wanted to talk freely, and that it was up to me to note down the points which should be changed or taken out before the interview was broadcast. The American television team accepted this arrangement. When the interview ended he asked if I had comments, and I responded that I had 18 observations. I proceeded to go over them one by one, and he approved all my suggestions. When I reached the eighteenth observation Bashir raised his finger in mock seriousness, and said whatever the eighteenth point was, and even if war were to be declared because of it, it must remain in the final interview; he could not lose all of them. I agreed. I no longer recall what the eighteenth point was, but I can never forget how well he took criticism. Whether such flexibility, observed on the basis of short acquaintance, would have carried over to his presidency is impossible to divine.

On 14 September 1982, while Bashir addressed a meeting in one of the Kata'ib party's offices in East Beirut, a bomb exploded, bringing down the ceiling and crushing the president-elect to death. Thus ended the saga and the enigma. Bashir died at the height of his fame, before he had been tested in the exacting role of president. While in life he had more enemies than friends, his tragic death at a time when he was building bridges and apparently transforming his policies brought sympathy from all quarters of the country, as his funeral in his village of Bikfayya demonstrated. President Elias Sarkis, worn out by six frustrating years as president, could hardly deliver his eloquent and emotional elegy.

The vocation of politics is impatient with death. Lebanon quickly changed course and focused on a successor. It was natural in the context of the power structure of September 1982 to rally around Amin, the elder son of Sheikh Pierre Jumayyil. Amin was less controversial than Bashir. As a member of parliament, he was more moderate and realistic, with extensive contacts in the Muslim community and in the region.

On 21 September 1982, Amin was elected president. Of the 80 deputies present, 77 voted for him. Although I knew a lot about the new president, I had never met him. When a few of Bashir's friends suggested to me that

we visit him, I gladly accepted. Amin was living in a humble apartment
in Bikfayya. Dazed and exhausted by the rapid events of the past few
days, he nevertheless embraced us warmly. Throughout the visit I kept
thinking that here was the brother of an assassinated president; he was
now himself president of one of the most insecure countries in the world,
and yet there were only two or three guards at the door. Any militia
leader would have had at least 30 guards, all better armed. 'Mr President,'
I said, 'you need more guards.' He stared at me and said: 'My dear Elie,
there is God above; when your hour comes, it comes, and no one can
protect you.' I thought it appropriate then to invoke the Prophet Muhammad. In a debate on freedom and on reliance on Allah the Prophet
was asked: 'O Prophet of Allah, if a Muslim travelling in the desert wants
to sleep, should he tie his camel to prevent it from escaping or depend on
Allah?' The Prophet answered that he should tie the camel and then
depend on Allah.

This was the first of many dialogues that were to follow in my six
years of association with President Jumayyil. Having no background in
Arabic civilization, Amin was always anxious to delve into it. He realized
how important it was in a country which was half-Muslim to have an
idea of Muslim culture and history.

1

Political Setting

Wars acquire greater intensity after dark. Maybe there is a correlation between darkness and the violent nature of man. Maybe it is just that the echoes of violence resonate more at night. The sounds of cannon-fire thunder in narrow inner streets, machine-guns go off like fire-crackers and, occasionally, fighters introduce measured, carefully calculated rhythms into the firing of their weapons, like drummers practising on a snare drum.

The night of 6 October 1982, was unusually calm in Beirut. The autumn sky was clear. It was 10 p.m., and I was having a drink with friends on the balcony of our faculty apartment when the telephone rang. On the line was Dr Wadi' Haddad, a former colleague of mine from the American University of Beirut who had later joined the World Bank. He informed me that he was working with the newly elected president, and that he was presently at the presidential palace in Ba'bda. He asked me whether I could come up to Ba'bda immediately, as the president wanted to talk to me. I urged postponement until the morning since I was not anxious to venture out alone at night and to cross roadblocks manned by armed and trigger-happy gunmen. The matter could not wait, he insisted. A few minutes later, I was anxiously driving through Beirut's dark, lonely and treacherous streets to the presidential palace on the outskirts of the city.

When I arrived I saw President Jumayyil pacing back and forth with Haddad at the entrance to the palace. The president was nervously playing with his key-chain, which encouraged me to do the same with mine. He looked young, fragile and rather small in the immensity of space surrounding him. He was in a pensive mood, and walked as if a burden of titanic proportions had fallen on his shoulders. I sensed, however, a hidden confidence. He welcomed me enthusiastically, and the two of us were left alone. The president and I walked and talked for a short while. He then said to me: 'I will be meeting the designated prime minister, Shafiq al-

9

Wazzan, tomorrow to form the government. I want you to be present in this meeting. I would like you to serve as foreign minister for my six-year term. After that you will serve as ambassador in Washington.'

I accepted the president's offer, but made it conditional on his response to the following question: was he committed to concluding a peace treaty with Israel? I would have to refuse his offer if he was committed to such a treaty. Not at all, he responded, adding: 'You know Bashir and I disagreed on virtually all political issues, and even Bashir was veering away from his ties with Israel.' 'In that case I accept,' I responded, 'and let us forget about the ambassadorial position in Washington. I don't have the temperament of an ambassador. When I leave the Foreign Ministry I will return to the American University of Beirut.'

On the way back to the university I wondered why the president had offered me this post. The man did not know me. Except for a short visit a few days before to congratulate him on his election, I had never met him. I knew something about him as a Maronite leader, but I had no idea if he knew anything about me. I later learned that he knew some of my friends and that he read some of my writings, and wanted me not only as deputy prime minister and minister of foreign affairs, but also as a close aide and friend. The new president, while a francophone, was anxious to collaborate with the American University and its graduates, and was banking on the USA to help him. Like Bashir before him he was veering away from France, the traditional Maronite anchor, and towards the New Imperium across the Atlantic. He was thinking politics, not history.

Upon returning to our apartment I decided to go out on to our balcony. Only a hundred yards away lies the Mediterranean. To the Lebanese, this sea was a highway driving emigrants outwards through Gibraltar, to West Africa, Europe, the Americas, Australia and New Zealand. But the Mediterranean also brought the Lebanese back. It brought them back with new-found wealth, new ideas and new institutions. To the east I could see the majestic outlines of Mount Lebanon, leaning into the coast, virtually pushing Lebanon's cities to the water's edge. Hundreds of towns and villages, at that moment peaceful patches of light in the dark, had been strained to breaking point in the past years. I wondered why such a beautiful place was destined for such a fate. How could so much beauty be associated with so much violence? Could the cycle be broken? Soon, I thought, I would be on the inside sharing in the difficult decisions; not on the outside, writing, lecturing and preaching homilies. But, I wondered, did it really make a difference if one was on the inside? How much power did our government really have? How much of our future was dictated by regional or international events outside our control? In the end, among the forces jostling for power in Lebanon, wasn't the voice of the constitutional government a mere whimper? Professors are trained to think in terms of questions. Soon, I thought, questions may become irrelevant. Only answers would be meaningful. My answer to myself was determination to do what was right as I saw it, and not to succumb to the sophisticated scepticism to which academics are prone.

Forming the Government

The next day I returned to the presidential palace to meet President Jumayyil and participate in the formation of the government. The meeting included Prime Minister Designate Shafiq al-Wazzan, the Director of the Surété Générale, Faruq Abillama, and the Director of the Army's Deuxième Bureau (intelligence), Colonel Johnny Abdu. Shafiq al-Wazzan had been prime minister in the last government under President Elias Sarkis. When Amin al-Jumayyil was elected, Wazzan submitted his resignation, but was asked by the president to form a new government. He accepted.

According to the Lebanese Constitution, the president appoints the ministers and designates one of them prime minister. In reality, however, the method of appointing ministers is different. After consultation with members of parliament and with leading figures in the country, the president designates a prime minister from amongst the prominent leaders in the Sunni community. Then, together with the prime minister, the president forms the government.

In forming a government the Maronite president takes the advice of the two key officials heading the Surété Générale and Army Intelligence, who are usually Maronites. Over time, the directors of the Surété Générale and of the Deuxième Bureau have become the vehicles through which the president exercises many of his powers, and they are generally his closest advisers. Although Abillama and Abdu were both in the Sarkis Administration, the president trusted them and valued their experience. I was the only novice in the small group.

Wazzan had already conducted his own consultations. He had met the parliamentary blocs and consulted former prime ministers, as tradition required, as well as leaders of parties not represented in parliament. Wazzan told us that if he were to implement the results of his consultations, he would have to recommend a government with an average age of 75 since all the leaders who had been on the Lebanese political scene since the 1930s wanted to be in the government. Such a government, he felt, would not reflect the image President Jumayyil wanted to project. A president in his early forties needed a government of young men who could work efficiently and reflect his dynamic image.

The president agreed. His chief concern was that such a government must be formed immediately in this very session. Everyone knew that a meeting was taking place at the presidential palace for such a purpose, and he insisted that the government must be announced at the end of our meeting. Any indication that the established politicians were being by-passed would create enough havoc to kill the Wazzan proposal.

For the next five hours names were proposed by each one in the group informally and at random. If a general consensus existed that the nominee was acceptable, Colonel Abdu was asked to check his records. Abdu would then disappear for a few minutes before coming back with a response. A negative response essentially disqualified the nominee. Similarly, a veto by the president or by the prime minister immediately eliminated a nominee. At that time objections were raised if the candidate was doctrinaire, partisan, controversial, or without professional qualifications.

When Maronite candidates were proposed I suggested the name of George Frem. I believed him to be a dynamic, honest, hard-working and self-made industrialist, as well as a philanthropist. A Maronite from Kisirwan, Frem had made a name for himself as a citizen concerned with the public good and as an active conciliator amongst the conflicting groupings. The president agreed with me and supported his nomination enthusiastically. The prime minister deferred to the president on Frem, since he seemed to fit the profile both men were looking for. They wanted a government of capable and qualified men.

When Wazzan nominated a Shi'i colleague from the American University of Beirut, the president asked me to check on his credentials. I telephoned another colleague from the university who worked with him. The colleague counselled against the nomination because the nominee had once attacked the Kata'ib party and its leader, the president's father Sheikh Pierre al-Jumayyil. I reported this to the group, and they went on to consider someone else. After a brief search for an alternative, Wazzan once again proposed the nominee who had attacked Sheikh Pierre. The president asked me to call the same colleague again and get a more definite evaluation. I did and returned with pretty much the same report. The president looked puzzled. The prime minister, who is known for his sense of humour, looked at the president and said: 'Mr President, in this long war do you know anyone who has not cursed Sheikh Pierre?' The president burst out laughing, and agreed to make the nominee a minister. The nominee, Dr Adnan Muruwwah, a medical doctor at the American University Hospital, turned out to be an excellent minister respected by all. When asked later about Sheikh Pierre, he laughed and said, 'Wouldn't you have done the same?'

The president and the prime minister hoped to form a government of six, in which each minister would have two or three portfolios. I categorically refused to take any ministry in addition to the Ministry of Foreign Affairs. To my amusement I was offered the Ministry of Agriculture, in addition to the posts of deputy prime minister and minister of foreign affairs; on the condition that I would contract with a consultant who would manage the agriculture portfolio for me. The president and the prime minister wanted me to concentrate on foreign affairs to effect Israeli withdrawal, especially in view of the fact that Israeli forces were in Beirut and its surroundings. I therefore felt I could not assume more responsibility than foreign affairs.

In the end a government of ten ministers was formed. To preserve the communal balance, now accepted as a norm of Lebanese politics, it included five Muslim and five Christian ministers: the breakdown was two Maronites, two Sunnis, including the prime minister, two Greek Orthodox, two Shi'is, one Greek Catholic and one Druze.

Protocol necessitated a measure of coordination with the speaker of parliament, Kamil al-As'ad, whose support the president and the prime minister needed in securing parliamentary approval of the government through a vote of confidence. As'ad did not like simply to be informed. The scion of a large and influential family in South Lebanon, Kamil al-As'ad maintained in his person both the characteristics of the feudal chief, and all the trappings of modernity. He was a brilliant politician who took care of his people and who ran parliament with a strong hand. In the past he had always been consulted beforehand on new governments, and he expected to nominate some. The president invited As'ad to the presidential palace and prepared for the tough meeting ahead. The meeting was a lengthy one – as the president would later tell Wazzan, 'It was like pulling teeth.' The president and the prime minister got the government they wanted.

After this long and unusual day I returned home. Home was now to be the old house in B'abda that my wife and I had bought in 1963. To this day I take pride in reminding my guests that this was the house in which Sheikh Bisharah al-Khuri, the first president of independent Lebanon, lived as a child. Fate placed it only five minutes by car from the presidential palace, and 20 minutes from the Ministry of Foreign Affairs.

The cabinet was announced late that night. Early next morning, 8 October, at precisely 7.30, my wife was on her way from our bedroom to the kitchen for her morning coffee when she encountered a blond stranger sitting in our living room. He was ushered in by the maid, as I had no guards yet. I was at that dangerous transitional stage in the transformation from dean of faculty to deputy prime minister and minister of foreign affairs. My wife exchanged a few words with him and returned to tell me that he was an aide to David Kimche, the director-general of the Israeli Foreign Ministry. The young man, she said, sounded professional and talked like a foreign service officer. He had told my wife that Kimche wanted to pay me a visit. Kimche, I learned, had opened an office in the wake of Israeli occupation of Lebanon in a building just behind my house in B'abda.

My wife was nervous. For the past few weeks she had been fighting her own battles with the Israeli army in B'abda. The Israelis had entered our house, just before we moved into it in October after a long absence on University Campus, taken what they needed from it, and abused the garden on which she had worked so hard. I calmed her down and sent her back to tell the visitor politely but firmly: 'The Minister of Foreign Affairs cannot meet an Israeli official. Lebanon has no official relations with Israel. Israel has violated the Armistice Agreement between our two countries and has occupied one-third of Lebanese territory, including its capital. Whatever I have to say to the Israelis I will say it through the American representative. Kindly leave.' My wife must have done well, because the man left and did not return.

When I later informed the president of this incident he told me that he was facing worse problems with the Israelis. They had placed roadblocks on the road from Sin al-Fil, where he lived, to the presidential palace. The president told me that he had asked American Ambassador Robert Dillon to persuade the Israelis to remove these roadblocks. One could not help seeing in this an almost too perfect symbol of Lebanon's predicament.

Israeli pressures on the new Lebanese government were not especially subtle. The Israeli army was present in force in and around Beirut in October 1982, and large Israeli military encampments were concentrated in a radius of three or four kilometres around the presidential palace. In my daily drives to the office I often found myself blocked in the narrow streets of B'abda by the large Israeli Merkava tanks, which somehow seemed to develop mechanical troubles just as I was about to go past. Trapped behind these enormous vehicles, there was little I could do but suppress my fury until the Israelis decided to let me by.

One day a soldier eyed me from the turret of his tank and asked: 'Sir, when are you going to Israel?' I feigned deafness, although I could not suppress a smile. I had a flashback to my student days at the American University of Beirut in the mid-1940s. These were formative and decisive years in the history of the Middle East, and the conflict over Palestine dominated our student life. Until 1947 there were still Jewish students from Palestine studying at the American University of Beirut. One of them was a young man named David.

As the conflict between Arabs and Jews intensified, Arab students at
AUB began to enlist in the Arab volunteer army of Fawzi al-Qawuqji,
while Palestinian Jews began to withdraw quietly from the university to
join their own armed organizations. In such critical moments, when the
power of politics tests the bonds of friendship, it is reassuring to see the
human and the universal prevail. I recall seeing David in the cafeteria one
day; he looked terrified. He was afraid that he would be the target of
reprisals by angry Arab students, and confided in me that he wanted to
leave for Palestine but did not know a safe way to go. We spoke for a
while, and as I listened to him describe his vision of a Jewish state I
thought to myself: here we are, two friends with different visions, both
caught in the rapid flow of history, and each with little choice except,
perhaps, to remain humane amid the conflicts surrounding us. I assured
David that he would be in Palestine tomorrow. Early the next day a taxi
was waiting for him at the University's main gate. David, three other Arab
students, and I got into the taxi and drove south to Lebanon's border
with Palestine. There the four of us embraced David tearfully and bid
him goodbye. He walked away towards his destiny and we returned to
our own. The three other students in the taxi were the most radical
Palestinian leaders on campus and were the founders, even then, of Arab
nationalist and anti-Zionist organizations. Today they are among the best-
known members of the Palestinian leadership. I looked back at the soldier
on the turret. For a moment I thought that this boy could be the son of
David. I smiled, and, at last, continued on my way.

From my first day in government to the last, I had an intriguing
relationship with the bureaucracy. I arrived for the transfer ceremony at
the Foreign Ministry in my old car, driven, for the occasion, by a part-
time gardener. I was greeted with looks of disbelief by the welcoming
committee made up of the ministry's high officials. Soon things would
change. My new position demanded that I be accompanied by bodyguards, travel in a luxury government car, and have an entourage of
hangers-on. Indeed the rule seemed to be the larger the entourage, the
greater the prestige.

The offices of the Foreign Ministry, like the offices of most Lebanese
ministries, are located in a number of buildings originally designed for
other uses. The foreign minister and his immediate aides work in an old
and charming house in the historical Sursock neighbourhood of Beirut.
Yet while the house would be ideal as a home for a well-to-do family of
five, it is utterly unsuited for government operations striving for even
minimal efficiency. The few offices it provides are large, have high ceilings,
and are more attractive than practical.

One of the first obstacles I encountered after my appointment as foreign minister was the attitude of members of the Maronite political hierarchy. To the Maronites I was an outsider: a Greek Orthodox, a graduate of the American University of Beirut, and an anglophone prone to torturing the French language. This was in stark contrast to the Maronite leaders who spoke French, had graduated from the Jesuit French-language St Joseph University, and saw the American University of Beirut as a bastion of Palestinian militancy and Arab nationalist causes. I was advised early on to visit Sheikh Pierre al-Jumayyil and gain his approval. Sheikh Pierre was the leader of the Kata'ib Party, the largest Maronite-based political party in Lebanon. If things went well with Sheikh Pierre, it would go a long way to improving my reputation with the Maronites.

Sheikh Pierre greeted me by saying:

> I must be honest with you. When I heard that my son appointed you foreign minister I was deeply disturbed; that night I did not sleep. I have nothing against you my son, but you are from the American University of Beirut; your friends are Palestinians, many of them are in the PLO; and your French is virtually non-existent. I told my son he was wrong in choosing you. Then I heard you in parliament and changed my mind completely. You amazed me, you are a good Lebanese. You have my blessings.

A few days after our government was formed the president asked me to plan for a visit to the USA. Before we travelled I felt the need to take time out and write a few guidelines on our foreign policy.

1. Israel must withdraw completely from Lebanon in accordance with UN Security Council Resolutions 425 and 509, i.e. immediately and unconditionally to satisfy an international juridical imperative and to ease tension in Lebanon and in the region.
2. The United States must be convinced of the validity of the first point and should help Lebanon realize it.
3. Lebanon, with Arab, and particularly Syrian support, must be given the means to ensure stability in south Lebanon and prevent PLO raids from Lebanon against Israel.
4. If Lebanon fails to convince the USA of the validity of an Israeli withdrawal under Security Council Resolutions 425 and 509, then Lebanon must consider discussions in the context of the Israel–Lebanon General Armistice Agreement of 23 March 1949, it being understood that such discussions are provided for under the terms of the Armistice Agreement.
5. Discussions leading to the withdrawal of the Israeli army should be followed immediately by discussions for the withdrawal of the Syrian army and of all non-Lebanese armed elements from Lebanese ter-

ritory. After that, the government must seek to disarm all Lebanese militias.

6. Lebanon must have clear and special relations with Syria based on close historical considerations. I felt strongly and intuitively that a knee-jerk anti-Syrian position would do more harm to Lebanon than good. Our policy must aim at excellent relations with the Arab world and distinctive relations with Syria; in the Arab world we should work closely with Saudi Arabia, which enjoys at present great influence in the Arab East and in the West, particularly in the USA.

7. Lebanon supports the Palestinian cause and any arrangement which satisfies the legitimate national rights of the Palestinian people, and which is acceptable to them. Support for the Palestinian cause, however, must not be at the expense of Lebanon's sovereignty. Lebanon will not accept a PLO military presence on its territory, or PLO military activity from its territory against another state. The Nine Points negotiated between the Lebanese government and the PLO, with the help of American Special Envoy, Philip Habib, and which involve Syrian and PLO withdrawal from Beirut, are already a major step in that direction.

8. An effective foreign policy must be backed by national consensus. Despite the fact that internal differences may exist on foreign policy Lebanon must be able to speak with a united voice when addressing the world community.

9. As Syria and Israel are in effect allies of the Soviet Union and of the USA, respectively, Lebanon must maintain direct communication with both superpowers to help in the process of disentangling the regional forces locked in conflict in Lebanon.

10. Given Europe's growing influence in world affairs, and the historical ties between many European states and the Middle East, Lebanon must explore all avenues to insure European participation and assistance in a settlement of the Lebanese conflict.

11. Lebanon must take its case to the capitals of all nations exercising influence in the Middle East region. By extension, Lebanon's participation in the Arab League, in the United Nations, and in the Conference of Non-Aligned States must be enhanced as these forums will be needed to promote international support for Lebanese objectives.

12. Lebanon must promote the notion that Lebanese security depends in large part on a secure and legitimate state system in the Middle East. Lebanon can only function properly and exercise its democracy fully if the countries around it are stable.

13. Lebanon must be genuinely committed to the principles of indepen-

dence, sovereignty, unity, equality and justice. These are principles to which Lebanon, as a democracy, has historically subscribed, but which unfortunately have not always been implemented.

14. Attention must be focused on the Lebanese crisis *per se*, in such a way that a solution to the Lebanese crisis will not become hostage to a solution of the larger Middle East problem.

These guidelines emerged from Lebanese facts. I presented the guidelines to the president and the prime minister. The president emphasized the importance of the UN as a forum, and of the USA as a mediator between Lebanon and Israel. The prime minister emphasized the importance of national unity, the need for Arab support, and continuing contacts with Syria. Although this was the first meeting for the three of us on policy issues, agreement between us was complete on virtually all aspects of foreign policy. Foreign policy in Lebanon had traditionally been the domain of the president, who worked closely with the foreign minister. Now Lebanon was under occupation and the old approach would not suffice. The prime minister must be closely involved and so should the entire council of ministers, and even parliamentary leaders, to ensure wide consensus and support for our policy.

After agreeing on the guidelines, I set about organizing the president's schedule and laying the groundwork for his meetings at the UN, in Washington and in Europe. I also began thinking more broadly about what our objectives would be during the trip and started preparing the statements and speeches which the president would make overseas; particularly the speech before the General Assembly. Finally, in line with the president's request, I prepared a list of those in the delegation. Of all the chores of a presidential trip abroad the most difficult is the one that should be the simplest, preparing the list of those accompanying him.

Presidential trips are headaches for aides; even more so when they involve the president of a country that has been in conflict for seven years. An aeroplane must be assigned and guarded; security teams must travel to the countries to be visited and coordinate security with domestic security forces. The delegation must be chosen carefully, if not to please all parties, at least to aggravate as few of them as possible. Speeches must be carefully written and checked with key leaders in the country to ensure broad support for the government's position.

The president had invited an American firm of consultants to help him write his main speech, intended for delivery at the UN General Assembly. After a week of assiduous work the consultants submitted a draft; the president read it quickly, with obvious displeasure. He felt it lacked spirit, and that it was a collection of ideas without any real focus. The president was getting nervous as our date of departure was nearing, and he asked me to try my hand at the speech. I closeted myself for a few hours and wrote what I believed the president should be telling the General Assembly. When I read it to him he was elated, not only because he had a speech he liked, but more importantly because he felt it showed that cooperation between him and me on foreign affairs would be smooth and fruitful.

On Sunday 17 October, at 11 a.m. the president's motorcade made its way slowly from B'abda presidential palace through Beirut's southern suburbs, to the airport. Somehow the motorcycle policemen and the presidential guard in their sleek Range Rovers instinctively knew when to increase the noise level of the motorcade to do justice to the pomp and circumstance required by the occasion. Units from the army also were deployed along the entire route. Another army unit greeted the president at the airport while a military band played the national anthem. All members of the government were expected to see the president off, and as is often the case in Lebanon, the more politicians at a departure ceremony, the better. After the brief ceremony, endless rounds of handshakes, and, at times, more passionate embraces, the president finally boarded the special Middle East Airlines flight to New York.

Throughout the flight the president, Ghassan Tweini and I, joined for short periods by other aides, worked continuously at a small table on the upper deck of the Boeing 747. The president enjoyed hard work and wanted to review in detail every aspect of the impending visit. In New York we were met by Mrs Salwa Roosevelt, the chief of the White House protocol, and by our ambassadors and officials in the UN, the USA and Canada. In the Waldorf Astoria Hotel, where we were staying, we were flooded by hundreds of Lebanese who were anxious to meet the president and offer their help; it was a tribute to the New York security force that order was maintained and access strictly controlled.

The president, however, was a politician, and politicians crave crowds. To the horror of the New York security officers, he escaped from their clutches from time to time and mingled with the Lebanese and Lebanese American crowds filling the lobbies of the hotel. Lebanese emigrants are highly emotional people and they maintain a strong attachment to their ancestral land, and to the president as the symbol of national unity. Inside Lebanon the president may be opposed, loved or hated, but among Lebanese emigrants he remains the symbol of that particular Lebanon which their nostalgia had reinvented. As a people schooled in the treacherous ebbs and flows of history, the Lebanese have both an eye for trouble and a natural disposition to settle elsewhere. They tend to spot danger from a distance and quietly depart to more promising shores when they feel that there is nothing more to be done. In this sensitivity lies both their strength and their weakness: their strength as individuals guided by an indefatigable will to survive, and their weakness as a people often incapable of working together through political institutions to avert danger. If this left a certain feeling of guilt in the hearts of the emigrants, then perhaps those now occupying the halls, corridors, bars and restaurants of the hotel felt that they were somehow making up for that which their ancestors had left undone or half-done in their old homeland.

The president was elated. He kissed and hugged the Lebanese around him and was kissed and hugged in return. Like all politicians, he thrived on noise; by the end of the day he had lost his voice, his right hand was swollen and his body ached; and yet he could have taken more. This was all new to me. Campus politics had been child's play in comparison. On campus one knew when to go to bed, and when to rise. Travelling with the president meant uninterrupted schedules, sleeping normally at 2 a.m., holding unscheduled meetings at 5 a.m., and eating only when you had the chance.

On the evening of our arrival, Ambassador Morris Draper, a member of Philip Habib's team, came to see us. Philip Habib was Ronald Reagan's Special Envoy to the Middle East, charged with easing the tensions between Syria and Israel and helping Lebanon out of its impasse. Secretary of State George Shultz had dispatched Draper to inform us officially of the Israeli cabinet resolution of 10 October, and to seek our reaction to it. We had already read the text of the resolution in the newspapers, but we now wanted to know if the reports were accurate, and what position the USA took on it.

The Israeli cabinet resolution consisted of the following six points:

1. Israel seeks a peace treaty with Lebanon.
2. The government of Israel proposes the immediate start of negotiations for the withdrawal of all foreign forces from Lebanon.
3. The first to leave will be the PLO terrorists remaining in the Biqa' Valley and in Northern Lebanon.
4. The Syrian army and the Israeli Defence Force (IDF) will withdraw simultaneously.
5. All Israeli prisoners of war, soldiers missing in action, and the bodies of fallen soldiers will be delivered to the IDF before the IDF leaves Lebanon.
6. Security arrangements will be made prior to departure to ensure that Lebanon will not serve again as a base for hostile actions against Israel.

These points were to occupy us for many months in difficult and acrimonious discussions with the Israelis and the Americans, which will be described in due course. At the time, however, it was enough to inform Draper that the Israeli position was unacceptable to us, and that the Lebanese government had set clear parameters on its dealings with Israel. We would discuss them with UN officials and with President Reagan. We anticipated that President Jumayyil's speech before the UN General Assembly would be the first volley in our efforts to bring about some form of international consensus on the Lebanese crisis. Draper said he was merely delivering the message, and was not necessarily supporting it. The US position would be made clear by Reagan and Shultz. The president asked the UN for help to get Israel out, to help in the reconstruction effort, and to support Lebanon's independence, sovereignty and democratic way of life. His speech, outlining the objectives of the new Lebanese government, went well.

The UN Secretary-General Javier Pérez de Cuéllar told us he sympathized with our position; he hoped that Israel would abide by UN resolutions, but had his doubts in the light of its previous behaviour. UN Security Council Resolution 425, adopted on 19 March 1978 during the massive Israeli invasion of Southern Lebanon, called for 'strict respect for the territorial integrity, sovereignty, and political independence of Lebanon within its internationally recognized boundaries'. The resolution also called upon Israel to 'withdraw forthwith its forces from all Lebanese territory', and created the United Nations Interim Force in Lebanon (UNIFIL) 'for the purpose of confirming the withdrawal of Israeli forces, restoring international peace and security and assisting the government of Lebanon in ensuring the return of its effective authority in the area'. While at the UN, President Jumayyil also met the Arab ambassadors accredited to the international body. After the president had finished briefing the Arab representatives on the situation in Lebanon, each of the ambassadors, all accomplished graduates of their respective bureaucracies, raised his hand to ask a question. Instead each delivered a speech intended for people in his own country. The speeches reflected the gaping chasms in the Arab world, and the shallowness pervading the treatment of political issues.

When the turn of the Libyan representative came, he urged President Jumayyil to guide Lebanon along the Arab path and enhance Lebanon's Arab identity. This proved to be the straw that broke the camel's back. The president, who was listening calmly and taking notes, banged the table and sent papers and notes flying before turning to the astonished ambassadors. Usually polite and urbane, he could not control his fury. He began to chastise the Libyan ambassador and the others for their patronizing advice to Lebanon: 'Lebanon is more Arab than any of your countries', he asserted. He went on:

Our Arabism is natural; it is part of our life. It is not an ideology that we buy and sell in the marketplace; we are a people who cherish freedom; we may have an exaggerated view of our dignity and self-importance, but we do not interfere in your affairs. You should not interfere in ours. We do not need you to teach us lessons in Arabism.

The Libyan ambassador was stunned. He insisted that he had no intention of insulting the president, nor of teaching him a lesson. But the president was already packing his papers and motioning to Tweini and me to get moving. 'Enough poetry,' he said, 'let us go!'

Washington Discussions

After we had finished our work at the UN in New York, President Reagan sent a special plane to bring the Lebanese delegation to Washington. At our arrival at Andrews Air Force Base, we were met once again by Mrs Salwa Roosevelt, the charming woman in charge of White House protocol who had welcomed us in New York earlier. Her warm reception was rendered more significant by the fact that she is of Lebanese origin. Mrs Roosevelt guided us to the two White House helicopters which carried us to the grounds of the Washington Monument, where we were met by Secretary of State George Shultz. After a brief ceremony we were taken to the Madison Hotel.

As in New York, Lebanese Americans arrived at the hotel to counsel us on how to handle official Washington. Those with experience in government offered tips on how to approach Ronald Reagan, George Shultz, and Secretary of Defense Caspar Weinberger. There was a general feeling of euphoria at the time within the Lebanese American community since President Reagan and his aides had predicted an early end to the Lebanese conflict. In this context, Lebanese Americans led by successful men like Najib Halaby, Mike Halbouty and Danny Thomas organized an effort to mobilize American entrepreneurial skill for the reconstruction of Lebanon. Lebanese businessmen living in the USA and led by Issam Fares, a leading Lebanese entrepreneur and philanthropist, organized activities to ensure the success of the president's visit and to mobilize support for Lebanon. An effective Lebanese lobby was in the making.

Meanwhile, we prepared for our meetings with the Americans. Under the influence of Dr Wadi Haddad, the only Protestant in our team and therefore, as he rightly claimed, the most organized, President Jumayyil wrote down on separate cards the headings of subjects he wished to discuss with Reagan. I thought this was a good idea as long as the objective was to organize one's thinking, but not if it meant conversing with constant reference to cards. At any rate, I argued, they would not be appropriate in our breakfast with President Reagan the following morning. The breakfast meeting was intended to prepare for more substantive discussions that were to follow. At 8.30 a.m. on Tuesday 19 October, President Jumayyil and I arrived at the White House. We were met at the entrance by Vice-President George Bush and Secretary of State Shultz. They guided us to the second floor to the family quarters, where President Reagan welcomed us warmly.

Reagan was in a relaxed mood, and appeared to relish his role as president. It seemed to come naturally to him. Every move he made, every word he uttered, fitted perfectly into the whole scenario. He appeared to me to be a master of ceremonies, someone who liked to set the stage, assign responsibilities, and then sit back and enjoy the performance. He was confident and informal, in every sense an archetypical laid-back Californian. As far as I could see, his contribution to the meeting was more formal than substantive. Bush was careful. He smiled a lot, spoke encouraging words and was careful not to venture into substantive discussions. He seemed to defer greatly to Reagan. Shultz was polite; he preferred to listen. He seemed professional and he took his time before he engaged in any discussion.

Jumayyil, the president of a small, divided and shattered country, looked anxious. By nature guarded and formal, he seemed the complete antithesis of Reagan. The difference was accentuated by culture and language; Jumayyil was fluent in French but not in English, and was not at ease in these surroundings. His anxiety was compounded by the fact that this was his first meeting with Ronald Reagan, and it was important for him to succeed. The more Reagan joked, the more tense Jumayyil became. The American president directed us to a cosy room with a fireplace where a small breakfast table was set. As we four sat down at table Reagan pointed to a mural facing Jumayyil depicting Americans fighting the British army in the American War of Independence and said: 'This is how we beat the hell out of the British redcoats. You see how tough we are!' Reagan was making a joke. He wanted the whole breakfast to be informal, free, to get acquainted, to break the ice, as it were. Jumayyil did not fully grasp Reagan's style, however. He responded by saying that Lebanon was pleased to have a friend in a superpower which would help it defeat its enemies, as the American colonists had defeated the British, and began to go into the issues in detail. Reagan would have preferred to get acquainted, and to save the details for the meeting scheduled after breakfast.

Reagan assured us that his 1 September initiative to secure peace in the Middle East would be pursued rigorously, and that peace in Lebanon was a first step towards peace in the Middle East. The United States, he said, would help Lebanon diplomatically, although economic aid would only be limited. He remarked, however, that there were Americans of Lebanese descent, among them his close friends Danny Thomas and Mike Halbouty, who were encouraging private investment in Lebanon.

Reagan spoke in generalities. Serious work was scheduled after the breakfast. It is in the working sessions, not in the fireside chats, that more serious matters are dealt with. In the working session the president brings with him the appropriate secretaries of departments, their advisers, aides and note-takers. In such meetings, the machinery of state is fully engaged: officials present their positions, these are duly recorded, and the record constitutes a commitment. The notes are then distributed to the National Security Council, the State Department, the Department of Defense and other relevant departments and offices.

Our working meeting with the president included on the American side President Reagan, Vice-President Bush, Secretary of State Shultz, Secretary of Defense Weinberger, National Security Adviser William Clark and his assistant Robert (Bud) McFarlane, White House Chief of Staff Edwin Meese, Deputy Secretary of State Kenneth Dam, Special Envoy Philip Habib, Ambassador Morris Draper, the Assistant Secretary of State for Near Eastern and South Asian Affairs Nicholas Veliotis, US Ambassador to Lebanon Robert Dillon, and the director of the Agency for International Development, Peter McPherson. In addition there were members of the National Security Council and some half a dozen note-takers.

The Lebanese side was represented by the entire official delegation as well as our ambassador in Washington, Khalil Itani. Reagan welcomed the Lebanese delegation, spoke of the good time he had with Jumayyil at breakfast and gave him the floor. Jumayyil spoke confidently, referring to his notes and showing that he had done his homework. He recognized that the USA was committed to helping Lebanon. He acknowledged the efforts of Philip Habib and his associates, Dillon and Draper, in helping resolve the crisis emerging from the Israeli occupation. He also acknowledged the importance of the Multinational Force and the US Marine contingent in it. There was no doubt where the USA stood morally, he said. The question was, however, could the USA deliver? Would Israel comply with the US position and withdraw from Lebanon? If Israel should comply, would the conditions of compliance be such as to lead Syria to withdraw? Would an isolated USSR allow the USA to score such a diplomatic victory? Would Reagan, at the height of the new Cold War in 1982, give the Soviets a role in Middle Eastern Affairs? These were unknowns, and the president wanted reassurances.

Lebanon needed US help in reconstruction, and for re-equipping the army. A strong army would enable the Lebanese government to extend its sovereignty throughout the country in the wake of the withdrawal of foreign forces. We estimated reconstruction costs at $1 billion per year to start with, and gradually less after that. Uppermost in our mind was an extensive housing project that would eliminate the misery belt around Beirut. We had, of course, prepared the US team on what to expect from us. I had told Draper at the Waldorf Astoria meeting what our position was on the Israeli statement of 10 October, and what we expected from the USA in terms of political and economic support. Reagan was well briefed. He chaired the meeting and choreographed the proceedings perfectly. He was clearly in command of the few basic points needed for making decisions at his level, while he left the details for Shultz, Weinberger and Clark. He pointed out that he was impressed by Jumayyil, by his methodology in presenting the Lebanese situation and by his confident tone. Jumayyil whispered to me: 'You see, the cards help.' Reagan too was resorting to his own cards to ask questions and to direct the discussions.

Having listened to all views, Reagan defined the US policy on Lebanon in the following terms:

> The United States is willing to help Lebanon end the war and regain its stability. We want to help you as much as we can, but cannot maintain our troops in Lebanon for a long time since it would create the impression that we are an occupying force. Foreign forces must withdraw as soon as possible, and withdrawal in the South will have to be staged in light of Israel's security concerns. We want to help in reconstruction, but our help will be limited due to the serious economic situation the United States is facing.

He continued: 'The United States fully understands your position on negotiations and your need to preserve the national consensus as well as your credentials in the Arab world. We are counselling Israel not to press you too hard or too fast and thus risk endangering your internal unity or alienating your relations with the Arab world.' Reagan's statement on Israeli withdrawal, 'in light of Israel's security concerns', disturbed me. I reiterated our position on full Israeli withdrawal. Reagan reassured us on this point and urged us to discuss details with Secretary Shultz. It was important for us to see that Reagan understood our concern about preserving national unity and maintaining our good relations with the Arab world. We had a different perspective from that of the Americans, and perhaps a greater reverence for details as well.

President Jumayyil, Tweini and I discussed these details with Secretary Shultz, after our meeting with Reagan. There was a fundamental problem in our dealings with the Americans. While we looked at Lebanon as an end in itself, Washington saw it in a larger context, whether as an instrument for general peace in the region, or as a cog in the East–West conflict. When the Americans saw Lebanon, they thought of Islamic revivalism, Israeli security, perhaps even the flow of oil. Yet Lebanon was not simply a collection of regional interests: we were and are a people displaced, a country divided, an economy in shambles, and a democracy threatened.

George Shultz told us that the USA was concerned with the larger issue in the Middle East, namely the peace process. Whatever the USA did in Lebanon should contribute to the process. The USA wanted Lebanon and Israel to live in peace, and if Lebanon could not conclude a peace treaty now, it should do so later on. To get all foreign forces out of its territory would be a great achievement and, therefore, Lebanon should make compromises worthy of that goal and the Arabs should support Lebanon in making these compromises. Shultz continued that if Lebanon felt it could get a full Israeli withdrawal on the basis of the relevant UN resolutions, then it should go ahead and try to do so. But then Lebanon could not depend on the USA for help. Israel, he told us, never withdrew in accordance with UN resolutions. It withdrew only on the basis of bilateral discussions in which it alone determined what its national interest was. In the case of Sinai, Israel withdrew only in return for a peace treaty with Egypt. Shultz then outlined specific Israeli objectives. He took these objectives for granted as the price of total withdrawal from Lebanon: Israel, he said, did not like UNIFIL involvement on its borders. It wanted a security zone from the Awwali river, north of Sidon, to Rashayya in the East, and the UNIFIL to be stationed on that line and at points to the north, but not below. One brigade of the Lebanese army could be deployed in this security zone. No more was needed, because the PLO had already withdrawn. Israel wanted Colonel Sa'd Haddad, the head of the Israeli-financed South Lebanon Army (SLA) reinstated in the regular Lebanese army and given responsibility in the south. It wanted normalization of relations with Lebanon, which meant open frontiers and movement of men and goods. Israel's aim, he added, was a peace treaty with Lebanon. Shultz proposed that we work out an agenda of things that could be done in this direction and then go ahead and do them. The sooner Israel withdrew the better. He gave examples of what Israeli occupation of the West Bank, Gaza and the Golan Heights had done to these areas. He noted how Israel created new facts on the ground and then negotiated on the basis of these facts; and the facts, he added, kept changing in its favour. In this respect, the United States could be of assistance to the Lebanese, but it was necessary to act before Israel changed the character of Lebanon.

Shultz was sincere in his presentation. He wanted to help Lebanon regain its independence. He wanted to deepen and broaden Israel's legitimate presence in the region. He wanted successful negotiations between Lebanon and Israel under US auspices, which would provide a model for future negotiations on the Middle Eastern question. Shultz was almost whispering, but his voice revealed a strong conviction.

His convictions, in the abstract, were not without logic: the victor dictates, the defeated accommodates, and the peace-maker mediates. Shultz was mediating between a victorious Israel and a prostrate Lebanon. Although as head of the Bechtel Corporation Shultz had extensive business contacts with the Arab world, he was not aware of the deep psychological barriers separating Arabs from Israelis. The logic of victory and defeat does not fully apply in the Arab–Israeli context. In the wars with Israel, Arabs celebrated their defeats as if they were victories, and presidents and generals were better known for the cities and regions they had lost than for the ones they had liberated. They were glorified for their intents not their achievements. In losing the June 1967 War Jamal Abd al-Nasir became a hero. In gaining peace, but dissenting from prevailing Arab psychology, Anwar al-Sadat became a villain.

By the time my turn came to speak, I felt that there was much that I needed to cover to make Shultz understand our position and appreciate it. I tried to explain to him the nature of Lebanese politics, its historical context, and the deep psychological factors governing Lebanese and Arab political behaviour in dealing with Israel. I reaffirmed some of the points made by President Jumayyil in his earlier presentation to President Reagan. It was the position of the Lebanese government that a full Israeli withdrawal in accordance with UN resolutions must take place. We were anxious for US help. The USA had already established a track record by negotiating the withdrawal of the PLO from Beirut. Yet Lebanon could not agree nor afford to agree to a peace treaty and the normalization of relations with Israel. We considered our relations with Israel to be governed by the General Armistice Agreement of 23 March 1949. We did not want to negotiate with Israel outside the boundaries of the existing Israel–Lebanon Military Liaison Committee (ILMAC). We would agree to an expansion or modified format of ILMAC if it were necessary, but always with the involvement of a third party. This third party must be the United States, since no other nation had such influence with Israel and none was more concerned with the future of peace in the region.

Lebanon would not enter into any negotiations with Israel which might be interpreted as consenting to changes in frontiers, to normalization of relations, or to a peace treaty. We believed the Israeli proposal of a security zone stretching from the Awwali River to Rashayya, with UNIFIL deployed north of that line, to be tantamount to partition. Furthermore, the borders between Lebanon and Israel should be closed, not opened. The Lebanese government must be allowed to deploy its army in the south to ensure stability and prevent infiltration across the internationally recognized frontier between Israel and Lebanon. UNIFIL should be deployed in the south with our army to ensure the implementation of UN resolutions.

I then outlined regional considerations. Prior to discussions with Israel, the Lebanese government would have to consult with Arab leaders. As we discussed with the Israelis their withdrawal from Lebanon, we would also be talking to the Syrians and to the PLO to bring about their withdrawal. The timing of their departure was our concern, although the sooner everybody left, the better. Lebanon had committed errors in allowing the PLO to give Israel reasons to attack Lebanon; we would take care of that in the future and we would strictly implement the articles of the Armistice Agreement.

Shultz seemed restless. He didn't seem to understand; I sensed that he was caught in his own logic. Somewhere in the midst of these discussions he stared me straight in the eye and said: 'Elie, I must remind you Israel won the war, you lost.' 'George,' I responded, 'you were not listening, let me repeat ...'

Finally, we agreed with the Americans on a number of points. We agreed to start exploratory talks through an expanded version of ILMAC, with the presence of US representatives. We acquiesced to discussions on the understanding that our position would be identical to the one stated in Washington: Lebanon's frontiers were inviolable; Lebanon would not accept an imposed solution; negotiations should not endanger the internal national consensus or Lebanon's ties to the Arab world; and if talks were to take place, the agreed framework would be as follows: 'To deal with arrangements for withdrawal of Israeli forces from Lebanon, and for the reassertion of Lebanese government authority throughout its territory.'

Return through Paris and Rome

We felt we had made some progress in Washington on procedural steps. The USA was the key in dealing with Israel. Nevertheless, President Jumayyil wanted to consult France and the Vatican before returning to Beirut. Both had historical ties to Lebanon, and even though they could not help directly with Israel they could play a constructive role in other respects. Both France and Italy were leading members of the European Community, and one of our objectives was to establish contacts with the emerging and increasingly independent European presence in world politics. In addition, Paris and the Vatican were anxious to learn of our policies and of the US commitment in helping us implement them.

I should have rested on the overnight flight to Paris in preparation for the gruelling schedule next day. Too tired to sleep, I spent the entire route reading and chatting with whoever was awake. Perhaps subconsciously I depended on our francophone president. I expected to arrive early enough in Paris to rest and to change. I was wrong. To my surprise President Jumayyil and most members of the delegation had all slept, shaved and changed into clean clothes on the plane. They knew the programme; I did not. Shabby, unshaven and tired, I was whisked from the plane to the elegant Elysée Palace. Two hundred years after the French Revolution, the palace still seemed to house a royal court.

Paris viewed the new US role in Lebanon with suspicion. What did these merchant Yankees know about the complexities of the Middle East and the intricacies of the Levant? What was worse, as far as the French were concerned, was that we were merely stopping over in Paris on our way back from Washington. France liked to keep a foothold in its former colonies and mandates by any means at its disposal. For decades Paris had been the political and social beacon of Lebanon; the Lebanese were expected in Paris first, and only afterwards in Washington, London and Moscow. But times had changed. Ancient capitals resent change, and of all the European capitals none is more resistant than Paris.

In an efficient style each member of our delegation was quickly paired with his counterpart. I found myself in a palatial hall of the palace with the French Minister of External Relations, Claude Cheysson. Obviously briefed on my limited French, he looked at me intensely and asked, in French, what language we should speak. Not waiting for my answer, he continued: 'We shall of course speak French.' I responded that I would of course speak Arabic. He looked at me with disbelief, not knowing whether this was spoken seriously or in jest. I maintained my serious demeanour long enough for him to shake his head, mutter, and finally agree that we would speak English. He added, however, that if anyone entered the hall, he would immediately revert to French. I agreed, and then proceeded, to his great satisfaction, to brief him on our Washington visit in my shaky French. It was apparently adequate enough to convey the political message clearly and precisely, despite frequent assistance from English words. I briefed Cheysson on our talks in the United States. I explained the framework for exploratory talks with Israel agreed to in Washington, adding that they would take place in an expanded version of ILMAC, with US participation. I assured Cheysson that Lebanon would coordinate with France and would seek its counsel. Lebanon appreciated the French contribution to its political and educational life, but it now needed

American help to secure an Israeli withdrawal. I assured him that Lebanon would count a great deal on French support, and that relations between Lebanon and France were historical and special, and therefore should be strengthened rather than weakened. This was an objective, I concluded, to which I was deeply committed.

France, Cheysson responded, was ready to help Lebanon politically, economically, militarily, and in the field of education. Due to the delicate situation at present, France would not take any initiatives, but would respond positively to any initiative acceptable to Lebanon. He was ready to come to Lebanon whenever I invited him, and he asked me to contact him whenever I needed his help. He supplied me with a list of telephone numbers where he could be reached any day of the week.

As urgent business awaited us in Beirut, we only allotted one day to Paris and one to Rome. The Vatican has a special role in Lebanese affairs. Its distinctive ties to the Catholic communities in Lebanon, particularly the Maronites, have historically made it an important player and mediator in Lebanese affairs. At this juncture, there was little the Pope could offer us, except a renewal of his commitment to peace in Lebanon, and support for the American effort aiming at the full withdrawal of all foreign forces. Secular Rome had also acquired a special importance in Lebanon. The Italians had important contingents in the Multinational Force and in UNIFIL. I briefed Foreign Minister Emilio Colombo on our Washington visit. He asked many questions which reflected his wide knowledge, his deep interest in international affairs, and his intense seriousness. Colombo assured me that Italy would remain engaged in Lebanon through MNF and UNIFIL, and would provide us with aid.

I had, over the past seven years, developed a kind of relationship with guns and those who wield them. Pistols, rifles, machine-guns, cannons, troop-carriers and tanks had been part of my everyday life in Lebanon, and I had come to know almost instinctively when they were threatening and when not. There is a psychology associated with guns and those who carry them which one learns rather quickly. In Rome, however, I lacked such a perspective; hence my anxiety as young Italian soldiers flaunted their sub-machine-guns in my face. I was not quite sure whether they were defending me as foreign minister, or somehow engaging in that timeless posturing associated with all bearers of weapons. Similarly, I had always thought Lebanese policemen particularly notable for their use and abuse of power, until I saw the Roman police in action. I observed with great amusement the four motorcycle policemen assigned to me. These fine motorcyclists were a terror; they screamed at motorists, and signalled to them to move out of the way; when motorists hesitated, the policemen kicked their cars or aimed their motorcycles at them, all the time gesturing and threatening. The motorists screamed back, threatened, or responded with a variety of imaginative Mediterranean gestures, but fortunately nothing happened. In Lebanon such verbal abuse would have certainly ended in fist-fighting or in a wild exchange of fire.

Upon our return to Beirut, Prime Minister Wazzan felt it was the right time to submit a ministerial statement to Parliament defining the policies of the government, and asking for a vote of confidence. The meeting was called for 4 November. In his statement to the legislators, the prime minister outlined the government's policies, and asked, in addition, for special powers for a limited period to legislate by decree. When Wazzan reached the section in his statement on special powers, the deputies became restless. Some walked out in protest and some shouted at the prime minister: 'Why don't you just dissolve Parliament, and while you're at it why don't you ask for legal powers to grant marriage licences and even the right of divorce?' As the shouting grew louder and anarchy reigned supreme, Speaker al-As'ad adjourned the session.

The next meeting was as anarchic and as uncontrollable as the one before. Again the meeting was adjourned. On 9 November, after an exhausting debate, the government received a vote of confidence from 58 of the 59 deputies present, and was granted the special powers to rule by decree. Vocal opposition, it seems, had little impact on the actual voting. With this formality completed the government proceeded with the long and arduous process of negotiating the withdrawal of Israeli forces from the country.

2

Negotiating Israeli Withdrawal

The main foreign policy objective of the Lebanese government at the end of 1982 was negotiating the full withdrawal of Israeli forces from Lebanese territory. As an observer of the Israeli–Palestinian conflict, I was concerned that Israel would slowly incorporate or annex occupied Lebanese territory, as it had done to the territories occupied in the June 1967 war. The Israeli policy of creating new facts on the ground, and then proceeding from these facts, alarmed me, and we were anxious to get the Israelis out of Lebanon to forestall the possibility of such an occurrence.

The first step in this direction was our agreement in Washington to holding exploratory talks with Israel under a tripartite formula which would include Lebanon, Israel and the United States. Israel, on the other hand, was reluctant to involve the USA in the negotiations. It wanted to negotiate with us alone, a strong power versus a weak one, in the hope of exacting better conditions.

No group was more conscious of the dangers of negotiating with Israel than the Lebanese government. The decision to negotiate was not an easy one, but it virtually imposed itself when all other options proved inadequate in confronting the challenge of Israeli occupation. The Soviets could not help because they had broken diplomatic ties with Israel and had no influence on Israeli politics whatsoever. France, Italy and the Vatican admitted that over Israeli withdrawals from Lebanon they must follow the US lead. The UN was not then a credible instrument due to Cold War politics and to Israeli suspicions of a UN dominated by countries that did not share the Israeli point of view. Shultz was clear with us. He said that if we wanted to go to the UN, we could not then depend on the USA. This was serious in the light of American assurances to former President Sarkis that all foreign forces would be out of Lebanon by Christmas 1982.

Those among us who would be involved in the decision of negotiating with Israel – namely President Jumayyil, Prime Minister Wazzan, Ghassan Tweini, the coordinator of the negotiations, and myself – understood the ideological movements in the region and knew what could be attempted and what could not. The president had a reputation for being sensitive to the imperatives of Arab politics and to the balances inside the Lebanese body politic. Prime Minister Wazzan had sufficient credibility in the Arab and Islamic worlds that he could not be accused of seeking a separate peace with Israel. Ghassan Tweini was an experienced politician, a season-ed diplomat and a well-known journalist. I had lived the Arab nationalist ideas at the university and had written extensively on them. We under-stood the Arab mind well. We also understood why Jamal Abd al-Nasir was popular in defeat and Anwar al-Sadat was labelled a traitor. At the same time, we also knew the limits of ideology. We had witnessed the rise and decline of ideologies in the Arab world and beyond. We also knew our environment well: we knew what could be expected of it, for how long, and under what conditions. We were familiar with Syrian politics and we appreciated Syria's concerns. We had also followed Israel's growing role in the region. We understood its ties with the West and, more importantly, we had a sense of the ethos driving it. We read history, and we knew the appetite of the conqueror and the temptations of the conquered.

There was a general consensus in Lebanon for taking all necessary steps to get the Israelis out. As pragmatists the Lebanese were not opposed to negotiations with Israel: only a small marginal minority wanted a peace treaty, while at the other extreme, only a few believed then that Resolution 425 could be implemented without negotiations. The majority of the Lebanese, as evidenced by the parliamentary vote, hoped to get Israel out through a reasonable agreement negotiated with the good offices of the United States. A consensus was there. Perhaps its major weakness, how-ever, was that it was largely sustained by the feeling that success was imminent. We followed the consensus as much as we led it.

The president was restless and anxious to move quickly. In his first six months in office, he did not walk, he ran. He moved on all fronts, whether in Lebanon, in the region, or internationally. He believed that he could be both a liberator and a builder: he would secure an Israeli withdrawal with the help of the United States, and he would reconstruct Lebanon after seven years of conflict. Jumayyil's confidence in the US commitment was boundless. When Philip Habib told President Sarkis in the summer of 1982 that all foreign forces would leave Lebanon by Christmas, Sarkis, like his successors Bashir and Amin, thought Habib was speaking in the name of Reagan, that Reagan was speaking for the USA and that the USA could not fail. There was little appreciation of the role of Congress, of conflicts amongst departments, of the influence of the media and of the lobbies in the formulation of US foreign policy. A word from Habib was taken as an irreversible commitment.

Fears and Counter-fears

The question now shifted to negotiating a framework in which talks between Lebanon and Israel leading to an Israeli withdrawal could take place. Since the invasion of Lebanon by Israel in June 1982, the Lebanese government had dealt with the Israelis through the Israel–Lebanon Mixed Armistice Commission (ILMAC). We were ably represented in ILMAC.

By the end of October, we had come to an agreement with the Americans on a number of points: (1) the United States would be present in all meetings of the expanded ILMAC; (2) American involvement would continue at least until all Israeli forces had withdrawn from Lebanese territory; (3) the United States would arrange for the first meeting between the parties; (4) each party would keep its own minutes; (5) the USA would intervene to resolve difficulties that arose in the negotiations; (6) the role of the MNF would be under continuous review in the light of the withdrawal of foreign forces from Lebanon, and the logistical requirements of the Lebanese army.

Procedural problems remained, however. There was no agreement on the venue, time frame or procedural framework for negotiations. The question of venue was particularly difficult to resolve. Israel, which wanted to give the discussions a political colour, preferred the venues to be Jerusalem and Beirut. This would have implied implicit recognition of Israel, as well as recognition of Jerusalem as its capital, and was unacceptable. We, in turn, proposed Naqurah, a Lebanese town on the Israeli–Lebanese border and the original venue for ILMAC, but Israel opposed this. We proposed a number of alternatives: meeting in a neutral state; meeting in the eastern Mediterranean on a ship belonging to a neutral nation; or negotiating through Philip Habib, who would shuttle back and forth between Israel and Lebanon. All these proposals were immediately rejected by Israel. We then proposed to Draper that both sides could hold exploratory meetings on procedural matters and an agenda at the Lebanon Beach Hotel in Khalde, south of Beirut; and that subsequently, we could hold future meetings in Naqurah. Draper responded by proposing holding the meetings alternately in small towns in Lebanon and Israel. Before presenting his proposal, Draper told us that he had cleared his proposal with Syrian Foreign Minister Abd al-Halim Khaddam. We found the suggestion acceptable, and by 5 November Draper had also obtained final approval from the Israelis.

We were anxious to start the process; Israel was not. It was not keen to have the Americans present; it thought delays would strengthen its hold on Lebanon and weaken our position; and also it was not optimistic in getting what it wanted from the proposed negotiations. The Americans were aware of the Israeli attitude and Shultz pointed this out to Moshe Arens, the Israeli ambassador in Washington, telling him that Lebanon had done the best it could, that the USA found the Lebanese attitude reasonable, and that discussions should start immediately.

On 8 November, Draper informed me that the Israeli government had changed its position and now insisted on political discussions. Israel's position, he added, had hardened due to 'big problems within the Israeli government'. There were those who questioned the wisdom of the invasion; there were those who wanted to exact a high price for the great losses in life that the Israeli army had suffered; there were strong accusations against the government that it had entered a war without clear purpose. Begin and Sharon wanted to show that their war was right and that it would end in a peace treaty with Lebanon, hence their insistent demand for political discussions with us. Draper told us that Begin and Sharon were 'passionately' opposed to discussions with a Lebanese team that had a strong military character. The Israelis, he said, wanted political contacts with us and they promised to keep these contacts secret.

I was not surprised to receive this message. What surprised me was Draper's recommendation that we ought seriously to consider it, and his suggestion that I speak to the president about it. I responded that if Israel wanted to communicate its views to us, they could do it through him. Our position on political discussions and on secret talks was final, and there was no need to see the president. Draper asked again if the president should be consulted on this matter, and I said no.

Draper insisted that the purpose of such talks would not be the conclusion of a peace treaty. He assured me that he had used all the proper arguments with the Israeli leaders, but to no avail. This worried me. At one time the USA, through its envoy, said the Israelis would be out by Christmas; at another they did not seem to have a machinery in place to effect this promise. Clearly the USA was depending on Philip Habib to conciliate the views between us and Israel. And the views seemed distant indeed. As we were anxious to gain time we were ready to have a civilian, a retired diplomat, head our team, but still within the context of ILMAC, albeit an expanded ILMAC. Draper supported our proposal for an expanded ILMAC format.

Despite the setbacks, we were hopeful. We received word from the Americans that President Reagan had asked for a daily progress report on the negotiations, and that he was anxious to get all foreign forces out of

Lebanon by Christmas at the latest. As Christmas was only five or six weeks away, no one could blame the Lebanese for the spirit of euphoria that pervaded the political atmosphere at the time. Special envoy Philip Habib had predicted an even earlier deadline for an Israeli withdrawal, but daily reports on the hardening Israeli position were casting doubt in our mind that the deadlines could be met. It was also obvious that the USA had no solution except what it hoped to get through negotiations between two teams. We were also worried by the different interpretations the US team had of the Israeli position. I recall Habib telling us that Begin wanted so-and-so. Draper would scream back: 'No, no, no, that is not what Begin said.' Habib, irritated, would say: 'Of course that is what Begin said. I know what I am talking about. I have not lost my mind.' Draper would respond with muffled 'No's' to ease the embarrassment as Christopher Ross, the note-taker, wrote down every word. 'For Heaven's sake,' Habib would shout at Ross, 'stop writing.' I would take Habib aside, calm him down and try to find out what was really happening. The USA was certainly not the magician we had hoped for, but we had no other. At least it had made a commitment: it had its troops in the MNF, and it was serious about discussions.

By mid-November we and the American team were getting restless. The more Habib shuttled between Beirut and Jerusalem, the more he realized that his promise of early withdrawals was losing credibility. Habib felt that the lack of progress was due to the fact that he was not as directly involved as he should be. He had no qualms about blaming his assistants. Habib is a self-confident, loud and flamboyant individual, whose style is more akin to that of a shrewd politician than that of a career diplomat. He is notoriously hard on his aides, shouting orders, questioning some points and clarifying others, and he cultivates an imperious attitude in order to inspire fear and awe. He is also sceptical about any process in which he is not the central figure. Habib's ancestors came from South Lebanon and had kept their Lebanese style of life, and from time to time in their new Brooklyn neighbourhood he betrayed an empathy for Lebanon and the Lebanese that flickered through his intense loyalty to his American homeland.

My acquaintance with Habib dated from the last weeks of the Sarkis regime. At the time he seemed to be continuously involved in negotiating ceasefires between the Israelis, Palestinians and Syrians in and around Beirut. One day, while at the American ambassador's residence, I saw him talking on the phone to the White House. He looked furious and was insisting to the person on the other end of the line that Israel had violated the ceasefire: shells and rockets were falling all over Beirut, as well as near the presidential palace in B'abda. The official in the White House questioned Habib's assessment and assured him that according to his information the ceasefire was holding. Thereupon Habib took the receiver and thrust it outside the window and screamed: 'Listen carefully to the ceasefire. The noise outside is war, my friends. What the hell is the matter with you? Do I have to place the phone on the roof for you to believe me that all hell has broken loose here? Tell Reagan someone there is lying to him', and he slammed down the receiver. He looked at me and said: 'This is Washington for you. The guys there only believe what they read in the telex. Who the hell invented the written word? Was it you, the Phoenicians?' I liked what I heard. I have always liked straight, blunt language. Soon Habib and I were working together closely and had become friends. We understood each other perfectly, though we did not always agree.

As we entered December, I grew increasingly concerned about the delays. I got in touch with Habib's assistant, Ambassador Morris Draper. I wanted to know from him whether the United States believed Israel had designs on South Lebanon, and if so, what kind of designs? Could the USA assure us that Israel had no territorial ambitions and that we could ultimately get the Israelis out by negotiations before more dangerous facts had changed the ground under us? Was the delay intended to create more facts on the ground? Draper responded that although Israel had no territorial designs on Lebanon, it might wish to hold on to South Lebanon as a sort of protectorate. While in the past Israel believed that a strong Lebanon with a strong president was a good thing, it no longer thought so. Some Israelis wanted a sphere of influence in Lebanon, and did not mind at all if the Syrians remained in the Biqa' valley. His answer was sobering. The American tone was beginning to change, and they were no longer promising withdrawals by Christmas. When Draper hinted that Begin would be visiting Washington after Christmas, I knew the Christmas deadline had finally fallen off the American agenda.

Lebanon, I told Draper, could not follow the Israeli timetable, nor, I believed, could the USA and still maintain its credibility as a superpower. Draper admitted that Israel was engaged in delaying tactics. It feared, he argued, that the success of American efforts in Lebanon would strengthen Reagan's hand in addressing the Middle East conflict. Israel, he said, was willing to negotiate to satisfy the USA, but it did not want the negotiations to lead Washington to pressure Israel to make concessions in a regional peace settlement. Israel was not ready for a Middle East peace, he said. If the Israelis were alarmed about linking a settlement of the Lebanese crisis to the wider Middle East conflict, so were we, if for completely different reasons. A serious concern, which hung over our heads like a sword of Damocles, was that an Israeli withdrawal from Lebanon would be conditional on a future resolution of the Middle East problem. The solution of this problem involved peace and a regional settlement. This meant multi-party discussions over a long period of time. We were not in that mood. It was our very capital, not merely a distant frontier strip, that was under occupation.

On 7 December, I sent the following message to Shultz:

> Under no condition should the Lebanese problem be tied to the Middle East problem. The Lebanese problem could be solved immediately and its solution could give a tremendous impetus to the overall peace process. The USA should issue a statement saying it will not permit the annexation of any part of Lebanon or the establishment of settlements or the institution of special zones or protectorates that will, in any way, compromise Lebanon's unity, sovereignty, independence and democratic institutions.

I wanted such a statement to safeguard Lebanon from dangers already incurred in the West Bank, Gaza and the Golan Heights.

Draper and Dillon assured me that US policy on these matters should alleviate my fears, and that Shultz would authorize statements to that effect. They were uncertain, however, on a number of concerns we raised regarding Israeli intentions and tactics. They were uncertain on how Israel would use its presence to create communal conflicts, or how long it intended to delay in the hope of creating favourable negotiation conditions for itself. Draper and Dillon were eager to help, and felt that if I wanted more assurances I should talk to Shultz directly. As I wanted to go to Washington I took advantage of an official invitation to visit London on the way between 7 and 10 December and meet Prime Minister Margaret Thatcher. It was the first official visit to Great Britain by a Lebanese foreign minister. The objective of my discussions in London was to discuss British participation in the Multinational Force. We wanted such a participation, even if it were minimal and symbolic.

Accompanied by our ambassador in London, Khalil Mikkawi, and my assistant Ms Itamar Diab, I met the Prime Minister on Friday 10 December. She had with her Sir John Leahy and an aide, John Coles. The meeting, originally planned for 20 minutes, lasted one hour. Thatcher combined the grace of an accomplished lady with the toughness of a seasoned politician and moved from one mood to the other with complete ease. Her power of concentration was phenomenal, and her questioning was penetrating and relentless. She would stare me in the eye and bluntly ask: 'How much of the conflict in your country is civil, how much regional, and how much international? Who is involved in the fighting in Beirut, who in the Biqa'? Why did Lebanon collapse as it did? Could the collapse have been prevented? Is there an end in sight? Could our participation really help? If we join we must succeed; what are the chances?' I gave her objective answers; she was entitled to know the facts. When she learned from me of the presence of Iranian Revolutionary Guards in the Biqa' Valley she was furious.

Turning to Leahy, she asked him between clenched teeth: 'Why didn't you tell me? Nobody told me there are Iranians in Lebanon. What are they doing there? Who brought them in? How many are they? Why are we so poorly informed?' Poor Leahy was in despair, and looked at her silently, wishing perhaps that the ground would open beneath him and free him from this inquisition. At this crucial moment a servant walked in with a tea-tray. Thatcher shifted gear, unglued her eyes from Leahy, and reverting to the role of an accomplished lady poured me a cup of tea with one knee virtually on the floor, gently asking whether I wanted sugar or milk. I was amazed at her ability to control her moods; it had only taken a fraction of a second for her to change the atmosphere from that of a tempest to the tranquility dictated by English custom. She continued:

> You realize why I hesitate to send troops to Lebanon. We are spread out in so many places: in Europe within NATO, in the Falklands, Gibraltar, Cyprus and Sinai. Our boys are in great demand, because they are so good everybody wants them. In Sinai, no one would have gone had we not gone there first. My problem is this. If we get in, we will get involved, and I cannot take on an indefinite obligation. I cannot function in uncertainty. I want to be certain. I want to take the decision today, by myself. I must know that if I send troops to Lebanon, I can get out in a short period. Your problem seems to me to be long term, but you had a working democracy as you said, and I want to help you restore it. But by God, you do have enormous problems and now I hear Iran is involved. I will decide today. If my decision is positive, our participation will be symbolic and for a limited period of time.

The 'I' was so prominent in her presentation that I was confident she would send troops; she was clearly the decision-maker and I felt she wanted to be involved because our case was right and the prospect of success was good, due largely to the seemingly total American commitment. Thatcher did send a small contingent to Lebanon, and gave us continuing support in our negotiations.

I left London for Washington on 13 December and began my official talks on the following day with Assistant Secretary of State for Near East and South Asian Affairs, Nicholas Veliotis. I told him of our concern at the delay in negotiations. I assured Veliotis that I was not in Washington on a negative campaign against Israel, but on an urgent and positive campaign for Lebanon. This psychological position had to be made clear to calm the many forces in and out of government in Washington that upheld the Israeli position. Veliotis understood our problem and appreciated our sense of urgency. He agreed that a delay in negotiations could be dangerous to Lebanon. There was a feeling in Washington that the Lebanese problem was a test of American credibility. If the Reagan initiative were to fail in Lebanon, it would most likely fail in resolving the Middle East problem.

In my meeting with Secretary of Defense Caspar Weinberger I emphasized the danger posed by the situation in Lebanon to Middle East peace and stability. The danger could only be forestalled, I argued, if Lebanon were truly independent and sovereign. This would come about if we were helped to build a strong army to ensure that our territory was not used by others to attack our neighbours, and thus invite the retaliation which we had witnessed over the years. Our thinking in early 1983 was to build an army of 40,000 men and a special unit of some 20,000 men to protect our borders.

I described to Weinberger the pressures the Israelis were putting on our government to comply with their demands. These pressures included the arming of rival parties, the instigation of confessional fighting, and even direct threats against members of our government. Such tactics, I said, would greatly undermine our efforts. Weinberger admitted that time had been lost. He had confidence in President Reagan's commitment to Lebanon. From his defence perspective he saw support of Lebanon as part of the US effort to check Soviet inroads into the Middle East. He believed the USA could persuade Israel to withdraw, but he was uncertain of American influence with Syria. Reagan and he disagreed with Ariel Sharon's insistence that Lebanon should conclude a peace treaty with Israel. He acknowledged that Lebanon should be among the last of the Arab states to sign such a treaty. He also expressed concern about the Syrian policy of introducing Iranians into Lebanon: 'The Iranians in Lebanon can go wild and endanger the entire Middle East', he said, 'I hope Israel realizes that. If it does, it should withdraw and thus facilitate Syrian, PLO, and Iranian withdrawals from Lebanon.'

In the White House I met Clark and McFarlane. Prolonging the Israeli presence in Lebanon would open a Pandora's Box, I argued. Israel was playing havoc with the complex Lebanese political formula, and fomenting violence in the Shuf mountains. This could lead to massacres, I said, that would dwarf the tragedies of Sabra and Shatila. We needed withdrawals today rather than tomorrow, and tomorrow rather than after tomorrow. It was a question of what was right. Lack of progress would erode American credibility and would weaken our government.

In the middle of our discussions President Reagan walked in, and said to me:

> We are with you all the way to get foreign forces out of your country and to re-establish peace in your beautiful land. I have just called Habib and asked

him to work out an operational framework for the withdrawal of all foreign forces from Lebanon. We will help you with Israel, and we will do what we can with the others. Things are going slow. I want them to move faster. We are determined and committed to see this matter through. I want action. If you have specifics please suggest them to Phil Habib, he has my full confidence.

I took this opportunity to give the president an overview of Lebanon's importance in the region and why it deserved American support. He listened attentively, looked at me with a broad smile and said: 'I know you are a professor; I advise you to keep that in mind when you talk to Shultz. He is a professor too. I am sure he will listen carefully and will appreciate the urgency of your mission.'

Shultz was in Europe on an extended agenda and I therefore arranged to see him in London. We met at the American Ambassador's residence; there were no ambassadors, advisers or note-takers. We sat by a blazing fire and talked freely about all aspects of the Lebanese problem. I reviewed with Shultz the details of my visit to Washington, and together we analysed what had been said and clarified vague points. An atmosphere of informality and trust tended to prevail in my meetings with Shultz. Perhaps this was because of our respective backgrounds: we were both professors who had become chairmen of their departments; we had both been deans in our universities; and now we were both serving as foreign ministers.

On the urgency of speeding up the withdrawal process, Shultz assured me that Reagan had the 'bit in his teeth on this business'. Philip Habib, he said, was not in Israel just to talk. He was there to achieve results. The objective was to get all foreign forces out – not to discuss how to do it, but to do it, and do it fast. Shultz remarked that the Reagan administration was as much in a hurry as we were to see a conclusion to the Lebanese crisis. He assured me that Israel would not be permitted to endanger Lebanese unity, independence and general orientation. America, he said, cared for Lebanon and for what it represented and would not desert us. Habib, he said, would soon come up with an action plan.

The Sharon Paper

I returned to Beirut on Friday 17 December and proceeded directly to the president's office. When I walked in it was obvious that something was wrong. Present were President Jumayyil, Habib, Draper, Tweini and Haddad. The atmosphere was sombre, and even Tweini, who usually exuded an air of optimism, was despondent. I entered in my usual noisy undiplomatic way, shook hands and exclaimed, 'What in the name of

Christ is going on? Who has died and was left unburied?' The president, who appeared hurt and withdrawn, looked at Habib and said, 'Tell Elie everything.'

As if he had been waiting for this signal, the American envoy related to me in a most theatrical manner what had happened. His eyes were focused on me, and his lips were trembling. It was vintage Habib: 'Elie, you won't believe this!' he began, his hands cutting the air with emphasis. He went on:

> I arrived in Israel to plead your case. I cornered Sharon and told him, 'You must get out of Lebanon fast. Lebanon cannot give you a peace treaty. Reagan wants you to take it easy, do not attempt to pressure Lebanon. You have to act in such a way as to facilitate the departure of the Syrians, the Iranians, and the PLO.' My friend, the more I cornered him the more he looked at me and smiled. I suspected he had a trick or two up his sleeve, and I am always careful with him. He allowed me to talk and talk, and then you know what he said? You won't believe it! Elie, he said, 'Habib, you are not needed any more. Your mission has just ended. You are trying to work out an agreement between Lebanon and Israel for our withdrawal. I already have such an agreement. I have negotiated it secretly with the president through his friend, Sami Marun.' And then Sharon handed me this document. Here it is, Elie, look at it. Are you aware of it? Do you approve of its contents?

I was stunned. I had no idea that the president was negotiating on a separate track. He knew how sensitive and careful I was in negotiating anything with Israel. He knew that the only question I asked when he offered me the post of foreign minister was on the matter of a peace treaty with Israel. I took the document and began to read it. Habib, who by this time was ready to burst, could no longer hold back: 'Mr President,' he said, 'it seems you do not need me, good luck to you and to Sharon, I am going home.' As I am not without theatrical ability myself, I shouted at Habib to calm down and let me read the Sharon paper. I was furious too.

The document was dated 14 December 1982. It stated that both sides agreed to reach a package deal on the following: (a) normalization of relations; (b) security arrangements; and (c) withdrawal of Israeli forces. To reach this package, the delegations of Lebanon and Israel would constitute a committee which would meet until a peace treaty was signed. Meanwhile there would be open borders between Lebanon and Israel for the passage of people and goods.

Here was an agreement negotiated in secret without the knowledge of the foreign minister. I wondered whether I could continue in office. Was this a signal from the president for me to quit? Was the president more involved with Israel than I knew? All these thoughts flooded my mind as I read the Sharon paper. After reading the document, I told Habib that it was unacceptable to Lebanon. It referred to two delegations, one Lebanese, one Israeli, while we insisted on three; the Americans had to be present in all discussions. The document mentioned normalization of relations; we could not accept this. It referred to a peace treaty; we would not sign a peace treaty until all concerned Arab states signed such a treaty in the context of a just and equitable solution to the Middle East problem. It outlined a formula for a continued Israeli presence on our territory; this was a violation of our sovereignty and must, therefore, be rejected. To me the content, the spirit and the entire framework of the Sharon paper were unacceptable and I suggested that it be dismissed as a grave mistake and that we return to our original track and to Habib's mission.

I was angry and made no attempt to hide it. Habib seemed relieved to hear my views. The president explained that this was a personal and unofficial attempt to feel out the Israelis, that he himself did not agree with its content; he did not intend to subvert the Habib mission. This was not an agreement, he said, but a list of talking points. The more he talked the more furious I became. 'What talking points?' I responded, 'we have nothing to talk about under such headings. We are not heading towards a peace treaty, we are not normalizing relations, we are not permitting stations on our territory. Who interjected such irresponsible thoughts into a delicate diplomatic process?' This was not the first or the last time that amateurs entered our delicate political process and with terribly misguided steps. I considered walking out from the office and from the job. However, I put a good face on what was obviously a serious error. The president now seemed to empathize with me, and accordingly asked me to say or do whatever I felt was needed to bury the Sharon paper and rescue the Habib mission.

The fact that this had happened behind my back pained me for a long time. That back-channel communications are sometimes attempted is an understandable diplomatic tactic, but not when what is negotiated goes against the stated policy of the state, and not when such communications fail to gain the approval of the officials most involved with what is being discussed, in this case the prime minister, Tweini as coordinator, and me. In the interest of unity and solidarity, I pretended all was well, and at dinner that evening at the president's residence, I played my part in trying to thaw the frosty relations between the president on the one hand and Habib, Draper and Dillon on the other, not to mention the ice that had accumulated between myself and the president.

The Sharon paper was a mistake that we had to put behind us. It was imperative to proceed at a rapid pace and within the guidelines we had discussed with Reagan. While we tried to forget the Sharon paper, the Israelis did not. They proposed that we accept it as the basis for the trilateral discussions, but we rejected this proposal. Sharon responded by threatening to unleash the Druze on Jamhour, a Christian town, just above where the presidential palace and our Ministry of Defence are located, and the Shi'ah on Damour, a Christian village a few kilometres south of Beirut. Sharon's threats against us were continuous. He would often send messages indicating that if the president did not comply with his demand, then Israel would make sure that his authority would not extend beyond the gardens of the presidential palace. The Sharon threats preceded the trilateral discussions in late December, and continued throughout. At times Israel would unleash Major Sa'd Haddad, the head of its surrogate army in south Lebanon, who would deploy his forces to the outskirts of Sidon. At other times, it would heighten Christian and Muslim tension by showing films to Palestinians of Christian militiamen massacring Palestinian Muslims in Sabra and Shatila, omitting, of course, Israel's role in that massacre – a role which was clearly revealed in the Kahan Commission Report. After strong and direct intervention from Washington, Israel finally consented to negotiate within the tripartite format. Sharon, frustrated and furious, insisted on two conditions: the opening session should be held in Israel, and the Lebanese delegation should not thank the USA for its efforts. As we were eager to move, we agreed to hold the first meeting in Kiryat Shmona in the Galilee. It had already been agreed that the meetings would take place alternately in Kiryat Shmona (Israel) and Khaldeh (south of Beirut). The Americans urged us not to thank them, for they too were anxious to move after the delays. We were in no mood to thank anyone anyway.

The Lebanese–Israeli–American Discussions

The Lebanese–Israeli–American discussions began on Tuesday 28 December, three days after all foreign forces were expected to have withdrawn from Lebanese territory, according to Habib's optimistic estimate, in the summer. The optimism that had prevailed in October and November had gradually eroded.

The Negotiating Team   The president, the prime minister, Tweini and I constituted a supervisory body that set guidelines for our negotiating team, and followed up on its discussions in the tripartite meetings on a day-to-day basis. President Jumayyil asked Tweini to be the overall coordinator of our negotiating process. Tweini accepted this difficult responsibility, seeing it as a national duty. As befits Lebanese political psychology, our negotiating team was drawn from as many of the religious communities as possible. It not only had to be a representative team, it had to symbolize the national consensus on an Israeli withdrawal as well. The team was headed by Antoine Fattal, a retired ambassador, prominent jurist, and an intellectual with broad learning, including a thorough knowledge of Hebrew. We had appointed a retired ambassador as chairman of the team to emphasize the technical nature of the discussions and to keep the negotiations within the context of ILMAC.

Ambassador Draper informed me that the Israeli team would include a cabinet minister, and that Israel expected the Lebanese team also to be headed by a cabinet minister. I repeated to Draper that our team had already been formed in accordance with our guidelines. We would not appoint a minister to our team, nor would we join the discussions if Israel had a cabinet minister in its team. The discussions were not political. They were technical and in the context of ILMAC to get the Israeli army out. For the Begin government, negotiations with Lebanon were intended, in part, to prove that something had been salvaged from their Lebanese war. If the Lebanese–Israeli–American talks could be given a political colouring, then the Israelis could argue that this constituted *de facto* recognition of the Jewish state. After lengthy exchanges through Philip Habib, it was agreed that both teams would be non-political. The Israeli team was headed by David Kimche, the director-general of the Israeli Foreign Ministry, and like ours it included civilians and military members. Special Envoy Philip Habib supervised the process, while Draper actually headed the American team in the discussions. The American team included a large number of technical and military people. Habib was the flamboyant negotiator, Draper the careful diplomat, and Chris Ross the indefatigable note-taker who shadowed Habib and Draper with a small notebook in hand, recording, with a benign smile, every whimper uttered by anyone within hearing range. He recorded everything – the serious, the humorous, the relevant and the irrelevant, the personal and the impersonal. If his presence induced silence, he continued writing, perhaps describing the prevailing mood of the moment, or the people involved. He took such pleasure in writing that even in direct conversations with him he found time to write down your question, and his own answer as well. His ability to record would be the envy of every scholar who respects detail and honours precision. His notebook should occupy a prominent place in the American diplomatic archives.

The Agenda   In all negotiations agreement on an agenda is a difficult first step. The nuances in the wording commit the parties in advance. The agenda sets the tone of negotiations, discloses their intent and scope, and reveals areas of flexibility. As the weaker party, we were very careful lest we create false impressions by agreeing to a disadvantageous agenda. Once when Winston Churchill accused General de Gaulle of being too rigid, the French leader retorted: 'I had to be, I am too weak to be conciliatory.' This applied perfectly to us. Not only were we occupied and our country shattered by war, a long internal war, we also had carefully to consider our Arab environment. In a sense we were negotiating for the Arab world, and we knew we could easily fall into a Catch-22: if talks with the Israelis went too well, we could be accused of going too far with Israel; if we failed in securing an Israeli withdrawal, we would be blamed for not liberating our country. Yet who was it who would define success? Success is a concept bounded by time and place, and subject to a kaleidoscope of perceptions. Is it preferable to negotiate with an enemy, or to try to resist it by force? Is the Lebanese national interest in matters of war and peace an autonomous interest separate from the interests of Syria, Jordan, Egypt, Saudi Arabia and the other countries in the region? And if it is separate, can it be addressed on its own without the involvement of these states? All these questions loomed large from the moment we began to consider the agenda. From the first trilateral meeting on 28 December 1982 to mid-January 1983, we were occupied with the wording of the agenda and with the legal framework in which the discussions were to take place. Finally both sides agreed on the following wording:

> It has been agreed, in the light of their interrelationships, to address con-currently the following agenda items: termination of state of war; security arrangements; framework of mutual relations: ending of hostile propaganda, exchange of goods and products, movement of persons, communications, etc.; programme of evacuation; immediate dispositions for withdrawals and conditions for Israeli withdrawal, including a first-stage withdrawal; future guarantees.

While the agenda items were proposed separately by Israel, Lebanon and the United States, the delegations to the talks agreed to discuss all of them in an open-minded way, without prejudice or prior commitment. Each team, of course, had its own position on where to start, what to emphasize, what to discard, what to act on and what to defer into the indefinite future.

Negotiating Tactics   This formula gave each delegation enough flexibility to discuss any subject on the agenda 'without prior commitment'. Sub-sequently the Israeli team submitted its agenda, which listed the topics in the following order: normalization of relations; security arrangements; and conditions for the withdrawal of the Israeli forces. The Lebanese agenda, however, listed the items in the following order: schedule of withdrawals; immediate measures concerning the withdrawals; security arrangements; general framework of relations; definition of the role of the United States.

The cardinal point was the normalization of relations, which would in effect replace the Armistice Agreement with a peace treaty or something resembling it. We rejected the concept of normalization of relations and all formulations and variations that approximated it. I was often annoyed with members of our delegation who would telephone me from Kiryat Shmona to ask me if Lebanon would accept language in the agreement which they should have, on their own, refused out of hand. For example, on 20 January Fattal called to get my reaction to the wording of the following Israeli proposal: 'Pending the establishment of diplomatic relations between Lebanon and Israel, there will be established liaison committees of the two countries, and the members of these committees will enjoy diplomatic immunity.' The first half of the phrase virtually granted diplomatic recognition by acceding to the principle, while the second half confirmed it. Since the outbreak of the war, telephone communications inside Lebanon had been very poor; they were poorer still between Lebanon and Israel. Perhaps this is why I shouted my reply, first to be heard, second to calm my anger: 'This is utterly unacceptable, and you know it. Why are you calling me on it and thus give the Israelis who are certainly listening the impression that this subject is negotiable? You seem tired and you need a rest. Come and see me this evening!' Fattal, the seasoned diplomat, had committed a grave error. He admitted later on in the day that he was wrong. Somehow, and for a moment, he had not grasped the implications.

On another occasion, I was called on a question of language the interpretation of which was pregnant with possibilities. The Israeli formulation was: 'In view of the growing relations between the two countries, Lebanon and Israel will develop positive relations, including cessation of hostile propaganda.' I reminded my caller that only recently he and I had had dinner at a restaurant called L'Os, and hoped that he would understand that 'l'os' is the French word for bone, and that the restaurant served a simple 'bare bone' menu. He was expected to be frugal with language and not come up even *ad referendum* with language which would undoubtedly be subject to broad interpretation. 'What growing relations?' I shouted into the phone. 'What positive relations, what are you talking about? Are we getting an army out or getting an army in?' We were ready, somewhere in the negotiations, to agree to the termination of the state of war in return for a stable and guaranteed peace for Lebanon. The termination of the state of war, however, was a juridical condition like the Armistice Agreement. It did not bring with it more baggage than the concept implied. Instead, it was to be a basis for future reconsideration, should regional conditions require it when Israel and the Arab states were ready for a comprehensive settlement. Undoubtedly the informality that arises from frequent meetings between negotiating teams could at times blur positions and lead to some misunderstanding between those negotiating on the line and those taking the decision in the capital. I warned our team about the dangers that could arise from familiarity with the other side. They had to keep governmental guidelines in mind, and remember that words said in jest over coffee could make their way into minutes and memoranda and could influence policy. I asked them to make all their positions *ad referendum*. Once the discussions began we had to face details that seemed to have no end. Although we thought we had buried the Sharon paper, some of its stipulations were emerging here and there in the discussions.

Habib informed us that under the heading of security arrangements, the Israelis wanted three early warning stations on Lebanese territory in Nabatiyyah, the Baruk, and on a hill north-east of Sidon. Israel was thinking in terms of 250 Israeli soldiers to protect each of the three stations. In addition they wanted cooperation between the Israeli army and the Lebanese army in maintaining peace in 'a security region' roughly covering the area south of a line running from Sidon on the coast to Hasbayyah in the west. Under mutual relations, he continued, the Israelis wanted normalization of relations. He then looked at the president, the prime minister and me and asked: 'Well, this is the Israeli position; what do you say?' I responded: 'You know our position on these issues. If we are to accept such terms we will negotiate directly with Israel. A superpower by our side should give us the protection we deserve.' I repeated our position on all the issues and emphasized the regional dangers arising from the strategic use of our hills by any country other than ours. From the Baruk Israel could monitor all air movements in the eastern Mediterranean and gain a regional strategic advantage. We could not accept this, nor would our Arab neighbours.

I then asked Habib to join me for a walk. We took leave from the president and the prime minister and walked in the garden of the presidential palace. 'What is going on?' I inquired. 'What are these terms? How can you bring them to us?' Habib answered that he had no choice but to bring them. He was pleased with our response. He had expected our rejection, but needed to hear it directly from me so that he could relate it to the Israelis and proceed from there. Our response, he said, gave him the influence he needed in future rounds of talks.

As negotiations proceeded it became clear to me how small an Israeli priority was a united and sovereign Lebanon. When I asked Habib whether a united, independent, sovereign Lebanon was an American priority, his response was, 'Darn right it is!' Yet Habib's missions to Israel were getting increasingly difficult. For one thing, the Israelis were resentful of the American presence in the committees and subcommittees issuing from the tripartite talks. They did not want the Americans standing between them and their ambitions in Lebanon. In Habib's reports from Israel, he also began to note that Begin was increasingly withdrawn. Sharon, on the other hand, was proving even more aggressive than before. Habib and Sharon were always at loggerheads over Lebanon, and Habib, who did not take defeat lightly, resented Sharon's intransigence, which he feared could scuttle his mission. Sharon kept the pressure on us through emissaries. Every time I took a negative stand on an Israeli proposal a Lebanese emissary would arrive in my house or my office urging a more conciliatory attitude towards Israel. It did not take much to pacify an emissary, but clearly Sharon was making a dent in the political armour of the Lebanese communities. His message was that the negotiations would fail and Israel would end up doing in Lebanon whatever its national interests demanded. The implication was clear: if Lebanon did not agree to a peace treaty, God help Lebanon. An emissary would come to see me 'in confidence' and show me maps of future Lebanons were we to fail in signing a peace treaty. These future Lebanons showed it partitioned into small states, or parts of it annexed, with a small country left as a dependency of Israel, the new imperium in the Middle East. I did not take these threats lightly. I checked carefully with the ambassadors of the powers, and I was assured that these were largely Sharon's ideas, and were intended to scare us into agreement.

It was obvious from early discussions in the Tripartite committee that the Israelis did not trust Lebanon to control its territory in the South, and yet they would not permit a strong Lebanon to arise to protect effectively its southern terrain. Instead of the security zone that the Israelis kept talking about I suggested to Habib that we should render all of Lebanon a security zone by converting Lebanon itself into a strong sovereign state with regional and international support, and with a strong army that would prevent any hostile activity from its territory against any neighbouring state. The Lebanese government would then declare emergency measures for a six-year period to consolidate the army's hold over Lebanon without violating basic freedoms in the country, or its constitutional democratic system. This way, I thought, we would be putting Lebanon in intensive care, so to speak. Habib was sympathetic. He listened carefully, but went on to emphasize, again and again, Israeli determination to get a new agreement from their conquest. The American position was clear and consistent: without new security arrangements satisfactory to Israel, there could be no withdrawals. This is what Israel wanted, we were told, and the Americans were engaged, within these limits, in helping us get as reasonable an agreement as possible. Early in February we began to receive reports of possible Israeli withdrawals from the Shuf region.

On Sunday 6 February 1983, an Israeli general claimed that the Israeli army had offered to withdraw from Aley, a predominantly Druze mountain town on the Beirut–Damascus Highway, and to hand over authority there to the Lebanese army; but that the Lebanese army had declined the offer. When President Jumayyil heard this, he called me at 10 p.m. and asked me to deliver the following message to Draper: 'Tell the Israeli authorities that if the Israeli army will withdraw from Aley tonight, the Lebanese army is ready to enter Aley tomorrow, Monday 7 February, at 6 a.m.' I was able to reach Draper at midnight. He called me twice after that to say that he had been unable to reach the Israelis. In our third phone conversation at 3 a.m., Draper informed me that he had reached Foreign Minister Shamir, who had informed him that the Israeli army had no intention of withdrawing from Aley at present.

The threat of confessional fighting in areas controlled by Israel was a potent weapon against us. The Israelis wanted to exact normalization of relations from us, and were resorting to blackmail to get it. I addressed this issue on 14 February, in my meeting with ambassadors accredited to Lebanon: Israel, I said, insisted on normal relations with us; but we were not ourselves normal to establish normal relations with Israel. The issue must await regional developments. We were prepared to discuss ending hostile propaganda and move away from an age of slogans to an age of reason. We were prepared to agree on implementing the humanitarian provisions of the Armistice Agreement. But we could not, on our own, normalize relations with Israel. Lebanon was not Egypt. Lebanon could not afford to lose its historical ties to 20 Arab states to establish ties with one state – Israel; it could not lose its export market to Arab countries, representing over 90 per cent of its total, to gain an export market of about 5 per cent of its total. To us the question of normalizing relations was an existential one; it threatened our national unity, our relations with our Arab brethren, and ultimately our existence.

On 4 March, Draper met Tweini and me and presented the latest Israeli position. Israel wanted the following: Sa'd Haddad must be allowed to command the Lebanese army brigade in the security region; joint manoeuvres must take place between the Lebanese army and the Israeli army in the security region; the top of Mount Baruk must be considered as important to Israel's security; and concrete steps must be taken in the area of normalization of mutual relations. Once again, our response was negative on all points. Draper agreed. The problem between us and the Israelis, he said, was essentially psychological. It related to confidence. He urged us to think of words, concepts or language which would alleviate Israeli fears.

I couldn't help asking Draper, 'How about language to dissipate Lebanese fears?' Since the Israeli occupation began, some Israeli goods had entered Lebanon; Israel had opened its frontiers with Lebanon, and wanted to keep them open. As a result, Saudi Arabia and Jordan, the two most moderate and pro-American Arab states, were boycotting Lebanese goods, fearing that they may accidentally import Israeli goods. If the moderates were acting this way, how did the United States expect the radical Arabs to act?

The USA was doing its best, but it was not as good as it had expected or we had hoped.

3

In Search of a Consensus

Arab Contacts

As we negotiated with Israel in 1982 and 1983, we sought to build up Arab support for our efforts, and ensure that a future agreement would meet with the approval of the Arab states. General Arab support was necessary because Israel was an Arab issue, and any dealing with it had Arab implications and repercussions. The fact that there were Arab states that were distant in terms of geography and concerns from the Arab East did not affect in the least the public positions of these states towards the Arab East. For example Algeria, Libya and Yemen are distant and yet, in matters relating to Israel, and at the appropriate timing for them, they are capable of raising havoc on the sensitive matters of Arab–Israeli relations. We therefore decided early on to involve as many of the Arab leaders as possible in our tripartite discussions by keeping them informed, by seeking their counsel, and by soliciting their support for our efforts.

I followed a policy of holding regular meetings with Arab ambassadors. The ambassadors had no reservations at all about negotiating with Israel, nor about the subjects under discussion. They studiously took notes, and asked for clarification of certain points. I continued to hold these sessions until the May 17 Agreement was signed, so that we could not be accused of keeping our Arab brethren in the dark. There were states in the Arab world, however, with which President Jumayyil felt especially at ease. These were the conservative and moderate Arab states, such as Morocco, Tunisia, Saudi Arabia, Egypt and Jordan. From the outset, the president wanted to develop close relations with them.

At the beginning of November 1982, the president and I visited Morocco. Upon arrival at the official guest house, we were greeted by a dozen or so colourfully dressed servants, each carrying a large tray covered with dishes of dates and cups of milk. This was the traditional welcoming ceremony, and was laden with a symbolism that stretched far back into the history of the desert nomads who had crossed into North Africa bearing the message of Islam.

King Hassan II is a curious combination of orthodox caliph and modern president. All high Moroccan officials adhere to ancient caliphal protocol, and approach the king by bowing and kissing his hand or the end of his right-hand sleeve, depending on their social status. In stark contrast, however, the king meets his foreign guests with great informality. He embraced the president and they exchanged kisses. I shook hands warmly, assuming that protocol did not expect me to embrace as I was not a head of state.

I met the Moroccan foreign minister, Muhammad Busittah, who was confident, eloquent, intelligent and candid. Busittah was hopeful about American support for Lebanon, and urged us to cultivate good relations with Washington. He also felt that the PLO would cooperate with our efforts and withdraw its 6,000 remaining fighters from Lebanon, and redeploy them to Jordan and Egypt. Busittah was banking on Reagan and his Middle East initiative of September 1982, and had some advice for us on how to proceed with Syria.

The issue with President Asad, he said, was partly psychological: Asad did not want to be equated with the Israelis. Asad might wish to make a number of arrangements with Lebanon. Busittah did not know what Asad had in mind, but he assumed that these arrangements would be mostly in the area of security, which was uppermost in his mind. I told him that I did not believe we had a problem in that regard. Busittah added that Morocco would support Lebanese actions which were in Lebanon's interest. The only way to get the Israelis out was to negotiate with them through the Americans: 'You are not making peace now,' he continued, 'we are all moving towards peace on the basis of UN Resolution 242, even if some slight modifications have to be made to the borders of Gaza and the West Bank for security considerations.'

It was President Jumayyil's intention next to meet King Fahd of Saudi Arabia. When the Arab world is divided, Saudi Arabia can be relied upon to act as a mediator. When one is striving to build a consensus, Riyad is the capital to visit. Our government was anxious from the very beginning to engage Saudi Arabia in our efforts to secure Israeli withdrawal from Lebanon. Such engagement, we felt, would encourage the Americans, put added pressure on Israel, moderate the Arab position, and on the whole augment the scope and impact of Lebanese diplomacy.

How the Arab desert kingdom, once a forgotten domain on the periphery of the Ottoman Empire, attained the prominence it did in Arab and world affairs is one of the exceptional stories of the twentieth century. The unification of the tribes of the Arabian peninsula under the House of

Saud, the discovery of oil, the stability of the royal family and of state institutions have all contributed to the rise of Saudi Arabia as a leader in Arab affairs and as a decisive force in world financial markets. The Saudis have neither the inclination nor the population to become a military powerhouse in the region; but they do have the money to finance their more subtle version of diplomacy. They are low-key, and do not roam the Arab world looking for problems to solve. On the contrary the problems come to them.

Although King Fahd gives the impression of being distant and aloof, he is in reality a warm person and a gifted raconteur, with a good memory and a fine sense of humour. He is a sharp observer of the procession of persons and events throughout the Arab world and is frank and colourful in his accounts of them. In our meeting with him he recalled his happy days in Lebanon in the early 1950s, and praised the unique beauty that Allah had bestowed on our country.

In his remarks to us, the king noted that Saudi policy towards Lebanon was to ensure the withdrawal of Israel, and to help the country in its reconstruction. Lebanon's independence, security and unique political system had to be preserved, he said. Israel was an enemy, and posed a great challenge to the Arabs. He assured us that Saudi Arabia would cooperate with the Americans and the Arab states to help us secure an Israeli withdrawal from our territory. 'There is a Lebanese good, and there is an Arab good,' the king continued, 'and one enhances the other. In our efforts to help you we will try to understand the Lebanese perspective and try to promote it. When the time comes for reconstruction we will be the first to help. Meanwhile we will continue our aid at the humanitarian level as required.'

I had the opportunity during the visit of meeting a number of other Saudi officials who would later be of great assistance to us in our negotiations, both with the Arabs and the Americans. I spoke privately to the Saudi foreign minister, al-Amir Saud al-Faysal, and we succeeded in building up a mutual trust which was essential for our future relations. As Saud had studied at Princeton and I at Johns Hopkins, we not only were products of the same educational system, but also had school friends in common. In my extensive dealings with Saud, I found him meticulous and efficient. He was extremely cautious and precise in his use of language, and I always found him to be a perfect diplomat.

Building bridges to Saudi Arabia was not, however, our major challenge in the early stages of the negotiations. Rather, the Arab country with which Lebanon had the most ambivalent relations in late 1982 and 1983 was Syria. Since the emergence of Lebanon and Syria from the ruins of the Ottoman Empire, relations between the two states had had their ups and downs. While there were brief moments of cooperation, most of the time relations between the two were tense and governed by fear and misunderstanding. After the Second World War, Lebanon and Syria went in different directions: Lebanon towards its particular brand of mercantile democratic liberalism and Syria towards revolutionary Arab nationalism, mobilizing its resources against the Israeli threat.

Developments in Lebanon during the early 1970s were of particular interest to the Syrian regime, if only because they threatened to draw Syria into a confrontation with Israel. In 1976, as the war raged on in Lebanon, Syrian forces crossed the Lebanese border to contain the fighting and enforce a balance of power in the country. Asad's objectives were twofold: to ensure that the war in Lebanon did not spill over and bring Syria into side confrontations, and to extend Syrian power in the region and improve its political and diplomatic positions.

President Asad had claimed for Damascus a prominent role in historical-geographical Syria. Syria must be consulted and its approval must be sought for any major policies affecting Lebanon, the Palestinian problem, and to a somewhat lesser extent Jordan. Syria could not and would not allow itself to be isolated in regional matters in which its interests may be threatened through the decisions of other states. On the basis of this reasoning, the potential for tension between Lebanon and Syria in late 1982, as we talked to the Israelis through the Americans, was evident. The decision to negotiate was ours; we were dealing with Lebanese territory only, and we felt that to involve Syria was to complicate an already complex question, and to include it in negotiations it would rather not have in view of its nationalist ideological position. It was felt, rightly or wrongly, that it was not necessary to involve the Syrians fully before progress was made in the discussions with the Americans and the Israelis. We also knew that an agreement opposed by Syria would have little chance of survival. As we negotiated with Israel, we kept one eye on Damascus, and we wanted an agreement which Syria would not oppose.

On 29 November 1982, the president chaired a meeting attended by General Abbas Hamdan, General Sami al-Khatib, Ghassan Tweini, John Ubayd and myself. Khatib was the commander of the Arab Deterrent Force (largely Syrian) and a very close friend of the Syrian leadership. Ubayd, who was a prominent Lebanese journalist, was a friend of the Syrian leader and of the men around him. He was also close to President Jumayyil. The president wanted Ubayd to be his special envoy to Syria. As a friend of Jumayyil and Asad, he was the right choice. He was sharp, blunt, and had an unequalled sense of humour. While friendly with leaders on all sides in the Lebanese conflict, his views on Lebanon were authentic-ally his own: though he was a good Lebanese with Maronite sensitivities, he also had a broad Arab outlook when it came to Lebanese politics. With Khatib and Ubayd on his side, the president hoped to start a positive dialogue with Syria.

After this lengthy meeting Ubayd and I met at my house and decided that he would leave for Damascus in a few days to brief the Syrians on our thinking and to assess the mood within the Syrian leadership. Ubayd went to Damascus with generalities and returned with generalities. There was nothing yet to disagree on. Syria had no objections to the American role, or to the negotiation process as envisaged by us. In subsequent meetings with the Syrians Ubayd reported that they reacted favourably to the president's speeches, especially the one before the General Assembly, as well as to my statements to the press. As a presidential envoy Ubayd got his instructions from the president, and the president by temperament preferred generalities to specifics and avoided details that could disturb. Ubayd often stated that he was not well briefed and asked me for information, which I gladly gave. However, in a clear indication that they had recovered their military losses in Lebanon in 1982, the Syrians were gradually raising the stakes.

We also made contacts with Egypt. We needed Egyptian counsel in three areas: we wanted to learn from their experience in negotiating with Israel; we wanted Egypt to intervene with Israel whenever appropriate to reduce pressure on us; and we wanted to benefit from the goodwill Egypt had garnered in Washington. We understood that, to a certain extent, the Egyptians also needed us: their success in helping towards a solution to the Lebanese crisis would have been a very useful step leading to Egypt's reintegration into the politics of the Arab world.

In 1982 and 1983, the 'Gift of the Nile' was a gift no Arab wanted. Sadat had broken ranks with the Arabs and had signed a peace treaty with Israel, an act hailed in the West for its courage and denounced in the Arab world for its treachery. Egypt was ousted from the Arab League at the 1979 Arab summit in Baghdad, and in 1981 Sadat was assassinated. Husni Mubarak continued to honour the peace treaty, but remained extremely reserved in his relations with Israel, always trying to avoid the flamboyant and defiant style of his predecessor. Egyptian patience, however, triumphed in the face of Arab militancy and Egypt was reinstated into the Arab League and the vortex of Arab politics in the late 1980s. Lebanon had to be careful in consulting the Egyptians in 1982–83, since consultations could be wrongly interpreted as a desire on our part to acquiesce to a Camp David-type arrangement with Israel. The Egyptian leaders, conscious of our predicament, kept their distance. They also kept their humour.

In December 1982, Usamah Baz, the political adviser to President

Mubarak, and Boutros Boutros-Ghali, the minister of state for foreign affairs, arrived in Beirut. The Egyptians were there to see how they could help us in our efforts to begin negotiations on Israeli withdrawal. The president and I were enthusiastic about their visit, although Prime Minister Wazzan was cautious. After meeting Baz and Ghali, he told the press that he had been 'surprised' by their arrival. Wazzan was anxious to protect his back with his Muslim community, which was then anti-Mubarak.

Engaging Parliament

As a former member of parliament, the president was anxious for the legislature to be involved directly in our diplomatic offensive to garner support in the Arab world. If we worked with parliament from the outset, the president argued, then it would give us the backing we needed when we reached an agreement. As a result, I set about planning our parliamentary strategy with Speaker Kamil al-As'ad. Al-As'ad had one obsession, to get Israel out of Lebanon as quickly as possible. He had no qualms about negotiating with Israel. He wanted results. Al-As'ad was anxious to cooperate with the government, and he proposed that three parliamentary teams be dispatched to the Maghreb, or Arab North African states, the Mashriq, or the eastern Arab states, and the southern Arab states.

In forming these teams, the speaker had to consider confessional and regional representation, and to select delegation heads who enjoyed the confidence of all members. The three parliamentarians selected to head the teams were Louis Abu Sharaf, a prominent rightist politician; Amin al-Hafiz, a former prime minister and a deputy from Tripoli, who was known for his middle-of-the-road politics; and Rashid al-Sulh, also a former prime minister and deputy from Beirut.

Getting the parliamentary teams off the ground to the designated capitals proved a delicate and difficult operation. Deputies are not only representatives of their districts, but often they are also local chieftains with authority beyond that of the law. In preparing these trips, protocol and appearance were of paramount importance to them. Everything, from accommodation to travel arrangements, was open to debate. One team leader insisted that we recall our ambassador in the country he would be visiting, because he 'hated the looks of that man'. Another insisted on submitting an oral report only, since he didn't know how things would stand politically a few months down the road.

After a few meetings with the delegations I told the president: 'Ask of me what you wish, but spare me the agony of dealing with your former colleagues. All the Maronites wish to be treated as future presidents, the

Shi'is as future speakers of parliament and the Sunnis as future prime ministers.' 'What about the Greek Orthodox?' the President replied. 'Very fine people', I answered, to our mutual amusement.

The teams submitted their reports on 24 January 1983. Two of the reports were written, and one was oral. The results were positive, but in the end the reports were far more fascinating as an overview of Arab reaction to a serious crisis in their midst. It was interesting to compare the priorities of each state.

The delegation to the Mashriq reported the following: King Hussein supported Lebanon's efforts, and stood fully behind the mediating role of the Americans; only the United States, argued the king, could influence Israel. He hoped that the PLO and Syria would also withdraw from Lebanese territory, otherwise Israel would exploit their presence to extend its occupation. Saddam Hussein of Iraq pointed out that Lebanon should have the final word in a matter as important as withdrawal. The Iraqis supported us fully in this process, and Saddam criticized the Lebanese National Movement for driving the Christians into the arms of Israel. Lebanon could not face Israel militarily and had no alternative but to resort to diplomacy. No Arab state should interfere in Lebanese affairs. Had Iraq not been engaged in a war with Iran, Israel would never have dared attack Lebanon. The whole Arab world, Saddam continued, was responsible for the tragedy that befell Lebanon, and he admitted that Iraq too was not innocent of blame. The Iraqi attitude was that the PLO and Iraq's arch-rival, Syria, should withdraw first to facilitate Israeli withdrawal.

The Amir of Kuwait, Sheikh Jabir Ahmad al-Sabbah, also expressed readiness to help Lebanon in every possible way. It was unfair to expect Lebanon to face Israeli pressure alone. He believed that negotiations should proceed with great speed, arguing that every delay would bring new complications with it. The amir said he would contact the Americans and the Syrians to help us, although he was confident that the Syrian troops would withdraw 'two hours after the withdrawal of the Israelis'.

The other Gulf states had a similar attitude: Lebanon must move fast to get the Israelis out, and must not be left to suffer alone the consequences of the Arab–Israeli conflict. In southern Arabia, the delegation heard much the same tune. Oman and North Yemen fully supported the policy of the Lebanese government. Their position was that no Arab state had the right to impose a course of action other than the one chosen by the Lebanese themselves.

The delegation to the Maghreb visited Tunis and the Arab League headquarters there, as well as Algeria and Mauritania. The report by the Maghreb team was not as clear-cut as the report from the other two teams. While there was general support for Lebanese policy regarding Israel, it was difficult to get specific commitments from most of the Maghreb states.

The position of the Arab League was predictable. Its secretary-general, al-Shadhli al-Qulaybi, argued that Israel had set out to destroy Lebanon's model of government. Israel had to withdraw first, and then Syria would follow; there was no problem there. He insisted that the Arab League wanted to help Lebanon, and was always calling on others to help as well. Al-Qulaybi was polite, mildly positive, elusive and eloquent when it came to generalities and, like the organization he represented, totally ineffective. He neither supported nor opposed our negotiations with Israel. He handled the question brilliantly by ignoring it. He did, however, send his best wishes to President Jumayyil, who, in his words, had a difficult job; may Allah help him.

In Tunisia, the delegation met President Habib Bourghiba and Prime Minister Muhammad al-Mazzali. Both supported our negotiation efforts within the parameters we had set, and they expressed the fear that Israel aimed at the balkanization of Lebanon. The Tunisians also hoped that the USA could thwart Israeli policy, and President Bourghiba called in the American ambassador in Tunis to express to him Tunisian interest in the success of the tripartite discussions. The Tunisians understood that the Israeli occupation could not be ended by military means, and they argued that Lebanon should take intensive political and diplomatic action, in coordination with the Arab states, to get the Israelis out.

In Algeria the delegation met President al-Shadli Benjdid in the presence of his adviser Lakhdar al-Ibrahimi. Benjdid was cautiously supportive of our efforts. He expressed as much concern for the Palestinians in Lebanon as he did for Lebanon itself, and asked for just treatment of Palestinian civilians.

No attempt was made to visit Libya due to Colonel Mu'ammar al-Qadhdhafi's recent attack on the president. He had called President Jumayyil a Zionist agent. Previously he had called on the Lebanese Christians to adopt Islam and simplify the problem. Following his attack on the president I had summoned the Libyan representative in Beirut, Abd-al-Qadir Ghuqah, to my office. Ghuqah was most polite. I requested that Libya deliver an apology within twenty-four hours, otherwise we would have to take certain diplomatic measures. Ghuqah's response was masterful. I had never before realized how literature or poetry could be so helpful at critical diplomatic moments; and Ghuqah was indeed a poet. 'Colonel Qadhdhafi', he began with a twinkle in his eye more eloquent than his words, 'is the leader of the revolution. Hence he uses revolutionary language. He himself says, again and again, that his position as

leader of the revolution is not necessarily the position of the Libyan state.'
The Popular Committee was not a diplomatic mission, it was not accredited like other ambassadorial missions; rather, it acted as an information office. He, Ghuqah, was prepared to issue a statement upon
leaving my office, or to meet the president and issue a statement from the
presidential palace affirming Libya's respect for Jumayyil. As for the
ultimatum, he could not possibly get me a response from Tripoli in 24
hours. For weeks his office had had no telephone or telex contact with
Libya. Finally we agreed that Ghuqah would issue a conciliatory statement, while we recalled our ambassador in Libya.

Prime Minister Wazzan and I travelled to Tunis in late January 1983.
We wanted a strong base in the Maghreb, and Tunis was now the seat of
the Arab League and of the PLO. We left Beirut on the small luxury
plane which Rafiq al-Hariri had presented to the Office of the Prime
Minister. The plane was in a state of disrepair after the recent fighting,
and the Israelis had tampered with it, stripping it of its instruments. After
some hasty repairs we were told it was ready. Wazzan and I were rather
nervous. As we winged towards the western Mediterranean we joked about
our uncertain fortune, and wondered whether we were guinea pigs in a
test flight. Wazzan, whose sense of humour matches his seriousness, made
the long journey seem like a pleasant interlude. In Tunis, Wazzan and I
gave Prime Minister Muhammad al-Mazzali and Foreign Minister al-Sibsi
a full briefing on the ongoing talks with the Israelis. They listened, asked
questions, expressed admiration for our courage, and wished us well.

In general, Wazzan tends to elaborate his points by resorting to a story.
In explaining Lebanon's problems with the Palestinians to the Tunisians,
he closed his eyes and said:

> There were two brothers living near each other. A guest arrived and asked
> for shelter. One brother closed the door; the other was more tolerant, and
> invited the guest in. The guest stayed longer than anticipated. He then
> brought his wife, and then his cousins, and then even his friends. While
> originally he had occupied a little corner of the three bedroom house, he
> soon took over most of the house and was knocking at the master bedroom.
> This is our story with our brothers the Palestinians.

No visit to Tunisia is complete without paying homage to the founder
of the nation, al-Mujahid al-Akbar, the great fighter, the liberator Habib
Bourghiba who, though old and failing, was still Tunisia's president and
autocrat. He received us at his rural retreat in Nafta some 30 minutes by
plane from the capital, and welcomed us with a great deal of emotion,
eloquently speaking of the beauty of Lebanon. Bourghiba then lapsed
into talk of his war of liberation against the French. He mentioned how

he had ordered Tunisian youths to charge the French army, and how hundreds had died in the ensuing gunfire. 'These were my children', he cried, with tears rolling down his cheeks. We tried to get him back to the subject of our visit, but in vain. President Bourghiba was already lost somewhere deep in his own past, extracting from it stories he felt were appropriate for the occasion.

Wazzan and I were embarrassed, but our Tunisian hosts did not seem to mind. From time to time, Bourghiba's wife tried to bring her husband back to the present, but to no avail. No one had prepared us for this encounter. The old warrior was truly senile, and a mere shell of his assertive former self. He was able to control neither his thoughts nor his gestures. It was terribly unfair, I thought, to expose this great man to the outside world at such a moment of weakness.

The tragedy of Bourghiba is the tragedy of Arab politics, which recognizes only a linear process leading towards the top. How one gets down from the top, however, does not belong to the realm of politics, but is relegated to the world of taboo, disorder and chaos; indeed the removal of an ineffective leader is seen as a failure of politics. Thus it was with Bourghiba: he had reached the top, but he did not know how to get down. Later on an army officer took the step; Bourghiba was deposed in 1988.

After the encounter with the president, Wazzan and I returned to Tunis to meet the secretary-general of the Arab League, al-Shadli al-Qulaybi, and PLO Chairman Yasir Arafat. Al-Qulaybi's comments on the Lebanese crisis were not much different from those he had made to the parliamentary delegation earlier. He knew the problem, and feared Israeli infiltration into the Arab world through Lebanon. He wished the Arab states would help more. He would do all he could for us through his limited means. I interrupted him to say that if the Arab League really expected to help us, it should change its style. Its uninspired and lukewarm methods had led to the humiliations of 1967, 1978 and 1982.

Al-Qulaybi is a polite, humble and professional individual. He is a good listener and, when he was at the head of the Arab League, he conceived of his role as a conciliator, rather than as a leader or initiator. He was handicapped by his natural lack of aggressiveness. As I listened to al-Qulaybi, I felt that he was simply talking for the record, without real conviction. His low-key style and the general amorphousness of the Arab League confirmed my instinctual suspicion that large organizations do not solve problems; they merely take note of them and file them.

While talking to al-Qulaybi, our minds were on Yasir Arafat. Since our arrival in Tunis, a crisis of protocol had arisen. Since Arafat considered himself a head of state, he expected us to visit him in his office. We, on the other hand, expected him to visit us at our hotel; we represented a state, while he represented a movement. Wazzan was greatly disturbed by this, and felt insulted. He had been the one who had negotiated with Philip Habib to secure an honourable exit for Arafat and his men from Beirut. He had also accompanied Arafat to the ship taking him away from Lebanon, an act both of courtesy and of courage. He expected Arafat to be grateful. Al-Wazzan means literally the one who weighs, and, true to his name, he always weighed his words and his moves carefully. To solve the problem, Wazzan finally advised Mazzali to invite us all to his house, which the prime minister did.

Our relations with the Palestinians were going through a delicate period at the time. To give momentum to the tripartite discussions we were hoping to persuade Arafat to withdraw at least two thousand of his men in Lebanon from Tripoli and the Biqa' Valley. We were preoccupied by the logistics of the PLO withdrawal: where would the *fedayeen* be withdrawn from? How would they be transported? What security arrangements would have to be made to ensure their safe departure? And as always, who would finance the operation? We had had preliminary contacts with Sudan, North Yemen and Jordan, to see whether they would accept the PLO fighters who were to be withdrawn. But, as yet, there had been no progress.

Wazzan and I arrived on time, Tuesday evening, 1 February, at Mazzali's house, where we were met by Mazzali and Sibsi. Arafat, the revolutionary, arrived appropriately late. He was immaculately dressed, and had obviously given much attention to the details of his attire. He wore military garb and his ever-present *kufiyyah*, and had a gun at his side. Appearance seemed to mean a great deal to Arafat. It enhanced the mystery surrounding the PLO leader, and made an impact on others. Arafat is known throughout the Arab world for his flamboyant personality and for his overwhelming bear-hugs. I did not much fancy politicians who kissed and embraced, and after Arafat had embraced Wazzan I managed to limit our mutual greetings to a formal handshake. With formalities completed, Mazzali and Sibsi withdrew, leaving us alone with Arafat. He plunged directly into serious talk, dispensing with the customary pleasantries and asides in which Arab leaders excel.

Arafat complained bitterly of the attitude of the Lebanese government towards the Palestinians. He was angry with President Jumayyil for not answering his letters, and accused us of jailing some four thousand Palestinians including some prominent figures. He insisted that his decision to withdraw all PLO fighters from Lebanon was final, and was in no way related to how Palestinians were treated in Lebanon. As the PLO fighters were not a disciplined army, he would have to come personally to the Biqa' valley and Tripoli to persuade them and their families to leave. This would not be easy, and he would need to coordinate with the Syrians on withdrawals. Arafat then praised our foreign policy, expressing satisfaction with my public statements, but criticized our handling of domestic Lebanese affairs. He also reminded me that we had friends in common, including two from my university days, George Habash and Hani al-Hindi. He wished us well in the negotiations and spoke emotionally of the suffering of the Lebanese and the Palestinian peoples.

In the two-hour meeting many a misunderstanding was corrected, and the session ended on a positive note. Arafat wanted to know where our negotiations with Israel were heading, and where Syria stood. He clearly wanted to link his stand with that of Syria. Arafat played for time. He is an experienced politician, a great tactician and a masterful exploiter of time. He was clearly delaying action, awaiting developments, and particularly the position of Syria. As we parted, Arafat embraced me affectionately and deposited three kisses on my cheeks. Wazzan could not help remarking: 'Elie, my friend, you are lucky there are no photographers, otherwise the Christian Right in the Eastern Sector would crucify you.'

For the moment, however, it was the Israelis who were furious. They still wanted high-level discussions with us, and they complained to the Americans that if Wazzan and Salem could meet with 'terrorists', there was no reason why they could not meet with Israeli leaders. We depended on Habib and Draper to quell Israeli fears and to remove this new psychological barrier.

The Non-Aligned Summit

The Non-Aligned Summit was scheduled to meet early in March, and we were debating whether the president should attend it. Lebanon, however, had never been active in the Non-Aligned Movement, which was always more ideological and controversial than the Arab League and the United Nations. The Non-Aligned Movement was rich in rhetoric, poor in achievement. It did, however, provide opportunities for world leaders to meet and to conduct bilateral discussions. India, in particular, took its role in the Non-Aligned Movement seriously, and now it was host.

On 12 February, the Indian ambassador in Beirut handed me the proposed resolution the summit would adopt on Lebanon. He was a cordial individual with an easy smile, and sincerely believed he had a draft resolution that would be helpful to Lebanon. Yet as I read the text, my face must have reflected my growing displeasure, since the ambassador's smile gradually disappeared. I said: 'This resolution is unacceptable to Lebanon; it is not a resolution on Lebanon; on the contrary it treats Lebanon as a footnote to the Palestinian problem. It speaks of the struggle of the PLO, of the nationalist parties in Lebanon, but it does not address the question of Lebanon.'

I told him I considered the resolution an unfriendly act. There was obviously no genuine Indian concern for Lebanon, I continued, but only a romanticized version of the Arab–Israeli struggle in which the integrity of Lebanon did not figure. The ambassador was speechless and his facial muscles began to twitch uncontrollably. He was clearly offended and embarrassed. He tried hard to justify the Indian position, but there was no conviction in his argument. I told him that we would support the strongest resolutions on the PLO or on the Arab–Israeli struggle, but that we wanted a resolution on Lebanon written by the Lebanese, clearly stating our objectives. If we could have our way, we would attend, otherwise, we would not.. He promised to convey the gist of our discussion to New Delhi and to keep in touch with us. He soon returned, asking us to prepare an alternate draft with the promise that India would support what we recommended. We did so, and he promised that it would be accepted. A few days later, the council of ministers decided to participate in the summit. Prime Minister Wazzan was to head the official delegation, and would be accompanied by me and the appropriate ambassadors and officials.

On Saturday 5 March, Wazzan and I held a strategy meeting in preparation for the summit, which was to start on Monday 7 March. The following day, the President called me at 10 p.m. and informed me that Ghassan Tweini had persuaded him to attend the New Delhi summit personally. We were all to leave at midnight. The president, realizing that this would be a bit embarrassing for the prime minister, since it had already been announced that he would head the delegation, asked me to go and see Wazzan and invite him to come on the trip if he liked; in that case the president would issue a decree appointing Minister Bahaeddine Bsat acting prime minister.

I raced to Wazzan's house with the unpleasant message and he was predictably furious. He finally decided to travel to New Delhi with the president. By midnight we were all at the airport: the president, his usual jovial and dynamic self, and the prime minister sombre and resigned. The president delighted in his surprise move, and tried to mollify Wazzan. We were all on time at the airport, but the departure was delayed: the Middle East Airlines office was having difficulty locating flight attendants for a flight that late at night.

The following morning, the president, the prime minister and I attended the Non-Aligned Summit's plenary session, where we listened to speeches by Arafat and Castro. Arafat seemed to have lost a great deal of his lustre, and applause for his speech was polite. Castro went on for hours repeating worn-out clichés, and his commitment to communism and to his alliance with the Soviet Union made one wonder about the seriousness of his non-alignment. I was so bored that I stood up to walk out. Wazzan pleaded with me not to do so as he wanted company, and felt it would be impolite to leave. I insisted that I could not take any more and that I was leaving. Wazzan sighed as I exited, wondering how many more hours were left before Castro finally vacated the podium.

I had my first serious meeting with Syrian Foreign Minister Abd al-Halim Khaddam in the afternoon. I greatly enjoyed this session, in which we spent time discussing the politics of the Middle East. I found Khaddam to be a rather boisterous and happy person; he enjoyed a good argument, and revelled in finding the right joke or apt comment to describe a situation. His mind was incessantly searching for an appropriate dig to put his interlocutor on the defensive. Khaddam loved it when one fought back, and he egged people on to give himself yet more opportunities to counter-attack. Khaddam could also be a paradox: while outgoing, he was also secretive and while he excelled in ideological speeches, he was also a pragmatist. He was clearly a man with a great deal of leeway. He had Asad's friendship and manipulated this friendship with brilliance, always taking the tough road whenever he felt it was prudent to do so, and leaving the easy road for his boss.

Khaddam began by noting that he wished Lebanon had followed the path of struggle against Israel, rather than that of negotiations. He felt that Israel would try to impose unacceptable conditions on the Lebanese, and argued that we should reject them. He attacked the Lebanese Front for cooperating with Israel in the hope that it would liberate them from the Syrians and the Palestinians. Syria's advice to Lebanon was to negotiate, noted Khaddam, but indirectly; and he concluded: 'Anyhow, we wish you success on condition that Israel does not reap any gains; use Syria as an excuse for not making concessions.

Like Khaddam, I talked a lot, invoking history and using it to explain current predicaments. Like him, I was familiar with Ba'th thought and sympathized with its ideals. But Lebanon had a specific problem on its hands, namely how to get Israel out. We had examined all options, I explained to Khaddam, and we found American mediation to be the most credible. We were not certain of its success, but we felt it was a good risk. 'We are not ready', I said, 'to take an absolutist ideological stand and lose our country. We do not have the military capability to oust the Israeli army. We want to oust it by diplomacy. We do not want to lose Lebanon!' 'Nor do we,' responded Khaddam, 'we are with you and we want to help. You should perhaps consider other options.' 'I am ready for other options,' I responded, 'give me one.' 'The Arab League', answered Khaddam. I responded that he could not be serious. He, more than anyone, knew the fate of the Palestinians when they had relied on the Arab League; did he want us to suffer the same fate? Khaddam's reply was representative of Syrian strategy; it was a strategy that had allowed Damascus to bounce back repeatedly from adversity in the past: 'My brother Elie,' Khaddam said, 'learn from Muhammad Ali Clay: move in such a way as to create new opportunities; you should come out from these negotiations without conceding anything to Israel.'

Khaddam suggested we consolidate the internal Lebanese front and lead a sustained, if long, struggle against Israel. I told him I did not believe that struggle alone would get Israel out. We needed a superpower to help us reach an agreement that would achieve this end and ensure safety of our frontiers and the stability of our country. I ended as follows:

> Trust the Lebanese government; give them your full support. Lebanon is very complex; only the Lebanese know how to handle their complicated situation. We shall try to solve it by diplomacy. Our way of doing things is different from yours; we disagree on method, but we cannot disagree on goals. I ask you to understand our position. We want Israel out. Accept the policy we are following to get it out. Lebanon is fractured. Its existence has become precarious. Give the government the support it needs and judge it later.

'There is no problem', replied Khaddam. 'We support you. Of Sheikh Pierre's two sons, we liked Amin and disliked Bashir. We wanted Amin to be Lebanon's president, and to be a strong one. A weak president will create problems for you and for us. If you want to negotiate that is your problem. Our perspective is different from yours.' Although we disagreed greatly in future encounters, the pleasant personal ties that were formed between Khaddam and me in this first meeting never weakened.

Asad was quite different from Khaddam. He invited President Jumayyil and the Lebanese delegation for lunch in his suite. Like most Arab leaders, Asad had brought his cook along with him, as well as his own food and refreshments. Thus we sat down and enjoyed a Damascene meal in a swanky Western hotel in non-aligned New Delhi. I found Asad extremely jovial and always keen to enjoy a good laugh. He welcomed us effusively, and looking at me he said: 'We know a lot about you from your revolutionary friends at the American University of Beirut who are also our friends.' He continued with a gentle dig at the president's Kata'ib party, asking: 'As far as we know you are a good Arab, what are you doing with the isolationists?' Not to be misunderstood by Jumayyil, Asad laughed out loud, and assured the president that he was only joking. He was. Asad is always at ease, and humour is an inseparable part of his diplomacy. Through humour he gets a point across and he also sugar-coats it. He likes his guests to relax and to talk. Asad plays his cards generously, but the right card he guards very closely.

Asad turned to me again, and said: 'We admire your public statements and your diplomacy. It seems the Kurah district [of which I am a native] produces great men; no, not always. Let me see, it produced Charles Malik: he was a good philosopher, but a bad politician; it produced Antun Sa'adeh [who, though Greek Orthodox, was not from the Kurah]: he was a great leader with a large following in Syria, but he never really understood Arab nationalism.' I noted that Asad liked to talk. He seemed to enjoy discussing everything. He paid great attention to the incidental and the anecdotal as if he had already made up his mind on the larger issues, and preferred not to discuss them. He amazed me by his detailed knowledge of Lebanese politics. He and Khaddam remembered names and events as if they were reading from a book they themselves had written.

Asad was anxious to hear about our negotiations with the Israelis, and reaffirmed that he wanted an agreement which would not compromise Lebanon's sovereignty and independence. He said he was eager to leave Lebanon once the proper agreement was reached. Asad showed deep interest in Lebanon, in the balance of forces within it, and in the impact of developments in Lebanon on the future course of events in the Middle East.

One of the more bizarre encounters we had in New Delhi was the visit of Abd al-Salam Jalloud, the number two man in Libya, who was heading the Libyan delegation to the summit. Of all the Arab politicians I have met, Jalloud stands apart. He looks severe, sombre, mystical, distant and suspicious. A kind word and a smile seem to change him. He begins to laugh deeply, and, almost child-like, talks freely about everything and everybody, revealing a warm and pleasant personality behind the dour façade. In his meeting with President Jumayyil, Jalloud started by accusing him of treason for negotiating with Israel; by the time the meeting had ended, Jalloud was in complete agreement with the Lebanese position. He even offered to help explain Lebanon's position in the Arab countries which were unaware of the dangers and complexities of the Lebanese crisis. The president responded that the Arabs were already convinced of the Lebanese position, and that the only person Jalloud needed to convince was Qadhdhafi. Wazzan, who witnessed the Jumayyil–Jalloud meeting, said that Jalloud's conversion was even better than that of Saul on his way to Damascus.

4

The Withdrawal Agreement

George Shultz Intervenes

As our negotiations with Israel dragged on, Shultz grew increasingly restless. As he was meeting Israeli Foreign Minister Shamir on Sunday 13 March, Shultz contacted me through the American ambassador in New Delhi, where I was attending the Non-Aligned Summit, and enquired whether he could meet me in Washington immediately. I told the ambassador I would go to Washington provided Shultz was not contemplating a joint meeting with Shamir. I was assured, after consultations with Washington, that this was not the case.

I met Shultz on Saturday 12 March. I repeated to him our position on a number of contentious issues which had come up in the negotiations: these included the future of Sa'd Haddad, joint manoeuvres between the Israeli and Lebanese armies, our position on the status of the Baruk and the normalization of relations between Israel and Lebanon. I told him that Sa'd Haddad was our problem and that what we did with him was not the concern of Israel; we certainly could not contemplate joint manoeuvres between the Lebanese and the Israeli armies, for we were not conducting a peace treaty and certainly were not allies who could enter into joint activities, especially in matters as sensitive as military and security cooperation. We could not accommodate Sharon's desire to have watchtowers on our territory, whether in the Baruk or any other place, and thus endanger our own security and expose the strategic position of the Arab states, particularly Syria. Normalization, I argued, was out of the question, and it could only take place in the context of a comprehensive peace between Israel and the Arab states. However, I also had a positive message that I wanted Shultz to convey to Shamir: Lebanon would never again permit its territory to be a base for operations against Israel, by the PLO or any other grouping. I explained to Shultz how we intended to strengthen the Lebanese army so that, supported by UNIFIL, it could maintain order throughout the country. Such assurances, I felt, would give an added impetus to the negotiations. Shultz later told me that my statements had been used to good effect with the Israelis. The secretary of state then urged me to meet Shamir as one step towards speeding up negotiations. This was an important confidence-building measure, he said. I told him that this was not possible, and that even if we were to meet, I didn't think it would be helpful.

The following day Bob Basil, a Lebanese-American businessman who was close to the Israelis, told me that the Israelis were wondering how I, as a friend of Bashir, could be so critical of Israeli policy and refuse to meet the Israelis. Basil also informed me that David Kimche, the chief Israeli negotiator in the withdrawal talks with Lebanon, had complained to him that because of Wazzan and me, Israel felt it was being treated like a mistress with whom a man does not wish to be seen in public. Israel, Kimche said to Basil, was sensitive about its image. It did not want to be treated like a mistress or a pariah, but to be accepted in the region and dealt with openly. I explained to Basil that neither Lebanon nor any other Arab state could act as Kimche expected until Israel had settled its deep historical conflict with its Arab neighbours, and not one by one, but with them as a group and as a conscious collective act.

In discussions with Shultz the question of how to involve Syria was discussed. The Americans were divided on how to deal with Asad. Shultz, who tended to look at Syrian policy in Lebanon from an international perspective, felt that we should have something in hand with Israel first, before going to the Syrians. Philip Habib, however, held a different view. He wanted the Lebanese to talk to the Syrians on a regular basis. He recommended that we engage the Syrians, and get a sense from them of how much they were willing to tolerate: 'You should tell them enough, so that they will not say later on they did not know.'

There was consensus in our government not to involve the Syrians in detail as we felt, rightly or wrongly, that Syria would not wish to be deeply engaged in such details, or become party to the discussions. We also felt that Syrian involvement would delay the process greatly; and anyhow we intended to consult fully and openly with Syria once we approached agreement on detail. It was also widely believed in our circle that Syria's final position on any agreement between us and Israel would be determined by its regional outlook and by its own assessment of the strategic situation in the region. Syria had regional concerns that Lebanon could not meet, and these were in the domain of the superpowers in their relations with Israel and with the Arab world as a whole, rather than with us.

While I was in Washington, I was joined by Sa'ib Salam, a leading

Lebanese statesman and former prime minister. Salam was not only from one of Beirut's most prominent Sunni families, but he was also instrumental in bringing about a rapprochement between Christians and Muslims, following the election of both Bashir and Amin Jumayyil. His presence in Washington at that time was intended to convey to the Americans the broad consensus that existed in Lebanon for the position we were taking in the tripartite discussions.

On Wednesday 16 March, Salam and I met President Reagan in the Oval Office. Reagan welcomed us in his easy comfortable style. He told us that he had met Shamir, and that the Israeli foreign minister had expressed concern about the security of Israel's northern frontiers. Shamir wanted specific arrangements, Reagan continued, but of course nothing should be done at the expense of Lebanon's sovereignty. 'The problems between Lebanon and Israel are complicated, and a solution seems difficult,' Reagan said, 'but I am a stubborn fellow. We will succeed.' When Salam questioned whether the United States would persevere in spite of the difficulties, Reagan smiled and said : 'I have no reverse gear.' Then he stared at me and said: 'Mr Foreign Minister, do you know of whom you remind me?' I said, 'Yes, Danny Thomas'. 'Right', he replied, and then he began to relate stories about his friend Danny, how he had come to Hollywood, the difficulties he had faced. And then he added: 'Don't be offended by the comparison – Danny is a very intelligent and capable statesman, and he is good-looking, too.' Salam was restless; he continued to talk about the difficulties we were facing in the tripartite discussions, and kept looking suspiciously at Reagan and at me fearing that the discussion would revert to Danny Thomas and Hollywood. Salam and I then had a meeting with Vice-President George Bush. Bush seemed to us to be an intense and emotional person. Although he wasn't well informed, he appeared enthusiastic and anxious to do something. He said:

> Is there something in your heart of hearts that you want our president to do or say? Tell me, and I will convey it to him. The president is deeply committed. Of all the Arab countries, the US has always identified with Lebanon because of its peaceful history, its commerce, its democracy, and because of the American University of Beirut. Lebanon is on our president's mind, and on mine; we both have a desire to have Lebanon live peacefully within its internationally recognized boundaries; we have deep feelings for Lebanon.

Salam was happy with what he heard from Reagan and Bush, and when asked by the reporters on the way out from the White House: 'What did Reagan tell you?' he answered, 'He told me that he has no reverse gear', and to clarify the promise to Arab reporters, he added that no reverse gear means in Arabic he has no 'en arrière'. I retorted, laughing, 'Saib Bey, you are becoming like Sheikh Pierre Jumayyil, mixing Arabic and French.' Salam smiled widely, lit his ever-present cigar, and walked away.

I returned to Beirut through London. In London I met Khaddam, who was on a visit to the British capital. I explained that the Americans were confident that the negotiation process would bear fruit, although they and we felt the Israelis would be difficult. Khaddam counselled that we maintain serious and open discussions with Shultz, whom he described as a good leader. Shultz's only problem, Khaddam added, was that he listened more than he talked. 'That's never been a problem for you', I said, to our mutual amusement. Khaddam urged me to keep him informed in writing of what was going on in the negotiations. I told him I depended on Ubayd to keep him informed. He said that Ubayd had told the Syrians what we had refused to agree to in the negotiations, and added:

> This is good. We want to know what you are accepting. Ubayd speaks to us in generalities. I want specifics, and in writing. We are in Lebanon to help you; use us as a means to pressure Israel. When you reach an agreement free of concessions with Israel, come to Damascus, and in half an hour we will agree on the withdrawal of our forces from Lebanon. The Americans keep asking about withdrawal. They are forcing us to play a tape for them – fine, we play it. We will withdraw, we will withdraw, we will withdraw!

Khaddam asked me if Lebanon had really reached an agreement with Israel, as he had been told by the French ambassador in New Delhi. I answered him that when we came close to an agreement with the Israelis, and definitely prior to signing it, I would come to Damascus and give him a copy of the draft. He would be the first to know, and not the ambassador of this or that country. I emphasized, however, that the responsibility for an agreement was ours. In reaching an agreement with Israel, we were taking into account the national interests of Lebanon first, and then the national interests of Syria. We were aware of the mutual and interdependent interests of our two countries. However, I wanted Khaddam to know that our problem with Israel was somewhat different than Syria's problem with the occupation of the Golan Heights. Ultimately Israel's occupation of the Golan had less of an impact on the independence of Syria than Israeli occupation of Beirut and the surrounding areas. In Lebanon's case, many of its vital centres were occupied, and once the vital centres of a state are occupied, the state is paralysed. What we needed now was Syria's help to end the occupation.

Khaddam assured me that Syria would do its utmost to help us realize this objective. Lebanon was an independent state, he said, and it naturally did what was in its interest. Syria, however, saw the matter from the perspective of the Arab–Israeli struggle. 'We support your efforts,' Khaddam concluded, 'but we are also bound by our perspective. I hope the two will not be in conflict.' We were hearing from our negotiating team that the Israeli negotiators were getting increasingly belligerent. They made fun of Lebanese sovereignty, they ridiculed our army, and were sarcastic with our negotiators.

I told Draper that the Israeli attitude must change if negotiations were to continue. 'I must tell you', I said, 'that the Israeli appetite is growing, and your intervention is not helping much. The South may be facing the same fate as the West Bank and Gaza. We must move before new facts mushroom on the ground.' Draper explained that Israeli sarcasm might be the result of a 'certain defensiveness'. 'Elie,' he said, 'you know comparative cultures, you know the sensitivities of the Israelis, you know the pressure the Israeli negotiators are under from their government. They are frustrated. They want a lot from you, and you are not giving, and they wonder who are you to refuse? They want to be friends with you and understandably, you cannot do that. The negative mood is purely psychological. It will pass. I want you to know that Kimche, a civilized man, is aware of this negative mood in his team and is doing something about it. Give him time.' 'Time is the last thing I have', I responded.

By early April a slight change in the Israeli attitude was noticeable. Perhaps it was due to a statement by Reagan suspending delivery of F-16 aircraft until Israel had withdrawn completely from Lebanon. Reagan's statement was made at the request of Philip Habib. By the end of March Habib was telling me he was sick of carrots, he wanted some sticks, and asked Reagan to provide him with some in the form of suspending delivery of F-16 aircrafts. Also by the end of March Israel had probed deep and wide into the Lebanese position and had come to the conclusion that we would not go further than we had already done.

A Draft Agreement

A draft agreement was ready by 3 April. Ghassan Tweini and I met Prime Minister Wazzan and went over it point by point, making changes. We were told by Draper that the draft was acceptable to the Israeli negotiating team, but that there were problems with the Israeli politicians. The politicians, namely Begin and Sharon, were going in different directions, we were told by Draper. Begin was withdrawing more and more into his inner self and blaming himself for the losses and mistakes in the Lebanese war. Sharon was getting more aggressive and wanted more from Lebanon to justify his conquest. The Kahan Commission, established by the Knesset to investigate the Sabra–Shatila massacres under Israeli eyes, was, in particular, critical of Sharon, and Sharon's reaction was to be tough with Lebanon and secure, through the negotiations, an agreement that would justify the Israeli adventure. The draft agreement still had loopholes. The questions of Sa'd Haddad, the Baruk mountain and UNIFIL were yet to be resolved.

We knew that further discussion of these topics could take a long time. Confidence in the US role was diminishing. Our government was beginning to face criticisms. Politicians had thought all foreign armies would be out of Lebanon by December 1982, and we were now in 1983. Some demanded the resignation of the government. Certain elements in the country were increasingly critical of me personally for my open attitude toward the Arabs, and I received a number of threats through various channels. President Jumayyil intervened on my behalf, but to be certain, he suggested that I should increase my guard detail. I informed Habib and Draper of the prevailing mood in the country and the need for results, and they promised to multiply their efforts. They too were disappointed by the pace. Indeed, Habib was frantic.

The president, meanwhile, was losing patience with the Israeli demands. In a meeting with Habib on 14 April, he vented his frustration without restraint. He kept looking at me to see if he was exceeding the desired bounds, but I was happy with his performance. Habib did not need the lecture. He knew exactly our mood and where we stood, but it was important for us to verbalize our position so that he could communicate it with his natural exuberance and sense of urgency to Reagan, Shultz, Begin, Arens and Sharon. 'I must be frank with you,' Jumayyil shouted at Habib, 'and tell you that the American position in the negotiations has not been as forthcoming as we expected.' He continued:

> President Reagan assured us that the principles of our sovereignty, national consensus, and relations with the Arab world would be fully protected. In the negotiations there was continuing American pressure on us to accommodate Israeli demands which would have brought us pretty close to compromising these three principles. America has applied more pressure on Lebanon than on Israel, and we have already conceded in this agreement all that we could concede. We cannot do more. We either have the agreement in accordance with the Lebanese text, or let us not have an agreement. I do not want to be the president who signs an agreement that violates Lebanon's sovereignty and dignity. I am ready to take great risks and lead a different kind of campaign, if necessary, to liberate my country. The Israeli conditions are becoming preposterous! There must be an end to their appetite and you Americans must put your weight behind your word. We are wasting our time on silly arguments. Your method in negotiating leads us to make one concession after the other. This has been a bitter experience. We did not expect you to be so lukewarm. Israel continues to interfere in our internal

affairs, and you do nothing. It was behind the massacre of our army unit in Aley; it is building an airport in Damour and a helicopter airport in Ayn Zhalta. Why are they doing that? Do they intend to stay? What are you telling them? Are you implementing Reagan's instructions? I wanted to work closely with you and yet I do not always get the right response. For the tenth time you bring up the question of Sa'd Haddad. I am tired of this issue. Haddad is our problem. He is Lebanese. I am telling you this is the last time I will permit you or anyone else to raise the Haddad issue with me. This subject is closed.

Habib was at a loss for words. He too was frustrated, and swallowed the reprimand with great difficulty. He was visibly angry, but maintained his composure. He promised not to raise the issue of Sa'd Haddad again. He moved from one subject to another without faring much better. To my surprise, however, he asked the president about recognition. The president exploded once again: 'What recognition?' he demanded. 'Are we signing a peace treaty? I would rather sign a peace treaty', screamed the president, 'and face all the problems openly rather than sneak an agreement that included recognition and all the other elements of a peace treaty. Recognition is out!'

After this stormy meeting, Ambassador Dillon and I met at my house and talked at length about the meeting and the president's anger. I told Dillon: 'I am fully with the president on his attitude and on his frustration with the process. He and I expected a superpower to be more effective with its client. You told us you understood our position and would not pressure us, and yet you do.' 'Believe me, we pressure the Israelis more', argued Dillon, and yet he fully sympathized with our position. He was one of the few ambassadors who reserved the right to hold strong views on what was right and what was wrong. And I suspected that he felt strongly that we were right. He was, however, the ambassador of a superpower and had to measure his words as well as his actions carefully and in conformity with instructions from Washington. I told Dillon that we had reached the limit; there was nothing else we could add to the draft text. This agreement could be signed today or next year, but as far as we were concerned, we would not give on any point. I added that I felt we were falling into a vicious cycle, and I invoked Nietzsche's concept of 'eternal recurrence': I remarked that the ancient Hebrews had totally rejected the Greek pagan cycle of eternal recurrence in history, but that the modern Israelis seemed to have embraced it. Dillon, who was a specialist in English literature, and who had a sharp mind, listened with a smile on his face. He said nothing. It occurred to me that the representative of a superpower cannot always say what is on his mind, even when he is with his closest friends.

Explosion at the US Embassy

On 18 April, as the president and I were examining new changes in the draft text with Philip Habib and his team, an officer walked in and informed us that a car-bomb had exploded at the American Embassy. There were many casualties, he said, perhaps among them Ambassador Dillon. Draper, whose wife Roberta was at the embassy, jumped up in a panic and sped towards Beirut. Habib decided to contact Secretary of State Shultz immediately to tell him that he was fine, as he was afraid that the media would put him on the list of dead. 'That would please many people,' he said sardonically, 'and I have no intention of doing so.'

Habib called Shultz from the presidential palace and assured him that he was okay. 'I hope he takes this as good news', growled Habib, although actually he and Shultz were close personal friends. We began to receive more information about the explosion. Someone on a suicide mission had driven a truck loaded with explosives into the embassy building. Dillon was miraculously safe, although his office had collapsed on top of him.

Dillon, having done what he could at the embassy, returned to his residence, where we were waiting for him. While he acted calmly, it was obvious that the ambassador was internally shattered: he had just lost dozens of his aides and associates, and had narrowly escaped death himself. None of us who listened to the account of his narrow escape could help wondering about the strange workings of destiny.

The United States sent an official delegation to accompany the coffins of the Americans killed in the incident. Dillon informed me that a brief private ceremony would be held for the victims at the airport, and that my wife and I were welcome to attend, if we wished to do so. I said I would.

On Saturday morning, 23 April, my wife, American-born Phyllis Sell, and I drove to the airport. On the way to the airport she told me how sad she was to participate in a ceremony of this nature, but that the sadness she felt was as a Lebanese citizen and the wife of the foreign minister of a country in deep agony, and not as an American citizen in Lebanon. Over the years she had become too Lebanized to worry about the problems happening in America or to Americans. The Lebanese dimension of the crisis had dwarfed all others. Our driver somehow missed the right route to the ceremony and drove on to the airport's main runway, where the American contingent in the MNF was located. The Marines were obviously tense, and two tanks rumbled in our direction, their guns pointing at us. Behind them were dozens of Marines in battle formation. I ordered the driver to reverse, which made us seem even more suspicious and brought more tanks from behind the sand-dunes. Cornered, I jumped

out of the car and shouted: 'I am the foreign minister coming to attend
the formal ceremony for the embassy personnel, lead me to the correct
route.' A gunner in the lead tank yelled back, 'The hell you are!'

Fortunately an officer climbed down, verified our identity, apologized,
and guided us in the right direction. It was a simple and dignified military
ceremony. The coffins were moved one by one from ambulances and
carried ceremonially to the waiting plane. Tears and anger were in the
eyes and on the faces of the American officials. We paid our condolences
and returned. The car-bomb was one more shot in the raging war that
had been in progress since 1975, and it was not the last.

Shultz's Diplomacy

On 28 April, President Jumayyil received from President Asad, by way of
an emissary, a handwritten statement, unsigned and undated. The message
read:

> The American team gave us the following information: We do not want any
> misunderstanding concerning our position. We will always want to discuss
> with you frankly. As we have always stated our position concerning the
> situation in Lebanon and as we are concerned lest our position is mis-
> understood as is often obvious from certain statements made, we would
> like now to clarify our position again: We consider any gains realized by
> Israeli aggression against Lebanon as constituting a danger against our
> national and Arab security. Such gains will force us to stay in Lebanon as
> long as these Israeli gains persist. It is natural that we adhere to this position
> to defend our national security especially since Israel contemplates and
> plans, from time to time, to expand through military force.

Wazzan, Tweini, Haddad and I met the president and reflected long on
Asad's letter. Obviously, this was a clear message not to go ahead with
the agreement. But we had already completed a draft. There were minor
points to be resolved; it was difficult to arrest the process. We hoped that
Asad would change his mind once he saw the text and heard our reasons
for going ahead with it. Some argued that President Asad had sent this
message to engage Shultz in a broader dialogue on the Middle East
question and, therefore, that it need not be a reason to stop the process.
Actually the letter added little to what Asad had told us before: no
concessions, no violation of sovereignty, and no measures that would
threaten Syria or Arab security. Khaddam had also made that clear in our
London meeting. But the timing of the letter was significant. We all felt it
was addressed to the Americans as much as it was addressed to us, and
as Shultz was on his way to Beirut, it was felt that direct discussion
between Shultz and Asad was desirable, indeed mandatory.

Shultz arrived in Beirut a few hours after Asad's letter was received. Philip Habib and I met him at the airport. On our way back from the airport, Habib joined me in my car while Shultz's motorcade left separately. There was much to talk about before our meeting with Shultz that evening. My driver moved leisurely through streets in the suburbs of Beirut which Habib knew were dangerous. When he looked back and found no security car behind us, he screamed: 'Elie, do you mean to tell me that you ride in this god-damned town without a security car behind you? Do you know who is with you in this car? Do you know how many people want my head? I sure hope you are not one of them!'

I calmed Habib down and urged the driver to speed up, which he enjoyed doing anyway. Soon Habib was uncertain which was the greater danger, a bullet in his back or a car crash. He was uncharacteristically silent until we reached the presidential palace. I learned, to my amazement, that when Habib is scared he goes silent and blank. From that date on, however, I had a security car behind me. Instead of protecting me, however, it tended to bump into my car at great speed and eat away what was left of my nerves. Bodyguards enjoyed speed, shooting in the air to clear traffic, shouting at normal mortals on the way, and I believe they contrived to create a conflict in which they would emerge as saviours.

In our discussions with Shultz, we told him that we wanted an agreement which would result in withdrawals, and which was also acceptable to Syria. Shultz responded that he felt we had a credible agreement. The only point, Shultz added, was that we could not allow the Soviets to impose their veto. Their objectives were not ours. He said that the Soviets did not want the USA to succeed and reach an agreement that would lead to a broader agreement on a Middle East settlement. The Soviets, he said, were spoilers. They could not help Lebanon and the other Arab states with Israel. The USA could. If they could not help, if the Soviets could not be a party, they would obstruct. They would attempt a veto, but we could not allow this to happen. The soviets had influence on Syria, he added, but Asad was independent. He was a free decision-maker and he could be persuaded that this agreement was good. While we were all a bit dubious, Shultz was pretty confident that President Asad would accept the agreement. It was obvious that there were obstacles ahead: nevertheless we had to finalize a draft so we had something to talk about.

Speaking for the Lebanese side, I went over the draft agreement with Shultz point by point, explaining what we could agree to and what we could not agree to: we could not accept that the agreement be signed by foreign ministers; we were not signing a treaty, but were making security arrangements. The agreement had to be signed by the heads of the delegations.

We opposed recognition. If we used the term, then we had a peace treaty. Shultz responded that Israel might, for internal political purposes, insist it had a peace treaty in hand and that it had won recognition from the Lebanese. 'If Israel says so,' Shultz enquired, 'would you contradict it?' I replied: 'What we say to our people must be the truth. We have been fair with them. They have already heard too many lies. I will tell our people the Israelis are lying.' Shultz nodded, not too happily.

We then discussed the more technical aspects of the agreement: the names of the committees and subcommittees, their membership, their functions, the role of UNIFIL, and the many thorny subjects which fell under the heading of mutual relations. The Israelis wanted us to agree to mutual relations when the agreement was signed. Formally we wanted to postpone discussions on mutual relations six months after a full Israeli withdrawal had taken place; in reality, however, we wanted to postpone the matter until the regional situation allowed for discussion in this area with all the Arab states concerned.

The general political atmosphere at the time was permeated by the fear that Israel might not withdraw from Lebanon, or might withdraw only partially. We began to sense that conclusion of a withdrawal agreement was not necessarily the highest priority in Israel, and that the Israelis preferred other alternatives. When Arens replaced Sharon as defence minister this orientation in Israel began to increase. We felt it in many small incidents. We checked with the Americans and they assured us it was not the case. They turned out to be wrong.

After a meeting with Shultz on 30 April, the president asked Shultz, Habib and me to meet him privately under a pine tree in the palace garden. We sat down, drank coffee, and talked freely. Shultz was in an optimistic mood after what he considered a fruitful visit to Israel. 'Suppose we have an agreement', Shultz said. 'We want to discuss with you how it would function in operational terms. What would the specifics of such an agreement be, not its general principles? The Israelis are suspicious. They want to hear from us how the agreement would be implemented on a day to day basis. They want examples. There are terms in the agreement that must be explained in an appendix.'

Shultz was also optimistic about the Syrian position. The Syrians had sent him a message welcoming him to Damascus. He thought that there were many things that President Asad wanted to discuss with him, and that the USA could be helpful to him. We, on the Lebanese side, were in no mood to discuss specifics before we were sure of the bigger picture. We were about to sign an agreement and we had important political questions to ask. I formulated six questions and gave them to the president to ask. I told Shultz that we would go ahead with the agreement only after we receive satisfactory answers to these questions. President Jumayyil then read the questions to Shultz while Habib wrote them down. The questions were:

1. If we fail to reach an agreement with Israel on full withdrawals, what is the course of action that the United States will follow to support Lebanon effectively?
2. If we reach an agreement, and Syria refuses to withdraw on the grounds that the agreement gives Israel gains in Lebanon, what would be the fate of the agreement?
3. If concluding an agreement leads to the boycott of our goods by Arab countries, how can the United States help?
4. If, ignoring the agreement, Israel withdraws partially and entrenches itself in whatever area of Lebanon it considers to be its 'security zone', how can you help us get Israel out?
5. Given Soviet influence in the region and Soviet opposition to your initiative in the Middle East, are you confident that this influence cannot defeat your effort in reaching an agreement between Lebanon and Israel?
6. Should the unforeseen happen, and Israel and Syria go to war, how can we protect Lebanon, knowing that such a war is going to be fought mostly in our country?

I told Shultz that the answers to these questions were as important as the agreement, if not more so. He agreed. He thought they were good and tough questions, and said that he and Habib would reflect on them and consult President Reagan. Some of the answers, he said, would depend on the agreement; some would depend on the moderate Arab states; and some would depend on what the United States would do.

President Reagan had said that the United States would help Lebanon out of the crisis, Shultz said, and it would. He added:

> We have no magic, we have influence and we will use it. We did not want this agreement to be a four-cornered affair. We are having enough difficulty with three sides already. I believe Syria will withdraw once it knows that we have an agreement to get Israel out of Lebanon. This is a major achievement; no Arab state has attained this without a peace treaty.

I explained that President Asad had opposed the peace treaty between Egypt and Israel; he was always against bilateral discussions with Israel; his note to us indicated he would oppose the agreement. Shultz agreed that Syria was not going to be easy, but if we had a good agreement that would get Israel out of the very heart of Lebanon then we would have general Arab support, including the Syrians. He admitted that a long diplomatic process was needed with Syria but he was confident of the result. The alternative, he said, was Israeli occupation not of a strip of Lebanon but of its very capital, with all the dangers that occupation implied. We were in a tight spot, but that was nothing new. We had been there for some time.

The same small group met again under the same pine tree the next day, Sunday 1 May. Shultz told us that he had reflected on our questions, consulted Reagan and was ready to respond. As to the agreement, we should not entertain the idea of failure. The consequences of failure would be bad for Lebanon, for Israel and for the United States. We had to succeed because the alternatives were bad. At best they confirmed the occupation, at worst they would lead to further wars in the region. Shultz continued:

> As to Syria, we will have to get Syria's approval for the agreement. We will negotiate with Syria, and we have some influence with Syria, more than is evident. Although the Soviets have influence in Syria, they do not dictate its policies. Asad acts independently; if he is influenced at all, he is influenced by the Arab states. We will work on that angle. I have not met Asad; I will, soon. I think I can work with him. I understand his concerns. He is a nationalist and I believe this agreement serves the national goal best. On the boycott issue, you are right to be concerned. We will try to help you. You are not trading with Israel. Mutual relations, we agreed, were for future discussion. We will explain this position to the Saudis and they will help you. They will not punish you for what you are not doing.
>
> Concerning a partial Israeli withdrawal, we anticipate that the agreement will be severely attacked in Israel. Israel wanted a peace treaty, not merely a security agreement. The government will have to face strong opposition, and it will have to account for the war and for the loss of life resulting from it. This should help you. The Israeli government has a tough time ahead of it, but it will abide by the agreement. Partial withdrawal by Israel is unacceptable to us. We are negotiating full withdrawal, and we will stay with you to ensure that full withdrawal takes place as is clearly stated in the agreement.
>
> We share your concern about a war erupting between Syria and Israel on Lebanese territory. The situation is potentially explosive. The Soviets are in Syria and they are manning some of the weapons which they gave to Syria. Should a conflict arise between Syria and Israel, the Soviets are likely to be drawn into it, and this is an ominous matter. We are thinking about it all the time, but I believe we can resolve the problem without provoking conflict. We will solve it by convincing the Syrians of the value of the agreement. Asad is a pragmatist, and I work well with pragmatists.

I listened to Shultz's assurances and was not fully convinced. Clearly he was doing his best, but he did not control all the cards. While Shultz did not assure us of success, however, he gave us enough encouragement to go ahead. At any rate, we were so inclined by the logic of our situation. There is, above the wills and whims of man, a certain autonomous force governing the conduct of nations. Such a force pervaded all the deliberations of the tripartite group and the committees and subcommittees issuing from it. They were discussing facts on the ground and ways of handling them, and facts are rude, they lack the pliability of theory and the flexibility of myth. Now that we had a draft approximating a final version we could brief the parties concerned and get their reactions. It was the moment of truth, and I realized that now we would be spared the polite generalities of the past.

In early May, we were ready to give President Asad a detailed account of the progress attained so far. I travelled to Damascus on 2 May and gave the Syrian president a full account of the proposed agreement. I was accompanied by John Ubayd and General Abbas Hamdan. My cousin Colonel Abdallah Salem piloted the military helicopter that carried us from the Ministry of Defence in Ba'bda to the Umayyad capital.

The 30-minute flight took us first over Mount Lebanon, with its array of pine trees, oak trees and fruit orchards. Below us were villages perched on hills, huddled in crevices, or lying sound and serene in peaceful valleys, their red tile roofs glistening in the sun. Then we flew over the Biqa' Valley, the historic path of imperial armies travelling south and north through the region, and now a region controlled by the Syrian army. Literally hundreds of Syrian gun-barrels were aimed at the sky, and from the fragile helicopter they seemed to be pointing at us. The helicopter then flew over the desolate and defiant Anti-Lebanon mountain range. It occurred to me that the Anti-Lebanon, which has historically shielded fertile Lebanon from the arid hinterland, had apparently succumbed to aridity itself.

Beyond the Anti-Lebanon is Syria. From the air, the plateau leading to Damascus reminded me of a huge fort. Missiles pointed towards the skies, and tanks or tank tracks were visible everywhere. Virtually every hill from the Biqa' Valley to Damascus was a fortress, a watch-tower, and a reminder that Syria's political course was quite different from ours: military, stoic, autocratic and intensely ideological, poised in a militant mobilized posture against Israel.

Every time I took this flight from Ba'bda to the Mazzeh airport in Damascus, my mind was overcome by the history of the area. How could it be otherwise? What other 30-minute flight anywhere on this planet looks down at a richer historical deposit, or at a greater kaleidoscope of the human spirit? To my deep sorrow, history was no consolation in this time of trouble, and the knowledge of it no real guide to the labyrinth ahead.

Hegel was right, history teaches no lessons. Somehow the immensity of political action generates a blinding glare which tends to block away all cumulative knowledge, except that which has been subconsciously implanted in the soul. At the Mazzeh airport our delegation was met by Foreign Minister Khaddam and a dozen dignitaries. The reception, as usual, was warm. Khaddam drove me in his own car, a bullet-proof Mercedes with Soviet-made machine-guns lining its interior. It was a reminder of the timeless linkage between legitimacy and power. Khaddam had often been a target of assassins, and he had learned to be careful. It had paid off: next to Andrei Gromyko and Sheikh Sabah al-Ahmad al-Sabah of Kuwait, Khaddam was, in 1983, the longest-serving foreign minister in the world. He was a survivor, and this had in no small measure been the result of his flair.

Khaddam drove me straight to President Asad's residence. Asad, true to style, was extremely cordial on a personal level, unyielding on the official. I gave him a detailed account of all the issues that had arisen in the negotiations. I informed him of all aspects of the agreement, and I outlined the Israeli demands which we had rejected. I also filled him in on our lengthy meetings with Shultz. I told him that proposed texts of the agreement were being prepared and studied by both sides, and that we expected to have a unified text within a week or two. I explained the introduction of the proposed agreement. I described the security arrangements and how they compared with those of the Armistice Agreement of 1949. I also described the functions of the Joint Liaison Committee that was to supervise the agreement, and the workings of the security arrangements. I explained the conditions governing the security region and the types of weapons in it.

Asad listened attentively. He stopped me and enquired in great detail about all military and security matters. He had been an accomplished fighter-pilot himself, and was particularly interested in all aspects of the agreement relating to airspace. He enquired about security arrangements close to the Syrian borders, and was obviously deeply concerned about military advantages which Israel might acquire in these areas. He was dubious about Lebanon's ability to meet Syria's security concerns. When I told him that the proposed agreement ended the state of belligerency between Lebanon and Israel, he asked if Lebanon was therefore required to withdraw from the Arab Defence Pact. I said no.

When I described the Joint Liaison Committee and the temporary supervisory teams, he wondered whether a hundred such teams might not arise. I assured him that they would not exceed half a dozen. He also enquired whether decisions taken in the Joint Liaison Committee were taken by unanimity. I said yes. Asad wondered why Israel refused to allow

UNIFIL to deploy in the security zone. He also asked if the agreement gave the Israeli air force the right to fly over Lebanese territory. I assured him that strict implementation of the agreement would prevent the Israeli armed forces from violating our territory, airspace and territorial waters.

The casual informality of the reception was put aside when Asad articulated Syria's position on the proposed agreement: 'We sympathize with the position of the Lebanese leaders,' Asad began,' and we appreciate the terrible conditions under which they find themselves.' He went on:

> Our point of view, however, is different from yours. In New Delhi President Jumayyil told me Syria can live without the Golan Heights and Egypt without Sinai, but that Lebanon could not live without the capital and the region to the south of it. This is not true. Each country has its particular problems, and in war people hang together. Our ancestors did so and ousted the foreigner. They realized this fact when they were poor and uneducated. Now they are educated and they can be more effective. I do not believe that Israel can fracture Lebanon and bring about small confessional states. Regional and international considerations make the rise of such states impossible. The very idea of fracturing Lebanon could lead to a regional war with dangerous international consequences. I am as concerned about Lebanon as I am about Syria. The Lebanese, when united, can push Israel out. Only struggle liberates nations. We liberated Syria from the Ottomans and from the French without having a major army. Now we have a strong army, we can do more. Liberation is the work of the people: it takes time and it demands sacrifices. Israel is an enemy of special qualities: its frontiers are not likely to stop at the Zahrani or Litani rivers; Israel aspires to an empire. The proposed agreement confirms Begin's leadership; it compensates him for his adventure into Lebanon; Israel cannot stay in Lebanon indefinitely. Its deployment in Lebanon is costly and its economy is on the verge of collapse. Our withdrawal from Lebanon is not a problem, but it is not in any way related to the Israeli withdrawal. Between you and Israel it is a matter of 'biting on fingers'. They are hurting you and you are hurting them. They are in pain and you are in pain. You should be able to withstand the pain; all the Arabs are with you. We should not deal with Israel. Even Husni Mubarak did not agree to visit Israel. He is a good man and I know him well; he was not responsible for the Camp David Accords.

Asad then asked why Lebanon had to reach an agreement with Israel. Lebanon's position was good, the government enjoyed broad national support, and it was respected in the Arab world. Why did we wish to compromise our position by consorting with the enemy? Lebanon, though occupied, was in a stronger position than Syria and Israel. Israel had not come to fight Lebanon, why was it Lebanon which had to pay the price? Asad went on, castigating the United States for allowing Israel to insist on new conditions. Withdrawal should take place in the context of UN resolution 425 only, he said. If Israel made gains in Lebanon, the Syrian army would not withdraw. Asad pointed out that he was not worried about the Israeli army in Lebanon; he was strong enough to defend himself. If the United States wanted the Israelis out of Lebanon, then that was fine; that was the way it should be. But the argument that the departure of the Israeli armed forces would reduce the pressure on Syria in Lebanon should not be raised. The Israeli army in Lebanon did not scare him, and therefore its withdrawal should not be used as an inducement to get his consent on an agreement he did not support.

What Lebanon was doing with Israel was worse than Camp David, Asad went on. Ending the state of war meant peace. 'We broke off our relations with Egypt', Asad remarked, 'because it concluded a peace treaty with Israel. We cannot break with Egypt and not break with you'. His argument was eloquent in the context of his ideological position. He had used a flurry of historical allusions to bolster a position he had already taken. For all intents and purposes, Asad's views were now cast in concrete.

I tried repeatedly to explain key points which he had dismissed lightly, but which were crucial for us and had consumed weeks of hard negotiation with Israel. While these details were important, they were not the issue for Asad. His perception was different; his position was different; his priorities were different, and he was not about to acquiesce to our position.

The genius of Hafiz al-Asad is that he gives you the most unpleasant news in the most pleasant way. It brings to mind a line from the medieval Arab poet al-Mutanabbi, who spent most of his life singing the praises of the governor of Aleppo. The line goes: 'If you see the teeth of the lion protruding, do not lull yourself into thinking that the lion is smiling.' Asad does show teeth, and he smiles, indeed laughs a lot. But the more congenial Asad is, the tougher his stand.

Anticipating Syria's opposition to the proposed agreement, I told the press in Damascus that when one-third of our country was occupied, including its capital, we did not have a choice between negotiating or not negotiating. We were negotiating within the parameters of our independence, unity and sovereignty. Our primary responsibility was to get all foreign forces out of our country. We were negotiating from a position of moral strength. We had come to Damascus to consult President Asad, and we would take his views into consideration. But we had to remember that the country which was occupied was Lebanon, and that the country which was suffering and whose existence was threatened was Lebanon. Negotiations, therefore, were our responsibility, although we recognized the interests of others in the process, particularly Syria.

Next day, I informed Shultz of Asad's position. Shultz remained hopeful that Asad would change his mind, especially since he was certain that the Syrian president would not be unduly influenced by the Soviets. Reagan and Shultz always saw a Soviet hand in forces working against their interests, though Shultz clearly recognized Asad's independent posture and his freedom to manoeuvre in Middle East affairs independently of the Soviets. I told Shultz that I believed Asad's position to be final. The secretary of state was upset by my report and enquired whether Asad had brought up the subject of receiving him in Damascus. 'Yes,' I said, 'and he was looking forward to meeting you.' We all agreed that Asad's tone had gone up a notch. The Americans thought that it was perhaps Shultz's presence in the region which had led the Syrians to escalate. Others felt that it was the Soviets who were responsible for Asad's uncompromising attitude.

On 3 May, in a meeting with President Jumayyil at which I was present, Secretary Shultz informed us that there was a breakthrough with the Israelis, and that we could have an agreement as soon as the next day. However, he added, the Lebanese would have to take the courageous step of agreeing to a meeting between Shamir and myself. This meeting, Shultz argued, would be essential to give the Israelis confidence. They needed to talk to a Lebanese official of high standing, not just a member of the bureaucracy, to reach an oral understanding on how Lebanon intended to implement the details of the agreement. Such a meeting would be secret. It could be held in Lebanon, in Israel, on an American ship, or in Europe. The choice would be ours. President Jumayyil looked at me knowing beforehand what my reaction would be. I told Shultz I could not meet Shamir, either secretly or openly. Were we to meet I would prefer such a meeting to be open. I would not do it, I argued, because such a meeting would give the agreement a political significance, and would provide the *de facto* recognition which we had refused to give throughout the negotiations.

Habib, with whom I had developed a close friendship during the past months, virtually hit the ceiling. 'Elie, my friend,' he said, 'you are about to conclude a historic agreement that will get Israel out of Lebanon completely without a peace treaty, a fact unequalled in contemporary Middle East history, and you refuse to give it the extra nudge needed to bring it about. It is completely in your hands. It is your choice.' The more Habib argued, however, the more certain I was of my stand. I believed a meeting would be more harmful than helpful as it would give the false impression that we were heading towards normalization of relations. Habib was fuming, as he was inclined to, when he failed to get what he wanted. In spite of the tension generated by my refusal, we put the finishing touches on a number of other details. One of the things we discussed was providing Sa'd Haddad, if need be, with a US visa to get him out of the country.

Throughout these meetings, Prime Minister Wazzan was extremely active. He urged the USA to exercise greater leadership and to restrain Israeli demands. Wazzan often lost his temper and used rough words with Shultz. Basically a kindly person, the prime minister would always find the right word to soften the impact of his criticism. Once, addressing Shultz after an attack on American policy, Wazzan said: 'I would like to apologize for my harsh tone. Often the patient insults the dentist who is pulling out his aching tooth. Take it in that spirit, Mr Secretary.'

Wazzan spoke with the wisdom culled from his long experience. He explained his points by providing historical analogies, and anecdotes which he attributed to his father. We not only had to translate what Wazzan was saying, but in the case of the analogies and the anecdotes we had to explain what he meant. Tweini enjoyed doing that, adding the appropriate flavour as he saw fit, while Wazzan eyed him suspiciously. When we had agreed with Shultz on the final draft of the agreement, Wazzan stood up to thank the secretary for his efforts. He asked me to translate. I said: 'Mr Prime Minister, I have been translating for my American wife for 29 years, and I have decided not to translate any more; our friend Ghassan Tweini will.' Ghassan agreed, but as he was an accomplished politician, Wazzan feared that he would modify his version to give the impact Tweini wanted. Wazzan spoke and listened to Ghassan translate, ensuring that he remained within the limits.

Wazzan spoke eloquently and courageously:

This is not the agreement I wanted, he said; I expected to get a better one through the good offices of the United States. This is not a happy day for me. It should not be a happy day for the United States. The United States, as the greatest democracy in the world, should have done more to help the most beleaguered democracy in the world. Nevertheless, I will support this agreement and will bear the consequences, because under the existing conditions it is the best instrument I have to free my country.

Shultz was not hurt; indeed he seemed rather touched. Although he was not an overtly emotional man, I felt that he deeply empathized with this courageous patriot. Shultz returned to Israel and I plunged into an intensive schedule of briefing leading Lebanese political figures and seeking their counsel. These figures included leading members of parliament, former presidents and prime ministers, and religious leaders. There was virtually unanimous support for the agreement, appreciation for the American role in the process, and respect for the team conducting the negotiations. This reaction was evident even among individuals who would later turn vehemently against the agreement, when the agreement seemed to fail. In politics nothing succeeds like success.

On Saturday evening, 7 May, President Jumayyil and I were together when we received a call from President Reagan assuring Jumayyil of his support. President Jumayyil was ecstatic. He thought the telephone call was very important, and that Reagan had committed himself to supporting the agreement. In fact, Reagan had merely confirmed by his call what he had told former prime minister Sa'ib Salam, namely that he had no reverse gear. It was not easy for me to temper the president's enthusiasm, however. I quoted Hamlet who, when asked by Polonius what he was reading, answered: 'Words, words, words.' I felt that even Shultz, the usually cautious statesman, had been too optimistic in his statements on the likelihood of Syrian acceptance of the withdrawal agreement. I tried to play down the possibility of success, and to emphasize the difficulties that lay ahead. On 8 May, Shultz informed us that the Israelis had accepted the agreement. The leaders of the Labour Party as well as Ariel Sharon were against it, but Shultz believed that Begin would get the agreement passed.

When the agreement took its final form, President Jumayyil called President Asad and told him that he was sending me to Damascus to show him the final text. President Asad welcomed this gesture. I left for Damascus on 12 May, accompanied by Colonel Sa'id Qa'qur, a member of our negotiating team, whom I had brought along in case Asad asked for clarifications on certain security matters. It was obvious from my recent visit to Damascus that Asad would not only reject the agreement, but would actively seek to oppose it.

When I arrived in Damascus, I met first with Khaddam. I told him that I was there to brief him on the draft agreement. We could read it carefully together, he could take extensive notes, and then we could discuss them. Khaddam's stenographer, however, was well-trained, and as Khaddam read the draft agreement at a normal speed, the stenographer took down the text word by word without missing a comma. I was amazed at his dexterity, and I was unaware that such skill could be acquired in the context of the Arabic language. Khaddam proudly assured me that the regime had developed this skill in its stenographers early on, and that Damascus had a number of them who had acquired this proficiency, but none like this one. He promised that he would send him to train our secretaries if we cancelled the agreement. With Khaddam, humour was substance; he had already rejected the agreement.

As Khaddam read he began to shake his head disapprovingly. When he reached the passage in the introduction on ending of the state of belligerency, he exclaimed: 'My God! Ending the state of belligerency! What have you done? This is worse than Camp David!' It got no better: Khaddam made a negative comment on virtually every article.

At the meeting with Khaddam early next morning, he told me that the Syrian leadership had met throughout the night, reviewed the draft agreement carefully, and rejected it on the basis of Lebanese, Arab and Syrian considerations: first, Lebanon was under Israeli occupation, and therefore any agreement with the enemy would not be in Lebanon's favour. The government was not balanced since prominent Muslim leaders were not truly represented in it. Second, the basis of the relationship established between Lebanon and Syria in 1943, namely that Lebanon would not be a source of hostility against Syria, was not respected in this agreement. Syria was in a state of war with Israel, and the agreement threatened the interdependence between Lebanon and Syria which had existed since the 1940s. Third, Israel's ambitions were regional. Israeli officials had said that the frontiers of Israel were defined in the Bible. The conflict with Israel was therefore regional. If there was to be an agreement, it had to be a comprehensive agreement. This was why Syria had previously opposed the Camp David Accords. 'Shultz told me', added Khaddam, 'that Israeli withdrawal depended on the prior withdrawal of the PLO and the Syrians. Do you know what I answered? – "In that case, Mr Shultz, there is no agreement, do not waste your time".'

After a long point-by-point debate we ended our meeting in the Ministry of Foreign Affairs and proceeded to our meeting with President Asad. Asad began by recalling pleasant memories of mutual friends of ours, which clearly indicated to me his determined opposition to the agreement. What I heard from Khaddam was nothing compared to the strong language I heard from Asad. He invoked Sadat's trip to Jerusalem and how he had betrayed the Arabs; he recounted ancient history when heroes had fought empires, and recent Syrian history when individual leaders had defeated the French army. Asad went on for two hours, virtually without interruption, making ample use of his knowledge of history, politics and warfare. All of it seemed to converge towards one thing: condemnation of the agreement.

I tried to defend the agreement article by article, but debate was useless. Asad was speaking from one perspective and I from another; there was no common ground. When I realized I was getting nowhere, I asked for a private meeting. Asad accepted immediately. This was my last and perhaps only chance to try to bridge the gap between us. I spoke at length, with passion, conviction and absolute frankness about Lebanon's predicament, and the need to secure an Israeli withdrawal. I let him know that I understood his position, his policies, and his revolutionary style, but I emphasized that this did not necessarily apply to Lebanon. We now had a chance to get the Israelis out of our territory without a peace treaty. We needed Syria's help. I pointed out the dangers of an Israeli presence in Lebanon both to us and to Syria. I expressed our government's desire to work with Syria very closely. Agreements, I argued, were always subject to interpretations in accordance with changing conditions. If Lebanon were strong, independent and sovereign, it would implement the agreement in a manner consistent with its independence and sovereignty. If Lebanon were divided, this would invite incursion from Israel and so pose a permanent threat to Lebanon's independence and sovereignty. I continued:

> You said, Mr President, that this agreement limits our freedom in maintaining good relations with Syria. I disagree. We are a free country; we want good relations with you; we are anxious to go beyond diplomatic niceties and develop firm relations with you. After we sign this agreement we will discuss, in depth, the future of Lebanese–Syrian relations, we want distinctive relations with Syria.

Asad replied:

> If you wish to sign, may Allah be with you. But I do not say it from my heart. I consider this agreement to be a peace treaty harmful to Lebanon, to Syria, and to the Arab world. If you want good relations with us these should be defined in written agreements, not in beautiful words exchanged between Hafiz Al-Asad and Amin Jumayyil or between brother Elie and his brothers in Syria. People come and go, while written texts endure.

The Agreement in Parliament

On 14 May the Council of Ministers approved the agreement. It also decided to send Minister al-Bsat and General Hamdan to Tunisia, Algeria and Morocco, and Minister Ibrahim Halawi and General Qa'qur to the Gulf states to brief them on the agreement. Meanwhile, as par-liament was to meet soon to approve the agreement, I was in the process of preparing a statement explaining and justifying it before the parliamentarians.

Before this, however, the president met Elias Sarkis to hear what he had to say about the agreement, and what he told us turned out to be prophetic. Sarkis spoke with the bitter experience of his difficult six years as Lebanon's president. He told us that all sides would be difficult when it came to the agreement. He feared that Lebanon could not regain the sovereignty it had begun to lose in 1969 when the PLO challenged the Lebanese government and the Cairo Agreement was signed. Saudi Arabia could help us, but not much. The Saudis were basically committed to the

Palestinians. The United States should help Lebanon with the Soviets, not with the Saudis. Instead the Americans were courting the Saudis and neglecting the Soviets. He counselled against calling for a session of parliament before seeking prior approval for the agreement from Syria. Many members of parliament, he felt, would change their minds once Syria opposed the agreement, and Syria already had opposed it. Sarkis, who seemed exhausted, concluded:

> You have a good agreement, the best possible under existing conditions. Allow me to say: Israel will not abide by it, Syria will oppose it, the moderate Arab states will change their mind on it. You will face difficult times. I did my best in my days, you are doing your best. This is our destiny. We have no substitute for this agreement. God help you, God bless you, and good luck in the difficult road ahead.

Sarkis spoke eloquently and emotionally. When we bid him goodbye, we felt that we were all together in a contest in which a chasm existed between our efforts and our hopes. The question was, should we succumb to destiny or battle on against the current? Was the question wrongly posed? Wasn't battling against the current itself a destiny, and a superior one at that?

Parliament met on 16 May to consider the agreement. In my statement, I urged the deputies to support the agreement. I explained to them what we had accepted and what we could not accept, and I pointed out the dangers of letting matters drift without a binding instrument governing Israeli withdrawals.

The articles of the agreement, I said, were based largely on the articles of the Armistice Agreement signed between Lebanon and Israel on 23 March 1949. The basic articles of the Armistice Agreement called for: abstention from the use of force; abstention from engaging in military acts against the other, either by the regular forces of Lebanon or Israel, or by irregular forces; the right of both parties to live in peace; the prevention of military acts from the territory of either party against the other; agreement on a security zone within which weapons were to be limited; the establishment of a mixed armistice committee of five members, two from each party, chaired by a representative of the United Nations Truce Supervision Organization (UNTSO); the committee to meet in Lebanon and Israel alternately; the right of the committee to appoint military observers from the two parties to supervise the security arrangements; the right of the committee to interpret and implement the Armistice Agreement; the right of the members of the committee and of the military observers to move freely in the zones defined in the agreement; the end of conditions which threatened the peace and security of the parties and the encouragement of new conditions allowing transformation from armistice status to a better status.

These were the conditions, I explained, which we had accepted in 1949 when our army was fighting the Israeli army on the northern frontiers of Palestine. We were now signing an agreement to get the Israeli army out of Beirut and, in our opinion, we were within the boundaries of Resolution 242 and the general principles of the Armistice Agreement. We had to go further in some articles and accept new articles, because of the radically different situation which now existed, but on the whole we had not strayed greatly from the letter and spirit of the Armistice Agreement.

Before we had started negotiations, I explained, we had seriously considered all the other options:

Some have proposed that the government should rely solely on popular resistance. This proposal presupposes a popular unity that is not exactly there after eight years of internal warfare. Were we to lead a popular resistance under existing conditions this would give the superior Israeli military machine the opportunity to suppress the resistance and expand its control over the country.

Some have proposed that we resort to the Security Council. You all know, however, that the Security Council is effective only when there is Soviet–American correspondence of views. Such correspondence does not now exist. We have learned enough from others not to fall into the same error again. We do not want to lose a nation and gain a cause which we then have to plead in international forums.

We are told that Israel will not withdraw because Israel is a camp on the move, an expansionist force that wants to overtake the surrounding Arab areas. The problem between Israel and the Arabs, we are told, is one of historic proportions and, in this context, if we lose, temporarily, a region or a country, it is not the end of the world. The important thing is not to lose our dignity or the determination to regain what we have lost, no matter how long the wait is. We, in Lebanon, are not ready to sacrifice south Lebanon for 20 or 50 years in the hope that we may regain it in the distant future, and regain it for what country? What name? What frontiers, and what characteristics?

We have often found ourselves, throughout the process, between a hammer and a hard place, but we stood steadfast, we stuck by our red lines despite the fact that we had no power except the power of having a just cause, the power of taking the right stand, and the power of saying 'No'. We should remember that the negotiations took place when Lebanon was occupied and while fighting, massacres and intimidations were the order of the day. The Lebanese negotiator, therefore, had an eye on the political position and an eye on his people who were being displaced, humiliated and killed.

We are not the first country in the Arab world to seek the help of the USA in evacuating Israeli forces from its territory. Every Arab state that fought Israel since the beginning of the 1970s has cooperated with the USA to effect the separation of armies, to ensure limited withdrawals, or to regain lost territory. Nor are we the first Arab country to ask the USA to maintain a presence on our territory through a security arrangement committee to ensure the implementation of agreed-upon security arrangements. All the Arab countries that fought Israel accepted security arrangements on their own territory. These arrangements contained the following: (1) areas in which weapons were limited; (2) buffer zones; (3) international or American supervisors; (4) bilateral security arrangements; (5) exchanges of letters with the Americans concerning the interpretation of security arrangements; (6) public or secret commitments to keep Palestinian military organizations at specified distances from the Israeli frontiers.

This agreement does not end Lebanon's problems. It does, however, provide a beginning for Lebanon to regain its sovereignty and its unity. When Lebanon is fully liberated, we shall then begin the process of liberating the Lebanese citizen. We must liberate him from the effects of the war and launch him on a new course. We must start the rebuilding of a Lebanon that will not fall again in the face of the political storms that gather here and there and about.

Parliament heartily applauded my speech. Unanimous support for the government in its efforts to regain Lebanon's independence and sovereignty was urged by the deputies. The motion was carried and, later, President Jumayyil asked me to his office. He said that he had intended to address the nation on the agreement, but that after listening to my speech and parliament's reception of it, he had decided he would not. Instead, he asked me to go on television and deliver to the nation the same speech I had delivered to parliament. I did so. The speech provoked popular support in daytime and intensive shelling at night; a signal that all was not well with the agreement.

Even before negotiations started between Lebanon and Israel, Israel had stated that a condition for its full withdrawal was the prior and full withdrawal of the PLO, and full withdrawal of the Syrians, as well as the return of Israeli prisoners in PLO and Syrian custody, and of the bodies of Israeli soldiers killed in war. These issues were also raised in the negotiations and rejected by us. We argued that we had no control over the PLO and the Syrians and that our negotiations with Israel were a separate matter. These were issues that we and the Americans intended to do our best to address, but we never considered the agreement to be conditioned on them. Nevertheless, Israel sent a letter to the American delegation stating that the Syrians and the Palestinians should withdraw before Israel did. When we learned of their letter we sent the following letter:

May 17, 1983

H.E. Ambassador Philip Habib
Personal representative of the President of the USA

Dear Mr Ambassador,

This is to confirm that it is the position of Lebanon that, unless Israeli
withdrawal takes place in accordance with the terms of the Agreement,
Lebanon will be at liberty to suspend performance of its obligations under
the Agreement. In that event, it is understood that Lebanon, the United
States, and Israel, will consult on an urgent basis.

   If the matter remains unresolved, Lebanon will be at liberty to declare
the Agreement null and void. Lebanon will continue to seek the restoration
of its sovereignty and the withdrawal of all external forces in all appropriate
ways.

Elie A. Salem
Deputy Prime Minister, Minister of Foreign Affairs.

May 17 was a busy and fateful day. What became known as the May 17
Agreement was signed by the heads of the three delegations, Antoine
Fattal, David Kimche and Morris Draper. As I sent my letter to Habib
expressing reservations, President Jumayyil received a letter from President
Reagan reassuring him of his support. Reagan's letter follows:

May 17, 1983

Dear Mr. President,

In view of its longstanding relations of friendship with Lebanon, the United
States participated fully in achieving an agreement between Lebanon and
Israel and signed itself as a witness. The United States will accordingly take
all the appropriate measures to promote full observance of the Agreement.
The United States fully supports the sovereignty, political independence and
territorial integrity of Lebanon. In this regard, the United States shares and
will continue to support the objective of the Republic of Lebanon that all
external forces must withdraw permanently from Lebanon. In the event that
external forces fail to withdraw in accordance with the arrangements of the
Lebanese government, the United States will consult urgently and take such
other steps as it deems appropriate to bring about the withdrawal of all
external forces from Lebanon.

   In the event of an actual or threatened violation of the Agreement, the
United States will, at the request of one or both of the parties, consult with
the parties with respect thereto in the Joint Liaison Committee or the
Security Arrangements Committee established pursuant to the Agreement,
or through other available channels, as appropriate. Upon being satisfied
that there has been a violation or threatened violation of the Agreement,
the United States will consult with the parties with regard to measures to

be taken by the United States or by the parties to halt, prevent or rectify the violation or threatened violation, to ensure full observance of the Agreement, and as it deems appropriate. In this regard, the United States acknowledges that Lebanon has entered into the Agreement on the premise that Lebanon will be at liberty to suspend performance of its obligations under the Agreement in the event the withdrawal of Israeli armed forces does not take place in accordance with the terms of the Agreement.

The United States will use its best efforts to avoid actions by other states in the region with which the United States has relations, which are designed to prevent implementation of the Agreement or otherwise harm Lebanon. Subject to Congressional authorization and appropriation, the United States will endeavor to contribute to the legitimate military and economic assistance requirements of Lebanon. In this regard, the United States will support, in appropriate ways, the economic reconstruction of Lebanon and the development of its armed forces in order to assist the Government of Lebanon in fulfilling its responsibilities under the Agreement.

In accordance with the terms of the Agreement, the United States agrees to participate in the Joint Liaison Committee and in the meetings of the Security Arrangements Committee to which it is invited by either party. In that framework, the United States will verify understandings reached between the parties during the negotiation of the Agreement concerning its interpretation or application.

Sincerely,

Ronald Reagan

These formal steps were accompanied by a growing feeling that the May 17 Agreement was in trouble. Israel's behaviour on the ground, its letter to the Americans, and Syrian opposition to the agreement, were all awesome obstacles and intensive diplomatic efforts were needed to remove them. We did what we could in Damascus and did not get approval. We and the Americans still hoped that the agreement could be amended to satisfy Syrian fears. We were wrong, but that realization came with hindsight. Meanwhile we continued to rely on the USA and its allies to complete the process we started.

I left for Rome on 19 May. At the American Embassy in Rome, I had a lengthy and secure phone conversation with Secretary Shultz. I wanted to know how he could help us implement the agreement. He responded that he was holding regular meetings with the Soviet ambassador to the United States, Anatoly Dobrynin, to minimize conflict between the superpowers on Lebanon. He had found the Soviet attitude encouraging, but was unhappy that Asad had refused to receive Habib in Damascus. Shultz wanted to work with us to maintain an Arab consensus around the agreement. The United States was active in building support for Lebanon in the Gulf Cooperation Council, and he was confident of making real progress with Syria in a matter of weeks. I certainly hoped so, I said, for without Syrian support the agreement was in deep trouble. In Rome, Foreign Minister Colombo was very supportive of the Lebanese position, and he sent a letter to Khaddam urging him to accept the agreement. Colombo felt that the ball was now in the Arab court, and it was up to the Arabs to decide whether the occupation of Lebanon would continue or not. He believed, however, that the European Community could select one foreign minister from among themselves to go to Beirut, Damascus and Riyad and help bring about implementation of the agreement. I supported his proposal.

I took advantage of my stay in Rome to meet officials at the Vatican. The Lebanese government was in contact with the capable Papal Nuncio in Beirut, Monseigneur Luciano Angelloni, and in our frequent visits to Rome, it was standard practice to meet the Vatican Prime Minister Cardinal Agustino Casorolli and Foreign Minister Monseigneur Achille Silvestrini.

No one at the Vatican meets you in his office – meetings always take place in a salon next to the office. Perhaps this is meant to enhance the mystery, and hence the power, of this small yet universal state. Casorolli, a fragile-looking priest with a sharp mind and penetrating eyes, listened carefully to my report, asked many questions, and then told me that the Vatican would do something to help us. What the Vatican usually does is to contact governments concerned with Lebanon, yet Vatican officials rarely indicate who they contacted, what they said, or what they intended to do. Vatican diplomacy is highly secretive, but the position of the Catholic Church on Lebanon was not. It was based on a commitment to dialogue between Christians and Muslims. Casorolli congratulated Lebanon on the agreement and wished us success in its implementation.

To honour an appointment with German Foreign Minister Hans-Dietrich Genscher in the limited time available to me, I rented a small plane to take me and my assistant Itamar Diab to Cologne, and then by car to Bonn. Genscher was at the time president of the European Community, and such a meeting was very important to help bring the European Community into the talks on implementing the agreement.

The plane I rented was a tiny four-seater with no facilities, except for a minibar with an ample selection of drinks, of which I made good use. The weather was terrible, and the plane ride was bumpy, which accounted for my generous intake of alcohol. In this ride, as in many others that I took in the course of my diplomatic experience, I acquired a healthy confidence in fate. It was perhaps the only way to absolve myself of responsibility for any erroneous travel decisions.

Genscher was quite different from Colombo. Colombo was the quintessential Italian: expressive, emotional and loquacious. Genscher was the quintessential German: sober, reflective and precise. With Colombo I developed an immediate personal rapport, while my relationship with Genscher was exclusively intellectual. As an avid reader of German philosophy, theology, history and political theory, I immediately found common ground with Genscher: we both agreed on the central role of ideas in history, and in the fate of Arab–Western relations. He had been well briefed before my visit and was prepared.

Genscher believed that we had a good agreement, and noted that had he been in our place he would have signed it. The question now was how to implement it. The Soviet position could be helpful, he thought, as the Soviets did not want a conflict in the region. As the president of the Ten he said he would talk to the Soviets and to the Americans. German support for Lebanon, he continued, arose from German respect for the democratic tradition there, and from German interest in the success of the American effort. Genscher felt that France would be more helpful with the Syrians than would Germany, and he volunteered to talk to Cheysson in this regard. Gensher added, however, that if as president of the Ten he could help with Syria, he would gladly do so.

Genscher told me that the EC must take a decisive and supportive position on Lebanon; it must initiate an independent European role in Lebanon, but one coordinated with the United States; the EC must support the US effort in implementing the May 17 Agreement; and it must establish direct contacts with the Arab states, particularly the Gulf and Maghreb States, in such a way that it would be helpful to Lebanon. To Genscher, Saudi Arabia and Algeria were the most influential Arab states in this regard. The United States could help with Saudi Arabia, while France could help with Algeria.

On Saturday 21 May I flew to Paris and joined the Cheysson family for lunch at the suburban Parisian chateau put at the disposal of the foreign minister. The chateau had extensive gardens to walk around in, and Cheysson and I made good use of them during my visit. He introduced me to his wife and children as the Lebanese foreign minister with the unusual French. He told his wife: 'Elie has invented a special French language, full of mistakes and English words, but easy to understand.'

When we began our discussions, Cheysson mentioned his good relations with Asad and Khaddam. Asad, he said, had encouraged his children to study French and, he noted, there were about 250 Syrian students studying for their doctorates in France. Cheysson also spoke of his good relations with the Soviet Union, particularly with Yuri Andropov, who had been careful to cultivate good relations with France despite France's recent expulsion of Soviet spies. While visiting Moscow, Cheysson had been interested to learn that the Soviets wanted to extend their influence throughout the Middle East, and not to limit it just to Syria and Iraq. He believed that this extension was in Lebanon's interest as it might tend to modify Soviet support for radical Arab movements and states. He advised the Lebanese government to maintain a national consensus on the agreement, maintain contact with Syria, and initiate independent contacts with the Soviets both directly through Ambassador Soldatov in Beirut or Ambassador Dobrynin in Washington. He also advised us to get in touch with Algeria, which had proved itself to be a credible mediator in international conflicts.

Cheysson proposed sending a private emissary to Damascus on a fact-finding mission and devising, on the basis of his report, a French initiative. France, unlike other European countries, did not coordinate, as he put it, with the United States or other European states in matters relating to Lebanon. They would all, however, be kept informed of French efforts. He thus wanted to emphasize both the independence of French policy-making, and to underline Lebanon's privileged place in French thinking.

While in Paris, I spoke on the telephone with the British foreign secretary, Francis Pym. He informed me that he had sent a private emissary to Damascus to convey to Asad the strong British support for the Lebanese position. As expected, Pym committed himself to support Lebanon and the American initiative in Lebanon and the Middle East within the framework of the European Community.

Genscher, Colombo, Cheysson, Pym and Shultz well understood Syria's regional interests, and they understood that Syria's role in Lebanon was an integral part of its role in the region. As a result, they were interested in opening a dialogue with Syria themselves. While they recognized the importance of Lebanese–Syrian discussions, they knew that Syria's regional interests could not be satisfied by the Lebanese alone, as they involved Israel, the PLO, the USA and the Soviet Union.

Upon my return to Beirut I found that Habib had already contacted King Fahd and President Mubarak and that both had suggested sending messages to President Asad, in the hope that it would bring about the implementation of the May 17 Agreement. Earlier we had made it clear to Shultz that we would not go ahead with the agreement if Syria rejected it. Without Syria's support, we maintained, the agreement would become a trap and a source of internal conflict and regional tension. We had to proceed cautiously, to try to modify the Syrian attitude towards the agreement, before completing formal steps relating to it.

When the president invited the Lebanese negotiating team for cocktails on 26 May, there was no joy in the party, and little confidence that withdrawals would actually take place. In consultation with Ghassan

Tweini, the Ministry of Foreign Affairs prepared a White Book on the negotiations. Copies were distributed to all those invited to the cocktail. The president, the prime minister and I autographed copies for all the members of the team. We already felt that the White Book was just for the record. We were in a despondent mood, faced as we were by the negative Israeli attitude, Syrian opposition to the agreement, American and European ineffectiveness, and the half-hearted measures of the Arab states.

5

From the May 17 Agreement to Geneva

American Assessments

As the agreement was facing trouble and as American attention, always short-spanned, could be diverted somewhere else, we felt the need to reconfirm US commitment. The USA, Habib told me, liked successes. If it felt Lebanon was getting too complicated the USA would drop it like a hot potato. 'You've got to keep Reagan personally engaged, he has many things on his mind, you've got to remind him of Lebanon. You are not too big on the screen, you know.' He insisted that I go to Washington to keep Reagan engaged and Secretary Shultz committed to an early resolution of the hurdles in the way of implementing the agreement. I, however, felt that my seeing Reagan might unfairly raise expectations in Lebanon, at a time when little progress was anticipated.

On the other hand we and the Americans had invested a great deal of time in reaching the agreement and we must see it through and, if necessary, amend it to meet Syrian objection. The agreement was not our objective; our objective was to get Israel out, and we were ready to attempt any course that would realize this objective. We thought then that an amendment to allay Syrian fears was a reasonable course to follow. We wanted parliamentary approval to go ahead with ratification, although we did not intend to ratify until we were certain the agreement as such or an amended agreement could be implemented with the desired consensus. Arab consensus predicated prior Syrian approval. The signals from Damascus were against amendment, but at times we could detect readiness to reconsider were certain articles to be removed. Maybe this was wishful thinking on our part, but we had no choice but to try. Even Habib, a highly sceptical and seasoned negotiator, thought that Asad's posture was tactical. Shultz was confident that Asad would change his mind once Shultz explained the regional benefits resulting from the agreement. Shultz figured his efforts with Asad should take about four weeks. To keep the

USA fully briefed on the problems we anticipated, I went to Washington in early June, and had a private meeting with President Reagan on 8 June in which he reiterated what he had told Sa'ib Salam and me earlier, that the United States would not 'reverse gear' in Lebanon, nor seek to extricate itself from the situation there. Lebanon, he said, would remain a priority on his agenda until the Lebanese crisis was solved. I told him we were ready to take risks, provided that these risks were sustained by policies that would lead to liberation.

In a meeting with Shultz on 11 June, he told me that he felt strongly that the May 17 Agreement should be implemented. He had spoken to the Soviets about the growing danger of terrorism in Lebanon. If the agreement was not implemented, the resulting vacuum would breed an anarchy that neither the Soviets nor the Americans would be able to control. He felt the Soviets appreciated US concerns. He also informed me that the European Community would soon be sending the German foreign minister, Hans-Dietrich Genscher, to Damascus to ease Syrian opposition to the agreement. Shultz believed that, as an independent country, Syria had legitimate points it could raise with Lebanon concerning the agreement, which might centre on security arrangements. If that point was reached, the United States was ready to help. The Syrians wanted to improve their dialogue with the United States, Shultz continued, and the USA had no problem with that. The United States also wanted to see what the Syrians had on their minds. The Americans were relying on the Saudis to test Syrian waters, while at the same time they were consulting with the Soviets to avoid a regional confrontation. Shultz felt confident that Soviet Ambassador in Washington Dobrynin did not want anarchy in the region, and this, he felt, was very encouraging.

I told Shultz we would not ratify the agreement unless we were certain it could be implemented. We did not want to have an agreement with no withdrawals. Shultz empathized with our position, but to my regret he seemed to be convinced that Israel would not withdraw until the Syrians and the Palestinian fighters withdrew first. Israel, he said, wanted security, and if it allowed the Syrians and the PLO to remain in Lebanon, its invasion would have achieved nothing.

I took advantage of my official visit in the United States to attend the graduation of my two sons. The elder, Adib, had been studying at Georgetown University, while the younger, Paul, had been at Harvard. My visits to these two universities awakened in me a strong yearning for academic life, and gave me a chance to discuss the Lebanese crisis with former academic colleagues from the American University in Beirut. I had a refreshing dialogue with them, a dialogue with historical weight behind it, but somehow dialogue hangs in the air when you are seeking concrete answers to concrete problems. Somehow the urgent problems of politics have a logic within themselves, a logic based more on power and on interlocking interests than on dictates of reason. This is not to belittle reason or academe. Indeed, without reason, on which academe thrives, the very politics of power would be deprived of the ethical dimension and the sense of fair play that humanize and civilize the political process.

Upon my return to Beirut I learned that Richard Fairbanks, previously a presidential envoy dealing with the Middle East peace process, had been asked by President Reagan to join Habib, Draper and Dillon to examine ways out of the Lebanese impasse. Fairbanks was a pleasant, relaxed and intelligent person. He was a Washington lawyer with a quick mind, who was a good addition to the US team. Fairbanks arrived in Beirut with the following assessment of the situation: (a) Syria would not withdraw in the context of the agreement; (b) Syria's position had been strengthened as a result of the Israeli invasion; (c) Syria was receiving increasing support from the Soviets, and its role in its regional influence had also been enhanced; and (d) Syria would not risk a confrontation with Israel, partly because it had not yet attained strategic parity with it, and partly because the USA and the Soviets were urging caution.

He felt that the Syrians were comfortable playing the waiting game. Time was on their side, argued Fairbanks. Asad might want the agreement amended, and if so, the United States was ready to discuss this matter with him. If the USA was not the right party to do this, then Saudi Arabia might be.

The Saudi Perspective

As we searched for ways out of the deadlock in implementing the agreement, we counted a great deal on Saudi advice. It was Shultz's conclusion that the Saudis wanted Lebanon to sign an amended agreement. Habib had met with King Fahd and discussed renegotiating the agreement, but had been dubious about Israeli acceptance of this. If Syria did not withdraw, Habib told Fahd, then there would be no Israeli withdrawal. Fahd believed that the question of a Syrian withdrawal must be negotiated between Lebanon and Syria, with Saudi mediation if this could be helpful. Fahd promised to call Asad and ask him to send a representative to Riyad to discuss with him future steps that would help Lebanon regain its sovereignty. He also said that he might send Crown Prince Abdallah to talk to Asad.

Secretary Shultz felt the United States had done its job in bringing about an agreement between Lebanon and Israel. Now it was the duty of the Arabs to make Syria withdraw. The United States would help, of course, but its role could not be as effective as it had been with Israel. The Americans did believe, however, that since Syria wanted a dialogue with Washington, Syria might be ready to compromise on the agreement and consent to pulling its forces out of Lebanon.

Meanwhile I was disturbed by the facts unfolding on the ground and by the shelling and the killing, and I could not react as did Professor Von Mises, who, when reminded that his theory did not square with the facts, answered: 'too bad for the facts!' Facts kill people, threaten regions, divide countries and determine the course of human affairs. I told Shultz of my fears. 'If we abrogate the agreement,' I said, 'Israel will stay in Lebanon; if we do not, Syria will continue to fight it. And if the agreement hangs in the air, the consensus behind it will collapse. The consensus is held by success or by the promise thereof.' Shultz assured me that the USA would do its best, and that within a month President Asad would change his mind.

I had maintained close contact with Saudi Arabia, and kept King Fahd and Foreign Minister Saud al-Faisal informed either directly or through Sheikh Rafiq al-Hariri, who was acting as the king's emissary to Lebanon. Indeed, I went to Washington in early June through Riyad and met King Fahd.

I saw the king in the presence of Crown Prince Abdallah, Saud al-Faisal, and Lebanon's ambassador in Riyad, Dr Zafir al-Hassan. I found the king in good humour, thoroughly informed about the agreement, and a little concerned about the section on mutual relations. He was in the mood to talk, and did not wait for my briefing to discuss the questions at hand. He was disappointed that neither the United States nor the European Community had put sufficient pressure on the Israelis to get them out of Lebanon with a minimum number of conditions.

The way to deal with Asad, he said, was to be direct with him and try to persuade him by rational argument. Jumayyil should send Asad a cordial letter explaining the conditions under which Lebanon signed the agreement. The letter should state that Lebanon was an occupied country, and as such had its own problems. Lebanon must get the occupier out, and the agreement realized this objective. It was true that there were articles that were better left out of the agreement, Fahd added, but the important thing was to get the Israelis out. Once this happened, parts of the agreement could be renegotiated, or interpreted in such a way as to guarantee the interests of Lebanon and Syria. Saudi Arabia would work with the USA to make the necessary amendments. A letter to Asad in this spirit should be helpful, he repeated. We would then wait for his response, and in the light of that discuss future steps.

King Fahd also informed me that King Hassan II had contacted Asad and expressed support for an agreement that committed Israel to a withdrawal from Lebanon. Crown Prince Abdallah had gone to Libya and would soon be travelling to Jordan, Iraq and Syria in search of a consensus that would help Lebanon. What was good for Lebanon was good for the Arabs, the king remarked.

After my discussions with the king, Rafiq al-Hariri drove me to his new palatial residence, which was in the last phase of construction. He and I were to meet frequently in the future in search of options to free Lebanon from the political-military net in which it was entangled. Rafiq was one of the few Lebanese who had come to Saudi Arabia, started at the bottom and climbed rapidly to the top. When he came to Saudi Arabia, he concentrated on contracting. He did a good job. He gained the confidence of the Saudi government, which honoured him by granting him Saudi citizenship – a rare prize, indicating trust. As a trusted Saudi and as a good Lebanese, he was relied upon a great deal by King Fahd to act as his special envoy to Lebanon and to handle special projects there. Even at times of great uncertainty Hariri kept his faith in the future of Lebanon and invested generously in the reconstruction of Beirut, rebuilding major sections of the devastated downtown area. One day, he drove up to the presidential palace followed by a truck. He surprised us all when his workers emptied the truck and constructed, in one of the palace halls, a mock-up of a new downtown Beirut as Hariri perceived it. The downtown area depicted in the model had been reconstructed along modern and efficient lines. Hariri was a dreamer, but with a difference: he often realized his dreams.

When I visited Hariri in his new residence, he seemed to be living more in his native Sidon than in Riyad. Here he was one of the busiest entrepreneurs in the world, and yet he still followed the course of Lebanese politics with the passion of one who wanted to get involved and change it. To him, the solution to the Lebanese crisis was not unlike a project: it could be contracted out and successfully completed on time. Hariri told me that he personally would follow up on my discussions with King Fahd and Amir Saud, as it was easier for him to come to Beirut than for a member of the royal family to do so.

While I was at my hotel, I received a telephone call from Amir Salman, King Fahd's brother, and Governor of Riyad. Salman called to tell me that he had read the speech I had made before the Lebanese parliament defending the agreement. He had found it to be an excellent statement, and one that Arab leaders should read carefully and reflect upon. He liked honesty and straightforward language in politics, and he had asked the king for permission to have the speech published in the Saudi newspaper. The king approved, and it was published in full.

Clearly, my visit to Saudi Arabia, and the Saudi attitude towards the agreement, helped secure overwhelming support for the agreement in parliament, particularly among Muslim parliamentarians as we shall see below. Immediately after my return to Beirut, a cordial letter, as proposed by King Fahd, was drafted and sent by President Jumayyil to President Asad on 14 June. We received indirect feedback from Asad through the US ambassador in Riyad, Richard Murphy. King Fahd had told Murphy that in discussions between Amir Abdallah and President Asad, Asad had said that he wanted a dialogue with the United States, and that he was ready to talk to the Lebanese. Yet Asad had made no direct reference to the president's letter. He had told Abdallah that he could not accept the agreement in its present form. In response, Abdallah had urged Asad not to reject the agreement out of hand, but to continue to think about it and use it to help Lebanon find a way to secure an Israeli withdrawal.

Fahd suggested to Murphy that the agreement be divided into two parts, one relating to security arrangements, the other to mutual relations. The first section on security arrangements could be implemented first, thus bringing about an Israeli withdrawal, while the section of mutual relations could be renegotiated. Murphy was non-committal, knowing how difficult Israel would be on this issue.

Parliamentary Approval

Prime Minister Wazzan was in an uneasy mood when I discussed with him the signing of the decree which would send the agreement to parliament as a first step towards ratification. The president asked Wazzan and me to lunch and convinced the prime minister to send the decree to parliament. Wazzan drafted the decree reluctantly. His Sunni community had always danced to the Arab tune, of which Damascus was often the writer and producer. He was leaving the next day on a mission to Paris, and I urged him, in jest, to linger in Europe and enjoy himself a bit and let me enjoy being acting prime minister. Generally a jovial person, Wazzan was too pained to smile. Speaker Kamil al-As'ad and I met several times to examine the steps needed to seek formal parliamentary approval for the agreement. When the parliamentary debate took place, the members of parliament had had two weeks to study the agreement and to ponder my defence of it, and prepare their decision. The debate took place on Monday and Tuesday, 13 and 14 June 1983. Attendance was very high, and the atmosphere was as electric as that of a close presidential election.

Three influential deputies gave long and eloquent statements in support of the agreement. Only two deputies voted against. They were Najah

Wakim, a Greek Orthodox Nasserite from Beirut, and Zahir al-Khatib, a Sunni populist from South Lebanon. Wakim focused his attack on me, and wondered out loud: 'How can our foreign minister carry the American nationality?' I replied: 'I am not an American citizen!' 'No!' he shouted back, 'You studied in the US, you married an American, you lived there, and you are an American citizen!' 'Yes!' I responded, 'I lived there, I married an American; she became Lebanese. I did not become an American.' 'You carry a green card,' he shouted. With a wide smile I answered: 'No, I do not.' He was stunned and looked at me in disbelief, before asking, almost in a whisper, 'Is it true?' 'Yes,' I whispered back. The whole chamber broke out in laughter, and ended this side-debate.

When the final tally was taken, of the 71 deputies present, 65 had voted for ratification, two had voted against, and four had abstained. Each of the abstaining deputies had informed me beforehand of his decision. The broad and enthusiastic support for the agreement in parliament was as much due to the conviction of the parliamentarians that it was, under the existing circumstances, a good agreement, as to their faith in the ability of the United States to help implement it. When their faith in the USA began to decline, however, support for the agreement also declined. The axiom that nothing succeeds like success seemed to be true.

By the end of June the consensus was beginning to crack. Rumours of partition were spreading throughout the country. The Israelis were speaking of partial withdrawal to Sidon, and there establishing a security zone under Israeli control covering South Lebanon.

Our dwindling expectations of seeing foreign troop withdrawals from Lebanon made us anxious, irritable and impatient. Habib was beginning to put pressure on the president. He was asking him to do more to sustain the consensus within Lebanon, to find new ways to persuade Asad to go along with the agreement, and not to expect miracles from the United States. The anxious president wanted to hear a different message. He wanted certainty, and he thought certainty came with superpower commitment. He was angry with Habib and refused to meet him.

I worked hard to reduce the tension between Habib and the president. Habib became very emotional at times: 'What is the matter, Elie?' he would ask me; 'The president does not want to meet me? I am trying to help.' Fortunately, these incidents did not last long, although unfortunately they were frequent. Frustration led to personal conflicts, and personal conflicts affected policy. Almost everyone I knew during that period who was involved in the process wished he could quit and be somewhere else. I admit that I too envied the serenity of my academic colleagues. One day as I was walking on the campus of the American University of Beirut, one of them asked me, not without sarcasm, 'Hey, Elie, when are you getting the Israelis out?' I was furious. What could I say? What I wanted to say and did not say was: 'My friend, you would be amazed how little is in my hands!' I recalled at that moment the words of one of my revolutionary classmates at the American University of Beirut. After graduation, and after a few *coups d'état*, a major Arab unification attempt, a few hijackings and other spectacular acts to his credit, he came to my office in the university and said: 'Professor I want to enrol in the graduate programme and get back to the world of books. After 20 years in the national struggle I have come to the realization that nothing is in my hands.' He was exaggerating, of course. So was I. What I believe both of us meant was that the issues in the Arab East were so complex and so interlocked with international politics, and so determined by the dictates of the Cold War, that the national players, no matter how well-meaning, were in effect marginalized.

We had worked hard. We had an agreement, but the agreement was not working. We needed viable alternatives which were acceptable to us, to the Syrians, and to the Israelis, and also to the Americans and the Soviets who were always, if not in the forefront, definitely in the background. As the USA would not give the Soviets a place in the forefront the Soviets fought them from the back lines.

Shultz, anxious to move fast, met with King Fahd on 4 July and with us on 5 July. He was scheduled to meet with Asad on 6 July. After our meeting with Shultz, I was driving my car, and my mind must have been somewhere else, because I found myself in a terrible automobile accident. My anxious young bodyguards, always wary of an attempt on my life, jumped out of their cars with their machine-guns at the ready. It was an automatic reaction, and I had to race from one bodyguard to the other to order them not to shoot and further complicate a bad situation. To calm one particularly nervous bodyguard, I needed the assistance of three of the man's colleagues. Meanwhile, a crowd had gathered, adding to the tension. In those stormy days everyone suspected an assassination plot. It was not. The radio and television immediately reported the incident, and some hinted at an assassination attempt. When I reached home my telephones began to ring incessantly, which led me to record a statement describing what had actually happened.

Prime Minister Wazzan called to congratulate me on my safety. A few minutes later, the president telephoned to inform me that Wazzan had just escaped a car-bomb explosion near his office. The bomb had malfunctioned and had exploded a fraction of a second after his car had passed, thus sparing a good man. Assassination threats were not new to any of us. I had had to live with them since my first few weeks in office. I found that once I overcame the first threat, the second, third and fourth ones became relatively easy to deal with. The first was of interest only because it was the first. One morning in my second week in office as I was reading the confidential messages sent to the president, the prime minister and the foreign minister only, I read the following: 'The leadership council' of a certain party 'has met and decided to assassinate the foreign minister, Dr Elie Salem.' I was reading the messages quickly as most of them were of local and parochial colour, and the fact that this referred to me did not register until some moments later. I stopped reading and reflected on the message. I was not scared. I was furious. Here I am doing my best, I argued to myself, to save my country and others want to assassinate me. I was boiling with anger. I went straight to the head of the party concerned and said, 'Here I am – assassinate me.' He was amused and befuddled. 'What are you talking about?' he inquired. 'The attempt on my life', I answered, and I detailed the confidential information I received. He laughed, denied any knowledge of it, and put the blame on our own secret service, saying that it sent these messages to scare officials so that it could then say: 'Do not worry, we have taken care of the threat.'

On 8 July, Draper briefed me on Shultz's meeting with Asad. Asad had been consistent. He had told Shultz exactly what he had told me earlier. Shultz did not fare much better in Israel. The Israelis said that they would redeploy their forces in accordance with Israel's national interests, and would not withdraw in the context of a full withdrawal plan negotiated with us. This report was not what we had hoped for. We wanted something to shore up the eroding consensus around the agreement, both within Lebanon and in the Middle East. Even Morocco, hitherto a strong supporter of the agreement, attacked it in a joint communiqué with Libya as being harmful to Lebanon's national interests. This was the same king who a month ago had called Asad and urged him to accept the agreement as it was.

The Role of the European Community

At around this time, we heard that Hans-Dietrich Genscher's planned visit to Damascus, as representative of the European Community, would not take place. The French had apparently derailed the visit, fearing that it would give Germany a prominent role in Lebanese affairs. Now that Greece had the chairmanship of the European Community, I hoped that it could carry the ball further than had Germany.

A visit to Athens meant a great deal to me. I had read and re-read classical Greek philosophy, poetry, history and politics, and made its literature and art an integral part of my intellectual life. In its post-classical era, Greece had espoused an orthodoxy to which I belonged, and had instituted a theology and church institutions which I greatly admired.

I arrived in Athens on Tuesday 12 July. I was met by Greek officials and by our ambassador to Greece, my old friend Shawqi Shwayri. My visit was designed to impress upon the Greek officials the importance of a solution to the crisis in Lebanon, and to urge the European Community to support our efforts.

My first meeting was with President Constantine Karamanlis, a friendly, seasoned and scholarly individual. He interrupted his vacation to see me. He also used the occasion to publicize, through my visit, the Greek role in the European Community. His office, lined with books, was warm and inviting, and I told him so. He burst out laughing, and remarked that the books were purely decorative; he had not read any of them. I liked his humility; his mind was acute, his questions were perceptive, and I really felt that this heir to Socrates cared for the freedom and democracy which Lebanon had enjoyed before its decline. Karamanlis did confess, however, that political power rested with the prime minister: 'He is a professor like you,' he said, 'and you will enjoy meeting him. Are you a Socialist?' 'No,' I responded, 'I am an individualist. In Lebanon, the parties are individuals, and individuals are parties, nations, and at times international organizations.' 'It is not too different here', he replied.

I then met Prime Minister Andreas Papandreou on Thursday 14 July. With his pipe and reflective demeanour, he looked every bit the professor he had been in the United States. He was obviously well briefed on Lebanon and on me, which gave the meeting an air of cordiality and informality. 'You come from the Paris of the Middle East,' he said. 'No,' I corrected gently, 'I come from the Athens of the East.'

Taking advantage of this opening, I described to Papandreou an ideal Beirut which reflected the ideal that was Athens. Professors on leave love to show off. They have little chance to do so in politics. So I thought that here was my chance to praise the glory of Greece and its contribution to the world. I spoke with conviction. I asked Papandreou to play a leading role in the European Community to help us. I told him: 'Our problem is urgent, complex and dangerous. If it is not resolved quickly the Middle East may be faced with a problem as devastating as that of the Palestinians.'

Papandreou promised to formulate a concrete plan of action, and to coordinate with the USA for maximum effect. He confessed that Greece had no Lebanese policy, although it had a Palestinian policy. It was aware of the US effort but felt completely outside the proceedings. Now that Greece was chairing the European Community, Papandreou promised to develop a Lebanese policy and to lend European Community support to the efforts of the USA. He felt that he could be helpful with the Palestinians, and would do something in that regard. He was conscious of the element of time. The more the withdrawals were delayed, the more difficult the solution would be. I felt that I had made a small dent in Greek official thinking and that I had given some guidance on how, as Chairman of the Ten, Greece could help.

From Athens I went to New York to brief directly UN Secretary-General Javier Pérez de Cuéllar. He had sent me word earlier to stop in New York as the Americans were not keeping him informed. He knew indirectly of our position from my continuous briefings to UNIFIL. Here was a crisis area with international implications, and a superpower had pre-empted his role. He wanted to take a UN initiative and to visit Beirut and Damascus, but he was aware that the time was not ripe. He would wait.

From New York I went to Washington to prepare for a visit by the president and the prime minister. Both were anxious to learn first-hand of the direction of the American initiative. In Washington I discussed with Secretary Shultz options in case the agreement could not be implemented. I informed him that if the agreement did not lead to withdrawals, then Lebanon would declare it null and void. Our policy, I explained, was to get Israel out through the agreement. If this was not possible we would immediately cancel the agreement, go back to the Security Council, call for the implementation of Resolution 425, and resort to resistance. We were aware, I said, of the dangers of this alternative course, but it was an honourable one. We would most likely suffer more; we would then depend on the element of time and on who could endure the pain of occupation more: Israel or us.

Shultz was concerned. He assured me that Reagan would not fail. He admitted the difficulties, but he saw a chance in convincing Israel to withdraw gradually. I opposed gradual withdrawal lest it meant moving from one temporary frontier to a more permanent frontier within Lebanon. He explained that gradual withdrawal would take place within a plan of total withdrawal. He was ready to send ships and planes to evacuate the PLO, if Arafat wanted to withdraw. He would work with Saudi Arabia to persuade Syria to leave. He hoped the Lebanese army could take over and stabilize areas evacuated by foreign forces, and said that he and his aides were impressed by the improvement in the Lebanese armed forces.

Shultz was working hard on the Lebanese issue, but nothing had materialized. He asked for time to reflect on the matter with his aides, and to consult with President Reagan, in the hope that he could provide us with specific answers. In Washington I also met Prince Bandar, whose appointment as Saudi ambassador to Washington was to be announced soon. Robert McFarlane, the assistant to National Security Adviser William Clark, was also at the meeting. McFarlane informed me that he had had a seven-hour secret meeting with President Asad. McFarlane believed that he had obtained a number of concessions from the Syrian president: Asad had accepted that Jumayyil's government was legitimate, and had also accepted that the Lebanese parliament was legitimate. The Syrian president had also noted that Lebanon had the right to sign an agreement that served its interests. McFarlane thought this was a breakthrough, and he was happy with his loot. I responded that Asad had told me the same thing, and I added that Asad, in defence of Syria's national and Arab interests, could oppose the three things he had 'conceded' to McFarlane. Bandar burst out laughing: 'True!' he exclaimed. Poor McFarlane, it was his first experience in the knotty diplomacy of the Middle East. Bandar concluded by telling us that he would probably be seeing Asad the next day, after which he would return immediately to Washington.

On Tuesday 19 July, President Jumayyil and Prime Minister Wazzan arrived in Washington to emphasize the urgency of moving the withdrawal process forward. Upon their arrival I went straight to Wazzan's suite in the Madison Hotel. The prime minister was despondent and in a bad mood. He felt that this whole gigantic effort was leading nowhere. He expected to be victimized in his community, not because he had done anything wrong, but because he had failed.

In politics, he told me, one should win. Then he added:

> But you will never understand this, you came to politics by parachute, straight from a university. I came on foot. I worked hard to become Prime Minister. I wanted to serve my country. Instead I see continued occupation, and the greatest power on earth does not seem able to help us. Indeed the greater the power the more impotent it seems to me. The consensus we worked hard on is eroding, and today I heard that there has been extensive shelling in Beirut and many people have been killed.

When he later pressed Shultz on the matter of securing an Israeli withdrawal quickly Shultz answered: 'There are many ways to skin a cat.' When I translated this for Wazzan, he retorted: 'Let's hope he is not doing it hair by hair.'

While in Washington President Jumayyil gave a press conference at the National Press Club. While the conference was taking place, there was extensive shelling in Lebanon. The Lebanese opposition, allied to Syria, was mobilizing against the agreement, and was beginning to use the impressive military power at its disposal. Members of the Christian Lebanese Forces were present in the audience at the press conference. One of them asked: 'Mr President, every one knows that Damascus is shelling

Beirut, what do you propose to do?' The president, who was inclined to respond to a challenge with a challenge of his own, responded emotionally: 'We shall reverse these shells and they will fall on the capital from which they came.' Although the answer received thunderous applause from the Lebanese Forces members in the audience, this was a diplomatic *faux pas* at a time when we were trying to negotiate with Syria. Tweini, who was sitting by me on the podium, wrote down something and passed it on to the president. The president read it and passed it on to me, without smiling as he usually did after reading Tweini's frequent notes. Tweini's note read: 'Terrific, Mr President, but what airport do you expect us to land in on our return to Beirut?' Tweini was a genius at finding the apt statement. He was also a good politician. He knew the president's response would escalate the crisis, endanger our return through the Beirut International Airport, and further harden Syria's position.

Wazzan, always the wise and cautious politician, could not believe his ears. He told me that he was determined to resign. I urged him to reconsider and maintain the united front we needed in Washington. To make matters worse, Wazzan was to hold a press conference shortly, and he expected to be asked about the president's threat against Syria. He decided to go ahead with the press conference anyway, and sure enough the first question was about the threat.

Without blinking an eye, Wazzan answered: 'What threat? The President meant that the Arab states constitute one solid block. If you endanger one you endanger the others. Syria is a sister Arab state and the president is doing all he can to work out a plan with Syria that will get Israel out of Lebanon.' Wazzan went on to give a long answer that diverted the question and confused the questioner. He then looked at me with his famous quizzical smile and said: 'How do you like this answer? It is untrue, but it is helpful.' Then referring to the president, he added, 'Tell our friend to stay on a helpful course, may Allah protect you.'

On Friday 22 July, we met President Reagan. He reaffirmed his commitment to Lebanon in general terms, before informing us that Habib was relinquishing his post as special envoy. He thanked Habib for a job well done, and announced the appointment of Robert McFarlane as his replacement. Richard Fairbanks was named as his assistant.

We did not get any new assurances in Washington, however, and we were uncertain of the results of the ongoing efforts to build a consensus around the agreement. Together with the Americans, we listed the options open to us. We had four proposals to deal with.

The American proposal was that Israel should withdraw first from all areas in Lebanon except the Biqa' Valley. After that, the Syrians would withdraw. The Israelis would not have to withdraw from the Biqa' Valley unless the Syrians withdrew fully. During the withdrawal period, the agreement would be suspended. It would be implemented or negotiated *pro forma* in a two-week period and reinstated without change.

The Saudi proposal was that all foreign forces would withdraw from Lebanon. The mutual relations clause in the agreement would be suspended. Six months after the withdrawal of foreign forces from Lebanon, this clause would be renegotiated. Security arrangements would be put into effect as withdrawals took place.

There was also a proposal, which Schultz called the Syrian proposal, and which he had formulated after discussions with Asad. The proposal called for the withdrawal of the PLO first. Israel and Syria would then withdraw. When full withdrawals took place, a plebiscite on the agreement would be conducted under the auspices of the United Nations. This implied Israeli withdrawal without an agreement and a return to the terms of the Armistice Agreement. I told Shultz that this could not be the Syrian position – he must have misunderstood. However, he insisted that it was.

The Israelis proposed gradual withdrawals. They would withdraw from an area, and see if the Lebanese army was capable of maintaining order there. If Israel was satisfied, it would then withdraw from another area, and so on. Final withdrawal depended on the withdrawal of Syria and the PLO and the full implementation of the agreement. There was also our option to cancel the agreement and to consider it null and void if it did not preserve the national consensus and effect full withdrawals. The Americans told us that would lead nowhere, that we would be fine with Syria, but in worse shape with Israel. The new McFarlane–Fairbanks team was to pursue these options with the parties concerned.

Testing Washington's Options

On 1 August, the new American team arrived in Beirut. It consisted of Robert McFarlane, Richard Fairbanks, Chris Ross, Philip Durr and Howard Teicher. It was a high-level team headed by McFarlane, a member of the Reagan team in in the White House. I knew him as an intense, serious and determined official in the National Security Council. The new team showed more direct commitment from the White House. The team discussed the American proposal with us, and wanted to know how we would fill the vacuum caused by Israeli withdrawals in the Shuf–Aley area. We told them that we had three brigades totalling 12,000 men ready to move into this area. We wanted to see the MNF deployed on the highways in a supportive role.

The team went on to Israel to sell the American proposal, and to get an eight to twelve-week withdrawal timetable from the Israelis. The last phase, which would be a pull-back from the Biqa', would depend on a Syrian withdrawal. The Americans thought that the Israelis were ready to talk, but were not willing to submit a schedule for a full withdrawal. They were ready to withdraw from the Shuf–Aley district and allow the Lebanese army to take over control there. Further withdrawals, however, were conditional on whether the army could keep the peace in this area.

We warned the American team, however, that Israel was arming both the Druze and the Lebanese Forces, and was laying the groundwork for a conflict in the Shuf–Aley area. Once a conflict broke out, Israel would announce that it had no confidence in the army, and would redeploy its forces as it wished. We suspected a trap. I told McFarlane that the Israelis had to withdraw cleanly, and not leave a time-bomb behind them. We stated this point again and again, and we provided the Americans with ample evidence based on the developments we were witnessing on the ground.

In early August, as McFarlane shuttled back and forth trying to sell the American option, John Ubayd made a short visit to Damascus to meet President Asad. Asad flatly demanded the abrogation of the agreement, and added that he would not meet with me to discuss anything relating to the agreement. He would welcome me in Damascus only to announce its abrogation.

When McFarlane and Fairbanks met Asad, they too realized that he was not budging. The US team concluded that Asad was comfortable in his position. He wanted to dictate the Arab agenda, and he knew that public opinion in Israel was against war. The new defence minister, Moshe Arens, was not Ariel Sharon, and he had no great commitment to the campaign in Lebanon. Arens had no qualms about a unilateral Israeli pull-back in Lebanon. Syria could afford to wait.

By this time, attention was shifting dramatically towards events in the Shuf and Aley areas. The Druze leader Walid Junblat, backed by the Syrians, was opposing the entry of the Lebanese army into these areas after an Israeli withdrawal. He had set down one set of conditions after another as a price for his cooperation with the government. Hariri arrived in Beirut on 15 August, with a message from King Fahd attempting to reconcile President Jumayyil and Junblat. Hariri brought with him Junblat's conditions, which included political, military, administrative and various other reforms. Hariri, and probably Junblat himself, knew that these conditions were impractical, especially as a number of Junblat's conditions demanded prior acceptance of other conditions submitted early in the war by the Druze and by the Lebanese National Movement.

Hariri, the indefatigable entrepreneur, was having his first experience in the labyrinth of Lebanese politics. He met President Jumayyil to try to engineer a reconciliation between him and Junblat. Meanwhile, the Druze leader was in Damascus anxiously listening to rumours, all subsequently proved false, that his palace in Mukhtara had been burnt, that Druze villagers had been evicted from their villages, and that the old and the young had been massacred. This further escalated the tension in the mountains, and defeated all efforts at conciliation between Junblat and the president.

The Syrians wanted us to abrogate the agreement, and the Israelis wanted us to act as if we had signed a peace treaty with them. Danny Sham'un, the son of former president Kamil Sham'un, reported to us that the Israelis were furious. They wanted to meet Lebanese leaders, and they wanted these meetings televised. They wanted to show their people that they had accomplished something in Lebanon, and they threatened that if we did not cooperate with them, they would make life difficult for us, starting in the Shuf. Danny told me that Israel was playing a different game from the United States, and that the Americans naïvely tended to believe whatever the Israelis told them.

The more the Americans seemed unable to secure an Israeli withdrawal, the stronger the opposition to the American role became. Parliament, which had strongly supported the American role in May, was now highly sceptical about the whole thing, and gradually began to lean towards the opposition. Meanwhile, former president Sulayman Franjiyyeh, former prime minister Rashid Karami, Amal leader Nabih Birri, and the Druze leader Walid Junblat formed a National Salvation Front with the objective of scuttling the agreement.

Opposition was accompanied by heavy shelling. This made my life at home in Ba'bda extremely difficult, and my drives from the house to the office or to the presidential palace extremely hazardous. In an eight-minute journey to the palace one day, I counted 23 shells landing to the right and left of my car. I often mused during these drives that I was perhaps the only foreign minister in the world serving under such conditions. I should also recall that my house was shelled continuously and we were so often in the process of fixing a wall, replacing a window, or changing tiles and glass that these wartime chores became routine. War hardens people, sets new standards, and the bottom line becomes sheer survival. Anything more was extra, and was joyfully welcomed. This is why little things in wartime acquire great significance.

While McFarlane was getting assurances from Begin and Shamir that Israel wanted a united and independent Lebanon with a strong central government capable of controlling the south, some Lebanese were bringing different messages from Israel. One envoy told me that he had heard Israeli cabinet ministers state that Lebanon should be cantonized: the Christians would have a canton in the mountain heartland. The Israelis would do their best to ensure that Zahleh fell within the Christian canton, but they could not guarantee it. The Shi'ah would have a canton below Damour, while the Sunnis would control the areas around Tripoli and in the Akkar. Syria would hold on to the Biqa' Valley. According to our informers the Israelis had thought a great deal about this scenario. Every time I heard these kinds of messages I checked them with McFarlane, Fairbanks, and Dillon. They always assured me that the only authoritative Israeli positions were the ones the US team was conveying to us. European ambassadors tended to corroborate the American interpretation of the Israeli position but were not always sure. They never fully discounted the fragmentation model, and some even suspected, as did ex-president Franjiyyeh, that the fragmentation of Lebanon had been laid down by Secretary of State Kissinger under Nixon.

The Suq al-Gharb Battle

The tension which had built up since the signing of the agreement broke out into widespread violence in late August and September 1983. Given the fears and hostility which had existed among the different Lebanese communities throughout the war, it was not difficult to kindle the fire.

One event was symptomatic of the almost surreal situation existing at the time: On 1 September, a certain Fakhry Fakhoury roamed the streets of Muslim West Beirut spreading the rumour that Christians were killing Muslims in the Hay al-Lija quarter of West Beirut. The Murabitun militia radio reported the rumour as fact, causing hundreds of Muslims to take refuge with the army. Sa'ib Salam called the president to inform him of what was happening. The president's face turned white, and he asked me to call army commander General Ibrahim Tannous, and have him stop the alleged massacre. The president was shaking, and before I could do anything, he got on the phone directly to Tannous himself. Tannous answered that Fakhoury had been arrested and that his rumour was groundless. The man was a paid agent, he said. There were so many of them. In this context, it was easy to understand why the Israeli withdrawal from the Shuf, which should have been the first step in the reunification of the country, became a major problem. Junblat was adamant, despite high-level intervention, that the Lebanese army would not enter Aley and the Shuf. Junblat feared that the army under Maronite command would ally itself with the Kata'ib and the Lebanese forces and suppress the Druze. President Jumayyil sent President Asad a letter on 1 September, asking him to withdraw Syrian forces from Lebanon. He wanted this letter to complete the legal formalities for withdrawal of all non-Lebanese forces.

The agreement provided such an instrument with respect to Israel. It was not working, but the instrument was there. Jumayyil did not expect Asad to comply. He knew of the other regional considerations influencing Asad's decision, but he wanted a formal instrument in place. The letter read as follows:

Ba'bda, September 1, 1983

His Excellency Hafez al-Asad, President
Syrian Arab Republic

I wish to extend to you and to the Syrian people my best wishes for your continued progress and prosperity.

The Lebanese government has, through the deputy prime minister, foreign minister, addressed today a letter to the secretary-general of the Arab League in which it confirms its decision and its request to ensure the evacuation of the Israeli army and of all non-Lebanese armed forces from Lebanon. In enclosing a copy of this letter for Your Excellency, I feel confident that you will respond positively to its content. The policy stated in the letter was formulated by Lebanon's constitutional authorities. I have personally declared it in international forums. Your positive response will eliminate an excuse that Israel might resort to, and will be expressive of your consistent position in defense of Lebanon's independence, unity and sovereignty.

As I look forward to hearing that Your Excellency has issued your orders to withdraw your forces from Lebanon, I also look forward to close relations between Lebanon and Syria. Lebanon and Syria are bound together by historical and geographic considerations and by mutual interests, and consequently the two countries should cooperate to ensure a future of peace and progress together.

Please accept, Your Excellency, the assurances of my sincere gratitude and high consideration.

Amin Jumayyil

On the same day, Jumayyil sent a similar letter to Chairman Yasir Arafat. He never received an answer from either Asad or Arafat. As foreign minister I wrote to the secretary-general of the League of Arab States informing him of our agreement with Israel, and of the urgency of full withdrawal from Lebanon by all non-Lebanese armies and fighters. In early September, Israel unilaterally pulled out of the Shuf and Aley regions without coordinating with the Lebanese Army. They had been announcing their intent to withdraw in accordance with their own national interests, and to establish new lines which we feared would be permanent somewhere south of Beirut. The coordination that the Americans hoped to ensure to prevent a vacuum that would lead to confrontation did not materialize. In the withdrawal process, the Israeli army left behind a bloodbath between Druze fighters and fighters from the Lebanese Forces.

Druze and Christians were massacring each other, and the army could do little to help: without a political agreement, it could not enter the areas of fighting

By 4 September, the fighting in the mountains was in full swing. Shells were falling on the presidential palace with such ferocity that one could hardly move from one office to the other. For days the president, his aides and I could not leave the palace shelter due to the intense shelling directed at us. Once I ventured out to get a file, but had I not spotted my briefcase lying amid the glass and debris, I would not have recognized what had once been my office.

One evening, as shells were pushing us further and further into the corners of our makeshift shelter, we were told by the guards that the American ambassador's residence was also being shelled and that the American team was coming to take shelter in the palace. At that time the embassy residence did not have a shelter of its own. The president and I ventured out and saw McFarlane, Fairbanks, Dillon and the entire American team, including secretaries, with helmets and flak-jackets on, coming to take temporary refuge with us. We spent most of the night in good humour despite the hell raging above and around us.

Generally, around 3 or 4 a.m., we would receive reports over the telephone from General Tannous who was at the strategic Suq al-Gharb front. Suq al-Gharb, ironically, had once been famous as a summer vacation spot, with a splendid view and charming hotels. More ominously, however, it overlooked both B'abda and the southern reaches of Beirut. If the Lebanese army lost its positions in Suq al-Gharb, the road to B'abda would be open, as would the road to Beirut. This would not only threaten government control over much of the capital, but it would also endanger areas controlled by the Multinational Force near Beirut Airport and, therefore, provoke international reaction.

On Sunday 11 September, at 3 a.m., Tannous called me to announce that the front was collapsing. He recommended that the president and I get out of the presidential palace and go by tank to the Kisirwan region, or we would be killed. Tannous described the attack on his positions, and noted that large units of the Palestine Liberation Army (PLA) and the Popular Front for the Liberation of Palestine had been able to penetrate a few points. I told him to hold his position at any cost, and that we at the presidential palace had no intention of evacuating. The collapse of Suq al-Gharb, I told him, had larger implications than a local conflict. He was encouraged, but he remained concerned. McFarlane noted that the collapse of Suq al-Gharb would expose the embassy and the US Marine contingent at the airport and asked the White House for permission to shell strategic points from US navy positions to prevent the collapse of Suq al-Gharb and the exposure of the Marine unit. I feared that the Suq al-Gharb battle could evolve from a conflict between the Druze opposition and the government into a conflict between the USA and its allies in the MNF on the one hand and Syria and its Soviet allies on the other. So intricate was the situation in early September that I virtually maintained hourly contact with McFarlane to keep the battle within strict bounds.

Meanwhile, the Lebanese Forces, who had deployed in the Shuf following the Israeli invasion, were being overwhelmed. Their leaders were calling President Jumayyil in despair, but he could only respond that his hands were tied. He could not send the army into the Shuf and Aley without prior agreement between the parties; indeed the army itself refused to do so without such an agreement. The president looked pale, and was deeply frustrated by his inability to deal with the compelling and conflicting demands which were directed at him. Prime Minister Wazzan reacted in a similar fashion. Sensing the impotence of the government and the ineffectiveness of international and Arab commitments made to us, Wazzan told me: 'Elie, record this in your memoirs: the superpowers have taken a solemn decision to liberate Lebanon from the Israeli occupation and have asked His Holiness the Pope to implement this decision!'

In response to the developing situation, the United States increased its contingent in the MNF and strengthened its naval presence close to Lebanese shores. Washington thought in global terms, and Syria's growing strength in Lebanon was interpreted as a gain by the Soviet Union. This perspective hurt us as it put Lebanon on the side of the USA in an American–Soviet confrontation. This was the last thing we wanted.

As the battle for Suq al-Gharb raged, our diplomacy focused on new issues. First, a ceasefire was needed in the Shuf, followed by a decision as to who would maintain order in the area – the army or the internal security forces? We also began to discuss the convening of a conference on national dialogue, which would discuss the fate of the agreement, and attempt to work out a new national understanding between the different Lebanese communities.

With the assistance of all the parties, we began to try to find solutions to these problems. This feverish diplomatic activity became even more intense due to the mounting tragedy on the ground. Retreating militiamen from the Lebanese Forces, accompanied by thousands of Christian refugees, took refuge in the ancient and picturesque Christian town of Dayr al-Qamar. Druze forces surrounded the village and threatened to overrun it. To prevent a major massacre, and relieve the pressure around Dayr al-Qamar, direct and indirect contacts were initiated between all the parties involved in the crisis. This included Syria, Israel, the USSR, France, the

USA, the Vatican, and particularly Saudi Arabia, which had for the past weeks been closely engaged through Rafiq al-Hariri in an effort to defuse the tension in Lebanon.

When McFarlane took on the job of special envoy, he was to help the Lebanese government secure the withdrawal of all foreign forces from its territory, through diplomacy. But by September, Lebanon had fallen back into war, and war brought forth new perspectives. It had forced us all to change course and play the game of the generals. It was said that war was too important to be left to the generals; unfortunately, the politicians didn't seem any better at it. Diplomacy became a victim of military force. Policy was determined by one's strength on the ground. War is the bottom line of politics.

In September, and under the pressure of war, we changed our policy. We put withdrawals on the back burner and concentrated on a ceasefire, on national dialogue, on the unification of the internal front, and on the refashioning of national consensus. Our original policy – of liberating Lebanon first and using this to forge a consensus around internal reform – had failed. The fighting in the Shuf in the wake of Israeli withdrawal deteriorated into a war between Druze and Christians, opposition and government, and in a very real sense into a conflict between the USA and its MNF allies on the one hand and Syria and its internal and external allies as well. The agreement became a problem – a matrix for new conflicts. The consensus around it was dissolving. The pressure on the prime minister to resign was great. I took his leave to honour a meeting with Cheysson in Paris, but no sooner had I arrived in Paris than I received an urgent message from him to return. I took the first flight to Cyprus. I arrived in Cyprus at night but as our army helicopters are not equipped for night flying, I came by an American cargo helicopter. My assistant, Itamar Diab, and I were ushered into the helicopter, and we found ourselves surrounded by a dozen or so marines. Later, as we approached the landing site at the Ministry of Defence in Yarzeh, the chopper made a sharp manoeuvre, sending a shiver up my spine and terrifying my assistant, before flying back out to sea.

Within a few minutes, Diab and I found ourselves aboard the USS *Iwo Jima*. Intense groundfire had aborted our landing, and we waited for an hour or so on the vessel, while the admiral in charge took pride in showing us the state-of-the-art technology of this huge helicopter carrier. He sent us back on a smaller helicopter with four gunners posted behind their 400-mm guns pointed at the dark city below us. The pilot flew a few yards above the ground, without lights, and virtually had to manoeuvre his way between narrow tortuous streets to get us to the ministry. The shelling was still intense, but we made it.

Immediately upon arrival, I met Wazzan, who told me that he had decided to resign. He was hurt as the Syrians were excluding him as well as Speaker Kamil al-As'ad from the proposed National Dialogue Conference. Bandar and Hariri were discussing with us and the Syrians the agenda for such a conference and the names of those leaders who would participate in it.

The shuttle diplomacy between 5 and 25 September had brought results. Bandar played an important role in this period without coming to Beirut. Only Hariri came. Bandar, as a member of the royal family, was not as free to move as Hariri. After all Hariri was also Lebanese and knew all the actors well, and felt no danger from any direction, though his comings and goings were not danger-free. We felt the need to get Bandar to Beirut. On 15 September I sent him a letter urging him to come to Beirut personally to discuss with us the many complex issues he and Hariri were addressing. He agreed and immediately came accompanied by Hariri, and bringing with him a series of proposals.

After extensive discussions, we decided to rework his proposals and send them back to him in Damascus the following day, 16 September. The Saudi memorandum was approved, after detailed consultations, by Beirut and Damascus on 25 September. A new process had begun, and was to lead to two conferences on national dialogue and to the cancellation of the agreement. The Saudi proposal included four points:

1. An immediate ceasefire on all the Lebanese territory and on all the fronts. Neutral observers would supervise the ceasefire. All Lebanese displaced from their homes since 1975 would be returned to their homes and villages.
2. A committee representing the army, the Lebanese Front, the National Salvation Front, and the Amal Movement would be formed to supervise the ceasefire.
3. The President of the Republic would immediately call for a National Dialogue Conference.
4. The President of the Republic would invite a representative from Syria and a representative from Saudi Arabia to attend the proposed conference. The ceasefire would take effect as of 6 a.m. on Monday 26 September 1983.

The conference was to be open ended. It was to discuss all the issues, including the fate of the agreement, the nature of political reforms, relations with Syria and the status of the militias.

The Geneva Conference

We were starting afresh. The questions we had to address now were the site of the conference, the names of the participants, agenda items, and pretty much the transfer of roles from Washington to Damascus, and how all this was to affect withdrawals. These were difficult questions, and how each was addressed could ultimately threaten the continuation of the whole process. Even simple matters took on a complexity of their own.

One of the first problems raised was, if the president was to preside over the conference, should the conference be held at the presidential palace? The president had been accused by his opponents of being partisan: in their eyes, he was guilty of signing an agreement with Israel, of favouring the Maronites, of protecting the Lebanese Forces, and of packing the bureaucracy with members of his Kata'ib party. Accusations are stronger than facts, and they determine positions and cast them in an iron mould. Two weeks after the adoption of the Saudi proposals, I met Bandar in Washington and discussed the issue of venue with him. Each of the participants wanted the conference to be held in a different place. Among the venues suggested were the presidential palace, Paris, Geneva, Lausanne, Beirut International Airport, and even the al-Diman Church in northern Lebanon. Bandar and I agreed that our first two options were the presidential palace in Ba'bda, and Jeddah (Saudi Arabia).

Walid Junblat refused to come to Ba'bda, fearing that a member of the Presidential Guard would take a shot at him. Hariri and I worked daily on the subject of venue with Saud al-Faisal, who called us regularly from Riyad urging speed before the situation deteriorated further. He and Hariri were soon to learn that what had been agreed upon on Monday could be changed by Tuesday. Even the self-confident Hariri confided in me that he had been fooled many times.

Equally important was the question of who would attend the conference. This created immense political problems. The Syrians objected to the presence of Prime Minister Wazzan. Kamil al-As'ad, the speaker of parliament, was also excluded. Syria opposed him because he had facilitated the election of Bashir Jumayyil and the adoption of the agreement in parliament. Al-As'ad was furious at this, particularly since his Shi'i opponent, Nabih Birri, the leader of the Amal Movement, was included in the conference. This was a harbinger of bad news for the speaker, as it meant that Syria would strengthen Birri, and support him in the future when it came time to choose a new speaker of parliament. Al-As'ad's rage turned against the president because he had accepted Birri in the talks, and he decided to boycott the president who, himself, was not faring much better. He was head of the official delegation and to chair the conference, but he was not able to get the agreement of the opposition to include his prime minister in the official delegation, or a member of the government, or even a member of parliament. The official delegation was, therefore, limited to the president and his staff.

After extensive and acrimonious discussions conducted largely by Hariri it was agreed that the proposed conference would have the president as chairman, with Pierre Jumayyil, Kamil Sham'un, Sulayman Franjiyyeh, Nabih Birri, Adil Usayran, Walid Junblat, Sa'ib Salam and Rashid Karami as participants. Raymond Eddeh, a Maronite leader from the Byblos area, living in Paris, was also invited to participate. Always a maverick in Lebanese politics, he refused to attend on the ground that the conference was useless as long as the country was occupied. The chairmanship of the president was a recognition of his position and of his legitimacy, although almost half the participants opposed him, and some openly called for his resignation. Pierre Jumayyil, as head of the Kata'ib Party, and Kamil Sham'un, as head of the Ahrar Party, were both members of the Lebanese Front which had a Christian rightist orientation and supported the president. Sulayman Franjiyyeh, a Maronite leader from North Lebanon, was a sworn enemy of Pierre Jumayyil, whose son Bashir had been accused of killing his son Tony Franjiyyeh. Nabih Birri was the head of the Amal Movement and a rising star in the Shi'i community. Adil Usayran was a Shi'i leader from Sidon and an independent politician and member of parliament. Walid Junblat was the Druze leader and the head of the Popular Socialist Party. Sa'ib Salam was a Sunni leader from Beirut, a prominent and independent statesman and a former prime minister. Rashid Karami was a Sunni leader from Tripoli and former prime minister. Franjiyyeh, Birri, Junblat and Karami were members of the National Salvation Front, which was allied to Syria and opposed to the president and to the May 17 agreement.

As Saudi Arabia and Syria were active mediators in arranging the conference it was agreed that both would attend as observers. Syria would be represented by the jovial and indefatigable foreign minister, Abd al-Halim Khaddam, and Saudi Arabia by the low-key secretary-general of the Ministry of Foreign Affairs, Mahmud Mas'ud. The observers were intended to play the role of mediators, conciliators and peace-makers in the formal deliberations in the sessions and outside. The chasm between the Lebanese Front and the National Salvation Front was widening, and the help of the observers was badly needed to hold the conference together and to keep it going.

On 19 October, it was agreed that the National Dialogue Conference would be held at the Intercontinental Hotel in Geneva. I called the Swiss *chargé d'affaires* and informed him of our intent of holding the conference there. On 21 October, the *chargé d'affaires* informed me that Switzerland's president, Pierre Aubert, was pleased to invite President Jumayyil to hold a National Dialogue Conference in Geneva. The president would be Aubert's guest between 29 and 30 October, and the conference would open on Monday 31 October. On Saturday 22 October, the new American ambassador Reginald Bartholomew arrived in Beirut. A week earlier ambassador Robert Dillon had left for his new post in Austria. He was a sad man; he had lost many of his colleagues in the car-bomb explosion at the US embassy in April, and all his efforts, as part of the US team, to secure an Israeli withdrawal had been unsuccessful.

Bartholomew, a dynamic person with boundless optimism, was anxious to take charge, although US policy in Lebanon was declining, and to get a new effort going in the wake of the proposed conference. His next day in Beirut was to bring him bad news and to shatter what little was left of US influence in Lebanon. On 23 October, one man on a suicide mission drove a truck wired with high explosives into the US Marine headquarters near Beirut airport, killing 241 marines. Another drove a similar truck into a building housing French paratroopers, killing 58 of them. These operations sent shock waves through the countries of the Multinational Force. It was also an inauspicious beginning for Ambassador Bartholomew. I called on him to offer my condolences, and under these tragic circumstances, to welcome him to Lebanon.

It was widely believed that the suicide operations had been conducted by Shi'i fundamentalists. In these operations, as in the bombing of the US Embassy in April, the perpetrators had voluntarily blown themselves up with their victims. Many questions were being asked in the capitals of the MNF nations: how could MNF forces in Beirut be protected against such missions? Would these suicide bombings continue? Should the MNF be strengthened or reduced?

Each question had its political implication. The two obvious responses were simple, perhaps overly so: either avenge the humiliation or withdraw. Yet for a superpower involved in the highly delicate Lebanese conflict, revenge meant pursuing a phantom. There was no clear target to retaliate against; and any such operation would risk killing innocent civilians.

Saudi Arabia and Syria were contacting all parties to ensure that the incidents did not affect the convening of the National Dialogue Conference. I assured them that the conference would go on. I asked Hariri to come to Beirut to work out logistics. The president was discussing the matter with King Fahd and President Asad. Asad, who had refused to talk to Jumayyil after the signing of the agreement, was now cordial and accommodating, as he expected the conference to cancel the agreement and wanted the president to go along.

The president hoped to meet Asad before the conference and thus strengthen his position, but Asad would not receive him unless he cancelled the agreement first. Disappointed, the president left Beirut for Bern, a protocol visit before the conference opened in Geneva on the evening of 31 October. The conference deserves a thorough treatment on its own, not as part of a memoir, especially as I was not on the inside to observe and take notes. The Geneva conference would be a good subject for a novel. It would take a novelist to describe the conflicts and contradictions, the players inside, and those outside, the hangers-on and the parasites, whose only excuse for being there was that they wanted to witness an event which, by all accounts, was of some importance. In the wings, hovering around the delegates, talking, nudging, persuading, conciliating and threatening was the ubiquitous Hariri. The Americans, the British, the French, the Italians, the Soviets and the Egyptians were all there in force, following the events and influencing them. The Swiss were discreetly available as 'experts' in conciliation and conflict resolution, ready to help at every impasse, when asked. Wealthy Lebanese deputies, with little to do back home, also made their way to Geneva. They were there, so to speak, to be part of the picture. Even Lebanese emigrants touring Europe came to Geneva in busloads to look at the 'warlords' and wonder how they had been transformed into peace-makers. It was my job to meet some of these people, to brief them, to receive their advice and to pass it to the president.

Security was tight. Participants had to walk through detectors similar to those used at airports. Some participants in the conference carried guns and had to be told politely but firmly to check their weapons in. The participants, many of them warlords unaccustomed to being told to remove their guns, were often irritated, and some even threatened to walk out. Ex-president Franjiyyeh refused to check in his gun and walked out of the conference. The president raced to the scene, embraced Franjiyyeh, apologized for the mishap and walked him back to the conference with his gun. Tension was heavy as Franjiyyeh, his gun at his side, eyed Pierre Jumayyil, the father of the president, and wished his death. Revenge is big in north Lebanon, where Franjiyyeh comes from. His tradition urged him to revenge, but his reason and his responsibility in the state held him back. He was not the only one among the participants who felt this way. Hence the personal tension was as heavy as the political. Wide chasms had to be bridged before any headway could be made.

Before the conference could open, everybody had to be properly cajoled. Rashid Karami was delayed in his suite while waiting to be accompanied by someone from protocol. He was furious and declared to someone nearby: 'I told you I did not want to come to Geneva, one gets humiliated outside one's own country.' Members of the Lebanese Front inquired about the elevators, to ensure that they would not find themselves in the same one as members of the National Salvation Front. Indeed, when they met during the conference, each pretended not to see the other.

Khaddam was friendly to everyone, and hugged everyone in sight, including the president and members of the Lebanese Front. Junblat arrived with many bodyguards. The Swiss had prepared a special route for him, but he surprised them and took another, delighted to have beaten the reputedly most efficient police system in Europe. He amused the participants by taking a small PSP flag and hoisting it at his desk. He winked and smiled at the president, whose resignation he had been demanding for some time.

Franjiyyeh wanted to ensure from the outset that Syria and Israel would not be discussed together: one was a friendly state, the other an enemy. Junblat felt that the agenda did not commit anyone. It was not radical enough. Sheikh Pierre Jumayyil thought it humiliating that Lebanon's Arab identity should be discussed. Of course, Lebanon was Arab, he noted, but why rub it in? Why raise it as an uncertainty? Who was going to lecture Lebanon on who was Arab and who wasn't? Lebanon invented Arabism, he declared. Nabih Birri said he would not discuss reforms while the South was occupied, but he did and he had good ideas on the subject. Karami called for freezing the agreement, generating heated discussion on freezing and its implications. 'To freeze', he told me, 'is to suspend in the hope that, in time, the suspended will fall and die.' Freezing, I said, implied cold; what he suggested was hot. Hot and cold, replied the sharp Karami, were the two sides of the same coin. Khaddam, a gifted lecturer, could not sit silent. He wondered whether observers should participate in the discussions, and before anyone answered he argued that they should, to help the discussion along and to reconcile views and he proceeded to attack the agreement. The first order of the day, he said, was to cancel the agreement, and then the participants should work out a new national pact based on equity and justice, not like the old one of 1943. The Lebanese, he said, should liberate Lebanon from Israeli occupation by struggle and resistance. Syria, he declared, would not withdraw an inch as long as the agreement was in place. Often the debate deteriorated into personal abuse. Indeed the personal and the public were intricately intertwined, hence the hovering tension that accompanied the sessions throughout.

The president pleaded with the participants to keep the minutes confidential until the conference was over. The participants, however, often rushed to the press following the sessions to publicize what they had said, what they planned to say and, sometimes, what they had not said at all. Some of these leaks led to outbreaks of fighting in Lebanon, and at times, fighting was initiated in Lebanon to influence the deliberations of the conference.

Deliberations centred on three main issues: the agreement, reforms, and ending the war. The three were interdependent; you could hardly discuss one without the other. If you addressed the agreement and its fate you immediately addressed ending the Lebanese war, which itself depended on reforms. The participants submitted written proposals prepared for the occasion covering all three issues.

On the agreement some wanted it preserved, some amended, some frozen or suspended, and some cancelled. The advantages and disadvantages of each position were passionately if not systematically argued. Reform was a broad subject. It covered virtually all aspects of the state – political, military, economic, social, educational and the media.

The subject of ending the war was equally extensive and intricate, and it brought forth the presence of non-Lebanese armies and militias. The Israelis were covered by the agreement, but the agreement had become controversial, and agreement or no Israel insisted on the prior departure of the Syrian army and the Palestinian fighters. Israel was the enemy. Syria was a sister Arab state, and yet it would not withdraw until Israel withdrew.

Each point under discussion was a cluster concept loaded with history, with precarious notions, and with fears. What seemed good to one party seemed dangerous to the other. We must recall that the debate in Geneva was between leaders who had been fighting not with words but with weapons for the past eight years, and each was virtually shouting from his trench.

In talking to the participants after each session I wondered whether the conference could agree on anything. So much rubble needed to be removed before you could address the issues soberly and in the national interest. The personal, the parochial, the partisan outlooks prevailed.

In spite of the confessional distribution in the conference the cards were stacked against the president. He could count only on his father, Sheikh Pierre, and on Sham'un, and the two were so old and so fiercely independent and outspoken that they often tended to irritate and embarrass him. The president frequently sent me on difficult missions to moderate his father, hoping that I, as an outsider, might be more successful than his son in changing the opinion of the 'rock' as he was known. Salam and Usayran were independent statesmen but sided on most issues with the opposition. Franjiyyeh was in opposition until it came to the powers of the presidency. On this issue he was uncompromising. Birri, Junblat and Karami constituted on their own a strong opposition, and with Khaddam's halo their power was multiplied manifold.

The Lebanese Front and the president were conservative. On the whole they preferred to keep the agreement, if necessary to amend it. They feared cancellation and thought it could expose Lebanon to greater dangers. To them Lebanon was Lebanese. Reluctantly they would accept the Arab identification, but they always saw in it an Islamic content and a Syrian connection which made them uneasy. They wanted good relations with Syria, but they were afraid of Syrian ambitions in Lebanon as Sham'un frequently warned. They were anxious to keep the presidency strong. They discussed the parliament, the council of ministers, and the prime minister from the perspective of the presidency. They opposed measures intended to limit the powers of the Maronite president. Clearly the presidency of the republic and command of the army were the two pillars on which the Maronite power structure depended.

On the other hand, the opposition was for the cancellation of the agreement and for resorting to national struggle to liberate the south. They wanted reforms to redress existing injustices. Lebanon's identity should be clearly Arab: not Phoenician, Mediterranean or Lebanese, but Arab, and should have special relations with Syria, its sister Arab state. The presidency should be open to all Lebanese. If it was restricted to the Maronites then its powers should be limited and perhaps the six-year term should be reconsidered. The parliament should be expanded from 99 to 108 and it should elect the prime minister. They wanted development projects for the outlying districts, namely Akkar, the Biqa', and the south, which are relatively poor, and relatively ignored by the state. They supported the abolition of political confessionalism and the opening of all positions of state to all citizens. If this could not be realized immediately then a rigorous plan must be drafted to realize this objective.

Irrespective of the questions under discussion the question of the agreement was always raised. It was clear that no progress on reforms could be realized before a consensus was reached on the agreement. Faced with this fact the president announced to the participants that the agreement was a problem. He would try to solve this problem to their satisfaction. He would call Reagan and find with him the solution to the problem. The participants, eager for a miracle, applauded the president for his decision and immediately agreed to adjourn, linger around in Europe, and await the miracle within a week or two at the latest. Thus the conference adjourned having agreed on one item only, the identity of Lebanon – by itself not a mean achievement at all. It was agreed that:

> Lebanon is a sovereign, free and independent country. It is united in terms of territory, people, and institutions, within the frontiers defined in the Lebanese Constitution and which are internationally recognized. Lebanon

is an Arab state, with an Arab identity, a founding and active member of the League of Arab States, and is bound by all its agreements. The Lebanese state must embody these principles in all fields without exception.

The Geneva conference adjourned on 4 November with the intent of meeting on 14 November after Jumayyil had seen Reagan. The conferees assumed that Lebanon was important enough to ensure a meeting between Reagan and Jumayyil at short notice. In the interim the conferees agreed on a subcommittee of the conference consisting of the advisers of the participants, chaired by Muhammad Shuqayr and an adviser of President Jumayyil. The subcommittee was to summarize the points in the proposals and come up with its own recommendations for discussion by the conference when it reconvened on the 14th.

The President thought he would return to Lebanon, get an appointment with Reagan and leave for Washington in a day or two, then return to Geneva to continue the proceedings of the conference. How and why he thought he could find a solution pretty much on his own, I do not know. He felt the conference was getting nowhere and he wanted to jolt it into action. As it turned out the Geneva conference was not merely adjourned: it had ended.

6

The Way to Lausanne

Coordination with Syria

Upon my return from Geneva I found that the Soviet ambassador in Beirut, Alexander Soldatov, was enraged by the US naval buildup in the eastern Mediterranean. President Reagan, fresh from his success in Grenada, was threatening retaliation against those responsible for having attacked the Marines in Beirut. Soldatov told me that the Soviet Union had interests in the region which it intended to protect, and he wanted to know the Lebanese position on the American buildup. I told him that such a buildup was likely to be part of a strategy that went beyond Lebanon, and that the Soviets were certainly more informed about this than I. One thing I wanted to make clear, however, was that any resort to force, whether by the Americans, the Soviets, or the Israelis, would be at the expense of Lebanon, and we would, therefore, oppose it.

Violence, however, was everywhere at that time. Pro- and anti-Arafat Palestinians were fighting each other in the suburbs of Tripoli and Arafat's followers had taken refuge in Tripoli. The anti-Arafatis were shelling Arafat's positions in the city, and the Tripoli oil refinery had caught fire, threatening the inhabitants of Tripoli with a cloud of toxic gas. Meanwhile, international negotiations were under way to bring about Arafat's withdrawal from Tripoli.

In the south, a man on a suicide mission had blown up the Israeli headquarters in Tyre, killing many Israeli soldiers. Israel had retaliated by cutting off South Lebanon from the rest of the country at the Awwali River just north of Sidon. The Israelis had also evicted Lebanese government employees from the offices of the Sidon administration, and replaced them with its surrogates. In their zone of control, the Israelis were shooting at everything that looked suspicious, and were thus making the lives of the inhabitants ever more difficult and perilous.

Wazzan's government had resigned, and although, for the moment, it remained in place as a caretaker government, it had lost all effectiveness. Wazzan wanted either to get out completely, or to form a new government including opposition leaders. Such a government would provide him with the support he needed in these turbulent times. Sensing that Wazzan was getting tired and irritable, I thought that he could be replaced by Rafiq al-Hariri. Although Rafiq was something of an unguided missile, he was dynamic and had exceptional contacts within Lebanon, in the Middle East, and throughout the world. I felt that his name would add credence to the president's efforts to introduce reforms, broaden the base of the government, and launch a programme of reconstruction. The president was not opposed to the idea, but he was not in the mood to change the government. He realized that forming a new government would require much bargaining, and for the moment he wanted to wait until he could negotiate from a position of strength.

The president felt good after the Geneva conference, and felt that he had somehow been re-elected: he had met those who had opposed him, and they had given him a mandate to work out a solution with President Reagan to the imbroglio surrounding the agreement. Jumayyil also saw a good sign in Reagan's appointment of Donald Rumsfeld as special envoy to Lebanon, to replace Robert McFarlane, who became Reagan's national security adviser. Rumsfeld was a former secretary of defence, a well-known politician, and a determined crisis manager. The president expected Rumsfeld to come up with a solution. But he had made a commitment at Geneva to see Reagan and find a solution himself. Rumsfeld should be in a position to help.

I invited US Ambassador Reginald Bartholomew to meet the president and me at the presidential palace. We met on 8 November. The president asked him to arrange an appointment with President Reagan. Bartholomew asked us why? – what could Reagan tell us? The agreement, he said, was an agreement among three parties, and Reagan could do nothing without Israeli approval. Discussions should take place within the context of the Tripartite formula, he noted, not with President Reagan. Should we wish to discuss other matters with Reagan, we were, of course, welcome to do so, but Reagan was a busy man, and he doubted whether we could see him before the end of the month. 'The end of the month!' exclaimed the president, 'I have people waiting around, we have to complete the Geneva process.' 'Sorry,' said Bartholomew, 'I will do my best, but I doubt if a meeting can be arranged in the time frame you have in mind.'

The president was deeply perturbed by this response. He had made a commitment in Geneva to meet Reagan, and he wanted to honour it. After much give and take, however, a meeting between Jumayyil and Reagan was arranged for 1 December 1983. Geneva was over. The president had another meeting on his mind as well. He had tried to bring the Syrians around on the agreement, but had repeatedly failed. He had confidence in his persona. He counted a great deal on personal meetings and on his ability to persuade his interlocutors, and he saw the meeting with Asad as an occasion to present his point of view to the Syrian leader. This was his chance finally to work out a deal with Asad either to suspend the agreement, amend it, or find an acceptable substitute for it. The president also understood that without Asad, he could not aspire to a national consensus in support of his efforts, nor would he be able to put together a broad-based government. The balance of power in Lebanon had shifted in Syria's favour, and President Jumayyil knew that he had to adapt to this new reality.

A meeting with Asad was scheduled for Monday 14 November. Asad's mood towards Jumayyil had changed after the Geneva conference. Asad was certain that Jumayyil would cancel the agreement, or at least he would seriously search for a substitute or a modality acceptable to Syria. To President Jumayyil's chagrin, Khaddam called on 13 November to say that Asad was ill and had been taken to hospital. Asad had really wanted to meet with Jumayyil, Khaddam said, and on the way to the hospital Asad had told him to call the president personally, explain the delay, and head off wild speculation.

Khaddam offered to come to Beirut to see the president. Accordingly I met him in Dhur al-Shwayr, and escorted him through the government-controlled area to the presidential palace in Ba'bda. Khaddam explained to us that Asad had had his appendix removed and was now recuperating. He would resume his official functions within two weeks and, Khaddam reassured us, Jumayyil's visit would be the first on his agenda. Actually Asad's sickness at the time was serious and there was a premature struggle for power in Asad's entourage that complicated matters greatly. It was exceedingly generous of Asad, during these dramatic hours, to send an emissary as high placed as Khaddam to ward off any wrong interpretation of the postponement of the visit.

Khaddam's visit to Ba'bda was intended by Asad to give a boost to the process started in Geneva. There had been a great deal of misunderstanding surrounding the agreement, Khaddam began by saying. The Americans had led the Syrians to believe that Israel would withdraw on the basis of security arrangements only. Israel was entitled to security arrangements, he continued, but it had no right to send the side letter conditioning its withdrawal on a Syrian withdrawal. Lebanon and Syria, he continued, should cooperate from now on and resolve all their problems, even those having to do with the agreement. Khaddam recommended that President Jumayyil should stop in Damascus on his way to Washington to meet President Reagan, and should also stop on his way back. This would ensure complete coordination between Syria and Lebanon. The president, who was anxious to coordinate with the Syrians, was pleased with the suggestion. Indeed, he knew that any understanding with Reagan that did not have Asad's support would not work. With the benefit of hindsight it was realized by us that coordination with Asad must be direct and complete. Such coordination with Asad was necessary but not sufficient.

Khaddam's visit was a polite gesture to cool things off until Asad recovered. Needless to say speculation about Asad's health filled Lebanon and the Arab world. In tightly governed states, the slightest mishap to the man at the top sends shockwaves throughout the entire political system. Asad's hold on power, however, was so great that few suspected a successful coup against him.

I flew to Damascus on 26 November and met Khaddam at Damascus Airport. Asad was still recuperating, and it was not possible to schedule an official visit to Syria by President Jumayyil before his meeting with President Reagan on 1 December. Khaddam recommended that we use Syrian opposition to the agreement as a reason to urge its abrogation in Washington. He also noted again that the agreement was in conflict with a letter the United States had sent to Syria on 10 June 1982, stating that Israel would withdraw from Lebanon in return for security arrangements and nothing more. Khaddam spoke to me in a measured tone as if he intended to communicate a message to Shultz through me. He said the United States intended to use Israel to attack Syria. This would be a mistake, since such a move would strengthen the Soviet presence in the region and lead to anti-Americanism among the Arabs. Syria preferred to maintain its freedom of action and not fall under strong Soviet influence, but were Syria forced to choose between Israel and the Soviet Union, it would chose the latter without hesitation. Khaddam remarked that the Syrian leadership respected George Shultz, despite the fact that his name was identified with the agreement. It was important that Shultz maintain contacts with the Syrians and the Lebanese to work out a new consensus on Lebanon. From there we could then proceed to solve all outstanding problems one by one. This was Khaddam the diplomat talking. He had expressed Syria's hard-line position in a nutshell; his tone was moderate and yet he had not conceded an iota.

On 27 November, the president and I left for the United States on a small private plane from a military landing strip at Halat, north of Beirut. As Beirut International Airport became too dangerous for official travel, the president had asked General Tannous, the commander of the army, to make a landing strip somewhere in the area under government control.

Tannous had found a little stretch on the Beirut–Tripoli highway which could be converted into a runway. Traffic was diverted and an airstrip was built, long enough to allow Lebanese Air Force Hawker Hunters and small civilian planes to take off and land. A white line in the middle indicated the right place for aircraft to touch down.

A month before, as my plane was about to land at Halat, one of my Lebanese pilots had remarked that the white line seemed shorter than it had a few days earlier when we had taken off. Between doubt and certainty as to where the plane should touch down, the pilot decided to land where the line began. Within seconds, however, we found ourselves speeding past the end of the runway, through a passage that had been cleared in case of such an eventuality, and perilously close to a banana field, before we stopped. What we hadn't known was that while we were away, the runway had been re-asphalted, and the white line was a few hundred feet short. The pilot expressed his anger by resorting to the most creative curse in the Lebanese language.

This time the plane and the pilots were Swiss. They had landed one day earlier to get used to the airfield. When we arrived, the pilots seemed a bit nervous. They were concerned about two things: there was a hill on either side of the runway, and also the runway ran over a perilous bridge. They were concerned about the wind and how it might behave in these two places. I told them that if in Lebanon we took such distant probabilities into consideration, we would never leave our houses. Reluctantly the pilots slid into the cockpit. As they started the engines, the pilot called me forward and told me that the plane was made to carry eight people, but that he had counted twelve of us; he didn't believe it was an ideal flying situation. I told him to depend on God, as ideal situations did not apply to us. He shook his head and took off. He may have resorted to a few creative curses in German, French or Italian.

We stopped in Rome to meet Italian President Sandro Pertini, Prime Minister Bettino Craxi, Defence Minister Giovanni Spadolini, and Foreign Minister Giulio Andreotti. It was touching to see the octogenarian President Pertini embrace the 43-year-old Jumayyil, and tell him of his love for Lebanon and of his commitment to stay with us to the end. The position of the Italian government was not as definite, however. Spadolini told us that if the situation deteriorated further in Lebanon, Italy would withdraw its contingent from the MNF. Italy went in when a solution seemed in sight, now matters were getting complicated. As a former professor of history he recalled the Italian wars and how much blood was spilled to unify Italy. He hoped our travail would be shorter, and wished Jumayyil well in his talks with Reagan. Before we departed he said, 'Don't forget I am still a professor, I also publish, here is my latest', as he offered me his handsome book on Florence entitled *Firenze Mille Anni* (Florence: A Thousand Years.) Craxi was more anxious than Spadolini to get 'out of there'. He wanted to redeploy his forces aboard Italian ships offshore. We suspected this was also the position of the other MNF countries, although they had all assured us, after the attack on the marines and the paratroopers, that no change would occur in the deployment of their troops. Also, despite a previous agreement, the Italians were now reluctant to sell us 80 armoured personnel carriers. It was obvious that something new was in the air. The spirit of confidence that had hitherto prevailed among the MNF countries was weakening, and as we left Rome we wondered what would be the mood in Washington.

In Washington, we had a luncheon with President Reagan which included Vice-President Bush, Secretary Shultz and Robert McFarlane. Our ambassador in Washington, Dr Abdallah Bouhabib, warned us not to expect much. We would get general support, but no specifics. The miracle we hoped for in Geneva was not going to happen, he said.

Reagan was in good humour. He was also well briefed, and what we got from him at luncheon was all we could get from Washington. There was no solution, but there was a determination to find one. Reagan said the Americans were pleased with the Geneva conference. They understood the problems Syria had with the agreement, and accepted the fact that it was now frozen. The new special envoy, Donald Rumsfeld, would work with us and with the Syrians, in coordination with Saudi Arabia, to find ways out of the impasse. Rumsfeld was in the region now with his famous yellow pad, taking notes, setting options, and applying his energy to come out with a solution.

Bush and Shultz spoke well of Geneva and of the Lebanese getting together to solve their problem. They did not wish the agreement to be abrogated – this would irritate Israel and undermine US efforts; nor did they want it implemented – this would irritate Syria and hurt Lebanon. We must find a third option. Rumsfeld was the right person to find this option, if we gave him time.

The Rumsfeld Mission

Rumsfeld arrived in Beirut in mid-November. He had served as secretary of defence under President Gerald Ford, and had since taken over the presidency of a large business firm. Rumsfeld did not look like a man in his fifties: he was athletic, dynamic and businesslike. If anyone could be called typically American, it was Rumsfeld. He was a politician who coveted success. He spoke openly of his ambition to run for the presidency of the United States. He had taken the job of special envoy because it had a chance to succeed, and it had visibility. I was told by April Glaspie that sometime ago, when she was still in the US Embassy in Damascus, Rumsfeld had visited Damascus. He had also met President Asad in her presence. After some difficult discussion between the two, Asad had looked at Rumsfeld and said: 'Why should I listen to you?' Without hesitation Rumsfeld had answered: 'Because one day I will be president of the United States.'

Upon his arrival in Beirut Rumsfeld came to our house to talk at length about the problem. He told me he had been reluctant to take the job. Reagan, however, had insisted. He had called him in Chicago, where his office was, and urged him to take on the challenge. Rumsfeld had answered, 'Mr President, if my appointment is to provide a fig leaf to get the Marines out of Lebanon, then I will not accept.' Reagan had reassured him that he had every intention of succeeding, and he wanted Rumsfeld to help him do so. The former secretary of defence had accepted, feeling that he now had a mandate.

Rumsfeld was well acquainted with the strategic importance of the Middle East from his experience at the defence department. His knowledge of Lebanon and Syria, however, was limited. In my first meeting with him, I outlined the situation he would be facing. He was a good listener, humble in his pursuit of facts, and confident in his ability to formulate policies on the basis of these facts. Nevertheless, his job was very tough indeed. He would have to settle virtually irreconcilable differences between some parties who were far less concerned with success than the Americans were.

Upon my return from Washington, I contacted Khaddam and Saud al-Faisal to brief them on our visit and to pursue the issues which had been raised in Geneva. I met Khaddam in Damascus on 9 December. He told me that President Asad, who was still recuperating, sent me his regards. He would have liked to receive me personally, Khaddam said, but was still resting outside Damascus.

I told Khaddam that we had discussed all options in Washington, but without reaching a conclusion. Rumsfeld would be in Damascus next week. I then listed for him the options we had discussed: a) abrogation of the May 17 agreement and full Israeli withdrawal on the basis of the Armistice agreement; b) suspension of the May 17 agreement and a renegotiation of the sections dealing with mutual relations; c) adding a section to the agreement stating that should a conflict arise between obligations undertaken by Lebanon under the agreement and obligations undertaken by Lebanon within the Arab League, then the obligations under the agreement must be considered null and void; d) amending the agreement in a manner acceptable to Lebanon, Syria and Israel.

I told Khaddam I would tell him objectively and precisely what Shultz had told us. He said the USA believed that Lebanon's problems were not with Israel, but with Syria. He said if we cancelled the agreement, then Israel would not be committed to withdraw from Lebanon. The Americans were displeased with the Syrians. They held the view that Syria had driven the USA into a corner, and it was as a result of Syrian policy that the United States had strengthened its ties recently with Israel. Syria was creating too many obstacles, and little progress had been made in the bilateral talks between Washington and Damascus. This was the message, I said, but Rumsfeld seemed to have elbow room in discussing the options. Khaddam listened carefully and reflectively, but was angry that American planes had recently attacked Syrian positions in Lebanon. The United States held Syria and Iran responsible for the attack on the Marine barracks, and the air-raids were in retaliation for this. Khaddam wanted the United States to know that Syria was not impressed by its use of force, and he noted that even a superpower could not challenge Syria in what it believed to be right. He then stated that Syria insisted on the cancellation of the agreement before or during the next meeting of the National Dialogue Conference.

From Damascus I left for Riyad to meet Saudi Foreign Minister Saud al-Faisal. Saud and Rafiq al-Hariri met me in the Conference Palace, where I was staying. I always found solace in talking with Saud, as he understood well the vicious cycle into which Lebanon had fallen. My frustration was increasing daily and it was clearly reflected in my talks in Riyad. We had an agreement and we did not know which course was best – to implement it, amend it, or cancel it. The alternatives were difficult but we needed to reach a consensus on one of them. We were worried that if we cancelled the agreement, Israel would entrench itself further in the south. It was unlikely that we could amend the agreement, given Israel's opposition to such a move. And we were unable to implement the agreement over Syrian objections. Whichever option we chose it had its dangerous consequences.

Saud felt that this objective could be reached by amending the agreement. He also believed that this was the Syrian position. I disagreed with him. Syria's position, I said, was to cancel the agreement. I had never heard the word amendment from either Asad or Khaddam. I then suggested, as a possible alternative, to aim at cancelling the Israeli side letter and suspending the agreement, with the understanding that certain articles in it would be renegotiated under the tripartite formula after a full Israeli withdrawal. This proposal might have a chance with the Syrians. It might also have a chance with the Israelis if the United States put its weight behind it. I explained to Saud that no agreement between Lebanon and

Israel could survive Syria's determined opposition. We should instead work on Rumsfeld to realize the proposal I had put forward. Saud advised taking the advice of King Fahd on such an important matter.

Before my meeting with the king, Hariri drove me to his new palace in Riyad. It was a grand structure, grand enough to show that Hariri was a good Saudi, who planned to remain in Riyad and invest in it. And yet it was intentionally not grand enough to compete with the palaces of the Saudi princes. When we arrived, his wife Nazik, who was pregnant, was busy selecting Persian rugs. Literally hundreds of rugs were spread around in the palace's salons, and although in pain, Nazik moved from one pile to another, selecting in a most perfunctory manner dozens of rugs of all sizes, without making the slightest effort to consult her husband. When I joked about her excessive freedom in decision-making, Hariri responded that he cared only for one thing, his huge indoor swimming pool. He could push a button and the ceiling would open revealing the sky. Thus, he remarked, he could swim bathed by the light of the stars. The entrepreneur was a romantic, I mused.

I met King Fahd on Sunday 11 December, in the presence of Crown Prince Abdallah, Saud al-Faisal, and the Minister of Information, Ali al-Sha'ir. The king was on excellent form. He was intense and anxious to examine the Lebanese situation. He reviewed the general Arab scene first, however, and its impact on Lebanon. He reflected on the Iraq–Iran war and on the danger of exploiting Islam and perverting it. He remarked that Islam was a religion of love, kindness and ethics. It respected other religions and respected individual leaders. Iran wanted to weaken the Arab world. This would have grave historical consequences, he believed, as it tended to strengthen Israel. Arab consensus was essential to remove Israel from Lebanon. It was the Arab consensus which had led the United States to pressure Britain and France to withdraw from Suez in 1956. An Arab consensus on Lebanon would be assured if the agreement dealt only with security arrangements. The Syrian perspective had to be taken into consideration, since Syria was strong and could defend its position. He noted that President Jumayyil had been wise not to ratify the agreement. Israel had to withdraw and then Lebanon could renegotiate the points of conflict in the agreement. The withdrawal of Israel from Lebanon would be a great victory for the Arab nation, because it would imply that Israel would withdraw from Gaza and the West Bank. If, on the other hand, Israel did not withdraw, then South Lebanon would be added to the West Bank, Gaza and the Golan Heights as parts of Greater Israel. The king felt that the ball was now largely in the American court. He nevertheless said that he would be available to help with Syria and to find a proper way out of our predicament. When I made my proposal he immediately agreed with me. He said the side letter was unfair, why involve Syria? The agreement should be suspended and if the Israelis withdraw then it would be re-negotiated on the basis of security arrangements only. The king proceeded to give a lengthy and reasoned argument against prevailing ideological politics in the Arab world and reviewed the historical steps that led to ideological posturing. He was critical of Abd al-Nasir and of the Iraqi leader Abd al-Karim Qasim. His review was not without humour. He recalled a speech by Qasim at the opening of a hospital for the mentally ill in Baghdad in which he said: 'This hospital is for you and for us.' Then he looked at me with a smile, and said that according to the rules of logic the man was insane.

Upon my return to Beirut, I briefed Prime Minister Wazzan on my discussions. I found him, however, engrossed in the internal problems arising from his resignation. Wazzan was, at the time, in an unenviable political never-never land: he had resigned as prime minister and, there-fore, had no mandate to conduct policy, and at the same time, he was a caretaker prime minister until a new government could be formed. He was critical of his opponents and their unwillingness to cooperate. Wazzan complained that whatever he did his opponents were unhappy. It reminded him of the story of Jiha and his donkey: Jiha and his son were riding on a donkey, and the people around said what bad manners they have, two people riding on a poor donkey. So Jiha then let his son walk while he continued riding on the donkey alone. The people looked at him and said, what bad taste, he rides and lets his son walk. So Jiha put his son in the saddle, and walked himself. Then the people started laughing at him for letting his son ride instead of him. Finally Jiha and his son decided to both walk and leave the donkey riderless; and the people laughed at them and said, they have a donkey and yet they walk. This is my situation, complained Wazzan, I ran out of options.

On 14 December, Hariri called me from Riyad to tell me that Saud would be in Damascus on 18 December, and that Khaddam would be inviting me to hold discussions with them at that time. In this meeting, he said, the discussion would be open. We would be examining all the options that we presented in Washington. He assured us that the atmosphere would be cordial; we had to keep moving and reconvene the National Dialogue Conference. The president was encouraged by Hariri's call, and felt it was necessary to bolster the new negotiation process by getting Arab support behind it. Accordingly, he called King Hassan II and asked to meet him urgently, and he travelled alone to Morocco on Thursday 15 December. Jumayyil liked King Hassan II personally, felt at ease with him, and always found excuses to stop by in Rabat to brief the king or to seek his counsel. He considered Hassan II to be a seasoned politician and not without influence on political issues in the Arab mashriq (Arab East). We were expecting the President to return to Beirut the following evening.

On Friday afternoon I received a call from Colonel Simon Qassis enquiring as to the president's whereabouts. Qassis told me that the president had left Rabat early that morning, and that his plane had been missing since 9.30 a.m. He had no idea where the president was heading. Dr Wadi Haddad, national security adviser to the president, walked into my office, greatly disturbed; he had just heard on the Israeli radio that the president's plane had landed in Tripoli, Libya. As we had just broken off diplomatic relations with Libya, Haddad wondered whether the plane had been forced down. I immediately called the prime minister, the speaker of parliament, the president's wife, and King Hassan II in that order. Wazzan was furious. He shouted down the phone: 'You and he just convinced me and the Council of Ministers that we should break relations with Qadhdhafi because he viciously attacked the president, and now you tell me the president is there sipping coffee with the Libyan leader. What shall I tell the people? What shall I tell the Shi'ah, who believe that the Imam [Musa al-Sadr] vanished in Libya?' I fully agreed with him. The president never told me he was going to Libya. 'Fine,' answered Wazzan, 'call Kamil al-As'ad [the Shi'i speaker of parliament] and listen to a speech tougher than mine.' I did. Wazzan had predicted correctly. I then called King Hassan. The king assured me that the president was safe. He had arranged the meeting between the president and Qadhdhafi and to guarantee his safety, he had sent his personal adviser Ahmed Ben Soda to accompany him. An hour later the king called me to say that the president and Qadhdhafi had been in a meeting for five hours, and that the president would afterwards fly to Paris. He would arrive in Beirut tomorrow.

Prime Minister Wazzan, Kamil al-As'ad, Qassis, Haddad and I were all furious that the president made this move without prior consultation. For a few hours, it was believed in the major capitals of the world that the president of Lebanon had been kidnapped. Furthermore, a meeting with Qadhdhafi a few days after breaking diplomatic relations with Libya was not serious. When the president arrived in Ba'bda, I told him that I regretted his visit to Libya at the present time. On the one hand it had a negative internal impact, particularly among the Shi'ah, who accused the Libyans of killing or 'hiding' their Imam. On the other hand, the president had created a small international incident given that he had been missing for almost an entire day. It had been embarrassing for me as foreign minister, to call King Hassan to find out where our president was. It made me look ignorant, if not irrelevant.

The president, who loved surprises, and the more spectacular the better, did not feel at all that he did anything wrong. To the contrary he felt he had made a major breakthrough with the radical camp, a psychological coup, he called it. He believed that he had had some impact on Qadhdhafi, and hoped it would induce the Libyan leader to stop financing the opposition within Lebanon. The president, the prime minister and I tried to find a formula to explain the visit to parliament, and decided to explain it within the context of the Geneva conference. As Libya had men fighting in Lebanon, we argued, President Jumayyil had visited Tripoli to discuss with Qadhdhafi the withdrawal of these Libyan fighters from Lebanon. Indeed, the president had raised the subject in the Tripoli meeting. Qadhdhafi had answered: 'Do I still have Libyans there? I did send some trainers to help the nationalist militias, are they still there? My aides never tell me anything, they keep me uninformed. By the way, you should read my Green Book, it is the best political essay of the century. Read it and apply its teachings and Lebanon's problems will be solved.' In parliament I explained to a cynical audience that the president had a successful visit to Libya. The kindest response was 'did he bring the Imam with him?'

In my talks with Saud and Khaddam in Damascus the following day, Khaddam gave the first faint impression that it might be possible to amend the agreement. His position was that Syria would withdraw immediately from Lebanon if a number of things were deleted from the agreement: the introduction, which Khaddam argued, constituted recognition of Israel by declaring an end to the state of war between Israel and Lebanon; the gains given to Israel, in virtually every article, the constraints put on Lebanon under security arrangements, and the existence of joint supervisory teams. After he had finished describing his amendments, I said, 'You are suggesting abrogation.' 'Yes,' answered Khaddam, 'let's face it, this agreement is bad and should be abrogated.' I suggested the three of us review the agreement and agree on amendments that were truly of concern to Syria and affected its strategic position. Then Rumsfeld would discuss our proposed amendments with the Israelis. Khaddam, in turn, proposed that the National Dialogue Conference should reconvene and define steps under which Israel should withdraw from Lebanon in the context of Lebanon's unity, independence, sovereignty, and commitment to the Arab world. 'If we send it back to the conference,' I argued, 'you know very well what happens, total babelism. The conference could not reach a solution; it could not negotiate.' I rejected his proposal, and he rejected mine. Khaddam wanted abrogation but wanted it accepted by all those concerned. He was delaying. He hinted at amendment, but meant abrogation. We agreed, however, to continue talking, and Saud invited us both to Riyad in early January.

As I reported to the president and the prime minister on my meeting in Damascus, I received a telephone call from the secretary-general of the

Ministry of Foreign Affairs, Ambassador Fuad Turk. President Reagan, he said, had just announced that the Marines would be staying in Lebanon until Lebanon regained its strength, or until it collapsed. Turk is a serious ambassador and very precise, but I doubted whether this statement attributed to Reagan was correct. He assured me it was. The reference to collapse was most disturbing. I contacted Ambassador Bartholomew for explanation. He was uncertain, he would verify and let me know. His answer to my repeated queries were getting less and less convincing. The US resolve was weakening. The Americans were telling us indirectly that if the National Dialogue Conference did not reconvene and come up with something useful and if a broad-based government was not formed in the wake of the conference, the USA would withdraw its contingent from the MNF.

The French were also talking about redeploying their MNF contingent to naval ships offshore, and they confidentially told us that the United States was also planning to withdraw its Marines. The Italians were reducing their contingent. The Italian Ambassador Franco Ottieri denied that the reduction had political significance. Italians, he said, looking for higher pay were flooding the Italian contingent in the MNF. 'We just have too many soldiers here,' he said, 'they are not all needed. We are sending the surplus numbers home.'

The security situation in Beirut was deteriorating. The authority of the army in the capital was contested and foreigners were threatened. The president and his government were rapidly losing control on the ground to the opposition. Saud al-Faisal, Khaddam and I were to meet again to find a way out agreeable to all concerned, and at the same time we were eager to reconvene the National Dialogue Conference as it represented all the groupings. Any solution needed a consensus and only the participants in the conference could bring about such a consensus.

I was in daily contact with our ambassador in Bern, Johnny Abdu, talking about the time and place of the next conference. We considered Geneva and Montreux, but finally decided that it should be held in Lausanne at a date to be determined after my meeting with Khaddam and Saud in Riyad.

I arrived in Riyad on Saturday 8 January and was met by Saud al-Faisal and our ambassador Zafir al-Hassan. Saud and I waited in the airport VIP lounge for Khaddam to arrive, and when he did the three of us got into Saud's car, which he drove himself. As soon as we started moving, Khaddam began a tirade against the Lebanese army, calling it a militia, and accusing it of promoting Sa'd Haddad, and planting car-bombs in the Biqa' Valley against the Syrian army. Meanwhile, Saud kept looking at me in his car mirror, signalling that I should remain patient.

By the time we arrived at the Conference Palace, it was obvious that the atmosphere was not conducive to conciliation. I told Saud privately that I was ready to return to Beirut immediately rather than exacerbate a bad situation. He again urged me to be patient, and said that King Fahd would see Khaddam that afternoon. After that, the three of us, Saud, Khaddam and I, would hold our meeting at Saud's house. Saud hoped to provide us with the warmth of his family home to ensure the success of this meeting.

We met at Saud's house at 6 o'clock that evening. I had with me our ambassador in Riyad and my assistant from the Ministry of Foreign Affairs, Elyse Alam. Khaddam and Saud were accompanied by their aides. Also present was Sheikh Rafiq al-Hariri. The house was humble by Saudi standards. It was a happy home full of children who kept walking into our meeting place, despite the tension which pervaded the session. Khaddam's talks with King Fahd had not softened him. He began our meeting with the same accusations he had made in the car. Khaddam showed no interest in discussing the modalities proposed in Damascus in December, nor those raised in meetings between him and Rumsfeld. He insisted once again that Israel must withdraw from Lebanon unconditionally, that the agreement must be cancelled, and that a Government of National Unity must be formed. The prime minister of the new government, as well as half the ministers, must be from the opposition.

Finally, in despair I told Saud in English: 'This is hopeless, this is a waste of time. If we continue like this we will worsen rather than improve relations. What are we lecturing for? Let the three of us go to a private room and talk alone without minutes and without speeches. I want results.' Khaddam, who often pretends he does not understand English, shouted back, 'Why do you say this is useless? Why go to another room? I am staying here!' I told Saud that I was tired and that I wanted to go back to my hotel and sleep. Khaddam said he was even more tired, and he left.

Saud, Hariri and I went to Saud's study and reflected on the meeting – why was it so bad, what was making the usually jovial foreign minister so angry? Each of us had his theory. Saud suggested that Hariri should meet me and Khaddam early the next morning for breakfast to change the tone of this evening. When Hariri and I met with Khaddam early on Sunday morning, he was relaxed and friendly. Instead of having breakfast at Hariri's house Khaddam insisted we have breakfast with him. We did. He told us in calm, sober words that the Syrian leadership had assessed the American commitment to Lebanon and had found it wanting. The Americans were short of breath, he noted, and they would be leaving Lebanon soon. Syria would not facilitate matters for the USA in Lebanon, and wanted to prove that the Americans had failed there. Anyhow, he remarked, 1984 was an election year in the United States, and this would freeze American policy in Lebanon. The USA, he said, was trying to work with the Jordanians and the Palestinians on a solution to the Palestinian problem. It was trying to isolate Syria by strengthening Egypt, Jordan and Yasir Arafat. Yet Syria knew how to handle the Americans. Syria would protect itself, and would block US moves in Lebanon. Syria was ready to help Lebanon with its internal security and its economy. The agreement had to be cancelled, not amended, and only then would a Government of National Unity be formed. Syria was not enthusiastic about the next dialogue conference. If its Lebanese allies wanted it, then that was fine, but Khaddam doubted that he would attend himself. This was a question which he and I could discuss during the Islamic Summit in Casablanca the following week.

After breakfast, Saud and I met King Fahd in the presence of Crown Prince Abdallah and Ali al-Sha'ir. The king had been fully briefed on the difficult meeting the previous evening, and he assured me of his continued support in finding a way out of the impasse. He also expressed confidence in Rumsfeld's creativity in trying to formulate options agreeable to all parties concerned. The king's primary interest at the time was to ensure the adoption of a ceasefire and a security plan that would give some respite to the Lebanese. Hariri was working on this virtually full-time. The king advised me to be patient, and told me that he had learned patience from his father, the legendary King Abd al-Aziz, founder of the Saudi Kingdom. A ruler must be patient and wise, he told me, and he believed that Asad was patient and wise. The king hoped that Asad would regain his health by the following week as he wanted to send Crown Prince Abdallah to Damascus to discuss with him the Lebanese situation.

It was obvious that the cards were now in Syria's hands. Asad's illness had in no way softened Syrian policy. In Asad's absence, Khaddam proved to be capable of speaking authoritatively and of shifting his tactics as he saw fit. He was not at all weakened by the brief struggle for power that had taken place in Damascus during President Asad's illness. His loyalty to Asad had paid off: he was the authoritative voice of Asad. King Fahd and Rumsfeld were trying to find out what the Syrians wanted. The lack of progress was leading to a further erosion of our government's credibility and to an increasing deterioration in the security situation and the economy. This was not a good time to be an official in Lebanon. Our government was in a shambles. Muslim ministers were keeping their distance from the president, and those of them who only recently sang the praises of the agreement were now denouncing it. The Americans talked big, but delivered little. The moderate Arab states voiced their support, but shied away from direct involvement in our affairs.

If in Riyad I was unable to reach an understanding with Khaddam, I felt that I would have even less of a chance to do so at the Islamic Summit in Casablanca. Our official delegation to the summit was headed by Prime Minister Wazzan, and he asked that I join him so that we could present a united front. We arrived in Casablanca on Sunday 15 January 1984. For me the conference was simply an opportunity to continue my discussions with Saud al-Faisal and Khaddam. Otherwise, the summit's agenda was of little interest to Lebanon. As a transnational organization, the Islamic Summit attracts the attention of regional organizations and the United Nations. Shadli al-Qulaybi and Javier Péréz de Cuéllar both attended the Casablanca Summit, delivered speeches, and conducted discussions on the side. They said nice things about Lebanon, expressed regret at our predicament, and urged more cooperation. This said, all was quickly forgotten. Saud, Khaddam and I met twice in very unsatisfactory and inconclusive sessions. Khaddam was not ready to talk about the agreement. He was in even less of a mood to help Rumsfeld find a solution to the Lebanese imbroglio, and thus enhance the US role in Lebanon and the Middle East. He wanted to put everything off, except working out a ceasefire plan that would reduce the sufferings of the Lebanese people.

In Casablanca Wazzan and I had ample time to discuss the fate of the agreement. He was rapidly leaning towards abrogation, and I was not far behind. It was becoming obvious to us that the choices were abrogation of the agreement or war. As these alternatives became clearer to us, I began pushing for immediate abrogation.

Upon my return I told the president of my conviction that the agreement should be abrogated. He agreed with me, but he wanted assurances from the Americans that in cancelling the agreement Israel would not harm Lebanon. When I told Bartholomew about our determination to abrogate the agreement, he emphasized Reagan's commitment to Lebanon. Reagan, he said, was not the kind of politician who would change his mind because of a change in public opinion. Bartholomew asked for three months so that Rumsfeld could have a chance to negotiate alternatives.

I was uncertain whether the Jumayyil regime could last two or three months in the face of growing opposition, unless a political solution were found: Walid Junblat was receiving weapons and money from Libya and the Soviet Union; Amal and the National Salvation Front had the strong military backing of Syria; and Beirut was in turmoil. It was felt in the government that the opposition would soon attempt a takeover of the western portion of the capital. On 2 February, the French ambassador told me that the Lebanese Communist Party had divided Beirut into sections, and had assigned party members to be in charge of them when the takeover started. On 3 February, the Muslim ministers in the government resigned under pressure from their respective communities. Each of the ministers called the president to apologize for their action, but they explained that they were afraid of the threats which had been made against them. Even Prime Minister Wazzan, who was a courageous man, could no longer resist the pressure. He called the president and read a statement of resignation which he submitted in writing on Wednesday 4 February.

Meanwhile, fighting between the Lebanese army and the Amal militia in Beirut's southern suburbs intensified. On 5 February, Nabih Birri, the leader of Amal, called for the president's resignation, and the following day, 6 February, the much-anticipated takeover of West Beirut took place. Within hours the militias of the opposition (Amal, PSP, PPS, the Communist Party) controlled all of West Beirut, as the Lebanese army's Sixth Brigade, largely Shi'i and pro-Amal, defected and joined the opposition. The president desperately sought to form a new government, but no Sunni leader would agree to head it, and no Muslim would join it. Syria still insisted on the abrogation of the agreement prior to the formation of a new government, or of the convening of the National Dialogue Conference.

With the fall of West Beirut to the opposition, the MNF became even more exposed than before, and pressure mounted to withdraw the forces. On 8 February, as I was driving north to Jounieh, I encountered the small British contingent in the MNF moving north too. I stopped, asked for the colonel in charge and enquired what they were doing. The colonel replied that his men were not leaving, but had received orders to redeploy aboard a British warship. I then contacted the British ambassador, who informed me that a military order had been issued to get British forces out from the chaos of Beirut.

The Eight-Point Formula

I called Saud al-Faisal and Rafiq al-Hariri and informed them of the serious consequences to the take-over of Beirut by militia leaders. Saud urged me to come to Riyad, and Hariri sent his plane to wait for me in Larnaca, Cyprus. Saud, Hariri and I met late in the evening of 8 February, and examined all our options. From this encounter, we came out with an eight-point formula:

1. Implement the security plan.
2. Cancel the Lebanese–Israeli withdrawal agreement.

3. Work out security arrangements in the South under which Israel would withdraw fully from Lebanon.
4. Introduce political reforms.
5. Reach an agreement with Syria on the withdrawal of its forces from Lebanon.
6. Adopt the principle of a simultaneous withdrawal of all foreign forces from Lebanon in a period not exceeding three months after reaching agreement on the withdrawal of Israel from South Lebanon.
7. The formula is to be considered a package deal; Syria will commit itself to implementing those sections relating to it, and to help in the implementation of the other sections. Saudi Arabia will commit itself to help in the implementation of the formula.
8. Form a Government of National Unity to implement the Eight-Point Formula.

The eight points were easy to formulate on paper. Unfortunately they involved many parties, each with its own agenda. What was equally disturbing was that Rumsfeld told us that he would not help us in bringing the Israelis around to the Eight-Point Formula.

On the ground, conflicting agendas were pushing the Lebanese even further apart. While Birri was tightening his grip on West Beirut, Junblat was expanding towards the sea. At that critical moment, Israel sent a message through one of the President's Lebanese friends, that if the president would meet publicly with Israeli defence minister Moshe Arens and ask for help, Israel would help the president in controlling a specified enclave. He had a map to prove it. The proposal was dismissed out of hand. At best such a proposal meant partition. It would have represented a total reversal of government policy.

On 10 February, Washington announced that it would withdraw its Marines from Beirut within 30 days. This decision conflicted with promises given to us by Rumsfeld and Bartholomew, and both were embarrassed by the reversal of policy. I urged the president to accept the Eight-Point Formula. He was very much inclined to do so. At the same time, Hariri met with the Sunni mufti of the republic, Sheikh Hassan Khaled, with the vice-president of the Supreme Shi'ah Council, Sheikh Muhammad Mahdi Shamseddine, with Nabih Birri, and with Beirut Sunni leaders, soliciting their support for the Eight-Point Formula. The Muslims were not opposed to it. Rumsfeld and Bartholomew promised to consult Shultz on the matter.

Before sending a letter to King Fahd informing him of his acceptance of the Eight-Point Formula, the president wanted assurances from the United States that his acceptance of the formula would not lead Israel to retaliate against Lebanon. Rumsfeld and Bartholomew, however, were not willing to give these assurances. Instead they repeatedly told us that the decision to cancel the agreement was a Lebanese decision, and Lebanon must assume responsibility for the consequences of its decision.

I told the Americans that if their policy was to support Lebanon, then they could see that unless the agreement was cancelled, Lebanon would have no way out of its current predicament. Bartholomew consulted with his superiors in Washington repeatedly, and finally came back with the following response: 'We understand why you are taking the decision on the Eight-Point Formula. It is important for you to keep Saudi Arabia engaged. We will continue our support to you.'

We were satisfied with the response. Armed with this policy line, I met former president Kamil Sham'un and convinced him to go along with the formula. Having convinced Sham'un, I spent virtually hours trying to do the same with Sheikh Pierre Jumayyil. Sheikh Pierre finally consented, but urged that someone should consult with Israel. It took another battle to ensure that he would not make this a *sine qua non* for accepting the formula. The Kata'ib leader was worried about the cancellation of the agreement, and consented to it reluctantly. He feared Israeli retaliation.

At that stage, the president prepared a letter which he sent to King Fahd, accepting the Eight-Point Formula. I delivered the letter by hand to Saud al-Faisal on Thursday 16 February. Saud then called Khaddam and told him that he had a proposal which he believed would help resolve the crisis. Khaddam listened to Saud and he read the formula and asked for time to reflect. He called back four hours later and invited Saud and Hariri to Damascus the following day.

On Sunday 19 February, Hariri called me from Damascus to report that the Syrians had agreed to go ahead with the Eight-Point Formula. However, they made this conditional on striking out points 5 and 6, which dealt with a Syrian withdrawal. Syria did not want to be referred to in any arrangement involving Israel. If these two points were eliminated, repeated Hariri, Asad would back President Jumayyil's efforts to reconvene the conference and form a Government of National Unity.

As we negotiated on the Eight-Point Formula fighting was going on unabated on the Suq al-Gharb, Bikfayya, and Kfarshima fronts. These villages became part of the negotiation process. Our intelligence people were telling us that the army might collapse at any time. Sunni officers, fearing for their families in areas under opposition control, were deserting the fronts in droves. Since Shi'ah and Druze officers had already deserted, there was a fear that only Christian officers would remain, thus diminishing the representativeness of the army. A political solution to this problem had to be found, and fast.

Hariri was calling regularly to find out about the fate of the Eight-Point Formula. I asked him to come to Beirut so that we could work together on implementing those parts of the formula which could be implemented, and thus start a process. He arrived on 20 February with a message from Saud. The message stated that Hariri was authorized to discuss the following points with us. They were points taken out of the Eight-Point Formula and listed in a certain order: reconvene the National Dialogue Conference; prior commitment from President Jumayyil to King Fahd that he would cancel the agreement during the National Dialogue Conference; the formation of a Government of National Unity; and the adoption of political reforms.

Riyad seemed to have taken over Washington's role as sponsor of a solution to the Lebanese crisis. Now initiatives were coming from Riyad and Washington was reacting. We accepted Saud's message even before consulting with anyone. Crown Prince Abdallah and Bandar delivered our acceptance to Asad. On 22 February, Hariri returned to Beirut with the following Syrian proposal which Asad had made in the form of a commitment to Crown Prince Abdallah: President Jumayyil would give Hariri a written unsigned statement in which Jumayyil would state that he would take constitutional steps to cancel the agreement immediately after his return from a state visit to Syria. Upon receiving the statement Asad would extend an invitation to Jumayyil to come to Damascus. After the abrogation was announced, Asad would help Jumayyil form a Government of National Unity and would speed up the convening of the National Dialogue Conference.

On 23 February, President Jumayyil called in Kamil Sham'un and Sheikh Pierre to seek their public support for the decision that he had already taken to abrogate the agreement. They agreed, but they wanted assurances from the USA that Lebanon would not be endangered as a result. Meanwhile, Hariri and I worked out in a side office on the text which the president would send Asad. When we finished, I called Bartholomew to the presidential palace and informed him, in the president's presence, that we had taken the following decisions: we would cancel the agreement; we were sending an unsigned text to Asad to that effect, and on that basis, we had a commitment from Asad to help us in forming a Government of National Unity and in reconvening the National Dialogue Conference to complete the work started at Geneva. The agenda of the conference would include reforms, the withdrawal of Israeli forces, and the withdrawal of all non-Lebanese armed forces from Lebanon. We had taken this decision after considering all other options, I continued. This we did in the best interest of Lebanon, and we were now seeking American support for our decisions.

Bartholomew responded that this was a Lebanese decision, and that therefore we had to assume responsibility for it. The United States would continue to support the government of Lebanon. The president insisted on hearing from Bartholomew a statement to the effect that the United States understood Lebanon's decision to abrogate the agreement. Bartholomew replied that he could not do this without first consulting with Washington. The following day he told us that he had done so and that 'Washington understood Lebanon's decision to abrogate the agreement. The USA will continue to support the government of Lebanon in securing the independence, unity, and sovereignty of Lebanon.'

Hariri and I completed the text of the letter Jumayyil was to send to Asad in the light of the Syrian–Saudi request. Jumayyil added the following passage to our draft: 'Lebanon expects to receive from Syria the support necessary to fortify its decision to abrogate the agreement against the pressures and actions that are likely to result from this act ...'

As he held the text, I realized that of all the difficult decisions the president had taken, the decision to abrogate the agreement was by far the most difficult. He had worked hard to obtain this agreement, and he was now taking a step in the dark. If he failed, Israel and Syria might remain in Lebanon, and the country would stay divided. To others, whether to accept the agreement or to cancel it was a political stand. To the president, it concerned the fate of the country, and perhaps his fate too. I understood what was going on in the president's mind: he probably wondered where was the superpower that had counselled and supported him? Where were the leaders of all the MNF countries who had risked a lot to deploy their forces in Lebanon? Where were the Lebanese leaders who had stood by the agreement in the past? Where were the 'brotherly' and 'sisterly' states of that nebulous amalgam known as the League of Arab States? They had all backed him when he was strong, and they had all changed their minds when he became weak! The president held the text as if he did not want to part with it. I said:

> Mr President, you are taking the right decision; I can testify to that. I know the facts. St Augustine defined freedom as the compulsion to accept Christ. As president your freedom lies in the compulsion to accept the facts. You have many bad options, and the one you are taking, given the facts, is the least harmful to Lebanon; please let me have the text.

I extended my arm and literally extracted it from his hand, before giving it to Hariri to pass on to Asad. The president did not respond; he was not listening, he was wondering whether there was light at the end of this new tunnel. Hariri, the master of the art of the deal, bolted out of the office, and drove to Damascus with John Ubayd. He carried the letter he wanted.

In the meantime, Bandar called from Damascus to find out what our decision was; I told him that the president had agreed to send the text to Asad, and that Hariri would soon be in Damascus to pass it on to the Syrians. Ubayd returned next morning and told us that the Syrians were satisfied with the text. They wished to know, however, what the president meant by 'Lebanon expects to receive from Syria the support necessary to fortify the decision to abrogate the agreement, etc.' By this statement, we wrote back, we meant we needed Syrian political support to face the opposition which would arise from announcing the abrogation of the agreement. We expected opposition from Israel and from forces influenced by it internally and internationally. Those who opposed the agreement were shelling the presidential palace and its surroundings. Fighting in one place starts fighting in another and the whole country was in turmoil. We were warned by some Christian Lebanese leaders – lay and clerical – that if we cancelled the agreement they too would shell us.

We were receiving intelligence reports that if we cancelled the agreement Israel might assassinate the president, the prime minister and the foreign minister. These reports could have been fabricated but we could not take a chance. There were also Israeli messages sent through emissaries threatening the unity of Lebanon were we to cancel the agreement and side with Syria. I asked Bartholomew to contact the Israelis to verify these rumours, and to inform them that our decision was made in the higher interests of Lebanon, and that it had the 'understanding of the United States'. I also asked him to inform the extremists in the Christian community of the American position on abrogation. These extremists thought we were acting alone and that the USA would encourage Israel to retaliate against Lebanon.

The most significant internal opposition to cancellation of the agreement came from the president's father, his family, the Kata'ib Party, the Lebanese Forces and the Maronite community. While Sheikh Pierre and Kamil Sham'un reluctantly approved of our policies, their displeasure was obvious, and they voiced it on all occasions. They were seriously concerned about the future of Lebanon without Israeli acquiescence and American support. Some members in the Lebanese Forces, who were pro-Israelis, accused me personally of engineering the abrogation, and I received appropriate messages from them. But the agreement, in my opinion, was already dead. The Israeli–Syrian linkage had paralysed it, and the environment that brought it about in May 1983 had radically changed in the winter of 1983. We could not get Syrian approval for it. Israel had acted independently of it and the USA had failed to deliver. The consensus behind it had collapsed. In cancelling it we were, in effect, burying a corpse. And it is true that, once I realized the agreement had become a problem, I took the lead in the president's circle to abrogate it. It was not a bad agreement; it may perhaps go down in history as the best agreement signed between Arabs and Israelis to get Israel out from Arab territory, not to mention getting it out from the very capital of an Arab country. But history is impervious to good and bad.

It was agreed with the Syrians that the Jumayyil–Asad summit would take place on Wednesday 29 February. The Wazzan government would abrogate the agreement after the president's return from Damascus. Then the National Dialogue Conference would convene, and this would be followed by the formation of a Government of National Unity.

We worked hard to prepare the Jumayyil–Asad summit. The president was going to Damascus as the defeated party, and yet he hoped to snatch a victory from defeat. With Syrian assistance, he hoped to restore a national consensus in Lebanon, bring about a halt to the fighting, and form a Government of National Unity. The country had been for months with no government except in name.

John Ubayd, General Uthman Uthman, the commander of the internal security forces, and I accompanied the president to Damascus. We went by motorcade from Ba'bda, through the heart of the Maronite area, to the Halat airstrip. The president wanted to show that he was not intimidated by the extremists in the Maronite community who were unhappy with his visit to Damascus. He and I rode separately in two identical cars. Once I realized the decoy character of the honour I hoped for speedy delivery. A ride in the tiny plane that flies from the airstrip at Halat seemed far more secure. We were received at the Mazzeh Airport in Damascus by Asad, members of the Syrian government, and members of the Arab diplomatic corps. President Jumayyil was received with pomp and circumstance, and after the ceremony a motorcade took us to the guest palace where the two presidents exchanged pleasantries. The irony of the event was lost on nobody. The young president had tried a course independent of Asad and failed. Now he wanted to be Asad's friend, but he did not know how far Asad was willing to befriend him. Each had his own agenda and sought a special benefit for himself from this rapprochement. Asad held a dinner in honour of President Jumayyil attended by about 300 people. With the exception of Najah al-Attar, a member of the Syrian government, and the sister of a Muslim Brotherhood leader vehemently opposed to the regime, there were no women among the guests. The guests who included all the ambassadors accredited to Damascus waited three hours for the two presidents to walk in. This evening confirmed my opinion of ambassadorship as I expressed it in my first meeting with the president. Poor ambassadors – how many burdens they must bear to meet the merciless compulsion of protocol. It struck me during the meal that the only relaxed group in this large gathering was the one that included President Asad, Ubayd and myself. I attributed this to Ubayd, who was a great instigator, a gifted raconteur and a master of the apt utterance. As I looked at my shoes and found them dirty, I said to Ubayd and Asad, 'Sorry, I should have polished my shoes.' Ubayd responded to Asad's roaring laughter, 'He who negotiates with Asad must polish his thoughts, not his shoes.' Asad kept urging Ubayd to recount the anecdote, and Ubayd obliged with the appropriate embellishments. The guests sat at separate tables, serene and quiet, their eyes fixed on Asad, whom they rarely met in person.

On Thursday 1 March, the two presidents met in the company of Khaddam, Ubayd and myself. In these meetings the Lebanese position, as expressed by President Jumayyil, was the following. We wanted to abrogate the agreement, and cooperate with Syria to reduce the dangers arising from the abrogation. We needed Syrian help in holding the National Dialogue Conference and in forming a Government of National Unity. We needed an effective ceasefire. Following the abrogation of the agreement, we needed a formula which would lead to negotiations with Israel through the United States, with the intention of working out security arrangements that would guarantee a full Israeli withdrawal from Lebanon. We wanted the Syrian army to be redeployed to specified areas within Lebanon as a first step towards a full withdrawal. We wanted the Syrian government to invite Christian leaders, especially those who opposed abrogation of the agreement, to come to Damascus and start a dialogue with them. We would continue our friendship with the United States as Syria would continue its relations with the Soviet Union. We continued to believe that the United States was a superpower ready to help us in our efforts to liberate our country.

Asad appreciated our decision to abrogate the agreement. The agreement was dead anyhow, he said, and neither Israel nor the United States had much faith in it any more. By saying that, I felt, Asad did not consider the abrogation to be a great or a generous act that must be rewarded. If something is dead, you bury it; burying the dead is not an achievement that should be rewarded. We might get thanks for conducting the burial ceremony – someone had to do it – but there would be no rewards. Asad stated Syria's position that the abrogation must precede any national reconciliation dialogue and the formation of a new government. The new government, he said, should be headed by Rashid Karami, who was experienced and a good conciliator. Asad added that the Lebanese opposition would refuse to join a new government unless there was prior agreement on certain principles of political reform. Asad promised, however, to talk to the opposition leaders to encourage them to help implement a ceasefire and to join a new government committed to specific reform items.

Asad then defined for us what he meant by security arrangements with Israel. Security arrangements should be understood to mean arrangements undertaken by the Lebanese government on its own territory and agreed to by Israel. These arrangements should not compromise Lebanese sovereignty. Syria would support Lebanon in rebuilding its institutions after agreement on a fair political formula was reached. He told us that the three presidencies agreed upon in the National Pact of 1943 would remain unchanged: the presidency of the republic would remain in the hands of the Maronites; the presidency of the parliament would remain with the Shi'ah; and the presidency of the council of ministers would remain in the hands of the Sunnis. The redeployment of the Syrian army in Lebanon would be discussed with the Government of National Unity. Such a redeployment would take place in the context of Syrian strategic considerations in its struggle with Israel and the United States. This meant, he continued, that Israel must withdraw first because its presence in Lebanon threatens Syria's national security. We agreed to go ahead first with the conference, complete the reform which included virtually every issue and affected foreign policy as well, and then form a strong government to put them into effect.

The Wazzan government would be legally reinstated and would itself cancel the agreement. This decision would then be sent to parliament. On Friday 2 March, Lebanon would send a message to the United States asking it to convene the Joint Liaison Committee of Lebanon, Israel and the United States, so that it may discuss the abrogation of the agreement, and launch a new round of discussions leading to security arrangements. The National Dialogue Conference would be convened in the middle of the following week, and a Government of National Unity would be formed after the conference.

We finished our meetings in Damascus in the late afternoon of 1 March, and departed from Syria amid the same pomp and circumstance as had greeted our arrival. Security on the road travelled by the motorcade was unusually tight due to the behind-the-scenes struggle for power. The car carrying the two presidents was surrounded by dozens of motorcycles and by about a hundred bodyguards armed with machine-guns. Absolutely no cars, other than those in the motorcade, were permitted on the road we travelled. I had encountered many types of security in the past months but this was unequalled. By the time we left Damascus, it was getting too dark to land at the Halat airstrip, so the president decided instead to fly to Rhodes. He invited us all to dinner at a cosy restaurant named Alexis, which was famous for its seafood. Diners recognized the president, cheered him, and joined us for drinks. Despite the fact that the unscheduled stopover raised speculation as to our whereabouts, we were happy to enjoy this all too brief respite on an island. Are islands always so peaceful?

Upon our arrival in Beirut the following day, I called Bartholomew and handed him a letter asking the United States to call for a meeting of the Joint Liaison Committee on 3 or 4 March. I wrote that my request was, 'in accordance with my letter to ambassador Philip Habib, President Reagan's Special Envoy, dated May 17, 1983', and was intended 'to discuss the abrogation of the agreement and to start fresh discussions leading to security arrangements'.

Bartholomew, whose face often betrayed his thoughts, smiled. He took the letter and said he would convey it to Washington. The USA, it seemed to me from his smile, was ready to 'understand' our course of action, but this need not be translated into 'readiness' to facilitate that course. After all, the USA was not a friend of Syria. It considered Syria a Soviet client, and worse still, a terrorist country; and some in Washington suspected Syria's strong hand behind the 'massacre' of the American Marines. The 'massacre' was a blow to Reagan; the man 'without the reverse gear' was not about to reward Asad. I also asked Colonel Simon Qassis to contact the Israelis through ILMAC and inform them of the proposed meeting. The following day, Bartholomew informed me that the United States would not attend the proposed meeting of the Joint Liaison Committee. Soon after that Colonel Qassis told me that Israel would not attend unless there was prior agreement on an agenda. Clearly Israel and the USA were not elated about our new course, and although the agreement called for immediate consultation through the Joint Liaison Committee whenever an issue of importance affecting the agreement was raised, they had no intention of adhering to the formalities. They too may have thought of the agreement as dead, so why honour its stipulations?

To avoid misunderstanding at this critical stage, I wanted to consult Khaddam on the text of the statement abrogating the agreement. I had worked on the text with the help of Nasri Ma'luf, a prominent deputy, a brilliant lawyer, and one of Lebanon's most experienced political leaders. John Ubayd and I reviewed the text a number of times, and when we were satisfied we called Khaddam and agreed to meet in Damascus on Sunday 4 March.

Early on Sunday morning, Ubayd and I boarded our helicopter for Syria. As we flew over the mountains, we found ourselves all of a sudden engulfed by clouds in all directions. Our helicopter pilots were not trained to fly at night or in clouds, and so I instructed the pilot to return immediately to base. The pilot was nervous too, but said that he could not change course because he was uncertain of the terrain below us. There was a tense silence for a few minutes, until a break in the clouds allowed the pilot to take his bearings. We swiftly returned to base, and decided to go by road to Damascus instead.

We went straight to Khaddam's office and discussed our proposed text. After extensive discussions, Khaddam said he needed to consult the Syrian leadership. Reference to 'the leadership' was common in Syrian diplomacy, and meant different things on different occasions. It could mean a meeting of the leadership of the Ba'th party, discussions between the three or four top officials in charge of the Lebanese question, or a telephone call to President Asad. While Khaddam consulted, Ubayd and I returned to the hotel for a rest. Instead, however, we had an unplanned and cordial meeting with leaders of the opposition, Walid Junblat, Nabih Birri and Asim Qansu, the head of the Lebanese Ba'th Party. They had all been shelling us mercilessly for the past few months, but the kisses and hugs we exchanged were almost surreal in their friendliness. They too were anxious about the new beginning – what would be discussed in the conference, would its membership change, when would the new government be formed, who would be in it? The discussion, though outwardly jovial, was cautious.

We then returned to Khaddam's office. After further talks, Khaddam, Ubayd and I agreed to the following text:

The Council of Ministers, taking into account articles 56 and 57 of the Lebanese Constitution which commit the president of the republic to promulgate a law passed by parliament during a specified period, or to return it; and whereas the president of the republic did not promulgate the law which the parliament authorized him to promulgate on 14 June 1983; and whereas the parliament has in that law accepted the agreement signed by representatives of the Lebanese government and of the Israeli government and by the United States, in its capacity as a witness to the agreement; and whereas the president of the republic did not return the law to parliament within the specified period; the Council of Ministers has, therefore, decided, in its meeting held on 5 March 1984, under the chairmanship of the president of the republic, the following:

1. The cancellation of the decision of the Council of Ministers dated 14 May 1983, approving the agreement referred to above and which was signed on 17 May 1983, by the representatives of the governments of Lebanon, Israel, and the United States in its capacity as witness; and the cancellation of the unratified agreement considering it null and void and as if it never existed; and the cancellation of all the obligations deriving therefrom.

2. The communication of this decision to the parties to the agreement.

3. The government of Lebanon will take the necessary steps in reaching security arrangements which guarantee the sovereignty of Lebanon and

the stability and security of South Lebanon, which will prevent the
infiltration across the southern frontiers, and which will lead to the
withdrawal of the Israeli forces from all the Lebanese territory.

Article 3 was the product of intensive discussion between Khaddam and
me. I wanted a language that we could use with the Americans and the
Israelis to start a process leading to withdrawal on the basis of new
security arrangements. Ubayd played an important role in bridging the
chasm between Khaddam and me on this point. This article became the
basis of a new policy and was incorporated in the ministerial statement
of the future government formed by Rashid Karami.

We returned to Beirut that evening and showed the text to the president
and the prime minister, who expressed satisfaction with it. We agreed to
hold a meeting of the council of ministers the following day to adopt the
proposed text. I called the ministers individually, and told them that the
Wazzan government had been reactivated for today to take an important
decision. Muslim members who had resigned and who were nervous about
coming to Ba'bda and meeting the president wanted to know in great
detail why they were invited, what went on in Damascus 'and are you
sure it is okay for us to meet?' 'Yes,' I told them, 'you are good enough
for three hours.' They all came.

At this time, Claude Cheysson was in Beirut for a brief visit, and he
came to my house to express his support for the step we were about to
take. Cheysson said that France was ready to help should Lebanon face
new dangers from Israel as a result of the abrogation. He had just met
with Shamir, and Shamir had promised him that Israel would not be
vindictive. Lebanon, Shamir said, was weak and divided and had no good
options.

On Monday 5 March, Wazzan and the Cabinet ministers arrived at the
presidential palace at 9.30 a.m. Jumayyil, Wazzan and Dr Joseph Jreissati,
the director-general of the presidency of the republic, worked on a legal
formulation to allow the government to convene as a council of ministers.
It was a terrible meeting; everything went wrong. Every statement was
misinterpreted or misunderstood, and virtually everyone was in a bad
mood. The president had had a bad night as pressure on him from his
immediate family and from the Maronite community had reached a
crescendo. Wazzan was furious at ministers who asked questions as if
they had never been members of the government. For example, one asked:
'Why did we sign an agreement which we had to abrogate?' Wazzan
exploded: 'Where do you come from, the moon?' Another asked if we
were to sign a similar agreement with Syria. Again Wazzan screamed:
'Have you just returned from China?' The decision to abrogate was taken

unanimously at noon, and announced publicly at 4 p.m. Immediately after it was made public, Asad called Jumayyil to congratulate him on his courage, and promised him full support in the future.

The next step was to prepare for reconvening the National Dialogue Conference, this time in Lausanne, Switzerland on Monday 12 March. The president wanted to give a historic speech at the opening of the conference and wanted Dr Charles Malik to prepare it. Malik was one of Lebanon's pre-eminent thinkers and statesmen. He was also unpredictable. Though a Greek Orthodox, Malik had become one of the more hard-line members of the Lebanese Front. President Jumayyil did not get along very well with Malik, in part because they did not see eye to eye politically. The president nevertheless respected Malik's brilliance, and he asked me to approach Malik on the subject of the speech and to offer him an honorarium worthy of his stature.

When I discussed the proposal with Malik, he responded that the decision was not an easy one. If the president's speech was to be historic, then the decision to write it was itself historic. Therefore, he could not take the decision alone; he needed first to consult Christ, and for that he wanted to be left alone for one hour to pray. I knew Malik well, but he always managed to surprise me. However, I was sure he would accept. I was to be disappointed: Christ had apparently vetoed the idea. Malik felt that he could not write the speech because he had not been directly involved in the government, nor was he familiar with the fundamental issues with which the government was grappling. Besides, Lausanne was not so historic an occasion as to require his participation. Most likely Malik, like the hard-line Christian right, was not pleased with the rapprochement with Syria. Malik also felt that Jumayyil did not appreciate him enough and did not seek his counsel before. Malik was close to Bashir and was his intellectual mentor and was not enamoured of Amin. Amin knew that and kept Malik at a distance.

We tried to broaden representation at the conference to include representatives from the Greek Orthodox, the Greek Catholic and the Armenian communities. I called Khaddam on this matter, as the names of the participants in the Geneva conference had been reached after a long and delicate diplomatic process involving the Saudis and Syrians. Khaddam had no objection to the inclusion of other representatives, if the opposition did not. Still, it was a Catch-22: the opposition was an amorphous grouping, some members of whom would agree with the move, others of whom would disagree. In the end the opposition would refer us back to Khaddam to take the final decision. Accordingly, it was agreed that to avoid further delays, the participants at the Lausanne conference would be limited to those who had participated in the Geneva conference.

The Lausanne Conference

President Jumayyil and I arrived in Lausanne on Sunday 11 March, one day before the opening of the National Dialogue Conference at the Beaurivage Hotel. Upon my arrival in Lausanne, the Syrian ambassador to the United Nations in Geneva, Adib al-Dawudi, called me to say that Khaddam had just been appointed vice-president for political affairs. This necessitated new protocol arrangements. The Swiss, who were good at that sort of thing, were quite helpful. They recommended that Dawudi and I get together, and then together with a Swiss protocol officer we would welcome Khaddam as he entered the hotel. We did this, and as I congratulated Khaddam on his new title, he joked that his only regret was that he could no longer battle with me as foreign minister.

International interest in the Lausanne conference was high. Claude Cheysson, Geoffrey Howe and George Shultz sent special representatives to observe the proceedings and to influence them. Mubarak sent a representative to help us with the Sunni participants, while the Italian prime minister Bettino Craxi dispatched a former ambassador to Lebanon to help deal with Walid Junblat. As members of the Socialist International, Junblat and Craxi were friends. But Junblat was a maverick, like his father, and no one could really influence him. Also like his father he had become a tough and brilliant manipulator of men and events. His idiosyncrasies added to his mystery, and his mystery added to his power. At the Geneva conference, he had brought along a camera to take photographs of the ageing participants. 'This is a rare occasion to have them all in one place,' he declared, 'soon they will become museum pieces.'

The president held a banquet for Khaddam on the occasion of his appointment as vice-president. All the participants, their wives, and their aides were invited. Although peace had not yet been made, they all had to walk in one door, shake hands with the host, and then move to their assigned tables. It was hilarious to see the president and his opponents kissing and hugging in the traditional Lebanese manner of greeting. Junblat, whom I knew well from university days, told me that he had not really kissed Jumayyil, because when he embraced he had been thinking of someone else. Birri told me that the president had hugged him so hard, maybe he thought he was a woman, and that he had run to the mirror to see if he had been transformed.

All the participants were in relatively good humour at the banquet, since they knew that a Government of National Unity would be formed and that they would all be in it. The war had created entrenched enmities, however, that could not be made to evaporate at a mere banquet. Former president Franjiyyeh detested Sheikh Pierre Jumayyil. Junblat and Birri accused the president of using the army against them and of giving cover to the Lebanese Forces. Sa'ib Salam, as a conservative elder statesman, was not enamoured of the new leadership, which was challenging him in Beirut. Even Birri and Junblat, who were outwardly allies, had had their conflicts, and were suspicious of one another. Junblat feared Shi'ah expansion into the Druze mountain, while Birri feared Druze political clout in Beirut.

Tension seemed to be as high in Lausanne as it had been in Geneva. The discussions during the conference were, however, long rambling discourses on such topics as political reforms, security and relations between Lebanon and its neighbours. Many a participant presented a paper on these issues. One of the top issues under reforms was the fate of political confessionalism that had governed Lebanon at least since the Mutasarrifiyyah system in the 1860s. It turned out to be as difficult as any other important issue. And all issues were subject to the spirit of conflict permeating politics on the ground in Lebanon.

I had a long session with Nabih Birri, the strongest supporter of deconfessionalization, in the presence of Hariri and Abdu. Birri wanted to abolish political confessionalism by decree. The only decision he wanted from the conference, he said, was to abolish confessionalism. After much discussion, Birri finally agreed that what we needed to do now was accept the principle of deconfessionalization. The process itself, he said, would take time and must be attained in stages. Birri did not want to return to his community and merely tell them that he had managed to get the Shi'ah this or that cabinet post; he wanted to return with a principle in hand; a principle that the Lebanese were equal, and that confessionalism was on its way out. Birri was a politician, however, and while fighting for this principle, he was also fighting for gains within the existing formula.

The Lausanne conference met under conditions not much better than those that prevailed in Geneva. Fighting in Beirut between the opposition and the government, and amongst militias themselves, was erupting now and then and souring the atmosphere. The participants discussed security problems in Beirut as much as they did the subcommittee's recommendation on reforms. In this heated atmosphere Sham'un proposed the establishment of a 'Federal Lebanese Republic', which Franjiyyeh and Karami opposed vehemently. Junblat proposed we call Lebanon 'The Arab Republic of Lebanon'. Franjiyyeh said that federalism would bring about a new devil – Israel – in addition to the American devil. Birri argued that the Sham'un proposal was more confederal than federal, and that both were objectionable. Franjiyyeh wanted to know if Israel was an enemy or not.' Birri accused Jumayyil of shelling the Shi'i suburb of Beirut. Junblat accused the president of shelling the Shuf region.

Khaddam implored the participants to rise to the level of the crisis and to talk sense. 'Syria', he said, 'is a small country but it acts big; so did Lebanon before 1975.'He urged them to 'act big'. As all participants had submitted reform proposals at this conference or in Geneva, each urged that his paper be used as a basis for discussion. Sham'un then proposed that Lebanon be a secular state 'in everything'. Karami answered: 'We accept in everything except in those things that contradict Islam.'

By 19 March the conferees were still debating without reaching an agreement. To facilitate matters the president asked me to meet Marwan Himadeh, an adviser to Walid Junblat, and to rewrite a paper prepared by Khaddam so that it would be acceptable to all. Himadeh and I read it carefully and made very extensive changes in it. Himadeh understood the opposition well. He was one of its leading members. He also understood Damascus and its concerns. I knew the president well, and was generally acquainted with the position of the Christian leaders.

I submitted the edited document to the president so that he could submit it to the conference as representing general consensus. This I called the Lausanne Document; its main headings were as follows.

- Lebanon's identity as an independent and sovereign state exactly as agreed upon in the Geneva conference.
- The conference adopts the decision taken by the Council of Ministers on 5 March 1984, cancelling the May 17 agreement.
- The government of Lebanon will make the necessary security arrangements in the south that will ensure Lebanese sovereignty, prevent infiltration across its southern frontiers, and lead to Israeli withdrawal from all Lebanese territory.
- The conference calls for an increase of the personnel of UNIFIL to improve its effectiveness.
- A new government of National Unity will appoint a constituent assembly with representatives from the various groupings to prepare a draft constitution for new Lebanon. Until this group submits its recommendations within a year, the following reforms will be implemented:
- Confessionalism will be abolished in all administrative posts except the posts of grade I (i.e. director-generals and their equivalent) which will be divided equally between Christians and Muslims.
- Taking into account the powers granted to the president in the constitution, the Council of Ministers is considered the highest political-administrative authority in the country. It sets the general policy of the state in all fields, it prepares draft laws, it supervises the institutions of state, it appoints grade I officers, it determines a state of emergency, etc.

- The parliament elects the prime minister. The prime minister-elect and the president together form the government.
- The prime minister shall have all the powers which he has exercised (although these powers are not written in the Constitution).
- The speaker of parliament will be elected for a two-year term.
- The parliament shall consist of 120 deputies divided equally between Christians and Muslims.
- A higher court to try presidents and ministers will be formed.
- A constitutional council to supervise the constitutionality of laws and the propriety of parliamentary elections will be instituted.
- A social and economic council will be formed.
- Administrative decentralization is to be enhanced and rendered more effective.
- Preserving the free enterprise system, realizing social and economic justice, and developing those regions that have been neglected.
- Dissolving the militias.
- Strengthening the security forces.
- The return of all the Lebanese who have been displaced since 1975.
- Restoring normalcy in the services provided by the state and facilitating communication between one sector of the country and another.
- Upon the completion of the conference a Government of National Unity will be formed to implement the reforms listed in the document.

The Lausanne Document was submitted by the president to the conference on Monday 19 March. Franjiyyeh attacked it on the grounds that it limited the powers of the president by transferring, in effect, executive authority from the president to the council of ministers. Franjiyyeh's position was challenged by ex-prime ministers Rashid Karami and Sa'ib Salam, and also by all members of the opposition who were in alliance with Mr Franjiyyeh, it seems on all matters, except the powers of the president of the republic. On this issue Franjiyyeh remained the quintessential Maronite. The discussion on the Lausanne Document deteriorated hopelessly and the president, realizing that the document was in trouble, adjourned the meeting. The delegates dispersed, each laying the blame on the other.

By that time, it was midnight. Khaddam despaired and went to bed. I was sound asleep also when the president called to tell me that the conference had failed and that the representatives could not agree on the document. I came to his suite and found him in despair. He urged me to get hold of Hariri and together seek the help of Vice-President Khaddam, to rescue some positions from the conference on which we could build when we return to Beirut. Hariri and I went to Khaddam's suite and woke him up in search of a way to salvage the conference. He was tired and counselled sleep. He told me to go talk to Franjiyyeh; 'Do not attempt to talk to the Sunnis and the Druze,' he said; 'they respect you, just leave it at that. I will try to talk to them, but frankly, I do not want to put more pressure on them than I already have.' No matter what happened, he concluded, he was leaving at noon the following day.

I went back to the president's suite, where he and Johnny Abdu were chatting. In total resignation we drank cognac, and fell asleep on our chairs. Early in the morning, Franjiyyeh saw Khaddam and told him that under no condition should the powers of the president be reduced. He added that he would see Asad on the matter. This was not well received by Khaddam, and he hurried back to Damascus. Birri and Junblat were also packing as they preferred the conference to fail than to come out with a statement that did not meet their expectations.

As I later reflected on the reasons for the failure of the Lausanne conference, I concluded that each of the participants had been largely pulling in his direction and guarding his parochial interests. Lebanon the state, the society, the shared experience, was hardly represented. The Christian right, which was close to the president, was drifting more to the right in this tense moment and making it more difficult for the president to move. The Muslims, for the moment, were on top. But they were not united, and each had his own desiderata.

Just before the conference adjourned on the 20th, two decisions were taken, as if to save face. They seemed important but every participant knew they were of no value as they were subject to developments on the ground in Beirut. These decisions were to form a security committee in which the warring militias were represented to supervise a ceasefire. To give it the semblance of importance, the security committee was to be chaired by the president of the republic. The second decision, which was in effect a decision to delay action on reforms, was to establish a committee of leading personalities to start working on a new constitution. Khaddam told me that the participants in the conference were useless, and most did not represent the new Lebanon. He thought it would be better to get Birri, Junblat and the Lebanese Forces together in some sort of dialogue, and arrive at a general arrangement through Lebanon's younger warlords. 'This is the way I see it,' concluded Khaddam, 'and I shall recommend this course of action to President Asad.' This was to lead a year later to the Tripartite Agreement.

Post-Lausanne Problems

On Wednesday 21 March, the participants left Lausanne for the unknown. Fighting had already erupted in West Beirut between Amal and the PSP on one side, and the Sunni Muslim Murabitun militia on the other. The fighting showed the extent to which the balance of power in the Muslim areas of the capital had shifted away from the Sunnis to the Shi'ah and the Druze. The Israelis, meanwhile, were sending messages that they would redeploy their forces in South Lebanon according to Israeli national interests. They also announced that they planned to organize a new surrogate army in South Lebanon under General Antoine Lahd, who had replaced the late S'ad Haddad as Israel's man in the area. The new South Lebanon army would consist of about 4,000 men recruited from those parts of Lebanon under Israeli control.

The Americans were increasingly displeased with the turn of events. They were concerned about growing Syrian influence in Lebanon, and about Soviet influence in the region. Bartholomew informed me that the United States would be withdrawing its contingent from the MNF within a week. The USA, Bartholomew said, had failed in Lebanon largely because there was no handle to grab on to. He also told me that there would no longer be a special envoy for Lebanon, and that Rumsfeld would instead be reappointed special envoy for the Middle East Peace Process. The American embassy would take over Rumsfeld's tasks as far as Lebanese affairs were concerned, but Rumsfeld might visit Lebanon in the future if such visits could contribute to the peace process.

Bartholomew's announcement brought to mind something Rumsfeld had told me earlier:

> Elie, we cannot be of great help to you. You know in American football there are the blockers and there are the dancers; the blockers are the big heavy guys who by sheer strength open holes in the defence. The dancers, however, are the light guys who carry the ball and run, and who move in and out of the defence with great agility. America in international politics is a blocker. We are best in handling big problems. You are a small country with small and complex problems. Your alleys, allegorically, are too small for us. You need dancers.

He did not elaborate. I took it as an honest attempt at self-criticism, as well as a critique of Lebanon's inability to get out from the web of conflicts it had created for itself or allowed to develop because of inaction.

America had decided to go low-key in Lebanon. It had, in fact, reversed gear. Reagan seemed to be conducting good public relations with us. When the chips were down the USA decided Lebanon was not of strategic importance to it. It had no oil, no great army, no great role in international affairs to deserve the extra effort. Lebanon's inability to maintain the consensus and its readiness to slide from one crisis to another was enough reason for the Americans to call it quits. This amorphousness of the Lebanese situation is what the US representatives meant when they said they could not get a handle on the situation.

In the weeks following Lausanne, the president was anxious to keep up the, albeit limited, momentum of the conference, and he wanted to meet with Asad to agree on a plan of action that would perhaps salvage the Lausanne Document.

On 18 April, the evening before our departure to Damascus to meet Asad, Bartholomew invited me to his residence. He showed me extensive underground construction and explained that the US embassy needed a bomb shelter. He added that when the USA decided to build a bomb shelter, it did so according to rigorous specifications. I asked him if he was trying to deliver the message that because of the change in US policy, and because of the new direction of the Lebanese government, the war in Lebanon would go on and on. Bartholomew enjoyed these questions, since they gave him the opportunity to play the role of the mysterious spokesman for a superpower, with secrets beyond our understanding: 'Who knows, my friend, who knows', he cryptically answered.

When I later told the president, Tweini and Ubayd about the bomb shelter, they thought it was a serious sign. Tweini, who always searched for the satanic in the affairs of man, was quick to interpret it as meaning that the Lebanese war would continue. The question, as far as he was concerned, was whether the United States was happy about it. Were they vindictive after their failure in Lebanon, or did the Americans still want to help? The question was left unanswered.

The president, Ubayd, presidential adviser Muhammad Shuqair and I left for Damascus on Thursday 19 April. The reception at Damascus Airport was, as usual, cordial. Although the visit was a working one, it was treated as an official visit. Asad was recuperating fast; he looked thin but strong, and comfortably in command. We had a host of urgent problems to discuss with the Syrians, and they were all interdependent. The Lausanne Document established a framework for solving them. For the past year and a half, we had been rigorously pursuing a process in which the United States had played a central role. Now we were searching for a substitute process, which would require close cooperation between Damascus and Beirut. Yet our new course seemed to lack the focus of the first, and many hurdles had to be overcome. We no longer had a superpower to help us overcome them, at least in their regional and international dimensions. Internally, we had first to agree on reforms, form a government to implement them, and then attempt to get Israel out. The complexities and the unknowns in this new path were staggering. The opportunities created by the consensus following the Israeli invasion of 1982 were truly exhausted. It was up to us to find new ones.

Jumayyil and Asad met privately for two hours as Ubayd and I spoke to Khaddam and the new foreign minister, Faruq al-Shar'. I described to them the problems facing us in the south, the deteriorating security situation in Beirut, the conflict between our government and Syria's allies in Lebanon, the deteriorating economic situation, and the weakening of the army through desertion. All these, I explained, necessitated urgent action to form a Government of National Unity. Only then could we address the matter of reforms, the mechanisms to get the Israelis out of the south, and new relations with Syria. Khaddam and Shar' took notes, preferring not to take a stand before our meeting with Asad. We then joined the two presidents in Asad's humble residence.

Every time I entered President Asad's office, which was increasingly often, I wondered who the designer was. The wallpaper wasn't especially attractive, and the arrangement of chairs was impractical, forcing the host and his guests to strain their necks to talk to each other. I always wondered how Asad could sit for hour after hour talking sideways to his guests. Meetings with Asad went on and on. Visitors were never told beforehand how much time Asad would spend with them. A visitor was made to feel that he could stay for as long as he wished, as if Asad had nothing else in the world to do but to chat. He appeared to his interlocutor to be inexhaustible and immovable. It was to Asad's advantage to make the visitor feel this way. In meetings we had had which lasted for three or four hours, during which cups of coffee were served at increasingly frequent intervals, I had always excused myself for a few minutes. Asad had never done so. I checked with others who had spent more than five or six hours at one sitting under the same conditions, and they confirmed my impression.

As I entered the room and saw the two presidents together, it occurred to me that the contrast between them was striking: Asad was comfortable and in a good mood; Jumayyil clearly was not. This was no surprise: there had been a confrontation between the two for the past year, and Asad had won. Asad's agenda was different from ours. Asad thought in strategic terms and therefore, in his mind, Lebanon was part of a bigger geopolitical picture, encompassing the Israelis, the Palestinians, the Iranians and others. In his constant efforts to gain the initiative in the Middle East, Asad could afford to take his time and allow regional contradictions to work themselves out, and in his favour. We could not afford to wait as long as he could.

Asad welcomed us to the meeting and started reviewing orally items from the Lausanne Document. He began by saying that he and Sheikh Amin had discussed the relations between Lebanon and Syria and agreed that they should be based on the higher interests of the two countries.

They had discussed procedures to attain this objective. On the powers of the president and the prime minister, he continued, Sulayman Franjiyyeh opposed the Lausanne language because it reduced the presidency to a secretarial position. According to the Lebanese Constitution, the president had all the powers. The prime minister and the council of ministers were hardly mentioned in the Constitution. Tradition, however, gave the prime minister and the Council of Ministers great powers. These should be defined in the new constitution. He believed the president was the head of the executive authority, but the Constitution should state clearly that he executed this authority in cooperation with the prime minister and the council of ministers. The Constitutional Document issued by President Franjiyyeh in 1976 called for the election of the prime minister by parliament. He did not believe this to be necessary. He and Sheikh Amin believed it was better to select the prime minister through consultation.

Asad went on to say that they had talked about the army and there was no problem there. The National Defence Council would supervise military affairs. In forming the new government this point must be taken into account, so that the ministers forming the National Defence Council were confessionally balanced. Sheikh Amin had suggested a large government in which *al-aqtab*, or political leaders with strong militias or large followings, would serve as ministers of state to deal with fundamental matters, while professional men would head the ministries, especially the service ministries. There may be a problem with *al-aqtab*. However, it was better that they be included in the new government, than excluded. There was the question of protocol – some were old and some were young. The old had their prestige, and the young had the power. Who would take precedence over whom? We should reflect on that. We must realize that there is the legitimacy of law and the legitimacy of revolution of those who wield power on the ground. We should keep that in mind. Asad argued for a while against a government of *aqtab*. 'Can you imagine your father in the cabinet? How could you call him to order?' 'Order,' retorted Khaddam, 'can you imagine Sham'un and Sheikh Pierre responding to a call of order? Stick with the young men, Mr President.' The president, preferring not to joust with Khaddam, looked at Asad as if urging a change in conversation.

On the bureaucracy, continued Asad, we had agreed that no administrative position should be reserved for any one confession, and that positions in the upper categories of the administration, i.e. grade I, director-generals, ambassadors, and their equivalent in the bureaucracy, should be distributed on the basis of half-Christian, half-Muslim. He understood that in Lausanne it had been agreed to form a committee or a constituent assembly to write a new constitution; this assembly should work on the basis of what we agreed today. He agreed with Sheikh Amin that no document should be issued from this meeting lest people begin to refer to it as the Damascus Document. Reform was a Lebanese affair, and any statements should be issued in Beirut. Asad would brief the opposition on Saturday, and we would brief the Lebanese Front as we saw fit. 'I prefer', said Asad, 'to have Sheikh Amin call all the participants in the Lausanne Conference and brief them on this meeting.' 'Who will guarantee their safety?' interrupted Khaddam. Asad smiled.

Jumayyil told Asad that irrespective of constitutional stipulations the government now functioned on the basis of power sharing, and that the prime minister had virtually the same powers as those of the president. The president argued that the 'constituent assembly' referred to in the Lausanne Document should be called the assembly, and that it should only make recommendations. Asad agreed. Jumayyil and Asad told us that the prime minister should not be elected by the parliament. His selection should be a matter of consultation between the president and the parliament, and the Lausanne Document should be amended accordingly. They told us that they had made minor changes in the Lausanne Document and that Khaddam, Salem and Ubayd should put these changes into final form.

Jumayyil and Asad talked at length about the new government. Asad regarded Jumayyil as a representative of the Lebanese Front, and wanted him balanced by a prime minister from the National Salvation Front. As the only Sunni in the National Salvation Front, Karami was the obvious choice, and Jumayyil saw no problem in nominating him. Khaddam wanted all the Muslim ministers to be chosen by the opposition. When Khaddam ventured into specifics, irritating Jumayyil, as Jumayyil opposed most of Khaddam's suggestions, Asad looked amused. Khaddam obviously had some elbow room, and Asad enjoyed seeing him elbowing others. Often Asad came to the support of Jumayyil by modifying some of Khaddam's suggestions. For example, Asad emphasized that Jumayyil was a president with certain powers which he must exercise 'taking into consideration, of course, the facts on the ground'.

When Ubayd and I met Khaddam to review the changes we found them to be minor. Apart from some nuances in the wording of the powers of the president that did not affect their substance, some changes in the procedure of selecting the prime minister, and in the role of the constituent assembly and its name, not much had been altered. The important points listed above as constituting the basis of the Lausanne Document had certainly not been changed. We completed our work with Khaddam by midnight.

The president told Asad he need not accompany him to the airport, but Asad insisted. If word got out that Jumayyil had not been sent off with the same honours as those with which he was received, said Asad, speculation would arise that the summit had failed. We had enough problems without creating new ones. Our delegation left Damascus after midnight for Larnaca, where we checked into the Sandy Beach Hotel. We waited in the hotel lobby till dawn, when we departed for home.

The Government of National Unity

After a day's rest, the president started consultations to form a new government. His advisers had already prepared half a dozen government lists, each reflecting the bias of its author. The president enjoyed busying his advisers with such responsibilities, which some of us suspected were useless since the president tended to do what was on his mind. Joseph Abu Khalil, who had worked with Sheikh Pierre Jumayyil, and who compared Amin to his father, often laughed when he saw an adviser assiduously preparing a government list. 'Don't waste your time,' he would say, 'the government is already formed in the president's mind.' But in this case, and from this time on, the president was no longer the main decision-maker in the forming of the cabinet. Damascus had its views on who was best suited to be prime minister, which of its allies should be in the cabinet and which post they should occupy. The prime minister too had acquired greater confidence, and his Muslim constituency had become vociferous about whom it wanted and what it wanted done.

Karami met the president on Wednesday 25 April. This gave rise to speculation that the two had agreed on a new government under Karami's premiership. On Friday, the president hinted to me that Karami wanted to take the post of foreign minister, in addition to the premiership. It was not uncommon for the prime minister to take one or more ministerial posts. Some preferred to take the Ministry of the Interior, others preferred the Ministry of Finance. The president assured me that I would continue as foreign minister in spite of Karami's desire to assume the post himself.

When, on Monday 30 April, the names of the ministers were announced on the radio, and I heard that Karami was to serve as prime minister and foreign minister, I was not surprised. As soon as the announcement had been made, the president called me and asked me to join him. When I arrived at the presidential palace, he told me that he had fought hard for me, but that Karami had wanted to be foreign minister himself. Karami thought highly of me, he added, and wanted to work with me in any capacity. The president and Karami had reviewed positions in which they thought I could be helpful, and they decided that I could serve best as adviser to the president on foreign affairs. Since foreign affairs were largely the domain of the presidency, the president explained, I would continue in effect to function pretty much as foreign minister. As I was on leave from the American University of Beirut and there was plenty of work to be done, I did not hesitate in accepting his offer.

The cabinet included the representatives who had participated in the National Dialogue Conferences in Geneva and Lausanne. The exceptions were Sulayman Franjiyyeh, who was represented by his son-in-law Abdallah al-Rasi, and Sa'ib Salam, who was replaced by Salim al-Hoss. Victor Qasir, a Beiruti merchant, was brought in to give representation to the Greek Orthodox community which was not represented in the National Dialogue Conference. The president told me that he and Karami preferred to have a small cabinet such as the one just announced and not one of 26 members, as he and Asad had discussed in the last meeting. He was hopeful that the cabinet would end the fighting, introduce reforms, and work on the withdrawal of all non-Lebanese forces from Lebanon.

The president and Karami were gambling on getting the youthful militia leaders together with the old guards Sheikh Pierre Jumayyil and Kamil Sham'un. The government was, by composition and platform, a continuation of the Geneva–Lausanne process. Its statement was to be based on the Lausanne Document amended by the Jumayyil–Asad summit of 19–20 April. This government left the post of deputy prime minister vacant. By tradition this post is reserved for a Greek Orthodox. I filled it in 1982–84. The post gives its occupant a protocol position fourth in the state hierarchy after the president, the speaker, and the prime minister. Now that Kamil Sham'un, a former president, was in the cabinet, the post of deputy prime minister was not occupied, in deference to the ex-president, so he would follow by protocol the prime minister, and not the Greek Orthodox deputy prime minister.

Under normal conditions, I would have called Karami to agree with him on a date for the traditional transfer of office in the Ministry of Foreign Affairs. Unfortunately, the war created *de facto* barriers which made it unsafe for Karami to come to East Beirut, where the ministry's offices were located. Instead, I went to the prime minister's office in West Beirut, gave him a detailed briefing on foreign policy issues, and answered his many questions on foreign affairs.

For many years, Karami had been living in Tripoli, virtually cut off from political developments in the world, and his questions reflected this. He knew, however, what he wanted with respect to Israel. He was against direct negotiations with the Israelis, and if negotiations had to take place to reach security arrangements in the south, he preferred to have a European country, perhaps France, act as mediator. If this wasn't possible, then Lebanon would ask for the help of the United States. I sought his permission to meet George Shultz when I visited the United States later that month, when I would be in Washington for a previous engagement, and he agreed readily. He also asked me to deliver a specific message to Shultz. His message was 'Lebanon is a friend of the USA and of Western democracies. It adheres to a democratic system and to free economic enterprise. It is also an Arab country with strong ties with Syria. Lebanon will always need the USA to help it get Israel out. In cancelling the agreement, we are not cancelling our ties with the USA. We and Shultz should look forward to new opportunities.' Karami spoke in generalities, but his message was genuine; I wanted very much to convey it because I wanted an opportunity to improve Karami's image in Washington, which was pretty negative.

7

A Change of Emphasis

Adviser on Foreign Affairs

From October 1982 to April 1984, the period in which I served as deputy
prime minister and minister of foreign affairs, the focus of Lebanese
political activity was on the withdrawal of Israeli forces from Lebanon.
Our assumption was that once Lebanon was able to secure the withdrawal
of all foreign forces from its territory, it would be in a better position to
deal with the internal problems, including constitutional reforms. We
always believed that constitutional reforms were important, but we also
felt that continued Israeli occupation of parts of Lebanon, and the presence of other non-Lebanese forces in the country, endangered the legitimacy and continuity of the Lebanese state. Very simply, we feared that
the divisions within Lebanon would be exploited by the foreign forces in
the country in their own self-interests; therefore the quicker they withdrew,
the better. The question of withdrawals proved to be far more difficult
than we had anticipated.

Once our policy of getting all foreign forces out of Lebanon failed,
the emphasis shifted to internal affairs. A new framework imposed itself
on us: we had first to consolidate the Lebanese house, ask for the implementation of Resolutions 425 and 509, and await developments. Within
this context, Lebanon's diplomacy was largely frozen. The new debate, if
indeed it could be so called, centred on the following topics: there was a
civil war in Lebanon; the Christians had more powers than they were
entitled to; confessionalism must be abolished; parliament and the
Council of Ministers must be strengthened; the constitution must be
rewritten to accommodate changes on the ground; Israel was the enemy
and it must withdraw without conditions; a national struggle against
Israel must be launched; Syria was a sister Arab state and its forces would
stay to help Lebanon regain its sovereignty. All the elements of the new
emphasis were basically correct. Some of them, however, were

exaggerated: they sounded simple in the abstract, but in reality were far more complex and difficult to implement. The change in the very hierarchy of the issues was itself a serious one, not accepted by all. The question of the priorities of issues was political and volatile, as is obvious from the issue of withdrawals – who would withdraw first, the Syrians or the Israelis? The Israelis wanted Syria out first. Syria refused to be discussed in the context of Israel although it stated it would withdraw after all the Israeli forces had withdrawn. More disturbing was that Lebanon's communities were divided on interpretation of the elements of this 'new' orientation. Instead of uniting the Lebanese people, these elements threatened to divide them further. This was obvious from the two conferences on national dialogue. Both had ended in failure. And what we had rescued from Lausanne, i.e. the Lausanne Document, could have been written in my study on the basis of proposals submitted and agreed upon with the Syrian leadership.

Previously we had sought to disentangle and then reform; now we were trying to reform first and then disentangle. We accommodated to the new emphasis because the policy leading to the agreement had collapsed. Also things had changed radically since the autumn of 1982. Jumayyil was not able to preserve the national consensus; the army became controversial; the USA could not deliver; and Arab interest in Lebanon was transitory. Relying on UN resolutions and on national resistance to get Israel out was always one of our options. It was not our first, because we felt it was not as effective as US intervention. This option was also Syria's preferred course of action. It did not preclude investigating various methodologies provided we stayed within the parameters of Resolution 425, and now the decision of the council of ministers of 5 March 1984, to provide for security arrangements in south Lebanon that would prevent infiltration across our southern frontiers and lead to Israeli withdrawals.

In an effort to regain the government's lost initiative, the president was anxious to cooperate with Syria and its allies in Lebanon. Most of them were now part of the government: Rashid Karami was prime minister, Nabih Birri was now the minister of justice, and Walid Junblat was minister of public works. President Jumayyil hoped, with Syrian cooperation, to salvage some of the objectives he once thought he could realize through the United States; but the euphoria was no longer there. New uncertainties arose: how would Israel withdraw? Who would apply pressure on it? What new order would Israel impose in South Lebanon? Would Lebanon drift into partition? Had the Lebanese problem become an integral part of the Middle East problem, and if so, would we have to be patient and await a regional settlement before we would see stability in Lebanon? The greater the uncertainty the larger the number of questions and the less certain the answers. I moved to the presidential palace on 3 May 1984, as adviser to the president on foreign affairs.

The advisory team around the president was largely amorphous, each of them tied to the president directly with no organizational structure to encourage team work. Although the president took pride in the House of the Future, a think-tank he had established in the 1970s, and in the administrative and technological innovations he had introduced to the presidential Palace, he was not really a team leader or a team player. He was a solo player, like most Lebanese politicians, and not a little suspicious of a team enjoying some autonomy apart from his person.

My academic background, my interest in research and writing, and my natural inclination to anonymity all helped me to adjust relatively quickly to my advisory role. I dealt mainly with foreign affairs, but as many aspects of domestic politics in Lebanon had a foreign dimension, I often found myself, from time to time, on missions of an internal character.

From the day it was formed, the government faced serious problems, and the president asked me to help in solving them. Former president Sulayman Franjiyyeh wanted Sheikh Pierre and Victor Qasir to resign and be replaced by two ministers whom he would nominate. Walid Junblat agreed to serve in the government, but refused to meet in the presidential palace in Ba'bda. He felt it was not safe, and worried that disgruntled Christians would try to kill him on the way. Birri refused to serve unless a new portfolio for South Lebanon affairs were created and given to him.

Not all problems could be solved. Franjiyyeh had to be assured that his interests would be defended. Junblat was satisfied by holding the meetings of the council of ministers in Bikfayya, the president's town, as the route from Mukhtarah, his own town, to Bikfayya was safe, and in Bikfayya he was under the protection of the presidential guard. Junblat, who was known for his humour and carefree attitude, would sometimes walk out from the cabinet meetings and ask the presidential guards which of them intended dirty tricks against him, much to the agony of his own anxious bodyguards. Birri got the Ministry of State for South Lebanon. Most security problems of going to and coming from Bikfayya were satisfied by using military helicopters to transport ministers and their guards. By guards I mean a small, tight-knit, highly armed militia for each of the main militia leaders, and not merely three or four tough guys.

Although the president's objective was to build up relations with Syria, I was instructed to maintain ties with the United States and Saudi Arabia. We knew that, sooner or later, we would require their assistance in bringing about the withdrawal of foreign forces. Although the Americans had withdrawn Lebanon from their priority list, Lebanon remained important for the United States in many respects. It could be the battleground for a Syrian–Israeli conflict, while at the same time, a PLO presence remained in the country. In addition, Lebanon was slowly becoming a centre for Islamic militancy, which was beginning to have worldwide implications. If Lebanon remained an anarchic free-for-all, this would threaten American interests in the region, as well as the peace process which was always in view though it was then on a back burner. Perhaps the United States was trying to forget the Lebanon experience, but it would soon find out that this was far more difficult a matter than simply pulling out the Marines.

The cultural–economic argument for continued interest in Lebanon was also a strong one. Well before the United States entered the Middle East arena in force after the second World War, it had already established a significant cultural and economic presence in Lebanon through the American University of Beirut (AUB) and through commercial interests. Through the AUB, Lebanon played an important regional intellectual role, attracting Arab students and thinkers, and influencing political and intellectual trends in the region. After Lebanese independence in 1943, Beirut, with its open political system, became the cultural and economic capital of the Arab world. Since the Second World War the liberal economic system in Lebanon had attracted American business, and Beirut had become the base of many American firms operating in the Arab world or the broader Middle Eastern region. Neither the USA nor Lebanon could afford totally to disengage from the cultural and economic activities which they had nurtured jointly for decades. Nor was the new Karami government, in spite of its anti-American rhetoric, truly anti-American. Karami was a pragmatist, and wanted help from wherever he could get it, and Damascus was not against engaging the USA in specific policies in Lebanon for it too wanted to maintain a degree of credibility in international affairs. Karami was happy that I sought his advice on going to Washington, and urged me to go and express his flexibility, his readiness to try new approaches, and his desire to cooperate with President Jumayyil.

Karami's image definitely needed a boost in Washington, where he was known as Mr Rhetoric. I found the Washington of the spring of 1984 a different city. Fear of Islamic militant terror had penetrated every nook and cranny of the American governmental system. Even entering the White House was an ordeal, and the area around it was sandbagged like a back-alley in wartime Beirut. Washington had bunkered against Iran and its arm in Lebanon, Hizballah, and against Iran's ally, Syria.

Officials in Washington listened politely to me, but clearly their mind was on Tehran. They believed that Karami's message was unrealistic. McFarlane commented that Karami seemed to want to will Israel out of Lebanon, but that Israel did not act this way. Shultz was disappointed by the outcome of his extensive efforts, and he noted that Karami's government had to prove its credibility. If Karami chose to go to the Soviets, he would not find sympathy in Washington, and if he went to the United Nations, he would not get results. Shultz spoke with sadness, knowing full well perhaps that he had not been able to get results either. I felt he was a decent man, who tried hard and failed, and I was not about to move the knife in the wound. He and I were in the same boat, and we understood each other's predicament well. Bartholomew later told me that Shultz had been nervous prior to the meeting. He was concerned that our session was going to be a difficult one. He had asked Bartholomew 'What does Elie want? Is he going to ask me, as usual, a hundred questions and expect me to answer them in front of 20 people taking notes?' He was referring, of course, to the difficult negotiation that preceded and followed the signing of the agreement. I did, indeed, ask difficult and specific questions because I was the weaker party and I wanted assurances. I only had one aide taking notes, my assistant Itamar Diab. The American side, however, had a dozen note-takers to keep the dozen or so agencies in the huge American bureaucracy informed of the negotiation process. I often complained to Shultz about the large number of note-takers. His answer was that the American bureaucracy, like the American polity, had its own checks and balances.

At the Department of Defense, I heard blunt language against Karami from the officers in charge of Middle Eastern affairs. They accused Karami of rhetoric void of policy. They said he was like the Palestinian leaders who talked much but did nothing and in the process lost most of Palestine. They were clearly ignorant of the real Karami, who was thoughtful, low-key and a statesman. I gave all my interlocutors a positive briefing on Karami whom I truly respected, but the cards were stacked against him in Washington. This was no time to introduce Karami or start a new process.

At the end of my Washington trip, it seemed clear to me that the United States had little remaining interest in Lebanon's affairs. The American officials I met with were distant, and spent much of their time sniping at Karami. 'You cancelled the agreement, now work it out with Syria', was the American message. While the message was predictable the president did not like it. The prime minister expected it. President Jumayyil felt that the United States was on the wrong wavelength. From now on, he remarked bitterly, he would see what the USA wanted and would do the exact opposite; then he would be sure of doing something right. I sympathized with him.

The president, who had always been close to the United States, was now distancing himself from Washington, and Bartholomew's visits to the presidential palace were often kept out of the press upon the instruction of the president. He was not anxious to be perceived as consulting with the Americans. He had done a lot of that for two years and it had led nowhere. Bartholomew was angry about this change in attitude. He let the president and the prime minister know that no Israeli withdrawals could be expected without US assistance. At a time when the United States was largely absent from Lebanon, I felt that it was Bartholomew who made policy himself, and who kept Washington engaged in Lebanese affairs, at least nominally. While in the past if I asked him a critical question he deferred the answer until he got instructions from Washington, I now found that he provided an answer to any question based on his understanding of the logic of the prevailing political situation. He was good at improvising and at generalities that were appropriate for the moment. He knew his parameters and moved at ease within them.

New Directions

Despite all our problems abroad, the nation's attention at this time was largely directed towards internal affairs. Fighting had not stopped despite the formation of the Government of National Unity. The security plan worked out after Lausanne was violated daily. Plans to form an 'Assembly' of 32 members to draft a new constitution were not going smoothly. Efforts to improve relations between the president and the opposition leaders, and between the president and the more hard-line members of his own Maronite community, were not yielding results. The president expected Syria to help him in his relations with Franjiyyeh, Karami, Hoss, Birri and Junblat. But most of these leaders had acquired large militias, had built up regional and international contacts, and had become auto-nomous potentates in their own right. Syria could not easily bring them into line to back Jumayyil. More to the point, however, Syria was not especially interested in strengthening the president at the expense of its trusted allies.

Those who backed the president within the government were either getting old, or had no strong power base. Kamil Sham'un and Sheikh Pierre no longer possessed the power they had once held within the Maronite community. Their leadership had been challenged by younger, more ambitious leaders, the products of the war – Fadi Frem, Eli Hubay-qah, Samir Ja'ja. Victor Qasir, a merchant with no political experience, was of little help to the president within the cabinet. Whenever Qasir spoke, Junblat advised him to return to his shop and 'sell sheets and towels', which greatly irritated the low-key urbane merchant of Beirut. The president considered replacing Sham'un, Sheikh Pierre and Qasir but feared that Sham'un and his father would not take the move well: 'I believe my father would die were he to be asked to resign', the president told me. Although Sheikh Pierre was dying, and knew it, he continued to attend ministerial meetings, give long lectures, and speak of a Lebanon that no longer existed.

Meanwhile, Israel was consolidating its position in the south. Lebanese politicians from the region met me frequently and described Israeli actions there. The Israelis, they said, were in the area for the long haul, and even if they withdrew they were likely to return whenever they saw fit. The Israelis were urging leaders in the south to establish local administrations, and Israeli goods were everywhere. Israel seemed bent on expanding its market in the south and normalizing relations with the sectors it controlled. The open market they asked for and did not get in the agreement they now had *de facto*; Israeli goods were being smuggled by many merchants to all parts of Lebanon, and our control system was too weak to check this flow of goods. Israeli generals, I was told by our politicians from the south, had brought Israeli scholars as consultants on how best the Israeli army could deal with the Shi'ah, the Maronites, the Sunnis and the Druze. The Israeli-backed South Lebanon Army was gaining strength. Israelis were telling the people in the south that the Lebanese government had ignored them, and that Israel wanted to live in peace with its northern neighbours. And yet to counter violence, the Israelis were pursuing themselves a policy of violence. They broke into houses, arrested inhabitants and killed or expelled those they suspected of anti-Israeli activity. If this trend continued, the southern politicians told me, South Lebanon would become like the West Bank and Gaza. They were anxious about their people, their property and their influence. They wanted action.

The Israelis were also playing communities off against each other. Israel had exploited Christian–Muslim differences to develop a sense of fear among the Christians of the south. Israel was also concentrating on the largest community in the south, the Shi'ah. The Shi'ah were divided into four large groupings: the Amal Movement, the fundamentalist Hizballah, the traditional Shi'a leadership, and leftist groupings. Israel was contacting all these groups, particularly the traditional leadership, to try to establish a *modus vivendi* with them in the area. The politicians were exasperated with the course of events. No one was talking about Israeli withdrawal except within the context of guerrilla raids or a *Jihad* (Holy War). In their opinion, this trend would keep the war going indefinitely, and Israel would then incorporate into its territory the region south of the Litani River. They urged us to start any format of negotiation that had a chance of bringing about a permanent Israeli withdrawal.

At about this time, I realized that I had not had a rest since I joined the government in October 1982. As I looked at my crowded agenda, it was obvious that I could not take a week off unless I made a conscious decision to do so. I stayed home the first week of August, and as usual rested by reading good books, and forgetting about contemporary affairs.

When I completed my vacation, I joined the president and his family for a private dinner. The past week, he said, had been terrible. He had fought with Karami, Hoss, Birri and Bartholomew. The president complained about everything and everybody. He was particularly distressed that Bartholomew saw him only to seek information and to offer advice; but he never informed the president about American policy in the region. 'I know what Asad wants,' the president told me, 'he wants influence in Greater Syria, but I have no idea what Reagan's plans are.' He continued:

> When I close my eyes all I remember is the Americans saying: 'Form a broad-based government.' Their policy has become a broken record. I did just that, I formed a Government of National Unity, and it turned out to be a tragedy. It is more a battlefield than a government. What did Muhammad say about his wives? Consult them and do the opposite? Let's keep that in mind when we talk with the Americans. As to my objectives, when I think about them and how to realize them, I tend to lose my mind. Instead of pursuing the big objectives, I am trying to manage the crisis as it unfolds daily. Decision-making on the big issues has shifted. It is taking place in every capital except Beirut.

The Government of National Unity was divided amongst itself and had rapidly become the Government of National Disunity. Some of its members fought in the cabinet when it met and in the streets of Beirut. Fighting for land was the logic of militia politics, and such fights always occur at the expense of the state. Fundamentalist movements were beginning to attack Western interests in Lebanon, and Westerners were leaving Lebanon quickly. The indirect result of these actions, however, was that the Lebanese government, as a unified legal body, was increasingly isolated, and was thus becoming quite irrelevant. As power shifted to Damascus, and as it became apparent that the Lebanese government had little influence in the country, many foreign countries began to ignore us. While in the past every important country had an ambassador in Beirut, now many states, for security reasons, sent their ambassadors to Amman, Damascus or Cyprus, and from their seats in these stable countries they made short visits to Beirut where they were also accredited. This practice angered and disappointed us, and confirmed publicly that Lebanon had lost its importance. Fortunately the great powers, and countries with special interest in Lebanon, did not follow this lead. The Americans moved their embassy from West Beirut to Awkar in the Eastern Sector; so did the British, the French and the Italians. Nevertheless, it was unmistakable:

the foreign embassies were increasingly retrenching themselves as radical and fundamentalist groupings discovered that hostage-taking could paralyse great powers, and even force them out of the Lebanese theatre.

On Thursday 20 September, another car-bomb driven by a suicide driver exploded at the US embassy in Awkar, killing 25 employees, two of whom were Americans. Ambassador Bartholomew had been meeting in the building with the British ambassador David Miers when the explosion occurred. Both had been taken to a local hospital, and I went there immediately. Miers was wrapped in bandages when I arrived. One of his eyes was swollen, and he had cuts on his face and hands. Bartholomew had been treated for some facial wounds, and had been sent home. Miers, who was still in a state of shock, was eager to talk about the experience, and he gave me a detailed, though at times incoherent, account of what had transpired. He had been meeting with Bartholomew in his office when the explosion shook the building. The wall behind Bartholomew's desk had surged forward and collapsed on the American ambassador, pinning him to the desk. Miers and a few others had helped disentangle Bartholomew, and both had then been driven to the hospital. 'It is a terrible time to be an ambassador', Miers concluded. Bartholomew was badly shaken. He had taken the decision to move the embassy to Awkar. He had brought in American experts to work out intricate security arrangements, and yet a lone sansculotte, driven by an idea and anxious to go up in smoke, had blown up the new fortress. How, he wondered out loud to me, was he going to protect the staff? I knew it was dangerous to be ambassador in Beirut at present, but that dangerous? In time Bartholomew built up a 500-guard detail – popularly known as Bartholomew's militia – which often terrorized Lebanese as its eager and heavily armed members escorted the ambassador in his comings and goings.

A group calling itself Islamic Jihad claimed responsibility for the Awkar operation. This organization, which would soon become famous for its kidnapping of foreigners in Beirut, had already taken responsibility for various daring operations against Israel and the Multinational Force in Beirut.

The Western powers were not the only ones to suffer from rising Islamic militancy in Lebanon. The Saudi Arabian embassy also became the target of repeated attacks by Shi'i fundamentalists. During one demonstration to protest at Saudi restrictions on Shi'is wishing to go on the pilgrimage to Mecca and Medina, the Saudi flag was burnt, the picture of King Fahd was replaced by that of Khomeini, and the embassy building was set on fire. After this, the Saudis closed their embassy in Beirut, and began to rely almost exclusively on Rafiq al-Hariri to conduct their political relations with Lebanon. Hariri, however, sensing where the power was, spent more time in Damascus than in Beirut. In Damascus he could move freely and meet radical leaders who had offices in Damascus as well as in Beirut, and he hoped through Syrian influence to curb their activities.

The Saudis and Karami were on bad terms. They expected him as prime minister and foreign minister to call King Fahd and apologize for the demonstrations, but he did not. In his speeches Karami always thanked Syria for its positive role in Lebanon, totally ignoring the Saudi role. What irritated the Saudis in particular was the way Karami had handled a Saudi financial gift. The Saudis had sent a gift of US $1,250,000 each to a few leading Lebanese politicians. He was one of them. Upon receiving the gift Karami declared: 'We were expecting a Saudi gift; we thought it was Saudi dates. It turned out to be one million two hundred and fifty thousand US dollars, which we immediately handed over to teachers and students to promote education in Tripoli.' This was an admirable and rare thing for Lebanese politicians to do. His public utterance, however, annoyed and embarrassed the Saudis who were accustomed to make such payments, often upon the insistent demand of the politicians themselves. When, after much mediation, Karami visited Saudi Arabia, he criticized the Saudis publicly for their extravagant display in honouring him. 'What are all these flowers for?' he asked. 'Couldn't this money be better spent on something more useful?' The Saudis then wondered whether it was his intention to irritate them, or merely lack of protocol on his part. Actually Karami was a frugal person. He lived in a modest apartment, and he spent little on himself and on his followers. It was against his taste to show opulence, and truly preferred to have such expenditure directed to help the poor and the needy. Also his association with Damascus was so strong that it did not disturb him much to irritate Riyad. And Damascus itself was jealous of its role in Lebanon and was not anxious for another Arab capital to share the role.

The United Nations Visit

As the new prime minister and foreign minister, Karami wanted to visit the United Nations and the United States to emphasize his policy of getting Israel out of Lebanon on the basis of Resolution 425. The meeting of the General Assembly in late September 1984 provided him with this opportunity. He invited Birri to join him on his mission, and to the surprise of American officials, he and Birri declared publicly that they would be meeting President Reagan, although no such meeting had been scheduled. A meeting with Reagan was rather unlikely as there was no American initiative in progress, and no particular desire at the time in

Washington to focus attention on Lebanon. Predictably, Reagan did not see them, but Secretary of State Shultz did. The rebuff was a blow to Karami and Birri, who were not at ease in the USA and who knew little about how that country functioned.

Shultz was cautious with Karami. He felt that the prime minister was soft on terrorism and even encouraged terrorist acts in his frequent declarations calling for armed struggle against Israel. Karami, on the other hand, was anxious to start a new relationship with the United States, and he told Shultz so. The secretary of state was wary. He merely conveyed the Israeli position to Karami: Israel wanted direct negotiations with the Lebanese government; it wanted the Lebanese government to recognize the South Lebanon Army; and it wanted security arrangements in the south. This time, Shultz added, Israel insisted on getting Syria's blessing for all these points. It had learned from its experience with the May 17 Agreement that any agreement with Lebanon which did not have full Syrian support would fail.

The USA did not merely convey the Israeli position to Karami; it supported it. Shultz believed in direct negotiations. He felt that the South Lebanon Army was justifiable for as long as there were illegal militias in the rest of the country. As for agreeing to security arrangements, he felt that this was the least that should be done to end Israeli occupation and prevent its recurrence. The meeting with Shultz did much to change Karami's mind about working with the United States. He began to think of the UN as a more viable option. To his surprise, he was to learn in the coming few weeks that neither the USA nor Israel was opposed to UN mediation, although Israel kept insisting on direct negotiations under a thin UN umbrella. Israel was leaning towards the UN since it did not want to strain its relations with Washington in case the negotiations failed.

President Jumayyil did not have much confidence in Karami's foreign policy. He found it naïve, antiquated and passive. He felt that Lebanon should not cut itself off from the United States and Europe. Besides, the president was an activist. He wanted to remain centrally engaged in foreign policy, and he enjoyed meeting world leaders and presenting Lebanon's case to them. He felt that Karami and Birri may have left a negative impression in Washington, and he wanted to travel to the United States himself to correct it. He wanted to go in November, in anticipation of a Reagan victory in the American elections, and offer Ronald Reagan his congratulations. There he hoped to start a new political process and, once again, engage the United States in Lebanese affairs.

I discouraged the president from doing this on the grounds that it would not be appropriate in the context of the existing government, nor would it come at an opportune time from Washington's point of view.

Washington wanted to distance itself from Lebanon, and it was unlikely that the Reagan Administration would choose to involve itself in our affairs again so soon. There was no credible process for the USA to follow, and there was no regional opportunity for the Americans to enter in the context of a broad initiative such as the one taken by Ronald Reagan in September 1982.

On 14 October, Bartholomew informed me that he and his wife would be out of Lebanon for a while. It was obvious that the Americans wanted to prevent the possibility of an incident which would focus attention on Lebanon during elections in the United States. Were Bartholomew to be kidnapped or killed in Beirut, the Democratic Party would exploit the incident to focus attention on Reagan's failures in Lebanon. Hence Bartholomew was advised to leave the country and save the Republican Party the embarrassment of another Beirut fiasco to be added to the embassy explosion, the Marine barracks destruction and the latest embassy explosion. A vacation is a convenient diplomatic tool, and when diplomacy or the failure thereof could affect politics, it becomes not only convenient, but necessary and urgent. I understood his plan and wished him well.

Meanwhile, Karami was trying to get a UN umbrella to secure an Israeli withdrawal from the south, and the president and I encouraged him to do so. It was an option, not a good one, but there was no better. Freedom, quite often, is the compulsion to accept the inevitable. The USA was out. The UN was there, with appropriate resolutions and eager to do something in the absence of the Americans. De Cuéllar was anxious to try: he sent his aides to us regularly searching for a UN role to get discussions between us and the Israelis going on withdrawals in return for security arrangements.

We wanted, however, to know if Israel was serious in accepting a United Nations umbrella, and if so, would the European states support our efforts through the UN. As the British foreign secretary, Geoffrey Howe, was planning to visit Israel, on 16 October I asked the British ambassador, David Miers, to ask Howe to find answers to our questions; and I proceeded with the questions which he wrote down carefully. Would Israel seriously negotiate with us at the military level under UN auspices? Had Washington changed its mind, and was it now ready to accept a larger role for the UN in the Middle East? Would the leading European countries, namely Britain, France, Italy, West Germany, as well as the Vatican, encourage UN mediation and take an active role in it? Were the European states aware that Israel was changing the nature of South Lebanon and that, with time, the south could become like the West Bank and Gaza?

Miers was overwhelmed by these questions. The interests of the United Kingdom in Lebanon were limited, he said. He would try to get answers to our questions, but he warned us that the United Kingdom was not prepared to be engaged in serious political matters in Lebanon: 'If there is something specific, simple, and inexpensive, we are ready to help, especially at the humanitarian level', he said. 'The last thing Lebanon needs', I retorted 'is help at the humanitarian level. We have a serious political problem, of regional and international dimension, and it is there that we need help. It is the regional–international impasse that caused the destruction and the displacement – let's treat the cause, not the symptom.' Miers was not ready for a dialogue of this nature. He agreed to convey my message. The answer from Howe came promptly and it dealt only with negotiations. Israel, he said, was ready to negotiate with a Lebanese military team on security arrangements. This was a change in policy, he advised, and urged us to accept.

When I met Karami on 18 October, he was optimistic. He felt that Israel would withdraw fully within the context of the Lebanon–Israel Armistice Agreement (ILMAC) of 1949. His conviction was strengthened by a letter which an assistant to UN Secretary-General Javier Pérez De Cuéllar had shown President Jumayyil that day. The letter, dated 3 August 1978, had been sent by Moshe Dayan to UN Secretary-General Kurt Waldheim. The letter stated that Israel considered the 1949 Armistice Agreement valid, and that Israel would respect it provided that Lebanon abided by its stipulations and prevented military activity across its borders against Israel. This meant that Israel may accept in 1984 the strict implementation of the Armistice Agreement, and that security arrangements made then could perhaps be applicable now. If so, this would be a reversal of the Israeli position since its occupation of large parts of Lebanon in 1982.

Reports from Washington, meanwhile, indicated that Israel was ready to withdraw gradually from the south, leaving behind the South Lebanon Army and a small mobile Israeli force. We were now faced with the same questions which we had faced when the Israelis announced they were withdrawing from the Shuf: to whom would the Israelis yield authority in the areas they evacuated? Would Israel coordinate its withdrawal with the Lebanese government through third-party mediation? The United States, we learned, was unwilling to mediate between Lebanon and Israel, preferring instead to mediate between Syria and Israel. Recognizing the new reality of power in the region, Washington was now ready to deal with Syria directly and to recognize its legitimate interests in Lebanon. The United States, Bartholomew had told me, would support a UN mediation role. The USA remained involved in Lebanese affairs, but would not move faster than the situation permitted. The Americans, Bartholomew continued, did not want to find themselves fighting windmills with a broken lance, like Don Quixote. They had learned their lesson: before the United States would do anything up front, it would first seek agreement between Israel and Syria.

The Naqurah Discussions

On 30 October, agreement was reached on a formula for negotiating with Israel under UN auspices. Israel had decided for internal political considerations to withdraw further in the south and cordon off a security zone on Lebanese territory that would serve as a protective buffer to Israel's northern towns and villages. To agree to talk to the Lebanese, under a UN umbrella, was good for its image. It showed willingness to cooperate, and it would satisfy its patron the USA without risking anything. Furthermore, any discussion with an Arab country would give the Israeli populace the impression that the Israeli state was gradually normalizing its existence in the hitherto distant and inimical Arab environment. Under the new formula the UN secretary-general would call for a meeting of Lebanese and Israeli army officers to discuss Israeli withdrawal and security arrangements in South Lebanon. The Lebanese side would state its position and insist on the validity of the 1949 Armistice Agreement, and the Israeli side would state its position. The UN representative at the talks would remain neutral, and he would listen to both sides and allow each to express its position. This was in effect the ILMAC formula provided for in the Armistice Agreement. I briefed leading Lebanese figures on the proposed formula, and Pérez de Cuéllar made it public on 31 October. Lebanese leaders were optimistic about the negotiations. They believed that the new Labour government under Prime Minister Shimon Peres would be more flexible than the Likud governments under Menachem Begin and Yitzhak Shamir.

The Naqurah discussions were held, under UN auspices, to arrange for Israeli withdrawal from Lebanon. Lebanon entered the discussions promising to implement the security arrangements under the Armistice Agreement. This was no mean feat. It meant our readiness to set aside the Cairo Agreement of 1969, under which Lebanon gave the PLO the right to violate these arrangements and attack Israel across our southern frontiers. Also it meant our readiness to extend our state authority in areas to be evacuated by Israeli forces.

We leaned heavily on UN Resolution 425, adopted unanimously by the Security Council on 19 March 1978, in the wake of Israel's invasion of southern Lebanon. The resolution called for Israeli withdrawal from all Lebanese territory and for the establishment of a United Nations Interim Force in Lebanon (UNIFIL). The force ultimately included some 6,000 officers and men from a number of countries. UNIFIL's role was to confirm the withdrawal of Israeli forces; restore international peace and security in the area; and assist the government of Lebanon in ensuring the return of its effective authority in the area occupied by Israel. Lebanon also relied on subsequent UN decisions, namely resolutions 505 and 509, also calling for an immediate and unconditional Israeli withdrawal from Lebanese territory.

The Naqurah Israel–Lebanon discussions opened on 8 November 1984, at UNIFIL headquarters, under the chairmanship of the UNIFIL commander representing the secretary-general of the United Nations. The UN delegation consisted of five officers, while the Lebanese and Israeli delegations consisted of six officers each.

The first obstacle we faced was Israel's position on the 1949 Armistice Agreement. The Israelis argued that Lebanon's participation in the June War of 1967 had rendered the agreement null and void. The problem was that this position was contradicted by Dayan's letter of August 1978. Lebanon rejected the Israeli argument since it had never cancelled the Armistice Agreement, nor, for that matter, had it participated in the 1967 war. The Israeli representative acted as if the letter did not exist. Indeed Israeli officials – including Dayan, the letter notwithstanding – had often declared that the Armistice Agreement between Lebanon and Syria was dead, and should be replaced by a new instrument. While Lebanon saw the Naqurah discussions as a UN process under the chairmanship of General Callahan, the Israelis portrayed them as direct discussions between Lebanon and Israel. Callahan, they insisted, was merely there to facilitate the talks, not to chair them.

The three delegations sat at three different tables and argued continuously about who was chairman and who was not. The Lebanese considered Callahan to be chairman. The Israelis considered the chairmanship to be on a rotating basis between Lebanon and Israel, with the UN present only as observers. Lebanon entered the discussions on the condition that they were conducted under UN auspices and UN chairmanship. The UN had kept the formula a bit vague to ensure that the discussions began, in the hope that matters like the chairmanship would be resolved in the process. The following is a sample of how each session began: Callahan: 'Good morning, let's begin.' As Callahan started each meeting he assumed he was the chairman; we always addressed him as such. The Israeli delegation, however, insisted that chairmanship rotate between Lebanon and Israel. Gilboa would start: 'If I am not mistaken, today I am the chairman, as General Hajj was the chairman of the previous session and, therefore, I hereby open the session.' Hajj would immediately respond by saying: 'Mr Chairman Callahan ...' etc., etc. This game continued throughout the discussions.

Israel's proposed security plan, after an Israeli withdrawal, was to divide the area from the Israeli frontier to Sidon into two areas: one extending from the frontier to the Zahrani river, the other from Zahrani to the Awwali river. The first was to be maintained by a territorial brigade consisting of elements friendly to Israel. The area from the Zahrani River to the Awwali River, just north of Sidon, was to be under UNIFIL control. Under no condition would Israel accept UNIFIL close to its borders. What Israel was in effect proposing was to detach the area from the Zahrani river to our southern frontiers and put it under a surrogate army similar, if not identical, to the South Lebanon Army under Lahd. This was a clear violation of sovereignty. The Lebanese plan was to deploy the Lebanese army and UNIFIL throughout South Lebanon, preferably from the area where UNIFIL was now deployed to the borders with Israel. The Israelis rejected our proposal, and we rejected theirs.

The Naqurah discussions ended in January 1985 in complete failure. In a way, they were bound to fail. Israel had no confidence in the Lebanese government, and it had accepted the Naqurah process merely to gain time and to show flexibility and goodwill, while it went ahead with its own plans to deploy as it saw fit. At the same time, Israel was putting up obstacles to prevent the Lebanese army from deploying to the Awwali river. With the failure of the Naqurah discussions Israel went ahead with the withdrawal and redeployment of its troops. The fate of the Christians in the areas of Sidon and the Iqlim al-Kharrub, north-east of Sidon, became a priority as soon as Israel's plan for withdrawal was announced. The president feared that the Iqlim would fall to the opposition forces, as had the Shuf before in the wake of LF–PSP confrontation. An opposition takeover would be likely to lead to another displacement of the Christian population.

When the Israelis previously withdrew from the Aley and the Shouf areas without coordination with us, it had led to the massacre and exodus of Christians from the region. There were about 150,000 Christians in the south, and in the wake of an Israeli withdrawal, it was increasingly likely that they might also be caught in clashes between the Lebanese Forces on the one hand, and between Muslim, Druze and Palestinian forces on the other. We worried that a new refugee problem would emerge in the south, and that the displaced Christian population would strain housing facilities in the Eastern Sector of Beirut and further exacerbate tensions between Christians and Muslims. We also feared lest intimidated Christians flocked to the south and joined Israel's surrogate army. Revenge in the affairs of man is often so strong as to blind objective interests and national principles.

I talked to Philip Habib on the telephone on 28 January 1985. While he was no longer an envoy he remained active in Middle Eastern affairs and maintained close ties with Shultz. It was his opinion that the Naqurah discussions were a joke. 'It would have been better for Lebanon had the talks never started at all', he insisted. What the Israelis were talking about was not full withdrawal, but permanent occupation of a part of Lebanon. 'I did my best to help,' Habib remarked, 'but I failed. I keep thinking of you guys, and all I can say is *Allah Ma'kum* (May God be with you).'

On the same day, I was told by Christopher Ross that Lebanon was no longer important to the United States. It was not an accident, he said, that the UN had been thrust into the Lebanese situation. The United States had let the UN become involved because it provided a convenient means for Washington to extract itself from the Lebanese crisis. The USA would come forth only if there was stability and peace, Ross told me, meanwhile we should be looking to the UN on the political-military front. Ross's advice reminded me of Wazzan's quip that Lebanon's complex crisis had been referred by the world's great powers to the Holy See for resolution.

I wondered about the attitude of a superpower that left a small country in trouble, only to come to its aid when the trouble was over. What Lebanon needed most was political assistance from the great democracies, and this it was not getting. Worse still, hostage-taking by radical forces operating within Lebanon, but controlled in large part by regional powers such as Iran, paralysed American activities in Lebanon and the region. One State Department official summed it up for me in the following way: 'It is sad but true that here is a superpower whose policy in a strategic region is caught in the issue of five kidnapped Americans.' American politics were largely preoccupied with hot issues, and the kidnappings were a hot issue, he said.

By the end of 1984, Lebanon was no longer perceived as a friendly country in the United States. A Gallup poll showed Lebanon ranking after Libya, Syria and the PLO as a source of terrorism. By 1985, the American officials I was dealing with talked about terrorism, and a resolution to the Palestinian problem. Only then, they hinted to me, could we proceed to solve the Lebanese problem. An exchange I had with George Shultz in January exemplified the new American attitude: 'Well, Elie,' Shultz began, 'let me hear your views. The main concern to me is the problem of terrorism and of the hostages now held by the terrorists in Lebanon.'

All I could answer was, 'Terrorism and hostages are not policy. Policy is to deal with the Lebanese problem in such a way that terrorism and hostage-taking will not take place.' I proceeded in the presence of Richard Murphy, the assistant secretary of state for Near East and South Asian affairs, to elaborate to Shultz what I thought should be the policy of the

USA. When I left Shultz's office, Murphy said: 'That was quite a lecture you delivered to the secretary of state. No one has done that before.' I told Murphy I was no longer a minister of foreign affairs bound by protocol. I was now an informal adviser, in effect, a free professor, Prometheus unbound, and I could say what I believed should be said.

Murphy, however, had no advice for me other than the UN route, which he admitted was not effective. Others within the US government who monitored Israeli policy repeated what we already feared: Israel was likely to withdraw from the south as it had from the Shuf, thus creating a violent situation leading to the forced displacement of the Christians southward to Israel's proposed security belt. A strong Christian presence on Israel's northern border would, in Israel's eyes, give Israel greater security and a sizeable human reservoir from which to get recruits for the South Lebanon Army. There seemed to be no light at the end of the tunnel. Indeed, the country appeared to be moving from one dark tunnel to another.

8

The Road to the Tripartite Agreement

Since Lausanne, the question of political reform had dominated the Lebanese political scene, and internal military conflict was justified in its name. The council of ministers, which met with great difficulty, tried to implement reforms on the basis of Karami's ministerial statement of 19 May 1984. This statement was based entirely on the Lausanne Document after it was refined by the Jumayyil–Asad Summit of the previous month. The ministers disagreed on the implementation of reforms. Sham'un, in particular, contested Karami's interpretations, and Karami's intent to coordinate closely with Syria. Sham'un said that there was a gap of one thousand kilometres between the ministers. To resolve the conflict, the president felt he had to appeal to President Asad for help. Jumayyil was ready to forge an alliance with Asad if the Syrian leader could encourage opposition ministers to cooperate with him, and extend government authority throughout the land. Jumayyil planned to meet Asad early in March 1985 to discuss cementing their relations and progress on reforms.

As preparations for the meeting went on, Walid Junblat's men were shelling the Christian Eastern Sector. The Eastern Sector covered generally the Eastern part of Beirut and the Christian quarter of al-Matn and Kisirwan, which is the Maronite heartland. As my wife and I were having lunch one day, our house in Ba'bda was hit. Doors were knocked wide open, glass shattered and gaping holes appeared in the ceiling in several places. We raced to the only room in our house with a cement ceiling – in most places the roof was merely wooden scaffolding covered with red bricks. Suddenly the phone rang. It was the president, furious with Junblat for shelling the presidential palace. What should we do? he asked. I responded that the only thing I had retrieved from the dining table was a glass of wine and shattered nerves. I was in no condition to discuss his enquiry on the telephone. As Junblat was an ally of Syria, the president believed the shelling was intended to weaken him prior to the summit in

189

Damascus. I recommended to him that he transcend the shelling and concentrate instead on forging a solid alliance with Asad.

The president wanted a friendship with Asad that would help him overcome internal obstacles. He admired Asad; he envied his hold on power, but resented his overwhelming influence in Lebanon. He knew that Asad was not especially enamoured of him, but he wanted results from the summit. He wanted to establish a Lebanese–Syrian task force to propose criteria of cooperation in security affairs, economic relations and information. He wanted Asad's support in unifying all Lebanon's forces, especially the pro-Syrian militias, behind the government. He wanted Asad to institute confidence-building measures to assure the Lebanese that their independence and sovereignty would not be lost. He also wanted agreement with Asad on basic reform principles relating to Lebanon's identity, its role in the Arab world, the presidency, parliament, the premiership, administrative centralization and decentralization, the establishment of new institutions, the social and economic system, the bureaucracy, the army, dissolution of the militias, and the return of refugees to their homes. In effect, he wanted the peace that was to follow the formation of Karami's Government of National Unity. Instead he had Amal fighting the Palestinians, Amal fighting PSP for turf, and the Sunni fundamentalists in Tripoli fighting Alawis for political control over the second capital. Furthermore the economy had been deteriorating and since the autumn of 1984 the Lebanese pound had been losing its value against the US dollar, thus causing financial concern that was to reach catastrophic proportions in the following years.

Prior to the summit, it was agreed that Khaddam would come to Bikfayya to work out logistical matters. On 5 March, I met Khaddam in Dhour al-Shwayr and accompanied him to Bikfayya. In his meeting with the president, Khaddam listened carefully to his ideas on reform, and the various other matters he wished to discuss with the Syrians. Among these was the establishment of new institutions which would give positions of power to the different communities. The Maronites had the presidency of the republic, the Shi'is had the presidency of the parliament (speaker) and the Sunnis had the presidency of the council of ministers (prime minister). The Druze wanted a senate instituted under a Druze presidency. The Greek Orthodox wanted either the presidency of the proposed senate or of the social and economic council. There were also other bodies – the Higher Court and the Constitutional Council. The politicians were clamouring for gains in the confessional pluralistic system and the president was reflecting their positions in his pre-summit talks with the Syrian vice-president.

When the president had completed his presentation Khaddam exclaimed: 'Mr President, these reforms confirm confessionalism and represent a step backward!' The president continued, saying that he wanted a package deal with Asad that would end the war and lead to withdrawals. Khaddam was not pleased with the idea of a package deal, and kept asking for a written document describing what the president had in mind concerning relations with Syria. He doubted whether a summit with Asad could be held soon, as Asad was busy forming a new government. To speed things up, however, Khaddam proposed to return to Bikfayya in a few days and bring with him Birri and Junblat. Syria saw the problem as one of conflicts between Lebanese warlords. Jumayyil, in Khaddam's judgement, was not ready to sign a special relations agreement with Syria. Jumayyil avoided this subject whenever it was hinted at. He wanted gains from his hoped-for friendship with Asad, but so did all the other Lebanese leaders who were allied with him. For such a balancing act it was better to hand it to Khaddam, the master tactician, and the experienced mechanic in the cantankerous Lebanese machine.

A mini-summit between the president and Khaddam was held in Bikfayya on 9 and 10 March 1985 and was attended by Karami, Birri, Junblat and General Ghazi Kana'an, the head of the Syrian military intelligence in Lebanon. This mini-summit was to discuss the ministerial statement and to eliminate the obstacles blocking its implementation. Soon the mini-summit turned into a disorganized and stormy two-day affair. Khaddam opened with a small lecture on Lebanon's fate. Man, he said, expanded his organization from the family to the village, to the tribe, to the city, and to the state. In Lebanon, he continued, we were doing the reverse. Perhaps the Lebanese, without knowing it, are dancing to the Israeli tune. 'Let's act like doctors,' Khaddam continued, 'let each of us say what the problem is, and then attempt to remedy it.'

Karami started by defining the problem as he saw it. Confessional representation and power-sharing should be expanded through laws; administrative decentralization should be applied, with the objective of developing all regions of Lebanon; and parliament should be reconstituted on the basis of numerical equality between Muslims and Christians.

Birri called for the abolition of political confessionalism, and insisted, 'I don't want anyone to be treated better than me, similarly I don't want to be treated better than others.' He was unhappy with the ministerial statement because it did not abolish political confessionalism. If political confessionalism were to be maintained then, Birri argued, we must establish equity amongst the confessions and, therefore, the Shi'ah should be treated equally with the Maronites and Sunnis in parliament.

Khaddam proposed a parliament which would be half-Christian and half-Muslim, but in which seats would not be specifically allocated to each confessional group. Birri liked the suggestion, but no one else did. Khaddam then argued for the abolition of confessionalism and warned that if we did not abolish it, the war in Lebanon would not end. Confessionalism would always give rise to a hundred Sha'bans and a hundred Musawis, he said, referring to two particularly militant Muslim leaders. 'Confessionalism is like fire, the more you feed it, the more it grows', Khaddam added. Abolition of confessionalism was a favorite theme of Khaddam and he excelled at expounding it, resorting to the boundless Ba'th secular ideology in which he was steeped.

Junblat complained that all we were doing was talking about the sex of the angels while the country was collapsing. The president retorted that the country was collapsing because the council of ministers did not meet and because the ministers were attacking him and each other with total disregard for the national interest.

The president proposed the adoption of a law to fight corruption. Khaddam exclaimed: 'If we do so, who will be left in the government or in the administration?' The president also urged the implementation of the clause in the ministerial statement on the ending of the war. 'Although we have a Government of National Unity,' he said, 'I hold most of my meetings in a bomb-shelter as the two ministers here [Birri and Junblat] keep shelling me.' The militias, he said, must return the tanks, armoured cars and trucks they had confiscated from the army, and they must transform themselves into unarmed political parties.

The president proposed incorporating members of the militias into the internal security forces, but Karami argued against this, pointing out that militias were partisan and could not be expected to serve the public interest. Khaddam responded that it was better to have the militias within the system than outside it. 'In that case,' Karami retorted, 'they will be in and we will be out.' Junblat argued that whether we liked it or not, some of these men would have to be incorporated into the system.

The subject was skirted and the discussion moved on to the Lebanese army. It was important to find answers to such questions as how could the army be united? How would it be equipped? And how could a reconciliation be brought about between the army and the militias? When a reference was made to compulsory military service, Karami, who was always careful about expenditure, wondered who would pay for it. Military service, noted Khaddam, was good for the character, and money could always be found. He recalled that he had had military training for 15 days, but that his commanding officer had put him in jail for half that period. This was not long enough, the president quipped, always eager to catch Khaddam off-guard.

Finally all agreed that it was Israeli meddling in Lebanese affairs that had led to confessional radicalism, and to the conflicts between the different communities. As always, the reference to Israel solved many problems. In former years the Lebanese politicians, always eager to put the blame on a third party, decided humorously to blame the Italians. Indeed, the phrase 'blame it on the Italians' had become part of Lebanese political parlance.

The president was disappointed with the meetings. He had wanted a summit with Asad and had ended having a mini-summit with Khaddam. He wanted a sort of alliance with Asad similar to the one between President Fuad Shihab and Jamal Abd al-Nasir, in the late 1950s, an alliance that would permit him to govern and get results; instead he had found that Khaddam was lukewarm to the idea.

The Intifadah

Despite his efforts to accommodate the Syrians, President Jumayyil had failed to change the Syrian attitude towards him. His reaction was to try instead to consolidate his position within the Maronite community and in the Kata'ib party. In his own Maronite community, however, authority was with the Lebanese militia, and particularly with Dr Samir Ja'ja, then the head of the military arm of the Lebanese Forces. The president and the head of the Kata'ib Party at that time, Dr Eli Karameh (who replaced Sheikh Pierre after his death on 29 August 1984) ousted Dr Ja'ja from the Kata'ib, but Ja'ja defied the order and proceeded, on 12 March, to take control of the northern parts of the Eastern Sector, from Jbeil to the Dog River. Ja'ja's rebellion, which came to be known as the 'Intifadah', was a challenge both to the president's entente with Syria, as well as to his leadership in the Christian regions of Lebanon. The president suspected Israeli involvement in Ja'ja's rebellion, but the US State Department denied any Israeli intervention.

Birri called the president and assured him of his and of Junblat's support against the Intifadah. The Syrian president called and offered to send any help the president needed to quell the rebellion. The president answered: 'It is best to pick our thorns with our own hands.' Joseph Abu Khalil proposed the convening of a conference of Christian leaders to come up with a unified Christian position on the developments in the Eastern Sector. The president liked the idea and a conference was held at the presidential palace. It included Christian parliamentarians, ministers, former ministers and religious leaders. It convened for four hours and issued a statement supporting the president and his policy orientation.

Emissaries kept telling me that the Syrians were disappointed that the president had not asked for help. The Syrians were supposedly ready to move in, crush the Intifadah, and withdraw from the Eastern Sector. I told them that such action would have a devastating impact on the Christian community and should be avoided. The best course, I believed, was to find a political solution to the Intifadah and treat the causes that had led to it. One way of doing it, I proposed, was to integrate the leaders of the Intifadah into the leadership of the Kata'ib, and thus help rejuvenate the ossified party. Bartholomew saw me on 18 March, after holding a meeting with Pakradouni. He told me that he had delivered a message to Pakradouni which stated that the Lebanese Forces rebels, through their actions, were hindering the political reform process. The United States deplored the resort to force, and believed that the Intifadah had weakened the president and the presidency.

Asad, who was now concerned about the Intifadah and its influence in the Christian community, called the president on Friday 22 March, and invited him to Damascus. The two presidents met alone over the weekend. On Monday, I had breakfast with the president. He was depressed, and he opened the Bible and started reading from the Book of Job. He wondered out loud about the frustrations of the presidency. Whenever he was in bad mood, which these days was often, I tried to find analogies which would help snap him out of his depression. I told him that I had just finished reading Gore Vidal's work on Lincoln: 'Lincoln', I said, 'faced problems like yours. His capital was surrounded, assassination attempts on his life were numerous, his generals quarrelled but did not fight, his government was in disarray, and his life in the White House was a nightmare.' The president was anxious to hear more. He wanted to read the book himself, but when he heard how long it was, he resisted the temptation.

The summit yielded nothing, the president told me. 'It is amazing', he admitted, 'how Asad keeps you busy with nothing. You talk with him and you think you agree on everything, then you walk out and you realize you have got nothing concrete, nothing at all.' The president felt helpless in the face of the crises erupting around him. The Syrians were not happy with the way he was handling the Intifadah. They thought the new leaders of the Lebanese Forces were taking control of the Kata'ib Party rather than the reverse, as the president had assured them. The president feared that the Syrians would attack the Lebanese Forces, and that this would be interpreted as an attack on the Maronites.

As the president was frustrated in seeing power in the Eastern Sector shift to the intifidah, so was Prime Minister Karami unhappy with the shifting balance of power in the predominantly Sunni cities of Tripoli, Beirut and Sidon. Karami and the Sunni leadership realized that they were losing ground in the urban areas to the Shi'ah and the Druze. In mid-

April, Amal and the PSP had crushed the major Sunni militia, the Murab-itun, in the process undermining Karami in much the same way as President Jumayyil was being undermined by the Lebanese Forces.

Karami's reaction was to announce his resignation, criticize the militias, and launch a few broadsides at Syria. The Sunni Mufti, Sheikh Hassan Khaled, also attacked the militias. Syria was accused by the Sunnis of having encouraged Amal and the PSP to eliminate the Murabitun, since the Sunni militia was collaborating with Yasir Arafat and the PLO. They argued that the attack on the Murabitun was an indirect attack on Arafat's forces, who were at the time in a bitter power struggle with the Syrians in Lebanon. Birri and Junblat were ecstatic with their victory. They ridiculed Karami and boasted of their intention to appoint a new prime minister. Karami did not resign officially but, as was his practice in difficult moments, he simply stayed home and called his act a resignation. As Israel withdrew further south, conflict arose in the areas it evacuated.

On 25 April, what had been expected happened. Fighting between the Lebanese Forces on the one hand and the Palestinians and the PSP on the other led to a Palestinian offensive against Christian villages east of Sidon, forcing the Christian inhabitants to flee towards Jezzine. The army units that were dispatched to South Lebanon to secure order disintegrated into Christian and Muslim units and became themselves a source of danger.

The president contemplated resigning. On 27 April, he told a Syrian envoy, Muhammad Khawli, that if Asad continued to support Birri, Junblat and Franjiyyeh against him, he would gladly leave office. As things stood, the president continued, he felt deserted and cornered, and did not believe that he could continue in office. He told Khawli that he had foreseen the unfolding of events in the south on 4 April, when he had sent his written message to Christian leaders. The message had been confidential, but the president now released it to the press to defend himself against attacks on his policies by the Lebanese Forces, and to minimize the fallout from further displacement of Christians.

On 28 April, Iqlim al-Kharroub fell to Walid Junblat's forces. Some members of the Kata'ib suggested to President Jumayyil that he resign, take control of the Lebanese army's strongest unit, the Eighth Brigade, and retrench himself in the Metn region, as Birri had done in Beirut with the Sixth Brigade, and Junblat in the Shuf with the Twelfth Brigade. The president rejected the advice out of hand. He insisted that he could not make a 180-degree turn in his political philosophy and remain true to himself. Though it was unlikely that the president would resign, he was not opposed to raising speculation that it was a possibility. This tactic had been successfully resorted to by Presidents Fuad Shihab, Charles Helou and Elias Sarkis.

Fearing that the president's resignation would isolate and expose them, the leaders of the Intifadah, Ja'ja, Hubayqah and Pakradouni, decided to cease their attacks on the president and, instead, to start coordinating with him. They met him in Bikfayya on Monday 29 April, and soon after that, they began to take public positions similar to those of the president. By mid-May, a startling new trend was evident within the leadership of the Intifadah. Eli Hubayqah, who now headed the Lebanese Forces command, began to issue statements that met with Syria's approval. At that point, Michel Smaha, a member of the Lebanese Forces, an adviser to the president, and a friend of the Syrian regime, paved the way for Hubayqah to travel to Damascus, and indeed to make a 180-degree change in orientation and shift from friendship with Israel to friendship with Syria.

This new policy of openness towards Syria masked an internal struggle for power within the executive council of the Lebanese Forces. Hubayqah's actions did not meet with the approval of Samir Ja'ja. The two men now represented the two extremes within the Christian community: Hubayqah had his power base in the Ashrafiyyeh sector of East Beirut. Ja'ja had his power base in the more rural Maronite heartland north of Beirut, and was less willing to compromise on his vision of Maronite security and self-interest. For the moment, Hubayqah controlled the decision-making within the executive council, and Ja'ja reluctantly went along with the new policy *vis-à-vis* Syria. But as subsequent events would show, he was simply biding his time.

The weaker the president's position became, the more vulnerable he was to attack. Birri and Junblat, continued their barrage of words and rockets against the Eastern Sector. Words, the president argued, were more devastating than rockets; they shattered the national confidence, exposed the divisions within the government, and eroded what was left of the prestige of the presidency.

Those working in the presidential palace had become adjusted to the shelling and sniping. They took them in their stride, and even with humour. Humour was a psychological shield for us, and provided a shroud of normality in a situation that was eminently abnormal. In encountering a colleague in the corridors of the presidential palace, one was as likely as not to greet him with a surprised 'I see you are still alive!' When, on 30 May, a foreign minister from a revolutionary Arab country paid a visit to the palace, we all wondered how a revolutionary would react to the shelling. He arrived under heavy guard and a hail of bullets. As he left his armoured car to walk the few steps to the palace door he looked frightened and pale, and raced indoors. During lunch with the president, a rocket hit the dining room knocking down walls, shattering glass, and spraying shrapnel throughout the second floor of the palace. While all the diners were disturbed, only he threw himself on the floor. The president, who enjoyed such scenes, tried to assure him that everything was fine, and that the two should resume their discussion. The foreign minister didn't agree; he wanted to leave as soon as possible, and return home. In the end, perhaps, the real question should have been who were the normal ones, we or our unfortunate guest?

A wave of kidnappings of foreigners started in Beirut. Since the American University of Beirut was the main employer of Americans, it became a target for the intensely anti-American Hizballah organization. I had cautioned AUB President Calvin Plimpton and others about the danger they faced as Americans. I had known Plimpton for some time and had always admired his courage and his readiness to risk his life to keep the university going. I also knew that his humourous carefree attitude could lead to his death. Early on, when he was in Beirut, I had called him to my office together with representatives from all the state security branches. The representatives told him that he should be well guarded; Beirut was dangerous and the Lebanese intelligence services were too weak to protect him. There was a risk that he could be killed. 'Well,' joked Plimpton, 'now I rank higher than an ambassador; last week they threatened to kidnap me; now they threaten to assassinate me.' One of the security officials advised Plimpton to hire twelve guards and arm them well. The official promised that he would have the men trained himself. 'No', said Plimpton. 'A few years back I visited Sheikh Shakhbut of Abu Dhabi and found that his guards carried old Ottoman guns. I said: "Sheikh, your guards need better guns than these." He replied: "I am a wise fellow; all my predecessors were killed by their guards, so I intentionally give them these impressive but useless guns."' We finally managed to provide Plimpton with guards. Nevertheless, he continued to argue that guards could not protect against fate.

Western ambassadors were also vulnerable. The US ambassador had a virtual militia of some 500 guards to protect him and his embassy staff. The ambassador himself carried a loaded gun which he handled like a top-secret document. A number of ambassadors enjoyed this whole scene. Their security details were no less impressive than those of presidents, and this often gave the ambassadors extra clout and extra pay. One man who did not enjoy the danger at all, however, was Comte Louis d'Elsius, the Belgian ambassador. He was always seeing me with news that some militia or other was after him. I advised him to go to Belgium until the danger had abated, and he was happy to take my advice.

University professors have no militias and, unlike ambassadors, they tend to be innocent, if not naïve, in assessing dangers against themselves. Accordingly I counselled American faculty members at the AUB to leave

Lebanon quietly. My wife and I made elaborate plans to get them out of West Beirut and to receive them at our home in Ba'bda. Many left under terrible conditions and needed a great deal of attention and reassurance. I secured special permission to send them by military helicopter to Cyprus.

As we concentrated on getting American faculty members out of Lebanon, a TWA plane was hijacked on 14 June by radical Islamic militants and brought to the Beirut International Airport. Some 40 American passengers were taken hostage and housed in various quarters of Beirut to foil any attempt by the United States or by Israel to rescue them. The hijackers demanded the release of 700 Shi'i prisoners in Israeli jails. This led to a confusing series of manoeuvres, statements and contacts, with each side masking its true intentions. The Israelis declared that a decision had been taken to release the prisoners before the hijacking took place. They added, however, that Israel would not implement the decision unless it was specifically requested to do so by the United States. The United States, in turn, publicly insisted that it would not negotiate with terrorists, but stated privately it would not oppose a release of the Shi'i prisoners. I believe that the Americans must have been considering a military operation, since Bartholomew repeatedly asked that all the remaining American citizens at the American University of Beirut should leave.

At that point, Nabih Birri, then the minister of justice, entered the scene and took over control of the hostages from the hijackers. Birri was playing a difficult game: by taking the hostages he was attempting to distance them from the more radical elements who had hijacked the TWA flight; on the other hand, Birri supported the demands of his radical co-religionists, and wanted the prisoners in Israel released. Birri was a moderate doing his best under difficult conditions. He wanted both to help the hostages, and to quell the rising radical tide in his community by identifying with the popular demands of the hijackers. While Birri acted as mediator in Beirut his image in the US media was that of a hijacker. Syrian intervention, together with the release of Shi'i prisoners in Israeli jails, led to the release of the TWA hostages on 30 June.

On 1 July, Bartholomew asked to see me at home urgently. He delivered the following message:

> The Beirut International Airport has become a source of danger to all air passengers. The United States has been singled out for air piracy and can no longer permit such actions to go unpunished. As of today the USA will initiate efforts with all countries concerned to stop flights to and from the said airport; the USA will refuse landing rights to the Lebanese airlines, MEA and TMA; the USA will attempt to influence Lebanon's neighbours to stop providing air information on flights passing through Lebanon's

airspace; the USA will attempt to cut off all aviation fuel from reaching Beirut. President Reagan and Secretary Shultz are taking these measures with regret, not to hurt Lebanon, but to hurt those in Lebanon who have become a source of danger to air travellers in general and to American travellers in particular.

I was furious. I told him that they were punishing Lebanon and the Lebanese, not the hijackers, and that our government would consider this move to be unfriendly. I urged him to talk to Foreign Minister Karami before the decision was made public. He said he would, but did not seem to be in a hurry, as if he did not mind having Karami, or 'Mr Rhetoric', as the Americans called him, slighted. Unfortunately Karami read about these decisions in the press, minutes before Bartholomew called him on 2 July. After Bartholomew's visit, I learned from the president that the ambassador had visited him earlier, and had delivered the same message.

The president then described his encounter with Bartholomew. When the ambassador had finished recounting the measures against the airport, the president had thanked him. A long silence had then followed. 'Don't you have any questions to ask, Mr President?' Bartholomew had asked. 'No', Jumayyil had answered. Another long silence had followed before Bartholomew excused himself and left. The president said:

> Elie, what do you expect me to say to him? Where would I start? I could have said, 'You wanted Birri and Junblat in the government, you got them; you wanted a broad-based government, you got it; you know who is respon- sible for the hijacking, and yet you punish the very state that cannot stop it; you keep weakening me and you expect me to deliver miracles.' I was so frustrated, I decided not to talk if only to preserve the very thin thread which remains between us and the United States.

While we understood American anger at the hijacking incident, we felt that the American measures punished the Lebanese state, not the hijackers. These measures, we thought, could even encourage hijacking and further weaken the state. We had intended to ask for a meeting of the Security Council to contest the measures, but finally we decided to lodge a com- plaint instead.

An amusing thing happened while we were drafting the complaint. The door of my office opened and a certain visitor walked in. He did not want to see me, he announced, but wanted to see the president on a matter of great importance. I urged him to tell me about it, as I could be trusted with state secrets. He looked at me quizzically and then shouted in a voice that brought half the palace officials to my office, 'Peace will not come to this land unless I am appointed minister of defence!' I realized then that the poor fellow was totally insane, and wondered how he had made it into the Palace. I quickly agreed with him and promised to have him appointed defence minister soon. Then I gently escorted him out of the building. When I told the president about our visitor, he said: 'Elie, as usual, you have acted hastily. The man is right. The time for the insane has arrived.'

Militias Meet in Damascus

Throughout the summer of 1985 Hubayqah was communicating with Syria, and plans for the meeting of representatives from the Lebanese Forces under Hubayqah, Amal and PSP were finalized. Vice-President Khaddam was the architect behind these meetings. He wanted the 'young men' in the militias to agree without the involvement of the government, the president and the established political leaders. He vowed to do that after the collapse of the Lausanne Conference in March 1984. He found Eli Hubayqah, a Maronite interlocutor, a confident young man with boundless energy and the conviction of the convert.

The Maronite community and the president were nervous. The future political formula of Lebanon and, therefore, the place of the Maronites in the pantheon of power was being negotiated by Hubayqah's emissaries in Damascus, neither of whom was a Maronite – Michel Samaha was a Greek Catholic and As'ad Shaftari was a Greek Orthodox.

The representatives of the three militias continued to meet regularly in Damascus, and by mid-October 1985, it was rumoured that they had reached agreement on major reform principles. President Jumayyil, Prime Minister Karami and Speaker Hussein al-Husseini were kept outside this entire process, and the president's efforts to crack the shield of secrecy surrounding the negotiations ended in failure. Hubayqah, meanwhile, began preparing the Maronite community for concessions, which he said he was making 'for Lebanon, not for this or that party'.

The president was anxious to be part of the political process. Not only was he president of the republic, but as a major leader of the Christian community, he was quickly losing ground to Hubayqah. As he was planning to address the General Assembly in October, he thought this would be a good opportunity to meet with Asad, coordinate with him on UN affairs, and try to find out what was going on in the militia talks. On 20 October, the president went to Damascus for a brief meeting with Asad. What Jumayyil wanted to know Asad was not ready to talk about. Jumayyil probed for information on the tripartite discussions going on in Damascus. Asad answered that he was not informed and that when the three militias agreed, then the president would be included. If he wanted more information now, a Jumayyil emissary should come to Damascus and talk to Khaddam. The president sent me word from Damascus to come and meet with Khaddam and get a briefing from him on the tripartite discussions.

When I met Khaddam he told me that the three militia leaders would soon reach an agreement on a document, and that a national conference would be held in Damascus to approve it. After this, a government would be formed to implement the document. Syria would have a peace-keeping role throughout Lebanon, even if it were kept at the level of observers. As usual, Khaddam was cordial, and he expressed disappointment that I was not in the government. He was unhappy with the Government of National Unity, and gave me his opinion of the situation in Lebanon:

> We agreed with Jumayyil to have a cabinet of 24 ministers. Instead he chose a government of ten, half of them senile. Who would make his own father a minister? Who would bring that tottering old man Sham'un into a cabinet? Though Jumayyil is not 'the star of the age', we support him, and we keep telling our allies we will not force him to resign. The constitutional process must be followed, and Jumayyil must complete his term. Had he led in reforms, we would not have reached the bad situation we are now in. The Maronites are not going to have security if they are going to insist on past privileges. Syria, as a secular state, cannot support confessionalism. Birri, Junblat and Hubayqah are young, they have daring ideas and they are aiming at abolishing confessionalism. Jumayyil talked to us about Karami's ministerial statement, but it is no longer adequate. Hubayqah is an intelligent fellow. Can you imagine me, an Arab nationalist, sitting with Hubayqah? Changes are indeed taking place; we will not discuss with Jumayyil or with you the contents of the document that is being worked out. When it is completed we will send it to you for comment. You might even submit it to a plebiscite.

'A plebiscite under the existing conditions', I responded, 'will give the results that you and I know. If there is a plebiscite, we should have neutral observers.' 'My God!' shouted Khaddam, 'are you going to bring back the Atlantic Fleet? Perhaps you also want the Russians', he added, laughing. 'No, there will be no observers.' I then argued against a document on the future of Lebanon prepared by three militia leaders. I believed that the militia leaders should have a role in the political process, but within a constitutional framework. Khaddam gave me no details on the agreement, but he was loquacious when discussing Lebanese politics and Syria's positive role in opposing the radicals in all communities.

The Maronites were increasingly nervous about Hubayqah's opening to Syria. The Kata'ib Party was now considering preparing itself to confront Hubayqah militarily, if necessary. Hubayqah was riding high, however. The Syrians released 31 Christian hostages to show the Christians that

Hubayqah could deliver. Asim Qansu, the head of Lebanon's Ba'th Party, withdrew a battalion of his militia from the Green Line to ease tension between East and West Beirut. The wave of opinion in favour of the Damascus process was so high in the autumn of 1985 that anybody who opposed it risked going under.

In the spirit of coordination, which we hoped to preserve during this critical period, I met Khaddam again on 30 October to brief him on the Lebanese situation as we saw it and to probe further into the Damascus process. Khaddam again gave me few details, but he expressed readiness to discuss with us the proposed agreement as a whole once it was completed. He wanted first, however, to commit the three militia leaders to the agreement in writing. He said, 'I want their signatures affixed to a document to stop each of them from saying I cannot do this or that because of Fadlallah or Shamseddine or Jumayyil. Then you will take the document to the president who will conduct his own consultations on it, and we will then hold a national conference in Damascus.' 'The conference should take place in Beirut', I said; 'Fine', he responded. 'Are you Lebanese getting sensitive?' 'We have always been', I replied. I told him that I expected the conference to last a week or so. Khaddam said no. It could finish its work in one brief session, perhaps an hour or more. I left Khaddam with the distinct impression that the document was to be accepted as it was, perhaps with minor, preferably editorial, changes. My job was to find out what was going on and not to press specific points of view but, once again, I had obtained nothing. I had discovered that when Khaddam wanted to be secretive, he talked a lot, but led one nowhere.

On Saturday 2 November, General Muhammad al-Khawli arrived in Bikfayya with the document, which would be known as the Tripartite Agreement. The president was in a bad mood, and I tried to change this and prepare him for a constructive meeting with Asad's emissary. I came close to him, touched his hand and said: 'You are happy, you are very happy, and we are going to show Khawli how happy and relaxed you are.' We both burst out laughing, and we were still laughing when Khawli was ushered in. I then left the two alone.

Later I rejoined the president and the Syrian envoy, and was surprised to see how uncommunicative Khawli was. Nothing in the styles of Asad or Khaddam had prepared me for the silent sphinx-like demeanour of Khawli. He had no answers to our questions; he just wrote them down and promised to relay them faithfully to Asad. The president had to think fast while he read the text, and the tension in the room could have been cut with a knife as he sought to engage Asad's emissary in a substantive discussion on the agreement. This was to no avail. When Khawli left, the president looked at me and said: 'Elie, we have a disaster here; it is much worse than I thought. I am too distressed to talk about it today. Take it home, read it, and let's examine it carefully tomorrow.'

I then met our security chiefs to evaluate support for the Tripartite Agreement. They said that the Lebanese Forces were divided on it and that many of their leaders had not seen the text. They argued that the document had been 'shoved down the throat' of Hubayqah, and that he was 'looking for someone to rescue him from his commitment'. He was supposed to go to Damascus to sign the agreement, but reportedly he had had second thoughts. This led the Syrians to send us an urgent message telling us not to show the text to anyone, because it had not yet taken its final form. At the same time, Damascus Radio announced that it was in no one's interest to block the agreement.

Former presidents Sulayman Franjiyyeh and Kamil Sham'un also criticized the Tripartite Agreement for abolishing confessionalism and for weakening the presidency. Pamphlets were distributed in East Beirut attacking Hubayqah and the Tripartite Agreement in the name of the 'martyred Bashir Jumayyil'.

The Tripartite Agreement

The document we received from Khawli was dated 26 October 1985. A handwritten note on the first page stated that it had been agreed upon by the Lebanese Forces, Amal and the PSP, and that it had been read in full on that date in the presence of Marwan Himadeh and Akram Shuhayyib representing the PSP, Muhammad Beydoun representing Amal, and As'ad Shaftari and Michel Samaha representing the Lebanese Forces. The document had been witnessed by Vice-President Khaddam, who had affixed his signature to it.

The document, entitled 'A Project for a National Solution in Lebanon', consisted of 25 pages divided into the following headings: Introduction, General Principles, Basic Principles of the Political System, the Transitional Period, Distinctive Relations between Lebanon and Syria, and an Appendix on Ending the War in Lebanon. The introduction called for the liberation of Lebanon from Israeli occupation, for the return of peace and stability to the country, and for the establishment of a true democratic system there. The general principles affirmed the sovereignty, freedom and independence of Lebanon and the unity of its people, land and institutions within its internationally recognized frontiers. Lebanon's identity was recognized as Arab. All efforts designed to lead to political decentralization, federation, confederation, cantonization and developmental decentralization were rejected as 'partitionist'. The agreement called for a new deconfessionalized political system. A senate would be established, and would share, with parliament, the right to deliberate on substantive matters such as amendments to the constitution, matters of war and peace, and laws on personal status. A new government would appoint a constituent assembly to prepare the new constitution.

The agreement went on to state that the total abolition of confessionalism, and the implementation of other reforms, would be completed by parliament within a five-year period. The powers of the president were to be curtailed, while those of the prime minister were to be defined more clearly than was the case in the present constitution of 1926. Real executive power was to be vested in the Council of Ministers. A ministerial council consisting of six ministers of state representing the six major Lebanese religious communities (Maronite, Greek Orthodox, Greek Catholic, Sunni, Shi'ah and Druze) would act on major political matters.

Distinctive relations between Lebanon and Syria were spelled out under the following categories:

- Foreign affairs: coordination in foreign affairs should cover Arab, regional, and international relations. Direct and confidential communication between those responsible for foreign affairs in the two countries must be established.
- Military relations: due to Syria's struggle with Israel, Lebanon and Syria agree to the stationing of Syrian military units in specific locations in Lebanon agreed upon by a Lebanese–Syrian military committee, in accordance with the strategic security considerations of Lebanon and Syria. The Syrian army will be deployed in Lebanon until such time when a reconstituted Lebanese army is ready to assume its role in the regional strategic balance.
- Security relations: the motto 'Lebanon's security derives from Syria's security and vice versa' should be translated into concrete agreements ensuring security complementarity between the two countries. Agreements will be concluded to ensure 'coordination and complementarity between the security offices in both states'.
- Education: mixed committees from the two countries will lay the foundations for a complete educational system in Lebanon. Private education in Lebanon will be preserved, and care will be taken to prevent private education from sowing the seed of partition amongst the Lebanese and from creating an atmosphere inimical to the Arabs and Syria.
- Information: 'as distinctive relations must be protected against disinformation coming from Lebanon, Lebanese information must attain a high degree of national responsibility and must adhere to the agreed upon principles defining new orientation of the state.

Reactions to the Tripartite Agreement

I thought the Tripartite Agreement could be salvaged, but I wanted almost every sentence rewritten. I felt that the principles were basically correct, but that many of them went too far to be acceptable. I also felt that a broader consultation could have produced a more acceptable document. I wanted the widest possible cooperation and coordination between Lebanon and Syria, within the parameters of independence and sovereignty. I had coined the phrase, 'distinctive relations with Syria and excellent relations with the other Arab states', which the president had accepted as a pillar of his foreign policy. The root verb *mayyaza* in 'distinctive' (*mumay-yazah*) and in 'excellent' (*mumtazah*) gave a rhythmic sound to the Arabic slogan. I recognized that, in the 1940s and 1950s, Lebanon and Syria coordinated their foreign policies, and their foreign ministers met regularly prior to regional or international conferences. Coordination between Lebanon and Syria in Arab affairs was essential, I believed. Yet Lebanon was different from Syria; it had a different economy, different cultural contacts, and different historical relations with the other nations of the world. In my view, there was no strategic need to coordinate, on a daily basis, in all the domains covered by the Tripartite Agreement. The concept of complementarity could be applied in certain areas, but not all.

The Lebanese outlook in many areas was different from the Syrian outlook, particularly in the fields of education and information. The Lebanese educational system had to be reformed, but it could not be like the Syrian educational system. The Syrian regime was a movement regime. It was ideological and military in its orientation, and the educational system and the media reflected these orientations. Ours was a liberal pluralistic democracy with a highly diverse educational system. A mixed educational committee meant Syrian intervention in Lebanese educational policy, but it would certainly not mean Lebanese intervention in Syrian educational policy. It is usually the strong that intervenes, not the weak. Lebanon had always been a country that published information which was unpublishable in other Arab countries. Compared to these Arab countries, it had always had a serious and independent media. In Lebanon, one could write or speak without government approval, or against the government, and not be imprisoned for it. Freedom in Lebanon had certainly been exploited to harmful ends in past years, but this situation demanded reform and improvement. Freedom could not, however, be recast and changed completely as the agreement threatened to do, and still claim to be freedom.

The president wanted copies of the agreement sent to ex-presidents Charles Helou and Kamil Sham'un and to Patriarch Khoreish. As we had been asked by the Syrians not to distribute the agreement, I advised the president not to send the text but to have an emissary read it to them. He agreed. Meanwhile, the press was freely commenting on the agreement, and ex-minister Michel al-Murr, who had played a role in its drafting, was reading it to everyone in sight. Reaction to the Tripartite Agreement in the various Lebanese communities was largely negative. Hubayqah was having difficulty selling it to his military commander, Samir Ja'ja, while former presidents Sham'un and Franjiyyeh, as well as the Maronite monks of Kaslik, the independent Maronite deputies bloc, and the Maronite bishops all opposed the agreement. Hussein al-Husseini, the Shi'i speaker of parliament, said the agreement had too many loopholes to work.

The Lebanese Forces began taking a more defensive tone on the Tripartite Agreement, pointing out that the distributed text was not what they had agreed to, since it did not include a number of amendments which they had proposed.

Pressure was mounting on the president to reject the agreement. I counselled caution, and urged him to deal with the facts in the best way possible. He had to maintain a presidential attitude, consult with all leaders, and keep his lines of communication open with Asad. The Kata'ib wanted the president to reject the agreement. I believed it should be amended. These two positions were put to the test throughout the coming weeks. Some Kata'ib leaders wanted the president to take over the Kata'ib Party before Hubayqah did. I felt that this was neither simple nor desirable. The president, I argued, should not be dealing with partisan politics, and should restrict himself to presidential affairs. This conflict in views led to heated debates between me and the Kata'ib partisans. I wanted the president to develop ties with Asad and exact benefits for Lebanon. Other advisers felt that the president should instead oppose Asad and become a hero amongst the Christians. I did not believe in sectarian politics, and thus I never really appreciated this line of thinking.

The text of the agreement, which had been kept more or less secret up to then, was published on 19 November by the newspaper *Al-Safir*. The American reaction to the accord came to us through Bartholomew. He noted that Syria wanted reforms in Lebanon, but that it also intended to get political gains through distinctive relations between Lebanon and Syria. Lebanon had a friend in the United States, and Washington would use its influence in Syria if it was needed. Bartholomew said that the president's decision to leave the door open on the agreement was good. Nevertheless, he believed that the Lebanese Forces had been naïve in the Damascus negotiations. They had not meant to make such extensive concessions, and had ultimately allowed the Syrians to do what they wished. The Lebanese Forces felt cornered, Bartholomew added, and he remarked that Hubayqah would not sign the agreement if it did not include the amendments recommended by his associates.

On 25 November Hariri called me from Paris to say that amendments could be made to the agreement, and that Sulayman Franjiyyeh would visit Damascus soon to discuss them. He also noted that when President Jumayyil met Asad he could suggest amendments as well. A national conference would also meet and introduce its amendments, and thus the document would be approved by the broadest possible consensus. All I could do was tell Hariri that I hoped he was right, because as the text now stood, it had many problems. Meanwhile, we heard that the Lebanese Forces had submitted their amendments to the Syrians, and that these had been accepted in principle by Khaddam. This seemed to support Hariri's claim.

In the light of this, I flew to Paris on 28 November to meet Hariri and discuss possible amendments. Hariri knew that the president was opposed to the agreement, and he wanted to know why. He felt that the president's fears were not justified since the agreement would be submitted to a national conference for approval. He asked the president, in the name of King Fahd, to be forthcoming about reforms, since the war would not end without them.

Hariri and I read the text amended by the Lebanese Forces, and made extensive changes of our own on virtually all the important points in the agreement. We spent over 20 hours discussing its contents, and I tried to be flexible, suggesting amendments which could still rescue it. Jumayyil approved the amendments I had worked out with Hariri and he felt that, with them, he had a reasonable text.

Khaddam asked Hariri if I could come to Damascus and discuss the amendments with him. I did so, and I believe my flexibility had an impact on Khaddam, since he began to talk about changes to the text which he had not been willing to consider before. Khaddam did not indicate, however, whether he would accept all or most of our amendments, but he was satisfied with our approach, and he asked for time to consult with his allies – namely Birri and Junblat.

While Hubayqah, Junblat, Birri and their advisers were meeting Khaddam in the last two weeks of December, I worked furiously on an amended agreement, which I completed on 27 December. My version was based on the Tripartite Agreement and on the discussions I had held with Hariri who, in turn, had been consulting with Riyad and Damascus.

On 28 December, the three militia leaders signed a final version of the Tripartite Agreement under Syrian supervision. Immediately the three militia leaders and the Syrians proclaimed that the document had to be accepted by all without amendment. In addition, talks were in full swing on forming a new government made up of the three leaders and their associates. Although they were not parties to the deliberations leading to the Tripartite Agreement, Prime Minister Karami and Speaker Husseini came out in support of it. Meanwhile they were consulted, and they had met with Syrian leaders who left no doubt about their interest in having the agreement approved by all its allies in Lebanon. Despite these developments, the president still hoped that he could get his amendments across in discussions with Asad.

On the same day, Bartholomew visited me at home to complain about the Christian leaders who had accompanied Hubayqah to Damascus. He was particularly annoyed by the position of the two former foreign ministers, Khalil Abi Hamad and Fuad Butrus. There were also a number of leading parliamentarians who went to Damascus, witnessed the signing of the Agreement, came out in support of it, and spoke openly of joining a government that would put this agreement into effect. Bartholomew feared that Ja'ja, who controlled the military arm of the Lebanese Forces, would initiate military action against Hubayqah. Ja'ja was clearly unhappy with Hubayqah's 'defection' to the Syrian camp and was biding his time before he unseated Hubayqah. Actually Hubayqah joked about Ja'ja leading a coup against him and was anxious to get the agreement behind him, get in the government, and gain a position of power within a legitimate authority backed by Syria. The ambassador wanted the president to express support for the agreement, but also to keep consulting with other Lebanese leaders so as to introduce amendments in discussions with Asad. The agreement, Bartholomew said, was like a train stopping at 50 stations. His advice was that we get on the train, and if we wished to leave, to do so at any of the 50 stations on the way.

On Monday 30 December, Faruk al-Shar', the Syrian foreign minister, delivered the new text of the Tripartite Agreement to the president. He also brought an urgent invitation for the president to meet Asad the following day. The president, hoping to buy time, responded that he was unable to do so. Shar' suggested the day after, and again the president excused himself, giving as an excuse his busy schedule around the New Year. Shar' then insisted that the meeting should take place on Thursday 2 January 1986, and the president reluctantly agreed. He knew that Asad would press him to approve the agreement without amendments, or with minimal changes to the text. Judging from Shar''s tone, there was no chance to introduce the amendments on which I had been working. Shar' left, and the president fell into a deep depression. In depression he becomes silent.

President Jumayyil was, once again, in an unenviable position. For the second time during his presidency, he had to decide whether to accept a fateful agreement which failed to fulfil his expectations. The pressure on him was intense: the Jumayyil family and its entourage wanted him to reject the agreement out of hand. I counselled a different course: I recommended that he try to work with Asad to amend all the clauses on which he felt strongly, and to gain time and call for a national conference on the agreement. I believed that under no circumstances should he reject the agreement out of hand and break with Asad. I felt that his rejection would spark off fighting and lead to gains by the opposition and to a further weakening of the presidency. My advice was based on practical considerations. I wanted an alliance with Asad, and through the alliance the president could influence the amendment of the agreement and the course of events. Without Asad he was exposed. His opposition, I argued, would lead only to his isolation and to the expansion of the opposition, with Syrian support.

The more I spoke to Jumayyil in this tone the more distant he seemed. From time to time he would break his long brooding silence and say: 'Elie, I am not on your wavelength.' This disturbed me, as we rarely disagreed on fundamental foreign policy issues. There was, however, a point in his mind which I could not reach. This was the point where the president's Maronite, Kata'ib and Jumayyil background met, and it was truly alien to me. The president had urged me to always pay attention to this dimension of his personality. A close and trusted friend of mine, Joseph Abu Khalil, the leading ideologue of the Kata'ib Party and the closest adviser to the president's father Sheikh Pierre Jumayyil, had never ceased to explain this side of the president's personality to me. His explanations had little impact on my thinking. So different were our backgrounds that it was impossible for me to ever fully empathize with the president's perspective.

A two-month period had elapsed between the time the first draft of the Tripartite Agreement was sent to us through Muhammad Khawli, and the date on which the final draft of the agreement was signed by the three militias in Damascus on 28 December 1985. The final version was essentially the 26 October version with minor modifications. These modifications principally affected the time allowed for deconfessionalization. The powers of the president were adjusted in a formalistic way to give him a little more to do. Cosmetic changes were made to the council of ministers. As to parliament, whereas the October text did not specify how many deputies the new legislature would have, the December agreement set it at 198, thus doubling the existing number of deputies.

The uproar within the Christian community against the agreement was deep and widespread. It was further exacerbated by the publication in the *Al-Safir* newspaper on 29 December 1985, of secret messages sent by

Hubayqah to Vice-President Khaddam, making commitments and concessions which were unacceptable to the Maronites. The tension was
mounting. The president needed all the time he could get to prepare for
his meeting with Asad on Thursday 2 January, but his time was taken up
completely by resolving problems arising from kidnappings and counter-
kidnappings between his guards and those of Eli Hubayqah's.

I was furious as I was unable to break into his routine until the early
hours of the morning of his departure to Damascus, when he was exhausted and his attention span extremely limited. I told the president that
I believed that he had four options in his meeting with Asad: (1) he could
reject the agreement out of hand and face bitter Syrian opposition which
would paralyse his presidency; (2) he could propose amending key points
in the agreement, and with these amendments, give the agreement his full
support; (3) he could accept the agreement in principle, with the proviso
that he would submit it for review and amendment to a national conference, after which the agreement would be processed through strict
constitutional procedures; and (4) he could review the agreement with
Asad, and then ask him for another summit to act on specific points in
an atmosphere of harmony and coordination between the two of them.
Given the political and military pressures against immediate adoption of
the agreement, and given the importance of the president's sponsorship
of the agreement, I felt that the third option was the soundest.

No sooner had I finished my presentation, than the president reacted
with great emotion: 'I do not have to accept any of this!' he exclaimed; 'I
cannot tolerate the Syrianization of Lebanon! If Lebanon is to be offered
to Syria on a platter it is not Jumayyil who is going to offer it. Elie, you
think you know me, you do not. I can overturn the table, I can reshuffle the
cards, I can wreak havoc! I have an apartment in Paris; I will do what I
have to do and then go to Paris.' I urged him to refrain from these
thoughts. 'You are not a spoiler', I said. 'You do not wreak havoc, you do
not run away from responsibilities.' He stopped me short and accused me
of applying too much pressure on him. He insisted that he had been very
serious in opposing the Tripartite Agreement from beginning to end, and
that I should not be surprised if after his meeting with Asad he returned to
Ba'bda, announced his resignation and appointed me prime minister. When
a Maronite thinks of appointing a Greek Orthodox prime minister he must
be joking, and I told the president so. I detected a faint smile on his face.

Jumayyil met Asad on 2 and 3 January 1986. Upon his return from
Damascus I met him at his home in Bikfayya. Jumayyil looked tired but
determined. He smiled at me and said, 'I took option four, and I asked
for time.' The president had told Asad that he had come on Thursday
because Shar' had insisted on it, but he was not ready to give a final

opinion on the Tripartite Agreement; he wanted first to consult with Lebanese leaders. There were points in the agreement which he could not accept. He had told Asad that he could not expect him blindly to sign an accord which three militia leaders had negotiated with the Syrians over an extended period of time. He had then promised to call Asad the following week to arrange a working session with him. Asad had agreed.

Khaddam had then intervened to say that Elie Salem had an agreement, and that he wanted to see it. The president had responded that Salem did not have an agreement but that he had been working on some ideas with Hariri, and we had made progress. The president had explained that he had not presented our proposal to the Syrians because he felt it would be better not to interfere and submit a plan which Damascus would reject anyhow. Khaddam had said that this was wise.

The president remarked that throughout the heated debate Asad had remained particularly calm:

> He is always so relaxed, as if he does not have a worry in the world. I envy him. No one will believe it, but he spent literally hours talking about Damascus as the oldest city in the world. The more I talked about current affairs, the more he tried to drag me into medieval history, ancient history, and even pre-history. What does he think I am – an archaeologist? He amazes me. One thing about him irritates me a lot: he treats me as one force among many, just like Birri, Junblat or Franjiyyeh; not as the president of the republic. He addresses me as Sheikh Amin, not as President Jumayyil. Am I the Governor of Beirut?

The storm against the agreement was gathering momentum. Junblat spoke about it in a lukewarm manner. The Sunnis did not like it. Franjiyyeh's opposition to it was obvious from the start, although he tended to modify his stance after his visits to Damascus. Most important, Ja'ja was now openly opposed to the agreement, and was preparing for a military showdown with Hubayqah. He seized control of the Lebanese Forces television and radio stations, the Lebanese Broadcasting Corporation, and Radio Free Lebanon. Simultaneously, the Kata'ib Party, under Eli Karami, was also increasing its criticism of Hubayqah.

Meanwhile, the Vatican appointed a patriarchal administrator, Bishop Ibrahim al-Helou, to act as caretaker of the Maronite Church until a new patriarch could be elected to succeed Khoreish. Bishop Helou was against the agreement, but he would not come out openly against it. 'I only have two guards at the gate, I do not want another Awkar here', he said, referring to the car-bomb at the American embassy in Awkar, in East Beirut. 'Besides,' he continued, 'we do not want to be accused of hegemony.' He was disappointed with the militia negotiators who knew little about Lebanon, and equally disappointed with the Maronite members of parliament who, in a recent meeting at the patriarchate in Bkerki, had each pulled in the direction of their political interests.

President Jumayyil's follow-up meeting on the Tripartite Agreement with President Asad took place on 13 January. On the morning of that day, fighting broke out in the Metn district between Lebanese Forces members loyal to Eli Hubayqah, and the Kata'ib Party. Fighting had also erupted on the Suq al-Gharb front: a clear message to the president to be conciliatory. I was forced to take a helicopter to reach the president in Bikfayya since all roads were closed as a result of the Lebanese Forces–Kata'ib fighting. I found Jumayyil highly agitated. He had convened a meeting of the Kata'ib leaders in the Metn who assured him they could hold their own against Hubayqah's men. The president was torn. He wondered whether he should go to Damascus under these conditions or not. I urged him to go. I felt the local scene was largely a reflection of the Damascus mood; his problem was with Damascus and he should deal with it there. After some hesitation he agreed with me. I rode with him in the helicopter from Bikfayya to Qulay'at, a Lebanese air force base in the north near the Syrian border, from where he took a special flight to Damascus. Before he left, I recommended to the president that he agree with Asad, work out a framework with him for forming a new government, and launch a new collaborative effort between the Syrian and Lebanese governments. I was not sure this was possible, but I thought it was a rational course to follow.

On Tuesday 14 January, the commander of the army, General Michel Awn, Colonel Qassis and I met the president at the Qulay'at airport. He arrived from Damascus in the midst of a rainstorm that was a harbinger of the political storm that was to follow. The rain was so heavy that we could hardly see him coming down the aeroplane ramp. Just before the plane landed, the Syrian colonel in charge of the Syrian contingent in the region insisted on sending a detachment of Syrian honour guards. We accepted the gesture, but erroneously thought that the discussions had gone well. Word was sent to the officers to give the president a deserved welcome. The Lebanese and the Syrian guards did their duty in the torrential rain. They must have cursed their fate.

The president, who was tired and soaking wet, seemed distant. He looked at me and said, 'I did not follow your advice.' He then turned to Awn and told him, 'Get ready, no ceasefire in sight.' We flew to Bikfayya by helicopter. Upon our arrival the president had a closed meeting with Awn, and another closed meeting with Kata'ib leaders from the Metn. Then the president met with me. The meeting with Asad, he said, had gone terribly. It was the most difficult meeting he had ever had with the

Syrian leader. Asad had not minced words. He had spoken of the legitimacy of the Lebanese revolution, in contrast to the vacuous legitimacy of the constitutional structure. In the past, Asad had referred to the Lebanese and the Syrians as one people in two independent states. This time he had kept referring to them as one people, without referring to two independent states. The Lebanese people, Asad had said, wanted unity with Syria, but Syria rejected it. Asad had talked about the big picture, about the destiny of Damascus, about geographic Syria, and kept referring to Palestine as southern Syria.

Jumayyil thought that Asad had spoken like a revolutionary, while he, brought up in the liberal democratic tradition, had spoken in a more Cartesian style. The president believed that he had been eloquent and courageous in presenting his views: 'I know how dangerous it is to oppose Asad,' he had told the Syrian leader, 'but I have no choice. When it comes to the independence and sovereignty of Lebanon, I cannot compromise, and the agreement seriously compromises our independence and sovereignty.' Confessionalism, the president had told Asad, could be abolished, but not by decree as the militia leaders wanted. In the past, authority was vertical between the president and the cabinet; but now, under the agreement, it would be horizontal with cabinet ministers dealing directly with Damascus. No Arab country was governed this way, why should Lebanon? The presidency should be strengthened to control the many centrifugal forces in the country, not weakened. The president told us that Asad had been furious with him, but that he, Jumayyil, had remained adamant.

After 15 hours of discussion both Jumayyil and Asad had started looking for a polite way to end their useless conversation. Jumayyil was under the impression that they had agreed on two points: the Syrians would invite the three signatories to discuss the president's views, and act on them since this was, as Asad put it, an internal Lebanese affair; and the president would submit the agreement to parliament. The parliament would be free to accept it, amend it or reject it. It is possible that Asad, always polite with his guests, left the president a way out, so that he could say he had come back with something. This was perhaps more polite gesture than policy. Clearly Asad was unhappy with Jumayyil for obstructing a process and was not about to change course to accommodate a president held in deep suspicion by virtually all of Syria's friends and allies in Lebanon. In the abstract the two points seemed valid; but when Khaddam, who knew Asad more than Jumayyil could ever hope to, announced to the press that there would be no more meetings between the two presidents and that Damascus would be holding urgent consultations with its allies, the signal to the president must have been clear.

Counter-Intifadah

On Wednesday 15 January 1986, the president and Samir Ja'ja dealt a serious setback to Syrian policy in Lebanon when they launched a joint military attack on Hubayqah's men. This effectively scuttled the Tripartite Agreement. The president used his Kata'ib militiamen from the Metn district, while Ja'ja used his loyalists in the Lebanese Forces. By the evening Hubayqah's forces were defeated. He surrendered to the army, and with 200 of his followers he was brought to the Ministry of Defence. On 16 January, he resigned as chairman of the executive committee of the Lebanese Forces, and was escorted to an army helicopter from where he was sent to Cyprus. From there he flew to Switzerland. On 22 January he arrived in Damascus, where he was received as a hero, and in a week's time he arrived in Zahle, rallied his followers and called from his new base for the resignation of Jumayyil. Meanwhile in the Eastern Sector Ja'ja was elected chief of the Lebanese Forces and Karim Pakradouni as his vice-chief. Khaddam, who had worked hard on the agreement, was furious with Jumayyil. He accused him of spoiling the efforts of 'the young generation'. In retaliation, Birri and Junblat unleashed their guns on the Eastern Sector. Khaddam invited the Muslim leaders to meet with him in Damascus and discuss the new developments. Ja'ja and his adviser Karim Pakradouni, on the other hand, considered holding a Christian conference in Bkerki.

The president was anxious to assure the Syrians that the Ja'ja–Hubayqah conflict was essentially an internal Lebanese Forces affair, and that lines of communication between Lebanon and Syria should remain open. The president was serious about reforms and distinctive relations with Syria, but not as outlined in the agreement. He wanted to be the one to negotiate such an agreement, and he was not ready to relinquish his position to the young and ambitious Eli Hubayqah, whose success could assure him the leadership of the Kata'ib Party and of the Christian community. These were precisely the two groupings President Jumayyil hoped to lead himself one day when his presidential term ended.

The president, hoping that the last-minute exchanges with Asad were serious, wanted to go through the formality of sending the agreement to parliament. This necessitated calling the council of ministers, seeking its endorsement of this step, and sending the agreement to the speaker to submit to parliament.

On 26 January, the president called the council of ministers to a meeting to study the Tripartite Agreement. A council of ministers headed by Karami and including Birri and Junblat was not about to meet to please the president. The president then sent an aide to deliver the agreement to the speaker of parliament, but Hussein al-Husseini refused to accept it. The aide left it on the speaker's desk and rushed back to the presidential palace.

Meanwhile preparations by the opposition for an attack on the Eastern Sector were in full swing. The signs were ominous: shelling was accompanied by calls for resignation, boycotts and military manoeuvres. The Ministry of Defence received a message from the Syrian commander in Lebanon accusing the Lebanese army of 'inimical moves' on the Bikfayya front. This note was particularly serious. Our assessment was that in case of an all-out attack, the Eastern Sector could hold on for a week. After that, only international diplomacy and goodwill could bring about an end to such an offensive.

The deterioration of the political situation began to adversely affect Lebanon's economy. There was a popular outcry when, in early February 1986, the US dollar, which had been gaining steadily against the Lebanese lira since 1984, reached LL 28. Again the brunt of the criticism was directed at the president, as if he had any power left to control political and economic events. But myths were difficult to dislodge. The Syrians were angry with the president and yet, ironically, he was not anti-Syrian. Deep down, Jumayyil liked Asad and admired him. Meanwhile, I looked for an opening to restore the Lebanese–Syrian dialogue, and on 5 February the opening came.

On that day, Israeli jets forced down a small Libyan plane suspected of carrying PLO leaders. It turned out that the plane was carrying a Syrian delegation. The Israelis were embarrassed by the incident, and soon released the delegation. The Syrians, and Asad in particular, felt personally affronted by the Israeli action. I advised the president to call Asad and condemn the incident. The president hesitated, fearing that Asad would embarrass him by refusing to take his call. I assured him that Asad would answer; anyhow he must continue to try for a dialogue with Asad as he could not make a single important political move without him.

The president stared at me for a long time, took a deep breath, and called Asad. Within minutes he was talking to the Syrian leader as if nothing had gone wrong between them. Jumayyil told Asad that he wanted to open a new dialogue with Syria, one that would lead to an agreement satisfactory to the two leaders. Asad responded that this was fine. But he added that the dialogue must start confidentially at the level of Syria's and Lebanon's respective intelligence agencies. If Syria found that there was a chance for progress, then the discussions could become political and open.

Asad was a patient man; he took blows well and never lost his temper. His reaction to the president's rejection of the Tripartite Agreement was not as apocalyptic as some hoped or some feared. Through Khaddam, he started a new long and tedious process of consulting with Lebanese leaders. The Syrians soon found that the unreserved support for the agreement which they had expected, or had been led to believe, was an illusion.

The Sunni leadership, under the chairmanship of Mufti Hassan Khalid, met with Khaddam as a group. The mufti spoke first and then former prime minister Taqi al-Din al-Sulh took the floor: There were articles in the agreement, he said, that were good, and there were articles that had to be amended. 'We do not need Birri, Junblat and Hubayqah to tell us that Lebanon is Arab', Solh continued. 'We are, and have always been, the front runners in Arabism. Legal details should be discussed freely by parliament and amended there.' Khaddam showed some flexibility on the agreement. He said that there had been a chance to amend, it but Jumayyil had lost this chance by launching an attack on Hubayqah. Actually the battle between Jumayyil and Hubayqah had been in the making for some time, and in such a conflict it is difficult to tell who started it.

Jumayyil's minor opening with Asad did not change his situation or his image: he was still a beleaguered president under pressure to resign. He was on the lookout for an opportunity to replace the Tripartite Agreement, or to start a process preferably involving him personally leading to an agreement.

The Hariri Proposal

As often happened during diplomatic bottlenecks, the Saudis appeared on the scene in the person of Rafiq al-Hariri. Hariri called me and we agreed to meet in Paris on 26 February. Hariri told me that he had been asked by King Fahd to bring about a reconciliation between Lebanon and Syria. Hariri had contacted Khaddam to assess his readiness for conciliation talks, and he said that Khaddam had declined all offers to cooperate with Jumayyil. Yet Khaddam believed that King Fahd was a special friend, and that he could not say no to him. Syria was ready to discuss with Jumayyil amendments to the agreement, provided that these amendments did not affect its substance.

King Fahd, Hariri continued, hoped that we would propose amendments which would take into account the facts on the ground; one could not always get what one wanted, he argued. If Jumayyil moved, King Fahd would support him, but if he didn't, the king would not oppose him, nor would he point a finger at him. Hariri told us that Asad had wanted Jumayyil to know that he had saved his neck many times before when his enemies in Lebanon had wanted to oust him. Asad also knew that when Jumayyil was last in Damascus, he was plotting to attack Hubayqah.

Hariri proposed that the president send a letter to Asad telling him that he accepted the substance of the Tripartite Agreement, and that he, Hariri, would deliver it to the Syrian leader. The president thought it would be a better idea to write such a letter and send it to King Fahd directly. Once it was in the king's hands, he could put his weight behind it, or use it as he saw fit with Asad. I met a number of officials to discuss this proposal. The Papal Nuncio Angelloni strongly supported the idea. He thought that such a letter would facilitate the mission of the Papal Foreign Minister Achille Silvestrini who was expected in Beirut and Damascus on a goodwill mission the following week. The Vatican, we were told, was getting mixed signals from the Catholics in the Arab East. The Greek Catholic Patriarch Hakim had told the Pope that the agreement was good for the Christians. Maronite spokesmen, however, were telling him that the agreement virtually spelled the doom of Christendom in the Near East. Angelloni himself was extremely nervous with the agreement as 'it reduced the powers of the Maronite president'.

When he arrived in Beirut, Silvestrini met Christian and Muslim leaders. His movements around Lebanon were limited due to the stepped-up activities of Hizballah. Hizballah welcomed the Papal envoy by taking French hostages in West Beirut and threatening to kill them. We were anxious to move fast to gain Syrian support in controlling Hizballah, and to reopen the dialogue that was interrupted after the defeat of the Tripartite Agreement. I impressed upon the envoy the need to move fast on reforms before a resurgent fundamentalism rendered Christian–Muslim dialogue impossible. Angelloni supported my plea and urged Silvestrini to use his influence with the Maronite leaders to develop a consensus on reforms and on Lebanese–Syrian relations.

To reduce risks on his life, Silvestrini arranged to hold one meeting with all the major Muslim religious leaders. The meeting included Mufti Hassan Khalid, Shi'ah Sheikh Muhammad Mahdi Shamseddin, and Druze Sheikh al-Aql, Muhammad Abu Shaqra. The Muslim leaders told Silvestrini that they insisted on coexistence with the Christians within a political formula in which no community would feel inferior to the others. They told Silvestrini that they understood his mission as being one addressed to all of Lebanon and not to one community only, and as such they favoured it. They felt that any agreement among the Lebanese had to be reached through the constitutional process, and they believed Syrian support to be essential for the success of any effort in Lebanon.

By 7 March, Jumayyil and I had completed our consultation on the proposed letter we were to send to King Fahd. We sent the letter immediately in the hope that Hariri and Silvestrini would both go to Damascus at the same time and would, therefore, combine their efforts to encourage negotiations and reduce the confrontation between the Syrians and the Christians. In the letter to King Fahd, we stated that we accepted the substance of the Tripartite Agreement, but that we disagreed on details.

The letter, dated 7 March 1986, referred to the Tripartite Agreement as a 'step forward towards a comprehensive solution', and asked for a new dialogue between the governments of Lebanon and Syria on the basis of the points we made in the letter. While we tried to reach Damascus through Saudi intervention, there was also an attempt by the Vatican. The Vatican mission, through Silvestrini, was in progress. He had already met Lebanese leaders and on 12 March he had his meeting with President Asad.

Asad, ever the pragmatist, had little to gain from the Vatican to contribute to the success of Silvestrini's visit. In Damascus, the papal envoy got the charm treatment, a historical lecture, a brilliant foray into the role of religion as a civilizing force, and nothing else. Silvestrini asked Asad whether Syria was willing to entertain any modifications to the agreement. He remarked that if Syria was considering modifications, the Vatican would offer substantive recommendations. Asad responded that Syria was not a party to the agreement. If the Vatican had any recommendation to make, it should talk to the three militia leaders who negotiated the agreement. Silvestrini fell silent. Khaddam had already told Silvestrini that Syria distrusted Jumayyil and would not negotiate with him. In the light of this, the envoy proposed making his recommendations directly to the militia leaders. When Jumayyil heard this from Angelloni, who was briefing us on the visit, he said he would resign if he were the obstacle. 'Indeed,' Jumayyil continued, 'I put my resignation at the disposal of the Pope.' Jumayyil did not mean a word he was saying. He was a politician, and knew better than to act on all the eloquent things he said.

Silvestrini's initiative fizzled out slowly. What the Vatican had planned as an ambitious drive to bring about a resolution to the new impasse in Lebanon soon became a more modest effort to bring about a consensus within the Maronite community. Silvestrini hoped to reconcile Jumayyil and Franjiyyeh, but his efforts failed. He tried to reduce Israeli influence in the Lebanese Forces, and he failed again. He hoped to convince Maronite leaders to work in unison, but he found that each had his own plan. He was surprised that the Maronite leaders had no unified vision. They uttered generalities, opinions, ideas, and they often said one thing while meaning the exact opposite, he said. Nevertheless, they felt relieved that the Pope was coming to save them. The Maronites, Silvestrini said, were steeped in medievalism. He found the Christian community in a state of paralysis. His sense was that the Christian community was heading towards a catastrophe. It was a frustrated Silvestrini who departed from Lebanon. He left behind an aide to create the impression that the Vatican initiative remained active.

On 26 March, our ambassador to Saudi Arabia, Zafir al-Hassan, delivered to us a message from the Saudis. In it, King Fahd thanked the president for his letter of 7 March. He had done the best he could with it, and had talked to the Syrians and prised the door open a little. The king assumed, however, that President Jumayyil would be making direct contact with the Syrians. King Fahd had been unusually forthcoming with respect to Lebanon, al-Hassan told me. He was spending most of his time now in the desert away from the demands of Riyad, and his mind was now on Iran, which had just invaded parts of southern Iraq. The king advised us to maintain contact with him through Hariri. This way our contacts would remain informal and low-key in case they failed.

9

Elusive Reforms

On 2 April 1986, General Awn, the commander of the army, showed me a letter dated 28 March from General Sa'id Bayraqdar, the commander of the Syrian forces in Lebanon. Bayraqdar accused the Lebanese army of shelling Syrian positions, and warned that if this was repeated, he would be forced to invade the Eastern Sector under the authority of the Lebanese army. Awn showed me his proposed answer to Bayraqdar, and I found it provocative and dangerous.

The president suggested that we write a letter to Arab heads of state through the Secretary-General of the League of Arab States, al-Shadhli al-Qulaybi. I advised against involving the Arab states. A letter to the Muslim Arab heads of states from a Maronite president boycotted by almost all Muslim leaders in the country, would not yield positive results. I thought a polite, objective and truthful answer from Awn to Bayraqdar would be more helpful. I helped to draft a letter stating that our army did not shell Syrian positions, and that all efforts should be directed to reducing tensions, not exacerbating them. Awn felt confident that he could hold off a Syrian assault long enough to evoke Western sympathy and support. The last thing we needed, I argued, was a Syrian assault. We should be cooperating with Syria rather than fighting against it. In the end, however, a diplomatic response was sent to Bayraqdar, and the Syrian threat did not materialize.

The regular quota of shellings, kidnappings and assassinations continued unabated as we awaited a break in the political deadlock. We knew that to break this deadlock the president needed to accept the Tripartite Agreement with amendments which did not compromise its substance. The president's letter to King Fahd had been communicated to Asad by the Saudis, but the Syrian leader had asked for more clarifications.

It was my job to encourage positive relations with Syria. I considered that the most rational course of action was to keep channels open with

Damascus and to try, by diplomatic means, to narrow the gap between their perspective and ours. We and the Syrians held different views on reform. They were ideological Ba'thists and we were a pluralistic democratic country with a different political outlook. They were betting on the young militia leaders to determine the future political course of Lebanon, and we were urging a broader consultation to include the leaders of all communities and groupings. The Syrian style, particularly that of Vice-President Khaddam, was to move fast. Our style was to move more cautiously, especially as the issues at stake could explode at any time if they were not resolved by broad consensus.

As a professor whose field of study is medieval Islam, I have always appreciated the 'personal' element in Arab politics. I once translated and annotated a medieval Arabic manuscript which dealt with the Abbasid Court, with the style of its caliphs, and with the role of relatives, wazirs and friends in influencing caliphal decisions. If Fahd, Asad, Mubarak and Arafat were not caliphs, imams or sultans, they were nevertheless their heirs, in terms of traditions and behavioural norms. It is true that the march of history changes people, but changes often tend to affect most the apparent, rather than the substantive. That which lies deep tends to resist change and accepts it late, reluctantly, and when it has no choice. After six long frustrating months of political paralysis and intermittent shelling I felt the need to depart from standard diplomatic channels. I believed it was time to see if personal contacts could get us out of the mess we were in.

In politics one develops a large network of friends outside government who become part of the decision-making process. Hariri, for example, gave a great deal of his time to help in the conciliation process. Hariri worked in the foreground, and Issam Fares worked in the background. Fares was a self-made Lebanese who worked in Saudi Arabia, acquired wealth and international business connections, and attained a highly respectable status in Lebanon, Saudi Arabia, Syria, the USA and Europe. Like a good Lebanese he used part of his wealth to help Lebanese in need and like a good nationalist he put himself at the disposal of the government to help in any way he could. He facilitated contacts with foreign leaders and advised on ways and means of communicating with his friends in Syria and Saudi Arabia. Through our ambassador in Washington, Dr Abdallah Bouhabib, active Lebanese in the USA kept us apprised of their views. Bouhabib was a good communicator and, unlike me, an indefatigable maker of phone calls. He consulted Fares regularly, and kept urging me to find a direct way for me to talk to the Syrians on the reforms stipulated in the Tripartite Agreement. One late evening Bouhabib called me to say that Hany Salam and a friend of his might be helpful. Bouhabib felt Salam and his friend (yet unnamed) could help me to talk directly to the Syrians.

Salam was a successful Lebanese businessman who, like many of his compatriots, had made his fortune in the Gulf. He was now conducting his international business transactions from his office in London. The Salam family was a prominent Beirut Sunni family, which had greatly contributed over the last century to the political life of the country. Hany or Hany Bek, as the Salams were known, had been living outside Lebanon, but he had maintained a base in Beirut to which he frequently returned. He had also maintained his contacts with Lebanese and Syrian leaders. His business contacts were extensive, and he was anxious to help. Hany was primarily a facilitator, a mediator, and worked through his own network of friends. Salam called me from London and offered to contact Khaddam on our behalf. His suggestion was to enlist Mahdi al-Tajir, a former United Arab Emirates ambassador to Britain and France, to help us resolve the impasse with Syria.

Tajir was known to be a wealthy entrepreneur and an avid collector of every item that Europe had cherished at one time or another. This included castles, palaces, cottages, rugs, paintings, clocks, silver, manuscripts and antique furniture of all kinds. According to Salam, Tajir had been a close friend of Asad since the early 1970s. I wanted to meet Tajir before we entrusted him with a mission. While I was visiting Abu Dhabi on 26 May, I asked a Lebanese entrepreneur named Mirshid Ba'qlini to take me to Dubai and introduce me to the fabled merchant of the Gulf. Ba'qlini was pleased to do so as he had done business with Tajir some time ago and had not seen him since. Tajir received us in his palace, the reception hall of which was built in the shape of a tent. But here all resemblance to a tent ended. The diminutive Tajir had a big ego, an eloquent tongue and a great knowledge of the past.

Tajir told us that he was close to all Arab leaders, especially Hafiz al-Asad. He would be glad to help us with Asad. Arab history was the history of people, he declared. And here he began a long lecture on the Caliph Ali, the son-in-law of the Prophet Muhammad, and on his martyred son Hussein, who was martyred at Karbala by Mu'awiya's son Yazid. This brought tears to Tajir's eyes, as if the martyrdom had occurred that morning rather than 13 centuries ago. Tajir was a truly unusual fellow: a believer and a sceptic; imperial in style, yet an ascetic; a sharp businessman, yet a poet and a mystic. He was anxious to take on the mission of reopening the Lebanese–Syrian dialogue. I urged him to meet Asad and feel his way.

In a move designed to inject new leadership at the top of the Maronite community, Mar Nasrallah Butrus Sfeir, a relative unknown, was elected as the new Maronite patriarch on 19 April 1986.

Soon after Sfeir's election the president and I paid him a long visit and briefed him on developments. I kept close contact with him, as he was the natural catalyst of Maronite political thinking. With the Maronites, the clerics have always played key political roles. Patriarch Huwayyik was instrumental in the creation of modern Lebanon from the wreckage of the Ottoman Empire. The internal war of the previous decade had torn the Maronite community apart and fragmented its leadership. A great challenge awaited the new patriarch. I told him that we had asked Tajir to help us with Damascus, and that the president would be proposing reform principles which we hoped would start a dialogue aimed at amending or replacing the Tripartite Agreement.

On 1 August 1986, in a speech delivered on the occasion of Army Day, the president spelled out his views on reforms and called on parliament to meet immediately and implement them through the constitutional process. These reforms, he said, enjoyed a wide consensus, and he outlined them as follows:

- Lebanon is a final home for the Lebanese, and must have sovereignty over all its territory. It is not part of another state, nor can it be united to another state.
- Lebanon's identity is clearly Arab and its commitment to its Arab environment is complete. Lebanon's government is republican, democratic and parliamentary, and all citizens must share equally in the governing process.
- Military conflict must be ended and the authority of the state must be extended over all Lebanese territory.
- Lebanon is committed to free economic enterprise.
- Lebanon must adopt and implement administrative decentralization.
- Lebanon must have distinctive relations with Syria.
- Diplomatic efforts must be mobilized to implement UN resolutions on South Lebanon.
- Lebanon must move gradually from confessionalism to a deconfessionalized order.
- The powers of the existing presidencies (presidency of the republic, parliament and the council of ministers) and of the presidencies of the new organs of state which will have to be established, have to be defined.
- Standards of accountability must be improved.

To start this process on an even keel, the president proposed that parliament meet immediately and introduce a constitutional amendment that would bring about equal representation in parliament between Christians and Muslims. The Algerian and Egyptian ambassadors praised the president's speech. They told me that the Sunni leadership were strongly behind it, but that they would not take a public stand in support of the president's proposals unless they were encouraged by Damascus to do so.

Prime Minister Karami, in direct response to the president's statement, appointed a Committee of Six from the council of ministers (Rashid Karami, chairman; Salim al-Hoss, Kamil Sham'un, Joseph al-Hashim, Joseph Skaf, Victor Qasir and Abdallah al-Rasi) to study the president's proposals, as well as other proposals, and to submit a reform plan to parliament within a month. He then sent his adviser, Dr George Dib, to deliver the following message to Khaddam: 'I am the prime minister of Lebanon and, therefore, of the Christians and of the Muslims. I therefore have to be moderate. I am taking this initiative on dialogue seriously. I want to have your reaction to it.' Khaddam answered that Syria supported any dialogue, especially if Karami was directing it. Damascus drew two red lines, however: there could be no return to the political formula of 1943, and no community could be allowed to prevail over other communities.

The Committee of Six fell from the first meeting into a heated and negative dialectic. Karami opened the discussion by saying relations between Lebanon and Syria should be holy. 'Holy Christ,' shouted Sham'un, 'are we here to discuss theology?' 'This is not theology,' retorted Karami, 'this is general orientation.' On almost every issue – confessionalism, identity, the power of the presidency – Karami and Sham'un disagreed. When Karami's group was deliberating on reforms, the papal nuncio in Damascus handed the Syrian foreign minister, Faruq al-Shar', on 1 August, a two-page memorandum representing the views which Silvestrini found to enjoy support amongst Christian and Muslim leaders. These views may be summarized as follows.

Lebanon must be rebuilt as an independent and sovereign state with its own identity. Lebanon may opt to have 'special relations' with Syria defined in bilateral agreements, but these must respect the independence and sovereignty of each of the two states. All foreign forces had to be withdrawn to allow the Lebanese government to extend its authority over its entire territory. Reforms respecting the demographic characteristics of Lebanon, its social structure, and the system of communal coexistence, had to be introduced in accordance with the constitutional process. The historical identity of Lebanon, its political pluralism, its individual freedoms, and the freedoms of the groups constituting it, had to be respected. Freedom of religion, of public expression, of education and of private property also had to be maintained. The principle of the distribution of the three presidencies amongst the three largest of Lebanon's sects should be protected, and the number of Christians and Muslims in parliament and in the cabinet should be equal. The memorandum also argued that it was desirable that new institutions allowing for broader political participation and decentralization be established.

Shar' promised to discuss Silvestrini's memorandum with Lebanese leaders. This meant: 'Thank you very much, your memorandum will be filed.' The Vatican tone was quite different from that of Damascus. The memorandum was conservative; it referred to 'special relations'. This is not as good as 'distinctive relations'. The reference to all foreign forces put Syria at a level of equality with Israel, and this was unacceptable to Damascus. The reference to demographic characteristics and to communal coexistence smacked too much of the past. Syria saw new realities in demography that must be accommodated. The historical identity of Lebanon to which the memorandum referred was itself in question. What was it – Phoenician? Christian? Islamic? Arab? Mediterranean? Syria preferred clarity, and Arab identity should be openly proclaimed. The question of the three presidencies may be conceded as tradition, but Damascus preferred not to have this matter move from the realm of tradition to the realm of law. This went against Ba'th secular orientation.

Tajir met Asad on 18 September, and we were anxious to know what had transpired. Hany Salam called me from California to report that Tajir had had a good four-hour meeting with Asad and that Asad had been positive. Was there a process? I asked Salam. Where could we meet Tajir to debrief him? Would the fighting stop? What was our next step? Salam responded that Bouhabib would call me and speak in code to confuse the intelligence services.

Bouhabib called the next day. 'The message to John Travolta', he began, 'is the following: I spoke to California, who said that the merchant had a good meeting in Damascus, and that it was advisable that Tyrone Power should meet with Roma to assure the Silk Man that we are complementing his efforts.' I interrupted Bouhabib's mystifying report to tell him that I had no idea what he was talking about. If this was a code, I added, then it had probably already been decoded by everybody except the poor fellow at the end of this line. 'Tell me who is who', I said. He obliged: Travolta was Jumayyil (handsome); California was Hany Salam because he had a villa in Palm Beach; the merchant was Mahdi al-Tajir (his family name literally meant merchant); Tyrone Power was Elie Salem (handsome as a joke); Roma was Khalid Agha, a leading Sunni personality I had met at Rome Airport; and the Silk Man was, of course, Hariri (a literal translation of his name in English, and not a good code at that).

'Now that your code is internationally known,' I said, 'let's forget it.' When I told this story to a Palestinian friend he said the same thing had happened to Yasir Arafat: an aide had called him on the phone from

Paris to say: 'The Tiger is arriving in Cairo tomorrow.' 'Refresh my memory,' Arafat screamed back, 'is the Tiger Abu Ahmad?' 'Yes,' answered the aide; 'may God have mercy on his soul.'

We were advised by Tajir that the president should publicly make a positive gesture towards Asad. Relations between the two had not been good, and Tajir felt that the president should take the initiative and break the ice. He should show that he respected Asad, and that he was not inimical as the Maronite leaders seem to be. The occasion presented itself on 23 September 1986, the fourth anniversary of Jumayyil's election to the presidency. The president addressed a large crowd in his village of Bikfayya. Jumayyil's military and security aides, who rarely received any praise, outdid themselves in rallying a crowd of some forty thousand, mostly Maronite villagers, from neighbouring areas. Although the crowd was largely anti-Syrian, it applauded loudly when the president solicited the help of 'my brother, President Hafiz al-Asad in putting an end to the Lebanese crisis'. It was indeed a courageous statement given the mood of the crowd at that time, and it was to the credit of the president that he received applause for uttering it publicly. Afterwards Tajir called me to thank us for the gesture and to say that Salam would come to Beirut to brief us on Tajir's visit to Damascus.

On 10 October, Salam arrived in Beirut and briefed us on Tajir's meeting with Asad. Asad, we were told, wanted a letter from Jumayyil indicating his commitment to reforms and to good relations with Syria. The president, however, was reluctant to send a letter as he was afraid of being rebuffed. His previous letter to King Fahd had not brought the desired results. Salam tried hard to convince Jumayyil, but only succeeded in persuading him that I should accompany him the following day to Athens, where we would meet Tajir and listen to his account of his meeting with Asad. In the light of that meeting we would decide what to do.

The next day, Salam and I took a military helicopter to Larnaca, boarded his private plane and took off for Athens. We picked up Tajir there and proceeded to London. After a spontaneous competition between him and me on medieval Arabic poetry which lubricated his memory, he gave me a long account of his meeting with Asad. Tajir began:

> I told Asad: 'Do you like President Jumayyil and do you wish to cooperate with him?' His answer was a strong yes. 'In that case,' I said, 'the two of you should get together, end the fighting in Lebanon, and put the country on the path to peace.' 'I have no problem with that', answered Asad. 'I can pick up the phone, call Sheikh Amin and invite him for a meeting tomorrow. But a war of twelve years is not going to end in a meeting between two presidents, no matter how long this meeting is. I am ready to cooperate, but I need specific assurances. Let Jumayyil give me a substitute to the Tripartite

Agreement. This agreement is not my agreement. It was reached by three Lebanese parties. It does not meet my ideals, indeed it is against my ideals. Internal reforms are a Lebanese problem. I care about one thing only, distinctive relations between Lebanon and Syria, because we have a common enemy, Israel. Israel, Asad went on, is already a dagger in my side and I do not want another in Lebanon. Syria is neither Tunis nor Morocco, and its relations with Lebanon are different than those between Lebanon and Tunis or Morocco. If things boil in Beirut they boil in Damascus also. The security of Syria is inseparable from the security of Lebanon and vice versa. I want a sovereign and independent Lebanon but within the framework of distinctive relations with Syria.'

Asad, continued Tajir, wanted from Jumayyil a written statement on the basis of which he would meet him. He wanted to ensure the success of the meeting before it was held. Tajir urged me to send a written statement to Asad that would put his mind at ease. This statement could be a letter, it could be a new reform project, or it could be an amendment to the Tripartite Agreement.

It was the inherent complexity of the situation which made President Jumayyil reluctant to make concessions which were not guaranteed to end the war. Furthermore, Jumayyil did not want to send Asad a letter which might be rejected by the Syrians, thus showing the basic weakness of the Lebanese presidency. On the other hand, Asad, who had publicly praised the Tripartite Agreement, was not ready to meet with the man who had defeated that agreement. Jumayyil was, however, anxious to realize peace in Lebanon, or at least make some progress towards peace. His presidency would expire in two years, and all he had to show for it to date was a record of frustration. He dreamt of a breakthrough, and the key to it was Hafiz al-Asad. This was how things looked to him in the autumn of 1986.

In frequent meetings in London with Tajir, Salam and a few personal friends of mine from academia, we outlined a list of options on how Jumayyil could start a dialogue with Asad. I suspected all along that nothing short of a clear written statement from Jumayyil to Asad explaining in detail how he perceived reform, and how he understood distinctive relations between Lebanon and Syria, would do. Our job was to find the right form, one which would be acceptable to two different men in different political situations. There was also the factor of timing. Was Asad ready to talk to Jumayyil? Asad thought in regional and strategic terms, and any move in Lebanon would be affected by his perspective of the regional scene.

Armed with these options, Tajir, Salam and I returned to Beirut. While we had varied options with varying emphases and nuances, the three of us agreed that the most viable option was to have Jumayyil send Asad a letter outlining what he saw as the major reform principles, proposing a process to reach a formal agreement on these principles, and assuring Asad of his intent to work out distinctive relations between Lebanon and Syria. After a long and acrimonious debate, President Jumayyil accepted our option.

In his letter to President Asad, dated 15 October 1986, President Jumayyil emphasized his readiness to work closely with Asad in resolving the Lebanese conflict and the broader regional conflicts. The letter expressed appreciation for Asad's and Syria's role in the region. It defined basic reform principles in the spirit of his speech of 1 August. Before we delivered the letter, we showed it to Patriarch Sfeir and to Kamil Sham'un. Both approved it. The president told me he had also informed Lebanese Forces leader Samir Ja'ja of the letter's contents, and that Ja'ja expressed no objections. President Jumayyil assumed that with the approval of these three figures, he had the backing of the Maronite community for his action.

On 23 October, Tajir personally delivered the letter to Asad. He was instructed to deliver additional 'oral notes' to the Syrian leader. These notes, which I wrote down for Tajir to use in explaining the president's letter, were largely of a psychological character, intended to build up confidence in Damascus. Tajir made a long oral presentation, handed the letter to Asad and asked that it be kept confidential. Asad compared Tajir's strong oral statements and the more reasoned statements in the letter and wondered why the letter was not as strong as Tajir's interpretation of it. Although Asad noted the discrepancy between 'letter' and 'notes' he nevertheless liked the letter. He thought it represented a step forward. 'If it is a good letter,' interjected Tajir, 'then I hope you will invite Jumayyil and reach agreement with him. He is ready to come, he has amendments that are reasonable.' 'We cannot meet and fail,' said Asad, 'nor can Jumayyil and I negotiate the Tripartite Agreement afresh. Our representatives should meet in a few sessions, and once they agree we shall then have a summit to crown the process.'

But before our representatives could meet, added Asad, he wanted to know in some detail where Jumayyil stood on distinctive relations and he wanted some details on his views on reform. We sent Asad a paper on distinctive relations between Lebanon and Syria dated 6 December 1986. Hany Salam delivered it by hand to President Asad on 10 December. The paper consisted of three sections: (a) political, (b) military and security, and (c) economic.

Our distinctive relations paper of 6 December was considered good enough by Shar' to serve as a joint paper, but as Lebanese–Lebanese

relations affected distinctive relations between Lebanon and Syria, Shar'
told Salam that he needed a paper from us on political reforms. Shar'
explained later to Salam that President Asad wanted distinctive relations
between two independent countries. He quoted Asad as saying 'We may
think of unity with Morocco before we think of unity with Lebanon
because we appreciate Lebanon's position regionally and internationally.'
National conciliation, said Shar', was one of the objectives of distinctive
relations. We prepared a paper on constitutional reforms dated 13 December 1986. Hany Salam delivered it to Shar' on 14 December.

Tajir proposed to Asad that I represent Jumayyil, and that Adib al-
Dawudi, Syria's ambassador in Geneva, represent Asad. He suggested that
we meet in secret in St Moritz, in the privacy of his own residence. Asad
responded that, although I had held a different view of the May 17
Agreement from that of the Syrians, he respected my position. He believed
that I was interested in developing Lebanese–Syrian relations, and thus he
welcomed me as interlocutor. Asad also believed Dawudi to be an excellent choice. Asad remarked that he had sent Dawudi to Geneva for
health reasons; otherwise Dawudi would have remained close to him in
Damascus. He agreed to have me and Dawudi meet in St Moritz, review
the Tripartite Agreement, consult with our respective leaders, and then
submit a proposal to the two presidents. He thought this would take
between one and four weeks. With this proposal in hand, a Syrian–
Lebanese summit would then be held to adopt it. Asad called Faruq al-
Shar' and asked him to summon Dawudi to Damascus so he could get his
instructions before the St Moritz meeting. He was to come on a regular
flight, Asad added, as he did not want publicity on this matter until an
agreement was reached.

Dawudi was called to Damascus to be briefed on the discussions he
was to hold with me in St Moritz. It was obvious that he had been far
from the intricate Lebanese problems, and needed more time to grasp
them. In the course of his consultations in Damascus it became evident
that the proposed meeting should be in Damascus. Asad informed Tajir
of the change of venue and for this purpose he had asked Foreign Minister
Faruq al-Shar' and General Ghazi Kan'an, the head of Syrian military
intelligence in Lebanon, to represent him. Jumayyil accordingly asked me
and colonel Simon Qassis, the head of our army intelligence unit, to
represent him. The Syrian team had Ambassador Walid Mu'allim, the
Director-General of the Ministry of Foreign Affairs, as a note-taker. Our
team had Dr Nicola Nasr, a legal aide of the president, as note-taker.

On 3 January 1987, Kan'an called Qassis and told him that the proposed discussions would start on Monday 5 January in Shar''s office.

The Salem–Shar' Discussions

Due to bad weather, our journey to Damascus on the 5th was long and circuitous. On arrival the Lebanese team was taken to the Meridian Hotel, a spacious modern facility with comfortable accommodation. As soon as we arrived at the hotel Shar' called me and invited our team to come to his office in the ministry. I knew the Ministry of Foreign Affairs well from my previous discussions with Khaddam. It is a humble building with crowded offices, except for the relatively spacious and Damascene-furnished office of the minister.

Shar' is a gentle and intelligent professorial diplomat. He lacks the flamboyance and the boisterousness of Khaddam, but he has a great deal of charm. As an aide of Khaddam he had learned a great deal about Lebanon, and as foreign minister he continued to consult and coordinate directly with Khaddam. He met me with a broad smile, and moved forward uncertain as to whether he should proceed with the standard Arab welcome of a kiss on both cheeks. I made it easier by extending my hand, as I preferred, in principle, not to indulge in hugs and kisses. Qassis and Kan'an hugged each other warmly.

Shar' started by saying that the Syrian leadership had met and appointed him and Kan'an to be the Syrian negotiators. It had also welcomed me and Qassis as the Lebanese negotiators representing President Jumayyil. I then made an extensive presentation on the political philosophy of Lebanon, its unique place in the Arab world, its Arab character, its distinctive relations with Syria, and its insistence on independence and sovereignty. Shar' explained that he was speaking as a conciliator, and accordingly he conveyed to us the position of the Lebanese opposition which we were to transmit to President Jumayyil.

Afterwards, Hany Salam, who was appointed presidential envoy, and I visited Khaddam. He welcomed me by asking: 'How are your in-laws?' By this, he meant the Americans, as my wife is of American origin. He welcomed Salam as 'Jumayyil's envoy' and asked him why the president couldn't be more like Eli Hubayqah.

'Look at this young man', Khaddam said, describing the former Lebanese Forces leader. 'The first Muslim he ever met was Rafiq al-Hariri, the second was me. He lived all his life with the Maronites, but he saw the light. He has a good sense of history. He opted for the Arab identity.' I retorted by asking him what identity had Jumayyil opted for, the Israeli identity? 'As usual you are trying to argue', retorted Khaddam light-heartedly, and he promptly changed the subject. At the end of this first round of talks, I returned to Beirut to report to the president. Meanwhile Salam proceeded to the Gulf to explain to regional leaders the negotiation process that was under way.

In a rapid succession of meetings with Shar' and Kan'an, we arrived at a number of basic principles. These principles we put in final form in a document entitled the 'National Pact' (al-Mithaq al-Watani) dated 22 January 1987. This was a brief paper of five pages which Shar' considered to be an excellent beginning and which, he felt, should lead to a summit between Jumayyil and Asad. We agreed to consult our respective constituencies.

I said: 'Faruq, I guarantee you the support of our constituency.' He replied: 'I do too, and we will only consult our important allies, otherwise we will never finish.' Syria's allies in Lebanon were numerous. They included political parties, militias, political groupings, religious leaders and individual leaders scattered throughout the country. The most important allies, however, as far as the reform process was concerned, included Birri, Junblat, Karami, Franjiyyeh and Hubayqah. He urged me not to consult with opposition members so as to avoid allowing its members to take a negative position which Asad would find it difficult to reverse later on.

The proposed National Pact included the following basic principles; Lebanon's Arab identity; gradual abolition of confessionalism through a commission appointed by parliament and chaired by the president of the republic; executive authority to be vested in the council of ministers chaired by the president of the republic, who does not vote; prime minister to be selected by president after binding consultation or to be elected by parliament; parliamentary seats to be divided equally between Christians and Muslims; establishing new councils; reforming the army and the security forces; ending the war with the help of the Syrian army upon the request of the president. The Lebanese army would supervise the ceasefire, dissolution of militias, collection of weapons, and the return of the displaced Lebanese.

I saw Papal Nuncio Angelloni and Maronite Patriarch Sfeir to fill them in on the details of the proposed National Pact. Angelloni approved the text without hesitation, and said it was an 'excellent document'. He congratulated us, and remarked that the Maronites would be mistaken if they did not support it strongly. He thought that the Maronites should be forward-looking, but he worried about the position of the Lebanese Forces.

Patriarch Sfeir also seemed pleased with the text. When we reached the article on the powers of the presidency, however, he exclaimed: 'What is this, the president does not vote?' I explained that voting was not really important. It rarely took place in the council of ministers. And the president as chairman could be influential. He then said: 'OK, they took away our voting rights, but we still chair the council of ministers. One must do something, I assume, to accommodate changes.' When we finished discussing the document, he said: 'God bless you, go ahead. I hope this agreement will work out.' I also discussed the document separately with Kamil Sham'un and Bishop Elias Audeh, the Greek Orthodox Metropolitan of Beirut; both found it reasonable. President Jumayyil, meanwhile, consulted Ja'ja and General Awn. He read the document to Awn in my presence, and Awn found it satisfactory. According to the president, Ja'ja also found the document satisfactory, but with some reservations. He was unhappy with the passage on 'Arab identity' and about the stipulation that the president would not vote in the council of ministers. With the 22 January document in hand, we hoped to open a new chapter in the relations between Jumayyil and Asad.

When discussions in Damascus resumed on Thursday 5 February I found Shar' in an agitated mood. I feared that our agreement had met with obstacles. I told Shar' that I had consulted widely on the document and that, while we had reservations on some points, I was authorized to tell him that the president accepted the document as it was. Shar' responded that he had received written responses from all the Lebanese parties and that it would take a computer to make sense out of them. He did, however, sift them and came out with something reasonable. Were we to accept at face value what they were suggesting, he added, we would never finish.

He then handed me a paper dated 6 February 1987, which was radically different from the 22 January document, and he urged me to take it back to Beirut and consult on the basis of this new text. This paper, he said, incorporated some, but not all, of the suggestions he had received from the opposition. Shar' argued that Syria was using its influence to persuade the Lebanese opposition to be reasonable, but that it could not impose its wishes on them. As I looked at the new text, I realized that the new document took us back to the Tripartite Agreement, which we thought we had transcended. The deadline for abolishing confessionalism was reinstated. The points on confessional distribution in parliament were at variance with the formula we thought we had reached in the 22 January text, and the language on the army was unacceptable. I said to Shar':

> There must be a point where we should stop. Continuing consultations with all kinds of groupings, some wanting agreement, some not, some important to national consensus and some not so important due to their numerical and ideological marginality, could become an end in itself without conclusion. We would be caught in a diplomatic version of *Waiting for Godot*, and you know Godot will not come.

I asked Shar' to keep the 6 February document confidential, as it would likely discourage those who had approved the 22 January text. He promised to do so. When I brought up the new text with president Jumayyil, he was indeed discouraged and was inclined to do nothing. He realized, however, that we had no choice. The process had to continue irrespective of personal frustrations.

So weak was the state, and so strong were the militias that only Syria could help the state maintain some resemblance of order. The fighting in Beirut in the winter of 1986 was intense, in particular between the former allies – Amal and the PSP. Each wanted to control Beirut. Their fighting caused over two hundred deaths and created havoc in the Capital. The Sunni leaders, who perceived the fighting as competition between the Shi'ah and the Druze to control 'their' city, appealed to Damascus for help.

On Friday 20 February, Syria responded to the appeal and sent its troops back into the capital for the first time since 1982. General Awn told me that the Syrian force, most of which was made up of élite special forces units, included some 12,000 troops, 100 tanks, and 90 artillery pieces. Awn judged that this force was strong enough to control West Beirut, but not enough to push into the Eastern Sector. The fear that Syrian forces might enter the Eastern Sector and strike the anti-Syrian LF under Samir Ja'ja was always there, and Awn refloated it. He was reassured by the nature of Syrian intervention that it was intended only for West Beirut.

Reaction to the deployment was mixed. Israel supported it because it hoped that the Syrian move would both weaken and contain the PLO. In addition, the Israelis were happy to see Syria caught in what they referred to as the 'Lebanese quagmire', especially once they ensured, through the United States, that the Syrians would not introduce surface-to-air missiles into Beirut. The United States was also happy with the Syrian move, and hoped that it would rein in Hizballah. As usual the Americans issued a statement supporting Lebanon's unity, sovereignty and independence.

The Soviet Union, however, was unhappy with the deployment, since it weakened Moscow's three key allies in Lebanon, the PLO, the PSP and the Lebanese Communist Party, which in this particular fight, was allied with the PSP. A Soviet delegation carried a critical message to the Syrian regime. Khaddam informed me later that he told the delegation, 'Had the USA sent us such a statement, we would have broken off relations with it. The USSR, however, is an ally, so we will not break off relations with you, but we do not accept your note or its implications.' Most likely the USA and Israel approved of the Syrian deployment because it threatened the Soviets more than it threatened them. The American ambassador later told me, however, that neither they nor the Israelis had been informed in advance of the Syrian move.

The president consulted with Christian leaders on how to respond to the deployment. I advised a moderate statement. When I read my statement, one of the president's advisers stood up and demanded to know whether I was for or against the president. I responded:

> Mr President, I am for Lebanon. Mr President, your strategy should be the following: you should work closely with Syria; try to make Asad your ally. He may not accept, but you will have to try in the interests of Lebanon, which is now forsaken by the international community. To gain its independence, Lebanon must work closely with Syria. Lebanon cannot dissolve the militias without Syrian support, and Syria must be assured of a friendly Lebanon, otherwise it will not trust it enough to give it back to the Lebanese. Lebanese independence must be taken by the Lebanese. But first the Lebanese must be united, must have a national and rational objective, and until we attain that status, or while working for it, we must coordinate with Syria. We must work with the facts.

The president accepted the moderate statement which, in effect, only registered a position and did not involve taking action. The Lebanese army was not then in a position to stop the anarchy. And if it could not, the president could not credibly condemn the Syrian army which was close by to enter the city and pacify it, if Syria was asked by the prime minister and other Sunni officials to do so. Naturally the Beirut crisis interrupted my discussions with Shar'.

Hany Salam, who was unaware of the manifold pressures on the president, tried a little too hard one day to push him to do more to accommodate the Syrian position. In response, he received a long lecture that went like this:

> Hany Beyk, my friend, I am not God. I am only human. How much can I do? The Syrians have been difficult with me. I send Elie to talk to them, and they enter Beirut without telling me directly or indirectly of their intentions. They asked for a letter, I sent one. They asked for another letter, and I sent that too. I never receive anything from them in return, not one signed scrap of paper. The more I give them, the more popularity I lose in my community. In return, they keep asking me to do things beyond my ability. They are driving me crazy. Elie asks me to be patient. Let him sit in my place and see how patient he can be. What have I got from them since November? Nothing except these cyclical discussions between Salem and Shar'. I am sorry to shout at you, but you must understand what your president is going through.

At the time, the Christian community was divided on reforms. Some thought that this was the right moment to introduce reforms, but others, like the Lebanese Forces, preferred to wait for a change in the regional situation before making any moves. Jumayyil thought of reforms as a minor part of the Lebanese problem. He told me that reforms could be settled in 'half an hour between me and Asad when the other big questions are settled'. In general I would have agreed with this, except that I thought that reforms were the key to the 'other big questions' to which the president was referring. The big questions were: would Israel withdraw? Would Syria withdraw? Would the PLO be active militarily in Lebanon again? Would Lebanon be sacrificed as a price for a Middle Eastern settlement? Would the internal war end? Many Maronites felt that they were called upon to make concessions and weaken the presidency, but having done that what would we get? Would we get the peace and stability we wanted? I was always afraid of the 'cyclical' in politics, and I thought reforms were good in themselves, a chance for what was right to be established.

This was my mood when I met Shar' on Thursday 5 March. I started the session by blaming Syria for not informing us of its decision to enter West Beirut. Shar' responded that Speaker Hussein al-Husseini had spoken to Ghassan Tweini in Paris, and that Tweini, in turn, had called President Jumayyil to get his approval. I was not aware of this communication. The president, I told Shar', would have approved the Syrian entry into Beirut to stop the anarchy and would have provided the proper legal framework for the Syrian entry had Damascus chosen to deploy their forces through the 'legitimate process' rather than through the 'political revolutionary process'. Shar' did not respond, nor did I follow up with the president on whether he was contacted or not. In this meeting and in future meetings I felt that Shar' was in no hurry at all. He wanted Jumayyil to impose his authority, contain the Lebanese Forces, and prove that he could implement any agreement that we reached. I realized that the Syrians had shifted the emphasis of our talks from the reform document itself, to a discussion of President Jumayyil's ability to implement reforms. From now on I had to argue not only our views on reform but also the president's ability to implement them.

General Ghazi Kan'an, who preferred to listen rather than talk, gave a long account of Karami's frustrations with Christian politicians, and with the Lebanese Forces in particular. He noted that Jumayyil had done nothing to consolidate his authority in the Eastern Sector and that he would be unable to implement what we were agreeing on in Damascus. He continued arguing that Syria could not tolerate an Israeli presence in the Eastern Sector, and he added that everybody knew that the Israelis had penetrated the Lebanese Forces, and through them, the Christian community. This constituted a grave danger to Syria. Jumayyil, he concluded, was well intentioned, but he could not deliver. I made a valiant attempt to improve the image of the president and to allay their fears that the president was approving, by inaction, LF connections with Israel. I challenged the accusation that the LF were an 'Israeli phenomenon'. I argued that they were young Lebanese, that all they cared for was Lebanon, and that in the future they may work closely with Syria. Syria, I argued, must see matters from their perspective, and give them and the president time to bring them around to the very perception which I was giving in Damascus as representative of the president.

After some twelve sessions, I told Shar' I was determined to stay in Damascus until an agreement was reached. I told him that I had the authority to deal with all remaining issues, although I believed we had agreed on all reform issues or were pretty close to doing so. Shar' could see that I was serious. He re-emphasized that he was simply a mediator and that he would need time to consult with all parties; he even suggested that he may have to 'broaden the circle of consultation'. I rejected this categorically, arguing that if we did this, it would mean reopening issues on which we had already agreed.

An unknown was preventing the discussions from reaching a conclusion. Could it be that Syria did not want an agreement with Jumayyil? Did it prefer to work out an agreement with a new president? Was Syria unprepared to agree to a document that would define its stand on all the players in Lebanon? We had no answers to these questions. I felt that our discussions had led to agreement on virtually all points, and where there was not an agreement, there was an understanding on the options which would be submitted to the two presidents to resolve.

The Hariri Effort

Realizing that the Lebanese–Syrian talks had reached a bottleneck, Rafiq al-Hariri called me to offer King Fahd's mediation. I met with Hariri in Cyprus on 24 May and he told me that the king was ready to help and, if necessary, to work out reform proposals with us which he would send to Asad directly. Hariri was confident that, given King Fahd's clout in Damascus, his intervention would lead to results. Together we prepared a letter to the king informing him of the progress attained in the Damascus discussions, and stressing the need to bring these discussions to a successful conclusion.

On 1 June 1987, Prime Minister Rashid Karami was assassinated by a bomb placed behind his seat in the army helicopter which was carrying him from Tripoli to Beirut. Despite the blast, the helicopter was able to land at the Halat airstrip. Immediately, the Lebanese Forces, the army and the president, were accused by the opposition of killing Karami. The president was accused of giving cover to the LF and to the army and for covering up the crime. Independent investigations were conducted by the army and by the Judicial Council, which dealt with crimes affecting the security of the state. Neither investigation was able to find out who was responsible for the crime. As in all Lebanese political killings, everybody denied responsibility while putting the blame on third parties.

President Jumayyil, acting quickly in cooperation with the Sunni leadership, appointed Dr Salim al-Hoss as acting prime minister, to ensure continuity in the government; albeit in a government that was no longer meeting. The assassination had an impact on the Damascus Discussions, and brought a halt to all action on reform. Asad sent his condolences to Karami's family and not to President Jumayyil, indicating either that he was irrelevant, or that Syria held him responsible for Karami's death. Sure enough, we soon received word that the Damascus Discussions would not be resumed until the assassins were found and punished. The president was anxious to keep his lines to Damascus open, and pressured General Awn to do something, even if it meant firing personnel in the helicopter command. Awn, however, did not want to demoralize the army by firing people he felt were not responsible for the crime. The president and Awn were not on good terms, and Awn had his eyes on the presidency. He wanted the army with him, and was not ready to serve the political purposes of the president by punishing officers he considered innocent. Awn suspected that a foreign agent had put the explosives in the helicopter in Tripoli to embarrass the army.

Tragic as the death of Karami was, we felt that it should not stop the Damascus Discussions. I asked Hariri to come to Lebanon so that we could see about Saudi intervention to reopen the talks. 'I will send you a helicopter to Larnaca', I said. 'A helicopter?' he shouted down the phone, 'do you think I am crazy?' 'No,' I answered, 'I will come to Larnaca.' I did. We agreed to put in final form all the points that were agreed upon in the Damascus Discussions. Then the king would call Asad and tell him that he had a reasonable proposal which he would like to present to him. Hariri would go to Syria as his personal envoy, with Jumayyil's proposal. The whole process would be kept strictly confidential.

Hariri said that should the president decide to accept the Saudi initiative, then it was necessary for him and the two of us to meet outside Lebanon. I proposed that the three of us hold a meeting on Hariri's aeroplane in Larnaca. Hariri was pleased with the suggestion. When I brought up the proposal with President Jumayyil, he hesitated. After a number of long sessions, however, I finally persuaded him to go along with Hariri's suggestion and meet with him on his plane.

On 10 June, President Jumayyil and I, with no bodyguards, took a helicopter to Cyprus where we boarded Hariri's plane. In order not to arouse suspicion, we took off in the direction of Sardinia. We worked non-stop from 10 a.m. that day to 4 a.m. the following day. Hariri and Jumayyil were both rather nervous in each other's presence. The persistent noise of the plane did not make the atmosphere any better. Finally we came out with a proposal based on the Damascus Discussions. As Hariri was supposed to submit the proposal to Asad on 13 June, we shall refer to it as the 13 June paper (see Appendix 1).

Our positions on reform as they found their way into the 13 June paper were as follows. We had accepted the principle of Arab identity exactly as adopted by the Geneva National Dialogue Conference. Of course we wholeheartedly adopted the 'finality' of the Lebanese nation, i.e. that Lebanon was here to stay as a state, not to be partitioned or united with another. Political confessionalism was to be abolished gradually in a manner that would not scare any minority. We proposed a formula for gradual elimination which was reluctantly accepted by the opposition. The Syrian team, as mediator and also as negotiator, was stressing the need to abolish confessionalism by a certain deadline. When our formulation was accepted, General Kan'an said: 'I am sure the members of the committee you are suggesting to work on the abolition of confessionalism will die long before confessionalism is abolished.' Shar' said: 'Fine, we have accepted your argument, but now I want you to write in your diary that under your formulations, confessionalism will never be abolished from Lebanon.' 'Oh, poor me,' I responded, 'I cannot ever hope to become president!' 'Nor your children', retorted the smiling foreign minister.

On power sharing we agreed, after extensive discussions on executive authority, that it be vested in the council of ministers. We did not agree on how the council would be chaired. We agreed that the prime minister be selected by the president after conducting binding consultation with members of parliament. We wanted the president to remain, in fact, the president. I argued that we must strengthen central authority and keep the president strong to control the centrifugal forces in the country. We agreed on 50-50 between Christians and Muslims in parliament, in the council of ministers, and in grade I in the bureaucracy (civil, military, security, juridical) and I urged that the council of ministers should supervise the bureaucracy to ensure equitable, if not strict, equality of distribution in all bureaucratic positions below grade I. We did not discuss distinctive relations as our paper of 6 February 1986 was considered satisfactory. We did, however, discuss certain general concepts that were to apply on future relations and we disagreed on a number of them, as the Syrians used ideological language such as 'strategic relations' and 'common destiny' and the like, which we found too broad. We did agree that there were historical and geographic considerations that necessitated establishing distinctive relations and signing agreements between the two countries in 'various fields'.

We agreed on the need for strengthening administrative decentralization without specifying what this meant. We agreed on the need to introduce a higher court to try presidents and ministers, a constitutional court to interpret laws, and a social and economic council to enhance development. We found the right language on education, information, the army and security forces, one which was radically different from the language used in the Tripartite Agreement.

When I briefed Patriarch Sfeir on the points we had reached in Damascus he was generally supportive. The following is a typical patriarchal response:

> We cannot accept the abolition of political confessionalism; all the Arab world is confessional. Why should we be singled out? We Christians are a value, not a number, and therefore the principle of 50-50 is essential for us. There are two values, Christianity and Islam, and these two must be equal irrespective of their numbers. We insist that the Maronite president should have enough power to provide guarantees to the Christians in times of crisis. Lebanon should have an army that is clearly its own, and not an extension of the army of another state. We are ready to be patient and wait; we waited in the past and preserved our independence, even if it was incomplete. We will wait again. God put us in these valleys and hills, and here we shall stay.

When Hariri submitted the 13 June paper to Asad, Asad said it was reasonable. Asad, however, believed that these events were directed against Jumayyil and himself alike. Asad believed that the question of reforms should be set aside while political matters were dealt with. Israeli influence in the Eastern Sector had to be dealt with immediately, and Asad said that he was ready to put all his resources at Jumayyil's disposal to eliminate Israeli influence in the Eastern Sector. Asad wanted to know Jumayyil's response to this message, and wanted to know how he would deal with the 'Israeli factor'.

Hariri was well aware that this was not the answer we expected. I told Hariri that he should not expect Jumayyil to attack the Lebanese Forces; whatever his differences with them, the president and they came from the same Christian community. His purpose was to contain the Lebanese Forces politically within the framework of an agreement which defined distinctive relations with Syria. The president, I told Hariri, wanted the Lebanese Forces to be treated like all other militias, and they must be absorbed politically into a new government formed on the basis of the principles we set in the 13 June paper.

Asad wanted Jumayyil to act decisively against the Lebanese Forces, and reiterated that Syria would help him do this. Asad believed that any agreement with Jumayyil, while Israel had influence in the Eastern Sector, was doomed to failure. Asad told Hariri: 'The Salem–Shar' discussions made great progress, and were about to be crowned with success, had it not been for the assassination of Karami.'

Asad also spoke well of the role the USA could play in Lebanon, particularly in securing an Israeli withdrawal. He expressed interest in greater cooperation with the United States. We learned later that President Reagan had told Prime Minister Thatcher at the Venice Summit that Washington wanted to improve relations with Damascus. Thatcher reportedly did not object to this, although she urged the USA to delay a dialogue with the Syrians until after the British elections. Reagan sent a letter to Asad expressing satisfaction at the expulsion of Abu Nidal from Syria, and listing issues which American envoy General Vernon Walters would discuss with the Syrian leadership when he visited Damascus soon. These issues included American–Syrian relations, the Iraq–Iran War, the peace process, and Iran's role in Lebanon through Hizballah. Shar' called the US chargé d'affaires in Damascus and told him that Asad was pleased with Reagan's letter and that he would gladly receive Walters.

I was not surprised to see that the Lebanese question was not on the agenda of American–Syrian discussions. I asked the American ambassador in Beirut, John Kelly, to request the State Department to contact Walters and add Lebanon to the agenda. At the same time, I drafted a letter for President Jumayyil to send to President Reagan prior to Walters's departure for the Syrian capital.

Walters met Asad on 5 and 6 July 1987, and on 7 July Kelly briefed me on the visit. Walters had emphasized the United States's support for the territorial integrity of Lebanon, and he had stressed that the institutions of the state must function properly, otherwise Lebanon would disappear. The USA, Walters added, was pressuring President Jumayyil to find Karami's assassins and bring them to justice. Asad told Walters that he had advised Jumayyil on how to handle this problem, but that Jumayyil had ignored his advice. Walters urged Asad to resume the Damascus Discussions, even though Karami's assassins had not yet been found; one issue should not be the hostage of the other, he had argued. At the same time as Walters was talking to Asad, April Glaspie met Shar' and encouraged him to resume the Damascus Discussions. Glaspie had served in Damascus before and was well acquainted with Syrian politics. As a high official in the State Department Near East section she was to play a significant part in our continuing efforts to reach an agreement with Damascus. The Syrians were adamant, however: there could be no resumption of talks until Karami's assassins were found and punished.

I realized that what Shar' and I had agreed to in Damascus required a different political context to be implemented. Peace in Lebanon required a number of simultaneous things: it needed intense regional interest and international backing. Mediators like Hariri and Tajir could push us forward, but the time was not right for a global solution to our crisis. The Damascus Discussions thus came to an end. They did not fail; the points we had agreed on were simply put into the freezer for the future. They all found their way into the National Conciliation Document reached in Taif, Saudi Arabia, in October 1989.

10

Between Washington and Damascus

Between 1982 and 1984 the Reagan administration was deeply involved in Lebanese affairs. When it failed to achieve its objectives in Lebanon, it withdrew militarily and diplomatically, preferring, for domestic American reasons, not to be visibly associated with the Lebanese débâcle. Washington's position between 1984 and 1987 was best expressed by Robert Oakley, a Reagan aide at the White House, when he said:

> We are as confused as the Israelis are about Lebanon, except we are more so. There are many demands on our time in Washington and we do not really have enough time to give to Lebanon. We, therefore, depend fully on Kelly [the US ambassador in Beirut] to blow the whistle and to tell us when something important is taking place. We get confused by the many religions, the many parties, the many leaders, and the many shifting alliances in your country. How can one explain that the LF [the Christian Lebanese Forces militia] and the PLO are now working together? We are not very sophisticated in Washington and we prefer simple solutions to simple problems.

Problems, however, are not solved by being ignored, nor does the complicated get simpler and less benign by being skirted. Iran made headway in Lebanon, and terrorist acts against American and European interests increased. PLO fighters returned to Beirut in large numbers; militias strengthened their hold on Beirut, the Eastern Sector and other regions. The period from 1984 to 1987 was one of ups and downs in Lebanon, of national dialogue conferences, and of brave but futile efforts to reach agreement on reforms and on the future of Lebanese–Syrian relations. Syria tried its hand at reforms through the Tripartite Agreement and failed. Jumayyil tried through the Salem–Shar' discussions and failed. By the spring of 1987, Syria was sending signals indicating its readiness to cooperate with the USA on Lebanon and on regional problems. Washington moved cautiously towards Damascus.

To assess the new American position on Lebanon and the Middle East before we sought to re-engage the USA, Bouhabib asked Issam Fares to finance and host a small two-day seminar on this question at his residence in Deauville, France. High-level American experts met Fares, Bouhabib and me in Deauville and gave us a full account of the Reagan policy at the time. Reagan had shifted his interest, we were told; he was concentrating on internal affairs. Shultz was in despair about Lebanon but anxious to move the Middle East Process forward; Lebanon was now way down on the Washington list of priorities. Damascus had acquired importance because it proved to be a capital that mattered. It had won in Lebanon; it was the key to the Middle East Peace Process. If Damascus was ready to hold a dialogue with the USA, the USA was ready, but it must act coy with Asad because he acted coy himself. In the warmth of the Fares household we gained new insights into the present state of mind of the Reagan administration, and new approaches on some specifics. Shultz had his mind set on an international peace conference on the Middle East. He wanted a success in the Middle East before the American elections in 1988.

The Americans appeared relatively optimistic that a breakthrough on the peace process would occur. Richard Murphy thought that the El Al incident, in which Syria was implicated in attempting to place a bomb in an El Al flight from London to Tel Aviv, had damaged Asad's image in the West, and that the Syrians were interested in a dialogue with the United States to turn this around. He told me that Washington, which had recalled its ambassador to Syria, Mr Eagleton, in protest against the El Al incident, would soon be sending him back to Damascus. Murphy, however, wondered whether Asad was interested in reaching an agreement with Jumayyil during the latter's final year as president. He wondered about the facts at Asad's disposal. He most likely perceived Jumayyil as ineffective; he perceived of Israel as making gains in the Eastern Sector through the Lebanese Forces. He perceived Jumayyil as an accomplice, not because he was sympathetic to the LF or to Israel, but because he was not able to check Israel's expansion in the Maronite community. He possibly perceived Iran as both friend and foe. He could not be very much at ease with the growing power of Hizballah. 'Our policy', added Murphy, 'is to prise Syria away from Iran. For this reason we want to open a dialogue with Syria. No one knows more than we do how frustrating it is to hold a dialogue with Damascus. The fact is Damascus is central to the peace process and to you.'

America chose General Vernon Walters, the US ambassador to the UN, to open the new dialogue with Syria in the summer of 1987. When I first met Walters, I realized he would get along well with Asad. He was a former general in the US army, jovial, pleasant, humorous, and completely

free of the formalism of diplomacy. When he analysed a situation, Walters
painted with a broad brush, leaving details to the diplomats. With the
Syrians he was used as a bulldozer, removing the rubble so to speak, thus
paving the way for the restoration of diplomatic relations at the ambassadorial level. Walters was confident that a new page had been turned
in Washington's relations with Syria, and he argued that Lebanon would
benefit from an American–Syrian dialogue. Walters admired Asad, and
felt he could do business with him. He also said that he had asked
Secretary Shultz to encourage the reopening of the Lebanese–Syrian
dialogue, which had been interrupted by Karami's assassination. He
wanted Shultz to talk to the Syrians in the context of the General Assembly session in September, about Lebanon and the need to reach an
agreement.

Upon his return to Damascus, Ambassador William Eagleton was asked
by Secretary Shultz to meet Asad and inform him of US support for the
following: (1) our reform proposal of 13 June 1987; (2) the need to end
the boycott of President Jumayyil; (3) the need to form a new government;
(4) a plan to unite Beirut.

The State Department found our 13 June proposal reasonable. American officials believed that once Asad saw our paper and heard that
Washington supported it strongly, he could not argue that President
Jumayyil had offered him nothing. I suggested to Glaspie that she explore
linkages which could move the process forward. Such linkages could
include European cooperation with Syria, the return of American com-
panies to Syria, the removal of Syria from the State Department list of
countries engaged in terrorism, congressional allocation of financial aid
to Syria, and American–Syrian understanding on some regional issues.

As I was working on this new process, the president sent me a copy of
a speech he intended to deliver in Canada. The text was in French, and
was written in an emotional tone by a speech writer who, in my opinion,
was completely off the mark. The speech dwelled to an excessive degree
on Lebanon's problems, on how it had been stabbed in the back, and by
insinuation insulted every country whose help we needed. Because it was
beautifully written it was deceptive. The form was brilliant, the content
was rotten. I called the president and bluntly told him:

> This speech will raise the value of the dollar to one hundred Lebanese
> pounds, it will end the American mediation process, it terrifies the Lebanese
> who still believe that there is some governmental authority left, it is full of
> question marks, as if it were delivered by a citizen not by the president of
> the republic, it has no stand, no guidance, no muscle, and is totally devoid
> of presidential style and content.

The president was stunned. He had just read the speech and liked it. Fortunately, he was convinced by my argument and dropped the speech. Instead, he called Kelly and told him that he was pleased with the process Kelly and I had started. He added, however, that experience told him that it was not likely to work, but there was no better alternative. He was very frustrated, and noted that if the process failed, he would have to form a new government, and publicly state his position on the situation. Kelly was understanding, but assured the president that the new process could bring positive results, and that we should stand by it.

On 11 September, Kelly informed me of Ambassador Eagleton's meeting with Asad. It had not gone as well as Washington had expected. Asad would not reopen a dialogue with Jumayyil until Karami's assassins had been punished. He had also said that Jumayyil must 'act decisively' with the Lebanese Forces. Jumayyil, Asad argued, had fallen into the isolationist camp, i.e. the pro-Israeli Maronite grouping. Jumayyil, in Asad's opinion, spoke well, but didn't do what he promised. Asad said that he had participated in eleven summits with Jumayyil, but had never really understood him. He hoped, nevertheless, that the USA would look over the Lebanese scene and see if there was anything which could be done, after which the Syrians and the Americans could together explore possible outlets from the deadlock.

Kelly saw in this a signal from Asad that he wanted to keep the process open, but that he was going to be a tough negotiator. According to Kelly, in his talks with Eagleton, Asad was negative on a variety of subjects covered in the agenda other than Lebanon. This included the PLO, terrorism, the Iran–Iraq war, and the peace process.

When Eagleton mentioned that Abu Nidal was still in Lebanon, Asad retorted: 'Lebanon is a sovereign country. My authority does not extend there.' When Eagleton spoke of Iranians using the Beirut International Airport for terrorist acts, again Asad disclaimed any responsibility for the airport, since it was not under Syrian authority. Eagleton had repeatedly tried to open doors to Asad, Kelly explained, but the Syrian leader kept slamming them shut. Kelly believed that there was still a slight possibility of arriving at an agreement on Lebanon with Asad and that it should be explored directly by President Jumayyil with Secretary Shultz in New York in September, when they could meet informally in the context of the General Assembly session. For our part, we wanted to be specific with Shultz, and present to him a timetable of what we intended to do, and when to do it. We thought such a concrete approach would convince Asad, who felt that Jumayyil spoke in generalities and never did anything.

On 28 September, the president, Ghassan Tweini, Abdallah Bouhabib and I met Murphy and Glaspie at the Waldorf Astoria Hotel in New

York. The Americans told us they would be meeting with Shar' the next day in the UN building. They said they needed some specific indication from us, such as a timetable, to show our commitment to implementing reforms. Shultz saw the American role in the current process as 'carrying messages back and forth' between us and Asad. He wanted quiet diplomacy and wanted to see what was 'on the minds' of the Syrians.

In our meeting with Shultz the next day, we agreed to give him a specific timetable on implementing reforms which he could deliver to Shar' with his support. Tweini, Bouhabib and I formulated the details of the proposal in what we termed 'the Eight Points'.

The Eight Points

1. President Jumayyil, upon his return to Lebanon, will issue a declaration in which he reiterates his determination to proceed with the specific constitutional reforms in light of our 13 June proposal.
2. Syrian–Lebanese negotiations will then be resumed at the appropriate level to reach final agreement on the details of political reform.
3. The United States will be informed of the progress of these negotiations and will be prepared to assist the Lebanese and Syrian negotiators in narrowing down the differences.
4. The president will accept the resignation of the present government and proceed to form a new government before 20 October. The programme of the new government will be the implementation of constitutional reforms which have been agreed to with the government of Syria, and will also include whatever measures are necessary to end the state of hostilities in Lebanon.
5. The new government will submit to the parliament draft constitutional laws and other necessary bills for reform, and will request an urgent final vote on them.
6. Following that, the membership of the parliament will be expanded as previously agreed.
7. Concerning the assassination or the murder of Prime Minister Karami the president is determined to activate the governmental juridical process to uncover and punish the assassins. He will ask for the formation of a parliamentary committee of inquiry in this matter and give it wide authority.
8. The president will take part in the forthcoming Arab summit of 8 November on the basis of the policy of the new government to ask for whatever Arab assistance is necessary to speed up the cessation of hostilities, address the consequences of the war, and start a programme of Lebanese reconstruction.

In his meeting with Shar', Shultz delivered the Eight Points from Jumayyil and indicated his confidence in the president's desire to implement them. Shar' expressed suspicion about Jumayyil and about the timetable. He wondered why it had been submitted, especially since Syria had not asked for it. Murphy, who was accompanying Shultz, emphasized that a time-table showed seriousness. He added that the reference in the document to holding an Arab summit was intended to speed up progress. Shar' was cautious. He wanted to consult with Damascus. Anyhow neither he nor any Syrian negotiator was ever in a hurry. Syria practiced the art of the strong. It acted confidently and in a relaxed manner, just as Asad himself acted, as if he had all the time in the world. After attacking Jumayyil for obstructing reform, Shar' reluctantly agreed to distribute Jumayyil's Eight Points to the opposition. Shultz felt that a step forward had been achieved.

When Murphy called me to say what Shar' was going to do, I objected strongly. To distribute our proposal to the diverse voices of the opposition was to strip it of all seriousness. The opposition spoke with many voices, and Babel in comparison seemed rational and coherent. Instead, I suggested that Shar' consult confidentially with half a dozen opposition leaders and not release it to the press. Since the 13 June paper had been kept confidential, so should our Eight Points. Murphy called Shar' and then called me back to assure me that consultation would be limited to Syria's main allies.

Meanwhile, in Beirut Ambassador Kelly briefed speaker Husseini on our meetings with Shultz and Murphy and on our 13 June proposal. Husseini told Kelly that the points raised in the 13 June document were what Prime Minister Karami and he had wanted, and he was pleased that the president had finally accepted them. According to Kelly neither Hoss nor Husseini seemed aware of our 13 June paper, and were pleasantly surprised by it.

On 1 October I was told by Kelly that Shultz and Murphy would be visiting the region. Murphy would go to Damascus alone, since it was too soon for Shultz to meet with Asad. Such a meeting must be prepared in advance, and some positive result guaranteed. It was not certain, however, that Murphy would come to Beirut. I insisted with Kelly that Murphy came, otherwise the process started in Washington would be endangered. Kelly agreed with me and advised Murphy accordingly. After some hesitation Murphy agreed to come to Beirut after going to Damascus. Shultz and Murphy arrived in the second week of October. Shultz was touring capitals concerned with the peace process, but he was not going to Damascus.

In Damascus Murphy met Khaddam, since Asad was on a state visit to Bulgaria. Khaddam was extremely negative when it came to Jumayyil, and did not believe there was much of a prospect of working with him. Nevertheless he promised to study Jumayyil's paper and send his response directly to the Americans.

After a few days I checked with Kelly to find out about the response. 'Whatever it is,' Kelly told me, 'it is going to be thin soup with a few grains of rice which you will be hard-pressed to find.' In fact he knew nothing yet; he was guessing. On 6 November, Dan Simpson, the chief deputy of mission in the US Embassy, called me to say he had received the Syrian response. I told him to deliver it directly to the president. A few hours later I called the president and asked for his reactions. 'I am still looking for the grains of rice', he retorted.

Damascus had responded to our proposals by calling for the abolition of confessionalism four years after parliamentary elections were held. They also made a number of demands which greatly weakened the office of the presidency. In addition, the Syrians called on Jumayyil to dissolve the Lebanese Forces prior to the implementation of reform. Syria accused the LF of having killed Karami, and demanded that the president 'confiscate their weapons and put their leaders on trial'. All these demands had been debated again and again, and our position was well known: clearly, Damascus was not eager to open a dialogue with Jumayyil.

The Amman Arab Summit

The American effort was transferred to the Arab League Summit in Amman. King Hussein was eager to score a success at the summit by arranging for meetings between Asad and Saddam Hussein, and between Asad and Jumayyil. Asad did not seem interested in meeting Jumayyil and urged Prime Minister Hoss to lead the Lebanese delegation. Hoss responded, 'Jumayyil is going, what should I do? Either I shall sit on his lap or he on mine.' Asad burst out laughing, and agreed with Hoss that he should not go to Amman, but should instead send a memorandum to the summit stating the Lebanese position as seen by the opposition.

Because of the boycott of the presidency, no Muslim would join President Jumayyil's delegation to Amman. The official delegation, consisting of the president, Tweini and myself, arrived in Amman on Saturday 7 November, and the conference opened in the afternoon.

Asad seemed unhappy and distracted. Yasir Arafat was all smiles, looking left and right for some leader to hug and kiss. Our location at the conference was the most photographed. Our place in the alphabet put us in the zone of troubles: Lebanon, Libya, Morocco and the PLO. We were the centre of attention, not for our achievements, but for the problems we posed.

The Lebanese delegation came to Amman with the assurance that King Hussein would arrange a meeting between Jumayyil and Asad. On Sunday, following a long meeting we had with Arafat in our suite, Crown Prince Hassan and Prime Minister Zayd al-Rifa'i arrived looking sombre. Asad, they reported, would not meet with Jumayyil 'unless he had new ideas'. Jumayyil responded that he would accept any ideas on reform that King Hussein and President Benjdid found reasonable – more of a political than a juridical statement – and it was probably accepted as such. The Jordanians, through Prime Minister Rifa'i, worked out a number of formulations on power sharing with us hoping to cut the Gordian Knot and resume a Lebanese–Syrian dialogue. All these attempts ended in failure.

In the evening Asad and Saddam Hussein were seen walking together and joking. I asked Tariq Aziz how these two old enemies had managed to meet at the summit. He told me that King Hussein had tried to bring them together, but had failed. Then Crown Prince Abdallah bin Abd al-Aziz had taken Asad and Saddam by the hand and said to both: 'Shake hands'. They had done so. Then he had added, 'Fine, now sit down and settle your differences', and had walked out.

While no meeting between Jumayyil and Asad could be arranged, Shar' told me that a new process involving American mediation had been started and that Syria was happy with it. There was no need to engage King Hussein or any other. If that was the only process, the president and I felt the need to reinforce it. Accordingly, I went to Washington to activate the American mediation. Bouhabib had prepared the ground well for this visit. Most of the meetings with Glaspie were held in Bouhabib's dining room, where we were warmly welcomed by his young wife Julie.

Philip Habib joined us and offered advice. He was sad about the turn of events in Lebanon. 'Elie,' he said, 'no one has heart any more. Poor Lebanon, poor you, you try but you get nowhere. At least you are always creating a process. You cannot make progress without process.' Habib found some hope in Glaspie, who was hard working, dynamic and persistent.

We worked on a draft paper which Murphy, Glaspie, Bouhabib and I found reasonable. It was based on our 13 June paper with greater detail on power sharing. It was agreed that the USA was to discuss the paper with Syria through its ambassador in Damascus, William Eagleton. Meanwhile, Hariri presented a reform proposal to Khaddam early in December, and Khaddam, we were told, had passed it on to Eagleton to have it discussed through the new process.

The Hariri Paper of December 1987

On Friday 11 December, Kelly called me to say that he had in hand a project which Hariri had submitted to Syria. We shall refer to it as the Hariri paper of 11 December 1987. The Syrians wanted our opinion on it. Damascus, we were told, would accept the Hariri paper if we did. Having seen dozens of such papers and produced quite a few of them myself, I was personally more interested in a credible process which would lead somewhere.

On 15 December, I called Hariri and told him we did not know how to react to his paper, which neither Syria nor the United States claimed. I told him that we had no problems at all with the language on distinctive relations with Syria. The question, to me, remained how to work with Syria to realize this option. I told Hariri that one could not negotiate by correspondence, ignoring the implementation of a credible process.

The Americans, like us, did not know how to react to the Hariri paper. Introducing the paper into the process, said Kelly, was like putting a third basket on a basketball court. I wrote to Murphy reaffirming our readiness to attempt every course open to us, adding:

> However, we fear delays and new beginnings whose intent may be to postpone the issue. The seriousness of the crisis necessitates a clear methodology and determined effort. We have no difficulty with the Hariri paper once we understand how it fits into a process, how discussions on it could proceed meaningfully, and particularly expeditiously. There are points in it which were agreed upon in the Lebanese–Syrian discussions in Damascus; there are points that are better stated in written communications with Damascus; there are vague points that require clarification. The main issue with us is not the content of this paper *per se*, but how to deal with a private initiative in the context of serious negotiations amongst states. This must be clarified first before we proceed into content, intent and the element of time.

On 22 December we received a note from Murphy urging us to respond in writing to the Hariri paper. Murphy was encouraged by Khaddam's statement that a positive response from us 'would generate positive Syrian suggestions. It is this Syrian promise which we have sought for so many weeks, which we believe should be explored', Murphy told us.

On 31 December we sent Murphy and Glaspie our response to the Hariri paper. We did it to keep the process going. In addition, Hariri had been calling me daily asking for a speedy response. The Hariri paper of 11 December is a lengthy document, and we need not go into it here.

From January 1988 on we were discussing nuances in the Hariri paper. The reform issues in it were now discussed along with two other issues –

the formation of a new government, and the election of a president in September. President Jumayyil, frustrated by a government that had boycotted him for more than a year, was anxious to change it and get a government that was willing to cooperate with him and take decisions. His advisers on internal politics urged him to form the type of government that any Sunni leader would be willing to form. The president had the constitutional power to oust the Hoss government and announce any government he wished, but if his announcement was not supported by political consensus it meant nothing. Hoss would not pay attention to the president's order, and in any open contest of wills like this one, a weak presidency was a certain loser. I advised against taking such a step except in coordination with Syria, and though the president was emotionally opposed to my counsel, he understood that there was no alternative.

As to presidential elections, almost all Maronite deputies acted as presidential hopefuls and their political behaviour was concentrated on elections eight months down the road. I recommended to the president that he take an active interest in the election of a successor to ensure the smooth transfer of power to a new president. Almost daily I told him: 'How to leave the presidency is more important than how you came into it.' The new president, I argued, should be a conciliator enjoying high credibility, particularly with Syria, and he should feel that President Jumayyil had facilitated his arrival. These two issues, forming a government and electing a new president, came to dominate our discussions with the Americans and the Syrians.

The president wanted to leave office on a note of success and hoped that agreeing to a package deal with Asad on reforms, a new government, agreement on a successor, and concrete steps for the restoration of Lebanon's sovereignty and independence would provide it. When I met Shultz in February, I told him that the president wanted reforms before he left office, and that he wanted to put in place a new government to implement them. I asked Shultz to send Murphy to Damascus and Beirut to move the process forward. I wanted to move fast since Glaspie, who was playing a dynamic role in the process, was about to be named US ambassador to Baghdad.

Washington's perspective was different from ours. To us agreement with Syria was central, but to Washington it was a means to open a broader dialogue with Damascus on Iran, Hizballah, the PLO, the West Bank and Gaza, and the peace process as a whole. I told my American interlocutors that Lebanon had for more than a decade been the dumping ground for the problems of the Middle East. It was easy to fall into the temptation of seeing Lebanon merely as a geographic expression. We wanted to prevent this, hence our insistence on a package deal comprising reforms, an end to the war, the formation of a new government and the election of a president. Reforms, I said, came first. Glaspie argued that it was difficult for a Ba'thi regime to accept confessionalism. I told her it was difficult for me too. I was as aware as anybody that Lebanon's confessional system deprived me and my children of many offices of state, but Lebanon was not Syria, and if it was our destiny to be confessional, if only for a period, then that was the cross we had to bear. Confessionalism would be abolished once we had a sophisticated political culture, a civic culture that would render confessionalism obsolete and irrelevant.

In our talks on the number of members of parliament I argued for the smallest number needed to attain equality between Christians and Muslims, which was 108 deputies. We preferred this minimum number, because appointing as few deputies as possible to fill the vacant and additional parliamentary seats would put less strain on our political system. I explained our position on every point to give Murphy and Glaspie a background on our thinking when discussing the package in Damascus. We showed flexibility on all points to give Murphy elbow-room in Damascus, and he felt confident that with this leeway he would get results. He went to Syria and I went to London and Paris. In Paris, I received a call from Murphy, who had just finished his meetings in Damascus and wanted to see me.

We met on Thursday 11 February at the residence of the American ambassador in Paris. Murphy briefed me in some detail: he had met Shar', Khaddam, and Asad on 6 and 7 February. The Syrians had said they were pleased with the US involvement. Murphy had stressed to them the danger of disintegration in Lebanon, the danger of Iranian fundamentalism, and the impact this may have on the presidential elections. The new president, he noted, should move into office on the basis of a new set of reforms. He asked Asad if he had decided not to reach an agreement with Jumayyil, to which Asad indicated that he was ready to reach an agreement with Jumayyil with the help of the USA. He added, however, that it was Jumayyil and the USA who had torpedoed the Tripartite Agreement, and Asad doubted whether Jumayyil wanted an agreement. Nevertheless he was willing to try again. Syria, he said, wanted to affirm certain principles: power in Lebanon should be shared equally between Muslims and Christians. The presidency should remain in the hands of the Maronites, but with reduced powers, and executive authority should be vested in the council of ministers. Asad wanted a clear answer from Jumayyil on the principles above and on deconfessionalism. Khaddam had intervened to say he wanted a paper on this from Jumayyil. 'No more papers,' Asad interjected, 'we have had enough papers, I have lost count.' How right he was.

Asad assured Murphy that Amal and the PSP would dissolve their militias, but that the other fundamentalist militias must be disarmed by the Lebanese state by force, and that Syria would help if asked. Asad insisted that deconfessionalism must take place in a short period of time, but he left the door open on a timetable. He felt that the Hariri paper and our response to it were serious documents worthy of consideration, and said that were we to respond positively on power-sharing and deconfessionalism, Syria would transmit our position to the opposition parties to seek their support. Then the representatives of President Jumayyil and the opposition could meet and reach a new agreement. Khaddam kept interjecting the issue of the assassination of Karami, but he insisted he was not linking the resumption of the Salem–Shar' discussions to the Karami assassination.

Murphy felt that he had made progress. I disagreed, sensing that he was allowing himself to become a postman, carrying messages back and forth. If the USA was convinced of a position, I argued, it should try and sell it in Beirut and Damascus; otherwise, it should not move. One could not visit Beirut and Damascus once a year and expect results. The Americans had to be prepared for a long stay, I argued. Murphy agreed. I then asked him to inform Kelly that the rules of the game had changed – the USA would not function as a postman but would press in Beirut and Damascus for what it believed to be fair, and we would work accordingly.

Once in Beirut, I briefed Kelly on my meeting with Murphy. He had just received an account of that meeting from Murphy himself, and admitted that there was one difference in the two briefings. David Wynn, who was taking notes in the Paris meeting, added, 'Salem was pacing back and forth, hands in pockets, lecturing Murphy with passion on how to proceed in the next stage of discussions.' If I did lecture at all it was not because Murphy was a student of mine at the Johns Hopkins School of Advanced International Studies, but because I felt strongly about what I was saying. The professorial role is an integral part of my personality. It has been with me since 1954.

After our meeting, Kelly immediately met Hoss and Husseini with a view to formulating a unified position on all reform points. When Tweini and I called at the embassy to see Kelly, he was in terrible shape. He had just returned from West Beirut, pistol in hand and extremely nervous. Colonel William Higgins, an American observer with the United Nations, had been kidnapped, and Kelly added that he himself had had a narrow escape as he drove through crossfire in West Beirut. He knew an ambassadorship in Beirut was exciting, but this was too much.

We had a good drink, and then proceeded to business. Hoss's idea on power-sharing, Kelly said, did not differ much from ours. On deconfessionalism Hoss and Husseini wanted a dynamic process leading to its abolition. They did not want to set deadlines and scare anybody. Kelly noted that he saw little difference between our position and Hoss's, and proposed that we prepare a memorandum on power-sharing and on confessionalism to send to Murphy.

The president was furious:

> I cannot go on like this, sending and receiving messages while nothing happens until my term of office expires in September. We must have a deadline to end the Damascus Discussions. They must end by April. I am not ready to sign reforms and hand them immediately to a new president to implement. I want at least two to three months to implement them myself. Why wait?

Kelly was understanding, and suggested June as a deadline for reaching agreement. He proposed that he should convey the president's sense of urgency to Shultz, whom he would be seeing in the next few days. We agreed to give Kelly an *aide-mémoire* on power-sharing and on the abolition of confessionalism, confirming positions already taken by me in Damascus.

Shultz visited the region between 24 February and 4 March 1988 with the view to laying the groundwork for a Middle East peace process on the basis of UN resolutions 242 and 338. During this visit, Shultz met Israeli, Jordanian, Egyptian and Syrian leaders.

On 29 February, Dan Simpson, the American deputy chief of mission, briefed me on Shultz's 27 February meeting with Asad. Shultz had presented our *aide-mémoire* to Asad and had noted that Washington was fully behind it. Asad had welcomed the US effort and promised to discuss the contents of the document with Murphy. There was no discussion of the Karami assassination. While Shultz toured the region in pursuit of the peace process, the Syrians were consulting with the opposition and preparing a response. A few days later Glaspie came to us. She was late from a visit to West Beirut, tired and nervous. The president was also tired and nervous, and felt slighted by her delay. He expected an apology and some small talk, but she was in a hurry and went straight to the subject of the paper and the Syrian position. To my shock and amazement he snatched the paper from her hand and in great fury signed his name to it. 'Here it is,' he said, 'I approve everything. The question is, does this end the war?'

Glaspie pursed her lips, turned pale, took a deep breath and looked at me. I winked 'forget it', and then she proceeded slowly into the paper. After the meeting, I told the president that in losing his temper he threatened to compromise the only progress we had made towards a settlement. He agreed, but he felt he had made up for it by showering

Glaspie with flattery afterwards. Kelly told me later that she had been exhausted. She had been travelling back and forth between Damascus, Riyad, Cairo and the two sides of Beirut for the past six days. In addition, Kelly had asked for a Syrian escort to accompany Glaspie and him to West Beirut. The escort, anxious to please, started shooting in the air to clear the way. Poor Glaspie did not know what was happening and was at the end of her nerves. She thought the shooting was aimed at her. After all she was in Beirut. She was American, engaged in a process rejected by the radicals in all camps and, therefore, this must be either a kidnapping or an assassination attempt.

Despite the frustration, the Americans were increasingly pleased with the process, and were hoping for a breakthrough with Asad through a settlement of the Lebanese crisis. If the proposal to convene an international conference on the Middle East did not succeed in bringing about a rapprochement between Washington and Damascus, maybe an arrangement in Lebanon would. In this way, Shultz could leave office feeling he had accomplished something in the region after his failure in 1983–84.

I met Murphy and Glaspie at Larnaca Airport on Sunday 3 April. They were arriving from Damascus, where they had met Khaddam and discussed our reform proposals with him. According to them, Khaddam insisted on a deadline for the ending of confessionalism, otherwise, he felt, it would endure and plague Lebanon for a hundred years. Finally Khaddam had agreed not to set a deadline for deconfessionalism, though it went against his convictions. Still, he argued that as the president was a Maronite, he should have no powers at all. 'Can he have a bed to sleep on?' inquired Murphy. Khaddam, who always enjoyed a good joke, had laughed. He was against granting the title of commander-in-chief of the army to the president because, he argued, a Maronite president would favour the Maronite community. When Murphy responded that the title was symbolic, Khaddam had retorted furiously that it was symbols like these that had led Lebanon to disaster. 'You do not want a president,' Murphy had said, 'you want a robot.' Murphy concluded that Khaddam was discussing the powers of the presidency and thinking of Jumayyil.

In early May, Glaspie spent a week in Damascus. She discussed Lebanon's need for a government which could govern; this meant a government which would meet, manage daily affairs and preside over the election of a new president. If such a government could not be formed, then the present one should meet. Progress on reform had to be achieved, she argued.

Political Concerns

We were in May 1988 and we were back discussing points we had exhausted in 1986 and 1987. I had done my best since the autumn of 1983 to help in the formulation of a reform that would end the war. I had worked hard with Hariri in the Geneva conference, and with Khaddam, Hariri and Marwan Himadeh in the Lausanne conference. I had counselled amending the Tripartite Agreement and proposed a dozen variations after dozens of conferences with mediators including the omnipresent Hariri. I had discussed in patient detail all aspects of reform in my meetings with Shar' and Kan'an. Repeatedly I had said what we could do, and what we could not. When all that effort failed I had turned again to US mediation. By May of 1988 I could no longer try. The message, I concluded, was the Syrians would not want an agreement with Jumayyil. Jumayyil kept hoping, and perhaps I too, that their position was not final. By May–June his hope seemed to be a desert mirage, the sooner discarded the better. I was no longer interested in pursuing the reform side of the negotiations. My interest was instead focused now on forming a government and, more importantly, on the election of a president.

Dan Simpson, in discussions on the presidential elections, claimed that the USA was innocent in this regard. It did not really know to what lengths the parties, namely Syria, Israel, the LF and the president, would go. 'I visualize our discussions with the Syrians', said Simpson. 'They will propose Sulayman Franjiyyeh and Eli Hubayqah, we will burst out laughing. Then we will propose Samir Ja'ja, and they will in turn burst out laughing; we will proceed with this game until the laughter subsides.'

Simpson also brought up the question of the commander of the army, General Michel Awn. He knew that the president and the LF distrusted him, and that his chances of being elected president were nil. He thought that President Jumayyil wanted a new government to take certain administrative decisions, one of them being the firing of Awn. He was right. Accordingly, Simpson suggested that the president send Awn as ambassador to some Latin American country instead of merely ousting him. The president welcomed the idea, but felt that the government would not approve any measure he introduced: 'If I say the day is clear,' he complained, 'they will say how dark it is for a spring day!'

An Arab Summit was held in Algiers between 7 and 10 June to discuss the Intifadah in the Occupied Territories. President Jumayyil, accompanied by Minister Joseph Hashem and myself, attended. The star of the opening session of the Summit was the Libyan leader Muammar al-Qadhdhafi. Of all the colourful leaders in the Arab world none stands out more brilliantly than he does – not only for his extremist policies, but for his personal style. He has unearthed ancient tribal attire and modernized it, they say with the help of Italian designers. He learned about the customs of the West from foreign troops in Libya and developed the art of shocking the West by violating their customs. He looked at the Arab scene and chose an ideology that no one could contest, but which no one took seriously, except himself. He understood the common and chose the uncommon. If the Saudis were deserting the tents for palaces he wanted to make the tent respectable again, and had one hoisted near his office. He saw the ascendant masculinity of the Arabs and chose to recruit young women to serve as his bodyguards. He saw new protocol dominating relations amongst heads of states and decided to violate it.

At the Algiers summit, Qadhdhafi sat aloof in his flowing white robes. He wore a white glove on his right hand. Jumayyil leaned towards him and asked why he was wearing a glove. 'Oh,' he answered, 'to cover a wound from the cursed American raid.' The Americans, infuriated by Qadhdhafi's antics against them, had bombed Tripoli and his residence, and had called on 'civilized nations' to break off diplomatic relations with Libya. I was not satisfied with the answer. So I whispered the same question to him again, and he whispered back: 'I must shake hands with all these reactionary leaders, and the glove is a protection. It keeps me clean.' During an exchange of niceties between Qadhdhafi and Jumayyil, the Libyan leader promised to send the president a tent to give him warmth and the Green Book, summarizing his own political philosophy, to give him guidance. The tent never arrived, but the book was received with the inscription: 'To the young leader who alone amongst the Arab leaders is capable of fathoming the depths of this great book.'

The real work in Arab summits takes place in the drafting committee, in which all delegations are represented. The most important statement was made by the Syrian foreign minister, Faruq al-Shar', who defined in crystal-clear terms Syrian policy on the Palestinian problem. Syria historically considers the Palestinian question as very much its own. His statement was in response to Faruq al-Qaddumi, the PLO representative who argued for the right of the Palestinians to take an independent decision on their own Palestinian problem. I took down Shar''s statement as follows:

> Syria is the leading Arab state in defending the national rights of the Arabs and particularly of the Palestinians. The Palestinian issue is of particular importance to Syria because the Palestinian people and the Syrian people are one. It is natural, therefore, for Syria to have an interest in the Palestine problem completely different from the interests of other states. There is something called Bilad al-Sham; it consists of Syria, Jordan, Palestine and Lebanon. Since the time of the Umayyads, Bilad al-Sham has been politically one unit and its pulsating heart has been Damascus. This is history; we are

not inventing it; it had always been so until the Sykes–Picot Agreement divided Bilad al-Sham into different states. The Sykes–Picot Agreement did not change the fact that the peoples inhabiting these four regions are one people and in substance one political entity. The Sykes–Picot Agreement was the biggest historical violation of this fact, and it is the responsibility of the people in Bilad al-Sham to end this violation and to restore the independence and the unity of the people constituting Bilad al-Sham. We do not want to interfere with the political regimes now existing in Bilad al-Sham, but it is our right and our duty to say that decisions affecting the people of Bilad al-Sham cannot be taken without regard to the position of Damascus which is the heart of this area. While the Intifadah is an important event and while the Palestinians have rights, they cannot reach a settlement that affects the political future of the Palestinians without the active participation and consent of Damascus. This is our position and this is our ideology and this is what we believe. This position may not please some of our friends in this meeting, but it is my duty to clarify our position lest there is any misunderstanding. The future of Palestine, like the future of the Golan Heights, like the future of South Lebanon, must be determined together because all of these issues constitute parts of the main issue of Bilad al-Sham.

This speech helped explain why Asad opposed the Camp David Accords, the Israeli Withdrawal Agreement of 17 May 1983, and the current steps which the United States was taking in the peace process.

Our attempts in Algiers to discuss reforms, the forming of a new government, and presidential elections with Asad were, once again, unsuccessful. Jumayyil and Asad did meet, but the latter did not allow the discussions to go beyond the personal and the general, another indication that he was looking to the post-Jumayyil period. The president asked for Asad's cooperation in forming a government, but this angered Asad. 'Why do you need a new government?' he asked. Jumayyil replied, 'Because the existing one has boycotted me for three years. Have you heard of a country on this planet in which the government does not meet with the president?'

We learned in Algiers that the Americans and the Syrians had agreed to pick up where they had left off on the reform process in September, after the election of a new Lebanese president. Bob Oakley, the White House aide, defined the new American position in blunt terms. Attention in the United States, he said, had shifted, and was now directed at convening an international conference on the Middle East, nuclear disarmament, the Iraq–Iran war and, most significantly, the American presidential elections. Lebanon was not a big issue, and no one in Washington believed that Lebanon was pivotal to the success or failure of American policy in the Middle East. The United States recognized Syria's presence and influence in Lebanon, and wanted this influence to be positive for Lebanon. It would now use its good offices with Syria to arrive at an agreement on a candidate in the Lebanese presidential elections. The process should yield three or four names on whom there was general agreement, and then a candidate could be selected from the group.

On 28 June, President Jumayyil's envoy, Joseph Hashem, met Asad to discuss the election of a new president. Asad proposed that Jumayyil send him the names of two or three individuals who enjoyed wide acceptance among Lebanon's different political factions. These names should be sent through General Ghazi Kan'an, the head of Syrian military intelligence in Lebanon. Asad reiterated his position that it was not necessary to form a new government. 'Forming a new government now is like hammering a nail in a coffin', Asad told Hashem.

As of July the presidential contest was wide open and the two dozen presidential candidates focused on the two main keys of the election process: Damascus and the American Embassy in Beirut. In Beirut it was assumed that Washington and Syria would select the next president, and the deputies were keen to know beforehand who was the chosen one, so that they could rally to his support at the right moment. In Damascus Khaddam, who in a different milieu could have been a gifted orchestra conductor, interviewed one candidate after the other and advised them how to work out their campaign with the members of parliament who actually elected the president. It was customary in Lebanese politics to agree on a candidate by consensus beforehand and then hold a parliamentary session to 'elect' him. Only once in 1970 was the election heatedly contested and the victor, Sulayman Franjiyyeh, won by one vote.

On 21 July, the LF took a public stand in rejecting three candidates for the presidency, Raymond Eddeh, Michel Awn and Sulayman Franjiyyeh. The president sympathized with their stand. We learned through presidential candidates meeting with Khaddam that Awn's chances were not good. Khaddam considered him indecisive because he had made, in his opinion, at least four mistakes: (1) he had failed to finish off Hubayqah's forces when they forced their way into the Ashrafiyyeh sector of Beirut; (2) he had failed to preserve the morale of his army after the assassination by the LF of General Khalil Kan'an, a close friend of Awn; (3) he had failed to take advantage of the assassination of Prime Minister Karami in an army helicopter to improve his reputation; and (4) when President Jumayyil lambasted Awn's presidential ambitions in front of his officers, the general had not confronted him. 'How', asked Khaddam, 'does anyone expect us to support such a candidate?'

Election fever increased as the elections approached. According to the Lebanese constitution, between 23 July and 23 August parliament becomes solely an electoral body. During this period a session can be called any time by the speaker to elect a president who will assume office on 23

September. If, for some reason, elections do not take place during this period, they can still be held any time before 23 September. Almost daily the president discussed with his advisers the three names he was to send to Asad through General Ghazi Kan'an, and daily these names changed. In Paris, Hariri was evaluating candidates and presenting his opinion on them to the Syrians and the Americans.

The Americans told President Jumayyil that Franjiyyeh would not be elected, while Jumayyil told the Americans that Raymond Eddeh and Michel Awn would not be permitted to reach the presidency. He meant that the Lebanese Forces, perhaps with his support, would oppose their elections.

Ja'ja had an interesting proposal which he asked us to pass on to Asad through Murphy. The proposal was for Asad to send us eight names, thus reversing the process previously suggested by the Syrian president, and we, i.e. the president and the Lebanese Forces and leaders in the Eastern Sector, would select three out of the eight. It would then be up to Asad to select the one he preferred from the three. The Americans felt the Ja'ja proposal had no chance with Asad and, therefore, dismissed it. At this stage, the coordination between Jumayyil and Ja'ja was good. Besides, the Americans would refuse to carry any name to Damascus unless it was cleared by both Jumayyil and Ja'ja. They considered that each on his own was not representative enough, but that the two together did represent the Christian position. Murphy met with the president in Beirut on 4 August, and issued a statement emphasizing the importance of elections taking place, the need to follow the constitutional process, and the responsibility of the Lebanese in 'selecting their new president'.

On 4 August, Murphy and I met in Beirut and agreed on 'talking points' for his discussions with Asad. These points dealt exclusively with presidential elections. We agreed to reject a hard-line candidate, as well as a candidate from the Kata'ib Party or from the LF. We also agreed that there was a need for a conciliatory president who enjoyed broad consensus not only in the Christian community but among the Muslims as well. The candidate had to be open to a dialogue with Syria and must agree to implement political reforms.

Murphy met President Asad on 8 August and was told that Syria supported Franjiyyeh for the presidency, but had not encouraged him to run. Asad respected Franjiyyeh and trusted him. He was a personal friend. If Franjiyyeh wanted to run Asad would stand by him, but Franjiyyeh was old and Syria would not encourage him to run. Syria did not want a candidate controlled by a militia. There seemed to be general agreement between Asad and Murphy on the 'talking points' discussed in Beirut, but no concrete steps were taken. The probability of a meeting between

Jumayyil and Asad to agree on a candidate now seemed remote and, therefore, any input the president had, he had to pass on through Murphy.

A few days later Simpson visited me to explain some nuances in Murphy's discussions in Damascus. Syria, he said, while it supported Franjiyyeh, if he chose to run, was keeping the door open for other candidates. Khaddam had suggested that we should be looking for three or four candidates, which Simpson found encouraging. Syria also was insisting that elections should take place within the constitutionally designated time. It was Simpson's opinion that Franjiyyeh would run but would not be elected. The USA, he added, was aware of a number of candidates who were moderate. These included René Muawwad, Michel Eddeh, Manuel Younis, Pierre Helou and George Frem. This list could also be added to as seen fit, he said.

Simpson also told me that the USA was not supporting Awn. The Americans found him to be a calm and honest fellow, but he was not a politician and they were suspicious of generals; they did not know how to govern by consensus. Once they took over power, they refused to give it up. Simpson assured me that the Israeli role in the presidential election was minimal. He said, 'We told them this time to stay out of it. We are dealing with this matter.'

On 15 August, the president met Karim Pakradouni, Colonel Qassis and myself and decided to send three names to Asad through the proposed process. He settled on Manuel Younis, Michel Eddeh and Pierre Helou. We called the Syrians to send them the list, but they were not interested. The Syrian rejection solidified the Jumayyil–Ja'ja alliance, and the two began preparing to block by force the session of parliament called to elect Franjiyyeh, scheduled for 18 August. On 17 August, Kan'an called Qassis and asked for the list of names, which Qassis sent promptly. On Wednesday the 17th, Franjiyyeh openly declared his candidacy. All day Jumayyil and Ja'ja worked on deputies to ensure that they would be absent from the session, thus preventing a quorum. At night the LF sent armed men around the Eastern Sector to prevent deputies from reaching the parliament building. Jumayyil and Awn also collaborated in this effort, though for different objectives. Jumayyil was hoping to have as president a person who was a friend and who would collaborate with him and give him a role as ex-president in public affairs. Franjiyyeh detested the Jumayyils and Ja'ja. Awn participated in blocking the election, fearing that a quorum would lead to the election of Franjiyyeh. He wanted to delay the process until he felt that he might himself have a good shot at the presidency.

On election day, some deputies who dared to challenge roadblocks set in their way were kidnapped until noon, when it was announced that the parliamentary session had been cancelled for absence of a quorum. When

I visited a deputy later that day to congratulate him on his release, he was frantically telling his story to every visitor. 'As I was driving to parliament, armed men stopped me and asked for my identity. I told them I was a deputy going to parliament to do my duty. "Ho, Ho," they answered, "a deputy, what a catch!"'

Deputy René Muawwad, fearing Syrian anger at Jumayyil, Ja'ja and Awn for blocking the election of Franjiyyeh, pleaded with us not to put his name on the list we passed on to General Kan'an. 'It would be the kiss of death,' he said; 'keep my name for serious discussion between Asad and Murphy.' The Syrians were angry with the president, Ja'ja, and Awn for their role in blocking the parliamentary session. According to some deputies returning from Damascus, Franjiyyeh remained the Syrian candidate, and if elections were blocked again, the Hoss government would continue in office and would assume the functions of the presidency as of 23 September.

On 28 August, Kelly informed me that Shultz had authorized Murphy to discuss names with Asad. He would ask the Syrian leader for his position on the three names sent by Jumayyil on 17 August. If his reaction was negative, then Asad could suggest alternative names. Murphy would then return to Beirut to get the reaction of Jumayyil and of other leaders. Murphy did not, however, envisage engaging in shuttle diplomacy between Damascus and Beirut. The USA was also contacting France, the Vatican and Saudi Arabia to help push the process forward and elect a president before 22 September.

President Jumayyil began thinking of the new government which would assume the functions of the presidency in case his term expired and no president was elected. The thought of keeping the Hoss government in place after expanding it to become more representative crossed his mind for a moment. Yet he was a Maronite and the representative of a Maronite political current which firmly believed that the community's destiny and that of the Maronite presidency were inseparable. In case no president was elected by midnight on 22 September, Jumayyil intended to appoint a government headed by a Maronite, as Bishara al-Khuri had done prior to his forced resignation in 1952.

Jumayyil's last two weeks in office were spent trying to find a solution to the presidential elections, or planning a transitional government in case elections were not held. Former president Charles Helou was considered for the post of transitional prime minister, and Simon Qassis and I were sent by the president to explore this matter with him. As soon as we entered he said:

> I know what you want. You want me to be prime minister. I cannot do it, I am too old, my wife is sick, but I have done my homework and here is my

list of candidates. I propose Ghassan Tweini. He has a great newspaper, and is not without experience. He talks a lot, but sometimes he makes sense. How about Elie Salem? He is new in politics, and of course he has a lot to learn, but why not? How about Joseph Hashem? Unlike Salem, he has not learned the art of maintaining silence. How about Abdu Uwaydat? He is a fine deputy, although the last time I saw him he seemed old and could hardly talk. How about General Awn? No, No, please erase that from the record. Do not whisper to the president that I proposed his name. How about Michel Eddeh? He certainly is large enough; he qualifies on all accounts, except he does not know how to stop talking. There is also Judge Jibran, he is a relative of mine, and a good judge, but most likely will not be a good politician.

And thus Helou went on and on proposing names and shooting them down. He was clearly interested; at least he wanted to be offered the position to have a greater say in the process. He was a moderate and well trusted by Jumayyil and Ja'ja. Helou was kept as reserve till the last moment.

While Jumayyil would have liked to extend his term for a short period if agreement could be reached with Syria and the opposition, to my knowledge he did not work for it, nor did he make any serious contact with any quarter for that purpose. Still, I was afraid that he may have discussed it with other advisers. To ensure that my position was clear, I entered his office one morning and told him that I had heard rumours that he intended to extend his term. I told him that I thought this would be dangerous, both to the country and to him. I argued that he should abide by the constitutional process, and the constitution did not allow for a renewal or extension of a presidential term. His efforts, I counselled, should be directed exclusively at ensuring the election of a successor and not to appointing a new government under a Maronite. Such a government would endanger the unity of Lebanon and lead us into a dark tunnel. The president cut me short, assuring me that he agreed with me fully and that I should work on that basis. Accordingly, I made public the president's position to all parties concerned, including foreign ambassadors, to make it part of the record. Kelly was pleased to hear this position stated officially and categorically, since Washington was full of rumours of Jumayyil's intent to stay on in office.

At the same time, Patriarch Sfeir was contacting foreign ambassadors to inform them that a transitional government, in case elections were not held, should be headed by a Maronite. He was very pessimistic and was feeling woefully ineffective: 'What more can I do?' he asked me. 'I wrote to Reagan, to Mitterrand, to the Pope, and I received no answers. If they want to leave us alone, fine, we will accept it. We survived in the past in valleys and on mountain peaks, and we will survive again.' I favoured keeping the Hoss government in place and expanding it, and mediators from West Beirut came to me to discuss this option. Still, the president insisted on a Maronite prime minister. He told me that I never understood the Maronite mind.

Lebanese Forces leader Samir Ja'ja was also after the president to discuss with him the formation of a new government. He wanted the president to be ready to announce a government as soon as it was realized that elections could not be held by 22 September. He wanted to be in such a government as he represented one of the forces on the ground. The president was non-committal, explaining that the appointment of ministers was in the hands of the president and of the designated prime minister, not the president alone. Ja'ja did not like this response. He wanted a clear commitment from Jumayyil that he would be in the cabinet. The more Jumayyil explained the problem, the more irritated Ja'ja became, knowing full well, that in this last constitutional act the president could appoint virtually whoever he wanted. This irritation was to grow in the next few days into open enmity.

The Murphy Mission

In the third week of September, Murphy went to Damascus for a final attempt to bring about agreement on a compromise candidate. In the interim, on 16 September Kelly left Beirut for health reasons, and Simpson became chargé d'affaires. No one in Beirut believed the reason given for Kelly's departure. Kelly assured me later that he did have a heart problem, and this was the only reason for his quick exit. We sent Murphy word that he should bring with him three names from Damascus for the presidency, and that we would agree with him on one. He replied that he would be in Beirut on 18 September and that he wanted to meet first with Hoss, then Husseini, which would then leave ample time for talks with the president. I suggested that he should brief me first upon arrival, and then proceed with his programme as suggested. This way I would have a chance to brief the president while Murphy was making his rounds.

When I met Murphy immediately upon his arrival in Beirut on the 18th, he told me the following:

> I had all in all seven meetings in Damascus with Khaddam and Shar', and one meeting with Asad. The first 14 hours of meetings produced nothing at all. The Syrians were immovable on Franjiyyeh. He was their only choice for the presidency. He was running, and they supported him. They wanted the Christians to stop blocking his election; they wanted reforms to be adopted before the elections; and they wanted executive power transferred immediately to the council of ministers. I rejected the three positions. The fact that Franjiyyeh's election was boycotted on 18 August showed there

was no strong support for him. With four days before the expiry of Jumayyil's term, there was no time to discuss reforms. Discussion on reforms would be resumed after the election of a new president. I started listing possible candidates for discussion, but the Syrians would not listen. Their candidate was Franjiyyeh. After long discussion on the list I presented, the Syrians finally agreed, and said there was only one name they wanted. It was best, I said, to identify two names. They said there would be one name only, deputy Mikhail Daher, not two, three or four names. They said that Franjiyyeh was a friend of President Asad; he would withdraw his name in the national interest. I agreed to communicate this to you.

This was the best they could do, said Murphy; they wanted the elections to take place before 22 September. They wanted Daher elected, he was a good man. If elections were blocked they would criticize publicly whoever blocked them. If we did not accept Daher, and if we went ahead and formed a government, then Lebanon would be heading towards partition and chaos. Murphy said that the choice before us was clear: either Daher or chaos.

I thanked Murphy for this message and proceeded to Bikfayya, where the president and his advisers were waiting. The president was disturbed by the finality of the choice. He wanted room to manoeuvre, and wanted a say in the election process. He had nothing against Daher, and had often spoken of him in the past as his candidate. But the finality of it reduced him to irrelevance.

While Murphy was meeting Hoss and Husseini, his assistants were briefing Ja'ja, Awn and Patriarch Sfeir, Awn called the president to consult on what he saw as a return to the Tripartite Agreement. He was identifying Mikhail Daher with the Tripartite Agreement because he was one of several Lebanese leaders who witnessed its signing. Then Ja'ja called to say the LF were opposed to Daher and wanted to consult on how to defeat the US–Syrian agreement. The LF was suspicious of Daher because of his role in the Tripartite Agreement and believed he was an ally of Eli Hubayqah's. Patriarch Sfeir reacted in the same way. He was furious and told us: 'They are giving us no choice, this is a diktat!'

Murphy's meeting with President Jumayyil added nothing new. The president was caught between two unhappy choices: accept Daher and provoke the anger of Awn and Ja'ja, or form a government and thus leave office with two governments competing for what was left of the authority of the Lebanese state. Murphy was criticized in the Marionite community for his failure in Damascus. He should have brought two or three names and let the Maronite leaders, including the president, share in the selection of one. This was a Maronite post, and the Maronites should have a say in it, the Maronite leaders argued.

Jumayyil's Last Visit to Damascus

In a meeting between Speaker Husseini and Ghassan Tweini on Tuesday 20 September, Husseini asked what would it take to make the president and the Maronite community accept Daher. Tweini listed five conditions he believed were needed to reach a possible consensus on Daher:

1. The paper presented by Daher to Khaddam on reforms should not be considered binding, but simply one paper amongst others.
2. The LF must be represented in the first government formed by Daher.
3. Hubayqah and his forces must not be permitted to return to the Eastern Sector.
4. Presidential elections must be held in the Mansour Palace, a neutral venue preferred by the Christian deputies, and not in the parliament building area, as it was not safe for Christian deputies to go there.
5. Jumayyil must meet Daher in Damascus, and if the president is satisfied with him, he would bring him to the presidential palace to meet with Ja'ja and other deputies. If the result of these meetings is positive, then he will be consensus candidate. If there is no agreement, then the president will return Daher by military helicopter to his home town, Qubayyat, in the Akkar region.

Husseini believed these conditions could be met. He wondered whether the president would accept them. Would he meet with Asad in Damascus the following day to confirm these conditions and ensure the election of Daher? Would he convince those opposed to Daher that this was the best course open to the country?

Tweini called me and started to relate the above in a home-made code. 'Ghassan,' I said, 'the country is about to collapse; we have a few hours to come up with a solution, and you talk to me in code. Speak openly, the whole world is listening anyhow.' He obliged. I then told him I would check with the president and call him back. The president was positive, and wanted to meet Tweini and me in the evening to discuss the matter.

That evening, in the presence of Karim Pakradouni, Simon Qassis, Joseph Hashem, Joseph Abu Khalil, Tweini and myself, a long debate took place. Pakradouni could not believe that Asad would accept to meet with Jumayyil at the last hour. If the meeting took place, it could not succeed. He bet one hundred LL. with Tweini that Asad would not receive him. There was general agreement that nothing would be lost in trying the Tweini proposal. Accordingly the president asked Tweini to call Husseini and tell him that the president was ready to meet Asad under the five conditions listed above. Tweini checked with Husseini and was told that a meeting with Asad for the following day, Wednesday 21 September, at 1 p.m. had been arranged. Husseini, who had been in contact with Khaddam, assured Tweini that the five conditions set by him were acceptable to Syria. After meeting with Asad, Jumayyil was to be reconciled with Hoss, Husseini, Franjiyyeh and Daher, who would also be in Damascus. We stayed with the president until 3 a.m., working out the details of his last formal meeting with Asad.

When I returned to the presidential palace at 11 a.m. the following day, I found the president and Tweini in a pensive mood. They told me that the whole plan had collapsed; Ja'ja had rejected Daher for the presidency and, therefore, it was useless to go to Damascus. After extensive discussion, the president decided to go. Asad, his cabinet, and all foreign ambassadors were expected at the Damascus airport any minute now, and we had no time to lose. Relations between Jumayyil and Asad had not been good, and Jumayyil could not afford to slight Asad by cancelling an arranged visit at the last moment. Ja'ja, the president told us, was not against the visit, but he was against Daher. The president, he said, could go and talk to Asad about a new president, but not about Daher, nor should he contemplate bringing Daher for consultation as proposed. Some of the advisers who had been anxious to travel with the president on what was believed would be a successful mission, now found appropriate excuses and withdrew. Only Tweini and I were left with a lonely and depressed president. He asked us if we were still ready to go. We said that we were, knowing beforehand that this was merely a face-saving journey to minimize damage, rather than to solve a problem, as we had hoped.

We arrived in Damascus an hour late. After a brief exchange of niceties betweeen Jumayyil and Asad, Tweini proposed that he and I leave to give the president a chance to talk to Asad in private. The two presidents then met for three hours. Throughout the meeting Asad's assistants brought him information on meetings between Ja'ja, Awn and Danny Sham'un, intended to torpedo Jumayyil's visit. Asad felt that a sort of coup had taken place and that Jumayyil could no longer control the course of events, especially as his term of office was set to expire by midnight the following day.

At the same time, the Christian deputies were meeting Patriarch Sfeir and awaiting the results of the summit. Tweini, who from Damascus was talking regularly to the deputies on the phone, told them to remain at the patriarchate in Bkirki, and that on our way back from Damascus we would land our helicopter there so that the president could brief them directly. On the way back Tweini wanted to know what had taken place. Fortunately for Jumayyil, the noise of the helicopter made conversation impossible, and the rapid course of events was such that Tweini and I never knew what transpired at that last summit.

We landed in Bkirki just after sunset and the president briefed the patriarch and the deputies. He said he had tried to convince Asad to accept more than one candidate, but that he had failed. The situation would be critical if no elections were held the following day, and Lebanon would have two governments, which may ultimately lead to partition, he said. He told the deputies that he left the matter in their hands, and that he remained at their disposal. At a critical moment he relinquished the leadership role that was his, and left the deputies confused and without direction. They looked to the patriarch for leadership, but he too was confused and, like the president, seemed eager to follow the collective will rather than lead it. Yet no collective will emerged.

Because of LF opposition, the Christian deputies decided to boycott the election of Daher, and all efforts were now focused on forming a caretaker government. I left the Palace at 3 a.m., returning to our home in Ba'bda. At 4 a.m. two rockets were fired at our house from a distance of fifty metres. The noise was so devastating I thought the house had collapsed. My wife, faithful to her practice in crises such as this, threw herself under the bed. I slept fatalistically. I was too tired to do anything else. My guards started shooting at random in all directions. This, I felt, was good for their morale, and had no relevance at all to the situation at hand. When in the morning I realized the extent of the damage and saw the leaflets attacking the Damascus visit of the previous day, I called the most likely suspects to complain. From them all I got denials and assurances of support. As usual in Lebanon the blame was laid on a third party.

22 September 1988

President Jumayyil's last day in office was the longest and the saddest of his term. As of 8 a.m. on Thursday 22 September, the presidential palace was like an oriental souk. Anyone who considered himself 'somebody' came to the palace to advise the president, to caution him, to drink coffee with him, and to play a role in the Lebanese national game of forming a government. Ja'ja and his deputy, Karim Pakradouni, came early. So did Danny Sham'un and his assistants. Parliamentarians walked in and out depending on the progress in the formation of a government. Former deputies, friends of the president, mediators in past crises, former president Helou, former ministers, presidential candidates, all were there in strength.

On a day when it was important for the president to be left alone, to reflect and act, he was instead holding court. While he should have been taking decisions on his own, he was allowing decisions to be taken by the amorphous mass which had formed around him. Deputy Pierre Helou was selected by the president to form a government, and he accepted reluctantly. Helou was a moderate, and did not want to head a government which would enter into a confrontation with the rival Hoss government. Hoss had announced that he would continue in office, and that any government appointed by Jumayyil would not be considered legitimate. Helou was having a difficult time convincing Muslims to join his cabinet, since no Muslim dared oppose the Hoss government which enjoyed Syrian support. When Helou was told that the Mufti Hassan Khaled would issue a fatwa forbidding any Muslim to join his government, he said to me, 'Oh, my God, did you hear that? Please tell the president I cannot do it – I am a man of peace, not of war.'

President Jumayyil reluctantly called Awn and asked him to come to the palace. When he arrived Jumayyil asked him if he would join a government headed by a civilian. Awn responded that he preferred not to; he was keeping his options open. He seemed distant and unconcerned, as if he had made up his mind to take over power anyhow. A week earlier, Awn had walked into my office and told me he intended to take over power if no president was elected because he could not expose the army to the chaos that would arise then. 'How would you do it?' I had enquired. 'I would take over the presidential palace and all government offices in the Eastern Sector. It is important to keep the army united and legitimacy in safe hands', he had answered. I asked him if he was telling me this so that I would pass it on to the president and he told me to do so, if I wished. When I told the president he didn't seem worried: 'Oh, he would not dare', was his response.

Danny Sham'un, who had been promised by Hoss that he could join his cabinet as foreign minister, was anxious to expand the Hoss government. He was in continuous contact with Hoss trying to convince him to bring in strong Christian representatives like Ja'ja, but Hoss refused. Then Sham'un announced to the restless crowd in the president's office that he would form a government. The president told him to try. Half an hour later he returned with a long list of ministers including Ja'ja and Awn, who were unlikely to be acceptable to the Muslims. Jumayyil told him that such a government would not work and that no Muslim would join it. In anger Sham'un proposed that in that case Awn should form the government.

Jumayyil, who had opposed Awn for the presidency and who was thinking of firing him from the army command, then asked him if he would form a government. Awn replied that he would form a government made up of the six generals, three Christians, including the commander of the army, and three Muslims, in the military council. 'What if the

Muslim generals will not agree to join?' asked Jumayyil. 'In that case,' answered Awn, 'I will broaden it and include people like Ja'ja in it.'

At 11.45 p.m., just 15 minutes before the expiry of his term of office, Jumayyil announced the formation of the Awn government. Ja'ja was furious. He shouted at President Jumayyil, 'A few days ago Elie [Salem], Simon [Qassis] and I were having dinner with you, and I asked you if you had a government; you said yes, and that you had the list of ministers in your pocket. It turned out you had nothing. This is not how governments are formed. Awn is my friend, I will manage with him, but I have problems with you.' Ja'ja then walked out in fury and slammed the door behind him.

The president asked Awn to call the members of the Military Council and inform them of their appointment. The Christians accepted immediately and they were in the presidential palace in a few minutes. The Muslims asked for time to think about it. They all answered a few minutes later, expressing their regret that they could not serve in the proposed cabinet.

In the cold silence that followed this outburst, the president called Awn and me aside. He walked between us with his hands on both of our shoulders. He told Awn: 'Elie is a professional. I want him to stay with you. He should remain in his office and counsel you on foreign affairs.' Awn welcomed the idea. I expressed my thanks to the president for his confidence and to Awn for his welcoming remarks. However, I was non-committal.

Exhausted, dazed and on the verge of despair, Jumayyil walked out of the palace a little after midnight, shaking hands with staff, officers and guards who had worked with him. It was a sad departure indeed. The president was virtually in tears. This was not the end he had expected. When he came to office he was confident and determined. He had grand plans. He saw himself as the knight on horseback who would save the maiden. Things did not turn out as he expected. The events were too complex. The determining factors extended beyond Lebanon. He could control only part of the game. He could, at times, enter it and be in the middle, but it soon slipped from his grasp again. He was a good Lebanese but not a good conciliator. He made enemies where he could have made friends. He allowed things to happen that ultimately marred his image and defeated his policies. How he and his term in office will be judged must now be left to the historians.

The following day I visited General Awn and told him I that I was taking a long vacation; I would not be continuing in my post as the president had recommended. The general thanked me for my past efforts and wished me a happy vacation. I wished him well.

Postscript

From 22 September 1988 to 13 October 1990, Lebanon had two governments: the government in place, headed by Dr Salim Hoss, and the government appointed by the outgoing president and headed by General Michel Awn. Each exercised limited authority over the area it controlled. For some time foreign ambassadors dealt with them equally, and as they became disappointed with Awn and his policies, they began to deal exclusively with the Hoss government. It is futile to argue which of the two governments was the legal one. By 1988 the authority of the president was so weakened as to render his constitutional acts weak as well. While his appointment of Awn was constitutionally valid, it lacked internal political authority, and enjoyed little external support.

The Muslim members of the Military Council, i.e. half the cabinet appointed by the president, refused to participate and, therefore, all governmental functions – 17 ministries – were in the hands of General Awn (Maronite), General Abu Jamra (Greek Orthodox), and General Maluf (Greek Catholic). The Awn government was expected to be transitory, to arrange for presidential elections, and be dissolved. Awn, however, harboured presidental ambitions, and his government became the vehicle of his presidency. Instead of thinking of himself as transitory he thought of himself as the axis of the new politics, and as the leader of the Lebanese and their future president. He developed a new style of communication with the people. He addressed them directly as their leader, not as their prime minister. He called for rallies; he flattered the people, ridiculed the politicians, attacked all external powers for intervening in Lebanon, and offered himself as the cure for Lebanon's malaise. The more he attacked the more loved he was by the people. He had nothing positive to offer so he focused on all that was negative in Lebanon, laying blame on the political and clerical establishments, which he accused of being part of the plot against the country. He wanted the opportunity to save it from the corrupt politicians who were in secret alliance with the occupiers and with the foreign embassies, from which they took their orders. He always appeared to the crowds in his simple military uniform, surrounded by army officers, thus giving the impression that the army under his command was ready to right the wrong and to take risks against impossible odds. He was the David to an indefinite Goliath, and this image was well received by all the non-sophisticated in Lebanon, irrespective of religion and locale. The more he oversimplified, the greater the acclaim and glorification he received. He identified the two most important idols – Syria and America – and attacked them both. At least this called for courage, and the people, longing for a hero of the 'mission impossible' found in him a leader ready to assume the mantle. If reason had failed in the past, maybe now the daring of Awn would give the crisis the nudge that would bring it to an end.

Syria attacked Awn, and the US ambassador closed the embassy and walked out, calling from a safe distance for the removal of the general. Awn, however, seemed to thrive on crises. He used the local crisis in March 1989 to launch a war of liberation against Syria. The war turned out to be an artillery duel between Awn's army, with token support from the Lebanese Forces, and Syria and its allies in Lebanon. As the duel was fought on Lebanese terrain and as the shells fell on the Lebanese and their homes, the real losers were the Lebanese. And when in January 1990 Awn declared his war of elimination against the Lebanese Forces, so called as he intended to eliminate them as a militia and incorporate their elements in the army, the main loser was the Christian community. This community had been weakened by the successive battles of the long Lebanese war, and now it was weakened further by an intra-Christian war involving the Christian part of the Lebanese army against the Christian militia. All religious communities were weakened by the Lebanese war. They all tried to be, in effect, little states; they all failed, but the one that lost the most was the Christian community.

As Awn was busy with his wars and his plans to become the liberator of Lebanon, the Lebanese deputies, the Maronite Patriarch, Syria, Saudi Arabia and the Western powers were working on a settlement that led to the departure of the deputies to Taif in Saudi Arabia in September 1989, where they met under the auspices of the Committee of Three (the heads of state of Saudi Arabia, Morocco and Algiers), established by the Arab League to resolve the Lebanese problem, and reached an agreement on the governance of Lebanon and on ending the Lebanese war. With minor juridical modifications, the Taif Agreement was essentially what Shar' and I had agreed on in the Damascus Discussions. The reason why these were rejected in 1987 and accepted in 1989 depended on regional developments and on perceptions that such an agreement would have to be implemented by a more acceptable government than existed then.

All efforts to get Awn into the Taif process failed. He objected to the process and to the content. When parliament decided to meet and formally approve the Taif Agreement, Awn issued a statement in the name of the council of ministers, which he headed, dissolving parliament. Parliament ignored Awn's decision and, with the support of the Tripartite Committee, Syria and the United States, met and approved the agreement. On 5 November 1989 it elected deputy René Muawwad as president of the republic. Thus the office that had been left vacant since 22 September 1988 was filled.

Awn opposed the approval of the agreement and the election of Muawwad, considering both acts invalid as parliament had been constitutionally dissolved by his government. On 22 November, just two weeks after his election, and after completing Independence Day ceremonies in Beirut, Muawwad was killed by a car-bomb explosion. Two days later parliament met and elected deputy Elias Hrawi president of the republic. For a few months Hrawi, for security reasons, lived in a Lebanese army barracks in the Biqa'; he then moved to a temporary residence in Beirut. Awn had been living and working in the presidential palace in Ba'bda since his appointment on 22 September 1988.

Hrawi tried hard to persuade Awn to relinquish his position and to join ranks with the legitimate government, but Awn kept insisting that his was the legitimate government and that Hrawi and Hoss were puppets. Hrawi moved fast to implement the Taif Agreement. The Constitution was amended to incorporate the Taif reforms. According to these reforms executive authority would be vested in the council of ministers; parliament would consist of 108 deputies and be half Christian, half Muslim; confessionalism would be abolished gradually and as a result of a national educational process supervised by a national commission; the militias would be dissolved within a specified time and the authority of the state extended over the entire Lebanese territory; the Syrian army would help the government of Lebanon extend its authority and would provide any help requested of it by the Lebanese government for the realization of this end.

On 13 October 1990, the Syrian army, on the request of the Lebanese government, entered Ba'bda region by force and ousted Awn from his position. He and his two ministers took refuge in the French embassy and asked for political asylum in France. Mitterrand granted the asylum and considered it 'a matter of honour for France'. After lengthy and acrimonious negotiations between Lebanon and France, Awn and his two ministers, who had also taken in refuge at the French embassy, left for France on 29 August 1991.

The presidential palace in Ba'bda was renovated, and President Hrawi moved in. The country was united and the militias dissolved. With the end of the war the process of reconstruction began, and it was not unexpected, therefore, that Hrawi called on Rafiq al-Hariri to form a government whose main mission was large-scale reconstruction.

As the international and the regional situations seem stable and propitious for Lebanon, the reconstruction effort is likely to succeed, but at a slower pace than the frustrated Lebanese had hoped. Financial support from the Arab Gulf did not come as hoped, due to changing conditions and priorities in the Gulf States. The end of Soviet–American conflict in the Middle East, progress in the peace process, and internal developments indicate that a new dawn may be emerging in Lebanon after the dark years that have devastated the country and marred its image.

Appendix 1

Main Principles for Solving the Lebanese Crisis
13 June 1987

This document, incorporating all the points agreed on in the Salem–Shar' discussions in Damascus, was put in this form by President Jumayyil, Rafiq al-Hariri, and Elie A. Salem and was carried by Rafiq al-Hariri to President Asad on 13 June 1987. This document was used as a background paper in the drafting of the National Conciliation Document (known as the Ta'if Agreement) agreed on by Lebanese deputies in meetings in Ta'if, Saudi Arabia, in October, and officially adopted by parliament on 5 November 1989.

Fundamental Principles

1. Lebanon is a sovereign, free and independent nation. Its territory, people and institutions are one and indivisible. Its boundaries are defined in the constitution and are recognized internationally.

2. Lebanon is Arab by identity and by allegiance. Its relations with Syria, steeped in history and cemented by mutual interests, are distinctive. These relations will be defined in long-term agreements in various fields.

3. Lebanon is a founding member of the League of Arab States, active in its work, and bound by its decisions and agreements. It is equally a founding member of the United Nations Organization, and bound by its charter. It is also a member of the Non-Aligned Movement.

4. Lebanon is a parliamentary democratic republic founded on the respect of freedoms, particularly the freedom of expression, the freedom of religion, and on the complete equality of all citizens in terms of their rights and duties.

5. The people are the source of political authority and the custodians of national sovereignty which is exercised through institutions stipulated in the constitution.

6. The separation of powers, the balance of powers, and the cooperation of powers of the institutions of state must be respected. The government shall be accountable to the parliament. The president of the republic may, with the agreement of the council of ministers, dissolve the parliament.

7. The economic system is free. It respects private initiative, guarantees private property, and aims at realizing equality of opportunity for all citizens.

8. All measures will be taken to liberate Lebanese territory from Israeli occupation, to extend the authority of the state on all its territory, and to implement the relevant section in the ministerial statement of 31 May 1984, which is based on the decision of the council of ministers of 5 March 1984.[1] Lebanon adheres to the resolutions of the Security Council, particularly resolution No. 425 which calls upon Israel to withdraw forthwith from all Lebanese territory;

---

1. Reference to the decision of the council of ministers prior to the cancellation of the May 17 Agreement to make arrangements in South Lebanon that will guarantee peace and stability there and prevent infiltration across Lebanon's international frontiers (namely the frontier with Israel).

Lebanon remains committed to the Armistice Agreement signed between Lebanon and Israel on 23 March 1949, under UN auspices.

Abolishing Political Confessionalism

1. The abolition of political confessionalism is an important national objective. To attain this objective national unity must be strengthened and the spirit of national identity must be deepened through the implementation of reforms within a specified period of time. A national task force chaired by the president of the republic, and including the speaker of parliament, the prime minister, and a number of members to be agreed on later, will be formed. The task force will start with the following measures:

— the unification of books of civics and of history;
— establishing an information policy for all news media with the view of enhancing national unity and transcending the prevailing confessional situation;
— removing confessional identification from the identity card;
— freeing all positions in the bureaucracy in such a way that no position will be specified to any particular religious sect.

2. Practical and gradual measures to end political confessionalism must be undertaken. Laws and regulations of confessional character will be abolished gradually. Subsequently a national (non-confessional) electoral law will be adopted.

Power-sharing

Until political confessionalism is abolished the base of the National Pact will be broadened to allow all confessions to be represented in a balanced manner in state institutions so as to ensure equitable power-sharing.

Executive Authority

1. Executive authority is vested in the council of ministers.

2. The council of ministers consists of the president of the republic, the prime minister and the ministers.

3. The council of ministers meets in a building specifically assigned to it.

4. The president of the republic chairs the council of ministers without exercising the right to vote. The prime minister shall, in agreement with the president of the republic, chair the meetings of the council of ministers. Decisions taken by the council of ministers chaired by the prime minister are referred to the president of the republic for signature. The president must sign these decisions within two weeks after reaching the presidency or return them within this period to a council of ministers chaired by him. Decisions of the council of ministers will then be final and binding, and the decree will be effective as of the date of the decision of the council. A limited period will be given to the prime minister and the minister concerned to sign decisions of the council of ministers. The minister will sign first, then the prime minister.

5. Ministerial posts in the council of ministers are distributed equally between Christians and Muslims and equally amongst the three main confessions (Maronites, Sunnis, Shi'is).

Powers of the Council of Ministers

The council of ministers holds executive authority and is responsible before the parliament. Amongst the powers it exercises are:

1. Setting the policy of the state in all areas – political, economic, defence, finance, development, education, social affairs, etc.

2. Submitting draft laws, adopting decrees, and taking appropriate decisions to implement state policy. When necessary, it may declare draft laws as urgent (to speed their passage in parliament).

3. Implementing the laws and regulations of the state and supervising all public offices.

4. Declaring and ending a state of emergency, declaring war, calling for mobilization, signing of agreements and treaties with due consideration to the powers of the legislative authority.

5. Coordinating, orienting and following up on the works of the ministries, the administrative offices and the public organizations associated with them.

6. Preparing the national budget and long-term development plans.

7. Appointing state officials, terminating their services, or accepting their resignation in accordance with law.

8. Decisions of the council of ministers will be drafted as decrees and submitted to the president of the republic to sign within a two-week period.

9. The council of ministers may, in certain circumstances, delegate to one of its members certain limited powers provided such delegation is done by a decree signed by the president of the republic, the prime minister, and the minister or ministers concerned.

10. Calling the parliament for an extraordinary session.

11. Dissolving parliament.

12. Decisions of the council of ministers are taken by consensus. If that is not possible, then by a three-quarters majority of the entire membership of the council.

The Powers of the President of the Republic

The president of the republic is the head of the state and its representative towards foreign nations and international organizations. He ensures that the constitution is followed, that law is applied and national unity preserved. He defends the independence of Lebanon, the safety of its territory, the integrity of its state, and the transfer of constitutional powers. He exercises the following powers:

1. He signs and issues decrees and laws in accordance with an agreed-upon time-table after they have been passed by the appropriate authorities. He may also return laws to which he objects within limits defined in the constitution.

2. He signs alone the decree designating a prime minister, he signs decrees appointing the ministers. He also signs the decree concerning the resignation of the government or its dissolution.

3. He chairs the higher defence council.

4. He is the commander-in-chief of the armed forces.

5. He receives the credentials of diplomats and he signs treaties with foreign countries.

6. He awards medals.

7. He grants clemency.

8. He addresses messages to parliament when he deems it necessary.

9. Together with the prime minister he may remove a minister from his post.

10. The president of the republic is not accountable except in the case of high treason and the violation of the constitution.

The Powers of the Prime Minister

The prime minister exercises the following powers:

1. He consults with parliamentary blocs in forming the government in agreement with the president of the republic.

2. Together with the president of the republic he signs the decree forming the government.

3. He prepares the agenda of the council of ministers in agreement with the president of the republic.

4. He acts as vice-chairman of the higher defence council.

5. He chairs the council of ministers in the absence of the president of the republic or when the president asks him to do so. The decisions taken in a council of ministers chaired by the prime minister are referred to the president of the republic to sign within two weeks from the time they reach the presidency. The president of the republic may return these decisions within the two-week period to a council of ministers chaired by himself. If the decisions are passed again by the council of ministers they become final and binding, as of the date in which they were passed.

6. He chairs ministerial councils to study issues with the views of submitting them to official meetings of the council of ministers for action. He follows up on decisions of the council of ministers.

7. He follows up with ministers, he coordinates amongst ministries, and gives directions to ensure proper implementation of policy.

8. He holds working sessions with officials of state as he sees fit.

9. He authorizes the secretary-general of the council of ministers to take the official minutes of the council of ministers.

10. He submits to parliament a ministerial statement detailing the policy of his government (to get a vote of confidence).

Nominating the Prime Minister and the Ministers

1. The president of the republic names a prime minister after holding binding consultations with members of parliament.

2. Once nominated, the prime minister-designate holds consultations (with parliament) to form a government in agreement with the president of the republic.

3. A government is considered to have resigned in the following cases:
— if the prime minister resigns;
— if enough ministers have resigned as to render voting in the council illegal;
— upon the death of the prime minister;
— upon the expiration of the term of parliament;
— upon the expiration of the term of the president of the republic;
— following a vote of no confidence in the parliament.

The Constitution

The constitution must be amended to incorporate the principles stated in this document.

Legislative Authority

1. Parliamentary seats are to be distributed equally between Christians and Muslims and proportionally within each of these two groups.

2. The number of parliamentary seats are to be increased (from 99) to 108. Vacant seats in parliament and additional seats are to be filled by candidates proposed by the council of ministers.

3. The speaker of parliament and the members of his office are elected for a two-year period subject to re-election.

4. The majorities needed to elect the president of the republic, the speaker of parliament, the prime minister and the ones needed for major national decisions are to be reconsidered.

5. A new electoral law ensuring widest and most effective representation to fulfil the objectives of this agreement must be adopted.

New Institutions (that need to be adopted)

1. A higher council to try presidents of the republic, prime ministers and ministers.

2. A constitutional court to interpret the constitution, to supervise the constitutionality of laws, and to act on all conflicts relating to the election of the president of the republic, to parliamentary elections, or other conflicts stipulated by law.

3. A social and economic council to include leaders from the economic and social fields, from syndicates and educational institutions. The law will determine the powers of this council and the number of its membership. The council is consultative.

Administrative Decentralization

1. The adoption of a broad administrative decentralization in the context of the oneness of the territory, of the people, and of the institutions.

2. The adoption of a comprehensive development plan for the country as a whole with the view of developing all regions of Lebanon socially and economically.

Army and Internal Security Forces

1. The reunification and the development of the army on the national bases stipulated in this agreement; and reinstating the national role of the army in defending the country and the people.

2. The adoption of a (compulsory) military service law.

3. Enhancing the military doctrine of the army in light of this agreement and of the political orientation of the state.

4. Forming a higher defence council headed by the president of the republic. The prime minister will be vice-chairman. The council will include the ministers of defence, finance, interior, foreign affairs and other members as required by law. The internal security forces and the sûreté

générale will be under the minister of the interior. These forces and the sûreté générale will be reconsidered in light of the stipulations above governing the army.

Nationalization Law

A new nationalization law covering all pending cases will be adopted.

Education

Enhancing education, ensuring its freedom, and availing it freely to all. Developing the programmes of public and private schools with the view of enhancing national identity and national unity.

Ending the Fighting

Implementing a comprehensive security plan that will end the fighting and restore peace and normalcy in the country. The plan involves:

1. Comprehensive ceasefire.
2. Collection of weapons.
3. Dissolving militias.
4. The return of all Lebanese displaced from their homes since 1975. The state will provide financial assistance to rebuild destroyed homes, and will guarantee the safety of the returnees.
5. The simultaneous implementation of the four items under 'Ending the Fighting' with the implementation of political reforms to ensure the credibility of all the articles stated in this agreement.
6. The assistance of Syria in the realization of the objectives stated in this agreement.

Appendix 2

Agreement between the Government of the Republic of Lebanon and the Government of the State of Israel

The Government of the Republic of Lebanon and the Government of the State of Israel:

Bearing in mind the importance of maintaining and strengthening international peace based on freedom, equality, justice, and respect for fundamental human rights,

Reaffirming their faith in the aims and principles of the Charter of the United Nations and recognizing their right and obligation to live in peace with each other as well as with all states, within secure and recognized boundaries,

Having agreed to declare the termination of the state of war between them,

Desiring to ensure lasting security for both their States and to avoid threats and the use of force between them,

Desiring to establish their mutual relations in the manner provided for in this Agreement,

Having delegated their undersigned representative plenipotentiaries, provided with full powers, in order to sign, in the presence of the representative of the United States of America, this Agreement,

Have agreed to the following provisions:

ARTICLE 1

1. The Parties agree and undertake to respect the sovereignty, political independence and territorial integrity of each other. They consider the existing international boundary between Lebanon and Israel inviolable.

2. The Parties confirm that the state of war between Lebanon and Israel has been terminated and no longer exists.

3. Taking into consideration the provisions of paragraphs 1 and 2, Israel undertakes to withdraw all its armed forces from Lebanon in accordance with the Annex of the present Agreement.

ARTICLE 2

The Parties, being guided by the principles of the Charter of the United Nations and of international law, undertake to settle their disputes by peaceful means in such a manner as to promote international peace and security, and justice.

ARTICLE 3

In order to provide maximum security for Lebanon and Israel, the Parties agree to establish and implement security arrangements, including the creation of a Security Regulation, as provided for in the Annex of the present Agreement.

ARTICLE 4

1. The territory of each Party will not be used as a base for hostile or terrorist activity against the other Party, its territory, or its people.

2. Each Party will prevent the existence or organization of irregular forces, armed bands, organizations, bases, offices or infrastructure, the aims and purposes of which include incursions or any act of terrorism into the territory of the other Party, or any other activity aimed at threatening or endangering the security of the other Party and safety of its people. To this end all agreements and arrangements enabling the presence and functioning on the territory of either Party of elements hostile to the other Party are null and void.

3. Without prejudice to the inherent right of self-defense in accordance with international law, each Party will refrain:

a) from organizing, instigating, assisting, or participating in threats or acts of belligerency, subversion, or incitement or any aggression directed against the other Party, its population or property, both within its territory and originating therefrom, or in the territory of the other Party,

b) from using the territory of the other Party for conducting a military attack against the territory of a third state,

c) from intervening in the internal or external affairs of the other Party.

4. Each Party undertakes to ensure that preventive action and due proceedings will be taken against persons or organizations perpetrating acts in violation of this Article.

ARTICLE 5

Consistent with the termination of the state of war and within the framework of their constitutional provisions, the Parties will abstain from any form of hostile propaganda against each other.

ARTICLE 6

Each Party will prevent entry into, deployment in, or passage through its territory, its air space and, subject to the right of innocent passage in accordance with international law, its territorial sea, by military forces, armament, or military equipment of any state hostile to the other Party.

ARTICLE 7

Except as provided in the present Agreement, nothing will preclude the deployment on Lebanese territory of international forces requested and accepted by the Government of Lebanon to assist in maintaining its authority. New contributors to such forces shall be selected from among states having diplomatic relations with both Parties to the present Agreement.

ARTICLE 8

1. a) Upon entry into force of the present Agreement, a Joint Liaison Committee will be established by the Parties, in which the United States of America will be a participant, and will commence its functions. This Committee will be entrusted with the supervision of the implementation of all areas covered by the present Agreement. In matters involving security arrangements, it will deal with unresolved problems referred to it by the Security Arrangements Committee established in subparagraph c. below. Decisions of this Committee will be taken unanimously.

b) The Joint Liaison Committee will address itself on a continuing basis to the development of mutual relations between Lebanon and Israel, *inter alia* the regulation of the movement of goods, products and persons, communications, etc.

c) Within the framework of the Joint Liaison Committee, there will be a Security Arrangements Committee whose composition and functions are defined in the Annex of the present Agreement.

d) Subcommittees of the Joint Liaison Committee may be established as the need arises.

e) The Joint Liaison Committee will meet in Lebanon and Israel, alternately.

f) Each Party, if it so desires and unless there is an agreed change of status, may maintain a liaison office on the territory of the other Party in order to carry out the above-mentioned functions within the framework of the Joint Liaison Committee and to assist in the implementation of the present Agreement.

g) The members of the Joint Liaison Committee from each of the Parties will be headed by a senior government official.

h) All other matters relating to these liaison offices, their personnel, and the personnel of each Party present in the territory of the other Party in connection with the implementation of the present Agreement will be the subject of a protocol to be concluded between the Parties in the Joint Liaison Committee. Pending the conclusion of this protocol, the liaison offices and the above-mentioned personnel will be treated in accordance with the pertinent provisions of the Convention on Special Missions of December 8, 1969, including those provisions concerning privileges and immunities. The foregoing is without prejudice to the positions of the Parties concerning that Convention.

2. During the six-month period after the withdrawal of all Israeli armed forces from Lebanon in accordance with Article 1 of the present Agreement and the simultaneous restoration of Lebanese government authority along the international boundary between Lebanon and Israel, and in the light of the termination of the state of war, the Parties shall initiate, within the Joint Liaison Committee, *bona fide*, negotiations in order to conclude agreements on the movement of goods, products and persons and their implementation on a non-discriminatory basis.

ARTICLE 9

1. Each of the Parties will take, within a time limit of one year as of entry into force of the present Agreement, all measures necessary for the abrogation of treaties, laws and regulations deemed in conflict with the present Agreement, subject to and in conformity with its constitutional procedures.

2. The Parties undertake not to apply existing obligations, enter into any obligations, or adopt laws or regulations in conflict with the present Agreement.

ARTICLE 10

1. The present Agreement shall be ratified by both Parties in conformity with their respective constitutional procedures. It shall enter into force on the exchange of the instruments of ratification and shall supersede the previous agreements between Lebanon and Israel.

2. The Annex, the Appendix and the Map attached thereto, and the agreed Minutes to the present Agreement shall be considered integral parts thereof.

3. The present Agreement may be modified, amended, or superseded by mutual agreement of the Parties.

ARTICLE 11

1. Disputes between the Parties arising out of the interpretation or application of the present Agreement will be settled by negotiation in the Joint Liaison Committee. Any dispute of this character not so resolved shall be submitted to conciliation and, if unresolved, thereafter to an agreed procedure for a definitive resolution.

2. Notwithstanding the provisions of paragraph 1, disputes arising out of the interpretation or application of the Annex shall be resolved in the framework of the Security Arrangements Committee and, if unresolved, shall thereafter, at the request of either Party, be referred to the Joint Liaison Committee for resolution through negotiation.

ARTICLE 12

The present Agreement shall be communicated to the Secretariat of the United Nations for registration in conformity with the provisions of Article 102 of the Charter of the United Nations.

Done at Khaldeh and Kiryat Shmona this seventeenth day of May, 1983, in triplicate in four authentic parts in the Arabic, Hebrew, English and French languages. In case of any divergence of interpretation, the English and French texts will be equally authoritative.

For the Government of   *For the Government of*
the Republic of Lebanon   *the State of Israel*
ANTOINE FATTAL   DAVID KEMHI

Witnessed by

For the Government of
the United States of America
MORRIS DRAPER

ANNEX: SECURITY ARRANGEMENTS

1. Security Region

a) A Security Region in which the Government of Lebanon undertakes to implement the security arrangements agreed upon in this Annex is hereby established.

b) The Security Region is bounded as delineated on the Map attached to this Annex, in the north by a line constituting 'Line A' and in the south and east by the Lebanese international boundary.

2. Security arrangements

The Lebanese authorities will enforce special security measures aimed at detecting and preventing hostile activities as well as the introduction into or movement through the Security Region of unauthorized armed men or military equipment. The following security arrangements will apply equally throughout the Security Region except as noted:

a) The Lebanese Army, Lebanese Police, Lebanese Internal Security Forces, and the Lebanese auxiliary forces (ANSAR), organized under the full authority of the Government of Lebanon, are the only organized armed forces and elements permitted in the Security Region except as designated elsewhere in this Annex. The Security Arrangements Committee may approve the stationing in the Security Region of other official Lebanese armed elements similar to ANSAR.

b) Lebanese Police, Lebanese Internal Security Forces, and ANSAR may be stationed in the Security Region without restrictions as to their numbers. These forces and elements will be equipped only with personal and light automatic weapons and, for the Internal Security Forces, armored scout or commando cars as listed in the Appendix.

c) Two Lebanese Army brigades may be stationed in the area extending from the Lebanese–Israeli boundary to 'Line B' delineated on the attached Map. The other will be a regular Lebanese Army brigade stationed in the area extending from 'Line B' to 'Line A'. These brigades may carry their organic weapons and equipment listed in the Appendix. Additional units equipped in accordance with the Appendix may be deployed in the Security Region for training purpose, including the training of conscripts, or, in the case of operational emergency situation, following coordination in accordance with procedures to be established by the Security Arrangements Committee.

d) The existing local units will be integrated as such into the Lebanese Army, in conformity with Lebanese Army regulations. The existing local civil guard shall be integrated into ANSAR and accorded a proper status under Lebanese law to enable it to continue guarding the villages in the Security Region. The Process of extending Lebanese authority over these units and civil guard, under the supervision of the Security Arrangements Committee, shall start immediately after the entry into force of the present Agreement and shall terminate prior to the completion of the Israeli withdrawal from Lebanon.

e) Within the Security Region, Lebanese Army units may maintain their organic anti-aircraft weapons as specified in the Appendix. Outside the Security Region, Lebanon may deploy personal, low, and medium altitude air defense missiles. After a period of three years from the date of entry into force of the present Agreement, the provision concerning the area outside the Security Region may be reviewed by the Security Arrangements Committee at the request of either Party.

f) Military electronic equipment in the Security Region will be as specified in the Appendix. Deployment of ground radars within ten kilometers of the Lebanese–Israeli boundary should be approved by the Security Arrangements Committee. Ground radars throughout the Security Region will be deployed so that their sector of search does not cross the Lebanese–Israeli boundary. This provision does not apply to civil aviation or air traffic control radars.

g) The provision mentioned in paragraph e. applies also to anti-aircraft missiles on Lebanese Navy vessels. In the Security Region, Lebanon may deploy naval elements and establish and maintain naval bases or other shore installations required to accomplish the naval mission. The coastal installations in the Security Region will be as specified in the Appendix.

h) In order to avoid accidents due to misidentification, the Lebanese military authorities will give advance notice of all flights of any kind over the Security Region according to procedures to be determined by the Security Arrangements Committee. Approval of these flights is not required.

i) 1. The forces, weapons and military equipment which may be stationed, stocked, introduced, or transported through the Security Region are only those mentioned in this Annex and its Appendix.

2. No infrastructure, auxiliary installations, or equipment capable of assisting the activation of weapons that are not permitted by this Annex or its Appendix shall be maintained or established in the Security Region.

3. These provisions also apply whenever a clause of this Annex relates to areas outside the Security Region.

3. Security Arrangements Committee

a) Within the framework of the Joint Liaison Committee, a Security Arrangements Committee will be established.

b) The Security Arrangements Committee will be composed of an equal number of Lebanese and Israeli representatives, headed by senior officers. A representative of the United States of America will participate in meetings of the Committee at the request of either Party. Decisions of the Security Arrangements Committee will be reached by agreement of the Parties.

c) The Security Arrangements Committee shall supervise the implementation of the security arrangements in the present Agreement and this Annex and the time-table and modalities, as well as all other aspects relating to withdrawals described in the present Agreement and this Annex. To this end, and by agreement of the Parties, it will:

1. Supervise the implementation of the undertakings of the Parties under the present Agreement and this Annex.

2. Establish and operate Joint Supervisory Teams as detailed below.

3. Address and seek to resolve any problems arising out of the implementation of the security arrangements in the present Agreement and this Annex and discuss any violation reported by the Joint Supervisory Teams or any complaint concerning a violation submitted by one of the parties.

d) The Security Arrangements Committee shall deal with any complaint submitted to it not later than 24 hours after submission.

e) Meetings of the Security Arrangements Committee shall be held at least once every two weeks in Lebanon and in Israel, alternately. In the event that either party requests a special meeting, it will be convened within 24 hours. The first meeting will be held within 48 hours after the date of entry into force of the present Agreement.

f) Joint Supervisory Teams

1. The Security Arrangements Committee will establish Joint Supervisory Teams (Lebanon–Israel) subordinate to it and composed of an equal number of representatives from each Party.

2. The teams will conduct regular verification of the implementation of the provisions of the security arrangements in the Agreement and this Annex. The teams shall report immediately any confirmed violations to the Security Arrangements Committee and ascertain that violations have been rectified.

3. The Security Arrangements Committee shall assign a Joint Supervisory Team, when requested, to check border security arrangements on the Israeli side of the international boundary in accord with Article 4 of the present Agreement.

4. The teams will enjoy freedom of movement in the air, sea, and land as necessary for the performance of their tasks within the Security Region.

5. The Security Arrangements Committee will determine all administrative and technical arrangements concerning the functioning of the teams including their working procedures, their number, their manning, their armament, and their equipment.

6. Upon submission of a report to the Security Arrangements Committee or upon confirmation of a complaint of either Party by the teams, the respective Party shall immediately, and in any case not later than 24 hours from the report or the confirmation, rectify the violation. The Party shall immediately notify the Security Arrangements Committee of the rectification. Upon receiving the notification, the teams will ascertain that the violation has been rectified.

7. The Joint Supervisory Teams shall be subject to termination upon 90 days notice by either Party given at any time after two years from the date of entry into force of the present Agreement. Alternative verification arrangements shall be established in advance of such termination through the Joint Liaison Committee. Not withstanding the foregoing, the Joint Liaison Committee may determine at any time that there is no further need for such arrangements.

g) The Security Arrangements Committee will ensure that practical and rapid contacts between the two Parties are established along the boundary to prevent incidents and facilitate coordination between the forces on the terrain.

4. It is understood that the Government of Lebanon may request appropriate action in the United Nations Security Council for one unit of the United Nations Interim Force in Lebanon (UNIFIL) to be stationed in the Sidon area. The presence of this unit will lend support to the Government of Lebanon and the Lebanese Army Forces in asserting governmental authority and protection in the Palestinian refugee camp areas. For a period of 12 months, the unit in the Sidon area may send teams to the Palestinian refugee camp areas in the vicinity of Sidon and Tyre to surveil and observe, if requested by the Government of Lebanon, following notification to the Security Arrangements Committee. Police and security functions shall remain the sole responsibility of the Government of Lebanon, which shall ensure that the provisions of the present Agreement shall be fully implemented in these areas.

5. Three months after completion of the withdrawal of all Israeli forces from Lebanon, the Security Arrangements Committee will conduct a full-scale review of the adequacy of the security arrangements delineated in this Annex in order to improve them.

6. Withdrawal of Israeli forces

a) Within 8 to 12 weeks of the entry into force of the present Agreement, all Israeli forces will have been withdrawn from Lebanon. This consistent with the objective of Lebanon that all external forces withdraw from Lebanon.

b) The Lebanese Armed Forces and the Israel Defense Forces will maintain continuous liaison during the withdrawal and will exchange all necessary information through the Security Arrangements Committee. The Lebanese Armed Forces and the Israel Defense Forces will cooperate during the withdrawal in order to facilitate the reassertion of the authority of the Government of Lebanon as the Israeli armed forces withdraw.

APPENDIX

In accordance with the provisions of the Annex, the Lebanese Armed Forces may carry, introduce, station, stock, or transport through the Security Region all weapons and equipment organic to each standard Lebanese Armed Forces brigade. Individual and crew-served weapons, including light automatic weapons normally found in a mechanized infantry unit, are not prohibited by this Appendix.

1. Weapon systems listed below presently organic to each brigade in the Security Region are authorized in the numbers shown.

Tanks
— 40 tanks
— 4 medium tracked recovery vehicles.

Armored cars
— 10 AML-90/Saladin/etc.

Armored Personnel Carriers
— 127 M113 A1/VCC-L, plus 44 M113 family vehicles.

Artillery/Mortars
— 18 155 MM towed howitzers (also 105 MM)/122 MM)/
— 12 120 MM mortars
— 27 81MM mortars (mounted on M-125 tracked mortar carriers).

Anti-tank Weapons
— 112 RPG
— 30 anti-tank weapons (106 MM recoilless rifle/TOW/MILAN).

Air Defense Weapons
— 12 40 MM or less guns (not radar-guided).

2. Brigade Communications Equipment:

— 482 AN/GRC-160
— 74 AN/VRC-46
— 16 AN/VRC-47
— 9 AN/VRC-49
— 43 GRA-39
— 539 TA-312
— 27 SB-22
— 8 SB-993
— 4 AN/GRC-106

3. Brigade Surveillance Equipment:

— Mortar locating radars
— Artillery locating radars
— Ground surveillance radars
— Night observation devices
— Unattended ground sensors.

4. In accordance with the provisions of the Annex, armored vehicles for the Internal Security Forces will be as follows:

— armored wheeled vehicles with guns up to 40 MM.

5. In accordance with the provisions of the Annex, there will be no limitations on the coastal installations in the Security Region, except on the following four categories:

— Coastal sea surveillance radars: 5
— Coastal defense guns: 15 40mm or less
— Coastal are defense guns: 15 40MM or less (not radar-guided)
— Shore-to-sea missiles: None.

6. The Lebanese Army Infantry Brigade and Territorial Brigade in the Security Region are each organized as follows:

1 Brigade Headquarters and Headquarters Company	Off. 14	Enl. 173
3 Infantry Batallions	Off. 31	Enl. 754 ea
1 Artillery Battalion	Off. 39	Enl. 672
1 Tank Battallion	Off. 37	Enl. 79
3 Tank Companies		
1 Reconnaissance Company		
1 Logistics Battalion	Off. 26	Enl. 344
1 Engineer Company	Off. 6	Enl. 125
1 Anti-tank Company	Off. 4	Enl. 117
1 Anti-Air Artillery Company	Off. 4	Enl. 146
Total: 4,341	Off. 223	Enl. 4,118

AGREED MINUTES

ART. 4.4   Lebanon affirms that Lebanese law includes all measures necessary to ensure implementation of this paragraph.

ART. 6   Without prejudice to the provisions of the Annex regarding the Security Region, it is agreed that non-combat military aircraft of a foreign state on non-military missions shall not be considered military equipment.

ART. 6   It is agreed that, in the event of disagreement as to whether a particular state is 'hostile' for purposes of Article 6 of the Agreement, the prohibitions of Article 6 shall be applied to any state which does not maintain diplomatic relations with both Parties.

ART. 8.1b It is agreed that, at the request of either Party, the Joint Liaison Committee shall begin to examine the question of claims by citizens of either Party on properties in the territory of the other Party.

ART. 8.1h It is understood that each Party will certify to the other if one of its personnel was on official duty or performing official functions at any given time.

ART. 8.2   It is agreed that the negotiations will be concluded as soon as possible.

ART. 9   It is understood that this provision shall apply *mutatis mutandis* to agreements concluded by the Parties pursuant to Article 8, paragraph 2.

ART. 11   It is agreed that both parties will request the United States of America to promote the expeditious resolution of disputes arising out of the interpretation or application of the present Agreement.

ART. 11 It is agreed that the phrase 'An agreed procedure for a definitive resolution' means an agreed third party mechanism which will produce a resolution of the dispute which is binding on the Parties.

ANNEX

PARA 1.b It is agreed that, in that portion of Jabal Baruk shown on the map attachment to the Annex, only civilian telecommunications installations, such as television facilities and radars for air traffic control purposes, may be emplaced. The restrictions on weapons and military equipment that are detailed in the Appendix to the Annex will also apply in that area.

ANNEX

PARA 2.d The Government of Lebanon affirms its decision that the Territorial Brigade established on April 6, 1983, mentioned in subparagraph c, will encompass the existing local units which had been formed into a near brigade-sized unit, along with Lebanese Army personnel from among the inhabitants of the Security Region, in conformity with Lebanese Army regulations. This brigade will be in charge of security in the area extending from the Lebanese–Israeli boundary to 'Line B' delineated on the Map attachment to the Annex. All the Lebanese Armed Forces and elements in this area, including the Lebanese Police, Lebanese Internal Security Forces and ANSAR, will be subordinated to the brigade commander. The organization of the existing local units will be adapted, under the supervision of the Security Arrangements Committee, in conformity with the Table of Organization for the Territorial Brigade as shown in the Appendix.

ANNEX

PARA 2.9 1. An area extending from:
33 degrees 15 minutes N
35 degrees 12.6 minutes E; to
33 degrees 05.5 minutes N
35 degrees 06.1 minutes E; to
33 degrees 15 minutes N
35 degrees 08.2 minutes E; to
33 degrees 05.5 minutes N
35 degrees 01.4 minutes E;
which is at present closed for civil navigation, will be maintained by Lebanon.
2. In order to prevent incidents, there will be continuous communications between the southern command of the Lebanese Navy and the Israeli Navy in order to exchange information concerning suspected vessels. The procedures for the abovementioned exchange of information will be established by the Security Arrangements Committee.
3. The Lebanese Navy will act promptly in order to ascertain the identity of such suspected vessels. In emergency cases, there will be direct communications between vessels.

ANNEX

PARA 3.f 1. The joint Supervisory Teams will carry out their functions in recognition of the fact that the responsibility for military, police, and other control operations rests with the Lebanese Armed Forces, police, and other authorized Lebanese organizations, and not with the teams.
2. If the Joint Supervisory Teams uncover evidence of a violation, they will contact the proper Lebanese authorities through the Security Arrangements Supervision Centers created pursuant to the Agreed Minute to paragraph 3.f.(5) of the Annex, in order to assure that Lebanese authorities take appropriate neutralizing and preventive action in a timely way. They will ascertain that the action taken rectified the violation and will report the results to the Security Arrangements Committee.
3. The Joint Supervisory Teams will commence limited activities as early as possible following the coming into force of the Agreement for the purpose of monitoring the

implementation of the Israel Defense Forces withdrawal arrangements. Their other supervisory and verification activities authorized in the Annex will commence with the final withdrawal of the Israeli armed forces.

4. Joint Supervisory Teams will conduct daily verification if necessary during day and night. Verifications will be carried out on the ground, at sea, and in the air.

5. Each Joint Supervisory Team will be commanded by a Lebanese officer, who will recognize the joint nature of the teams when making decisions in unforeseen situations, during the conduct of the verification mission.

6. While on a mission, the Joint Supervisory Team leader at his discretion could react to any unforeseen situation which could require immediate action. The team leader will report any such situation and the action taken to the Security Arrangements Supervision Center.

7. The Joint Supervisory Teams will not use force except in self-defense.

8. The Security Arrangements Committee will decide *inter alia* on the pattern of activity of the Joint Supervisory Teams, their weaponry and equipment, their mode of transport, and the areas in which the teams will operate on the basis of the rule of reason and pragmatic considerations. The Security Arrangements Committee will determine the overall pattern of activity with a view to avoiding undue disruption to normal civilian life as well as with a view to preventing the teams from becoming targets of attack.

9. Up to a maximum of eight Joint Supervisory Teams will function simultaneously.

ANNEX

PARA 3.f.5   1. The Security Arrangements Supervision Centers will be set up by the Security Arrangements Committee in the Security Region. The exact locations of the centers will be determined by the Security Arrangements Committee in accord with the principles that the Centers should be located in the vicinity of Hesbaya and Mayfadun and should be situated in populated areas.

2. Under the overall direction of the Security Arrangements Committee, the purpose of each Center is to:

a) Control, supervise, and direct Joint Supervisory Teams functioning in the sector of the Security Region assigned to it.

b) Serve as a center of communications connected to the Joint Supervisory Teams and appropriate headquarters.

c) Serve as a meeting place in Lebanon for the Security Arrangements Committee.

d) Receive, analyze, and process all information necessary for the function of the Joint Supervisory Teams, on behalf of the Security Arrangements Committee.

Operational Arrangements:

a) The centers will be commanded by Lebanese Army Officers.

b) The Centers will function 24 hours a day.

c) The exact number of personnel in each Center will be decided by the Security Arrangements Committee.

d) Israeli personnel will be stationed in Israel when not engaged in activities in the Centers.

e) The Government of Lebanon will be responsible for providing security and logistical support for the Centers.

f) The Joint Supervisory Teams will ordinarily commence their missions from the Centers after receiving proper briefing and will complete their missions at the Centers following debriefing.

g) Each Center will contain a situation room, communications equipment, facilities for Security Arrangements Committee meetings, and a briefing and debriefing room.

ANNEX

PARA 3.g In order to prevent incidents and facilitate coordination between the forces on the terrain, 'practical and rapid contacts' will include radio and telephone communications between the respective military commanders and their staffs in the immediate border region, as well as direct face-to-face consultations.

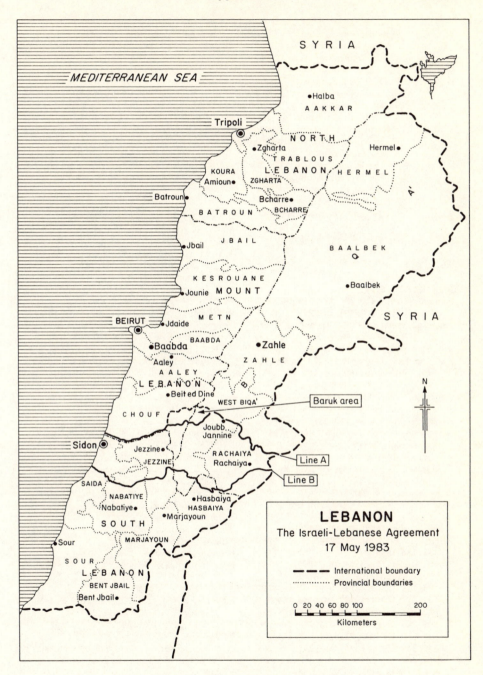

MEDITERRANEAN SEA

SYRIA

●Halba
A A K K A R

●Tripoli

N O R T H
●Zgharta   Hermel●
T R A B L O U S
L E B A N O N   H E R M E L
KOURA
Amioun● ZGHARTA
Batroun●
●Bcharre
BCHARRE
B A T R O U N
B A A L B E K
●Jbail   J B A I L

K E S R O U A N E
●Jounie   M O U N T   ●Baalbek

M E T N
●BEIRUT ●Jdaide   S Y R I A
BAABDA
●Baabda   ●Zahle
Aaley●   Z A H L E
A A L E Y
L E B A N O N
●Beit ed Dine
WEST BIQA'   ┌─────────────┐
C H O U F   │ Baruk area │
                                 └─────────────┘
Joubb
Jannine
●Sidon   ●Jezzine   RACHAIYA   ┌────────┐
JEZZINE   Rachaiya●   │ Line A │
                                 └────────┘
SAIDA   ┌────────┐
NABATIYE ●Hasbaiya   │ Line B │
Nabatiye● HASBAIYA   └────────┘
S O U T H ●Marjayoun
MARJAYOUN
●Sour
S O U R
L E B A N O N
BENT JBAIL
Bent Jbail●

N

┌────────────────────────────────────┐
│   **LEBANON**   │
│   The Israeli-Lebanese Agreement   │
│   17 May 1983   │
│   │
│ ▬ ▬ ▬ International boundary   │
│ .... Provincial boundaries   │
│   │
│ 0 20 40 60 80 100   200   │
│   Kilometers   │
└────────────────────────────────────┘

Index

Abdallah, Crown Prince, 101, 102, 103, 137, 143, 148, 249
Abd al-Nasir, Gamal, 27, 33, 138, 193
Abdu, Johnny, 11, 12, 141, 159, 162
Abillama, Faruq, 11
Alam, Elyse, 142
Algeria, 52, 58, 89, 96
Amal Movement, 120, 121, 122, 144, 145, 162, 177, 190, 195, 200, 203, 233, 253
ambassadors: burdens of, 151; dangers to, 197, 253; meetings with Arab, 52
American Enterprise Institute, 4, 5
American University of Beirut (AUB), 1, 4, 9, 14, 15, 16, 66, 70, 100, 105, 169, 174, 197, 198
Andreotti, Giulio, 133
Andropov, Yuri, 96
Angelloni, Luciano, 95, 217, 231
Arab League, 17, 56, 59, 60, 61, 63, 65, 116, 135; summit, 248–9
Arab nationalism, 55, 67
Arab states, 80, 83, 91, 98, 144, 205, 230; consensus of, 137; contacts with, 52; threat of boycott of Lebanon, 79
Arafat, Yasir, 61, 62, 64, 109, 116, 129, 143, 195, 225, 248
Arens, Moshe, 35, 73, 78, 113, 146
Armistice Agreement, 47, 50, 82, 90, 91, 112, 183, 184, 185
al-Asad, Hafiz, 53, 55, 65, 66–7, 79, 80, 87, 94, 96, 97, 99, 102, 105, 106, 110, 112, 113, 115, 116, 123, 124, 135, 143, 147, 149, 150, 151, 152, 153, 155, 157, 162, 164, 164–8, 189, 190, 191, 193, 194, 200, 206, 207, 208, 209, 210, 211, 212, 213, 215, 218, 220, 226, 228, 232, 235, 237, 238, 239, 240, 244, 247, 248, 249, 252, 253, 254, 255, 258, 259, 260, 261, 264, 265, 266, 267; discussions with, 81–5; illness of, 131, 132, 143, 164; letter from, 76, 77
al-As'ad, Kamil, 13, 31, 57, 104, 120, 121, 139
assassinations, 106, 107, 197, 220, 236, 237, 240, 255, 259

al-Attar, Najah, 151
Aubert, Pierre, 123
Audeh, Elias, 232
Awn, Michel, 212, 220, 232, 233, 237, 256, 259, 260, 261, 262, 263, 265, 267, 269; formation of government, 270
Aziz, Tariq, 249

Bandar, Prince, 109, 110, 120, 121, 148, 150
Baqlini, Mirshid, 222
Bartholomew, Reginald, 123, 130, 141, 144, 146, 147, 148, 149, 154, 163, 164, 175, 176, 178, 179, 182, 183, 194, 198, 206, 207, 208
Baruk, 48, 73; status of, 68
Basil, Bob, 69
Ba'th party, 155, 221, 252; Lebanese, 155, 202
Bayraqdar, Sa'id, 220
Baz, Usamah, 56
Begin, Menachem, 6, 35, 36, 37, 45, 49, 72, 73, 83, 87, 114, 184
Beirut: East, 5, 178, 186, 189, 202, 203, 233, 235, 239, 240, 266, 269; Israeli occupation of, 71; reconstruction of, 103; unification of, 244; West, 5, 7, 145, 146, 162, 178, 198, 202, 217, 233, 235, 253, 254, 255
Beirut International Airport, 132, 198, 245
Ben Soda, Ahmed, 139
Benjedid, al-Shadli, 59, 249
Beydoun, Muhammad, 203
Bilad al-Sham, 257–8
Biqa' Valley, 36, 37, 38, 62, 81, 111, 113, 115, 127, 141
Birri, Nabih, 114, 121, 122, 125, 126, 146, 155, 158, 162, 172, 173, 176, 178, 180, 181, 191, 192, 193, 195, 196, 198, 199, 207, 211, 214, 216, 231
bombings: of Kata'ib office, 7; of US embassy, 75–6, 123; of US embassy (Awkar), 179, 211
Bouhabib, Abdallah, 134, 221, 225, 243, 245, 246, 249
Bouhabib, Julie, 249
Boukhalil, Joseph, 209

Haddad, Sa'd, 26, 41, 44, 50, 68, 73, 74, 86, 141, 163
Haddad, Wadi', 9, 22, 139
al-Hafiz, Amin, 57
Hajj, General, 185
Halaby, Najib, 22
Halawi, Ibrahim, 89
Halbouty, Mike, 22, 24
Hamad, Khalil Abi, 208
Hamdan, Abbas, 55, 81, 89
al-Hariri, Rafiq, 60, 102, 103, 113–14, 119, 120, 121, 122, 123, 124, 130, 136, 137, 138, 142, 143, 145, 146, 147, 148, 149, 150, 161, 179, 180, 207, 211, 218, 221, 230, 236–41, 249, 256, 260; discussion paper, 250–5
al-Hariri, Nazik, 137
al-Hashim, Joseph, 224
Hashem, Joseph, 256, 259, 263, 266
Hassan, Crown Prince, 249
al-Hassan, Zafir, 102, 141, 219
Hassan II, King, 53, 102, 138, 139
Hegel, G.W.F., 82
al-Helou, Ibrahim, 211
Helou, Charles, 195, 205, 262, 268
Helou, Pierre, 261, 269
Higgins, William, 253
Himadeh, Marwan, 160, 203, 256
al-Hindi, Hani, 63
Hizballah, 174, 177, 217, 233, 240, 243, 251
Hobbes, Thomas, 2
al-Hoss, Salim, 169, 176, 178, 224, 237, 247, 248, 251, 253, 262, 264, 265, 267, 269
hostage-taking, 179, 187, 217
Howe, Geoffrey, 158, 182, 183
Hubayqah, Eli, 176, 196, 200, 201, 202, 203, 206, 207, 208, 210, 211, 212, 214, 216, 217, 230, 231, 259, 265, 266
al-Husseini, Hussein, 200, 206, 208, 215, 235, 247, 253, 264, 265, 266, 267
Hussein, King, 58, 249
Hussein, Saddam, 58, 248
Huwayyik, Patriarch, 223

al-Ibrahimi, Lakhdar, 59
India, 63, 64
Intifadah: counter- 214–16; in Lebanon, 193–200; in Occupied Territories, 256
Iran, 165, 174, 187, 219, 242, 243, 251; presence in Biqa' Valley, 39; role in Lebanon, 40, 240
Iraq, 58, 97
Iraq–Iran war, 137, 240, 245
Israel, 3, 6, 14, 18, 20, 21, 40, 44, 71, 82, 84, 97, 102, 105, 106, 118, 125, 126, 129, 130, 132, 134, 136, 140, 144, 146, 147, 150, 151, 154, 156, 159, 165, 177, 181, 184, 187, 192, 193, 198, 204, 225, 227, 233, 236, 239, 240, 242, 243, 254, 256, 261; arming Lebanese Forces, 113; bombing of Tyre headquarters, 129; conflict with, 55, 65, 66, 72; danger of war with Syria, 80; frontier with Lebanon, 28; invasion of Lebanon, 1, 14; negotiations with, 27, 29, 32, 56, 67, 68–98, 121, 152, 169, 181, 183, 184; occupation of South Lebanon, 37, 163; possible peace treaty with, 10, 20; proposal of security zone, 27; recognition of, 140 *see also* normalization of relations; resentful of US presence, 49; return of prisoners, 92; roadblocks in Lebanon, 14; security concerns of, 25, 26, 153; smuggling of goods from, 177; withdrawal of, 24, 25, 27, 28, 31, 32–51, 54, 59, 66, 99, 100, 103, 109, 110, 111, 112, 116, 123, 131, 135, 137, 142, 146, 148, 153, 160, 164, 170, 171, 172, 176, 180, 182, 183, 185, 195, 235, 240 (from Shuf, 119, 183, 186, 188; partial, 80; possible agreement, 68–98)
Islam, 3, 4, 26, 137, 160, 174
Islamic Jihad, 179
Islamic movements, 178, 179, 190, 198, 252
Islamic Summit, 143, 144
Israel–Lebanon Military Liaison Committee (ILMAC), 27, 28, 29, 34, 35, 45, 154, 183, 184
Italy, 32, 94, 124, 133, 134, 141, 182

Ja'ja, Samir, 176, 193, 196, 206, 208, 211, 214, 232, 233, 256, 260, 261, 262, 263, 264, 265, 267, 268, 269
Jalloud, Abd al-Salam, 67
Jiha, story of, 138
Johns Hopkins University, 253
Joint Liaison Committee, 82, 93, 94, 153, 154
Jordan, 46, 51, 52, 53, 55, 62, 103, 143, 254, 257
Jreissati, Joseph, 156
Jumayyil, Amin, 2, 7–8, 9, 11, 12, 18, 20, 27, 28, 33, 41, 42, 44, 50, 53, 55, 59, 60, 62, 66, 67, 70, 73, 76, 78, 79, 83, 85, 87, 89, 92, 102, 104, 110, 113, 115, 118, 123, 127, 128, 130, 132, 133, 137, 139, 140, 144, 147, 148, 149, 150, 151, 152, 156, 157, 164–8, 172, 175, 176, 181, 183, 189, 191, 193, 194, 195, 199, 200, 201, 202, 207, 208, 209, 210, 212–13, 214, 215, 216, 217, 219, 222, 223, 226, 227, 228, 229, 230, 232, 233, 234, 235, 236, 237, 239, 240, 242, 243, 244, 245, 246, 247, 248, 249, 251, 252, 253, 256, 257, 258, 259, 260, 261, 262, 263, 264, 265, 267, 269; address to UN, 18, 21; discussions (with Hafiz al-Asad, 210–11, 212–13; with Ronald Reagan, 22–8); elected president, 7–8; end of presidency, 265, 268, 270; last visit to Damascus, 266–8; letter to Asad, 116; rejection of Tripartite Agreement, 215; visit to Paris, 29

DATE DUE

GAYLORD			PRINTED IN U.S.A.